readings
on
premodern
societies

prentice-hall international, inc., London
prentice-hall of australia, pty. ltd., Sydney
prentice-hall of canada, ltd., Toronto
prentice-hall of india private limited, New Delhi
prentice-hall of japan, inc., Tokyo

readings
on
premodern
societies

Victor Lidz
University of Chicago

Talcott Parsons
Harvard University

prentice-hall, inc./englewood cliffs, new jersey

prentice-hall readings in modern sociology series
Alex Inkeles, Editor

ISBN: 0-13-761924-3
Library of Congress Catalog Card Number: 72-166139

Printed in the United States of America

10 9 8 7 6 5 4 3 2 1

table of contents

Part 3
archaic
societies

Part 4
historic
civilizations

Part 5
the
seedbed
societies

general introduction

TALCOTT PARSONS

Like other Readers in the *Foundations of Modern Sociology* series, this one is designed to accompany and supplement the original book, *Societies: Evolutionary and Comparative Perspectives*. Its main purpose is to make easily available to the student a selection of the literature on which the other book was based. Mr. Lidz appears as the "senior" Editor, not by virtue of age or academic position, but for the very cogent reason that he has done most of the work and that this fact should be accorded symbolic recognition.

The ground which the original book covered is vast, especially for so small a book, and the literature relevant to it is correspondingly vast. Since both Mr. Lidz and I are in a sense "general" sociologists, we are not qualified experts in the subject matter of any chapter, to say nothing of all of them. We therefore have had to rely on "advice" of various sorts—both the oral advice of experts, and information about the "reputations" of various contributions we ourselves have gleaned from the literature.

As in the original book, we have relied heavily on sources which make rather general statements, summaries of empirical evidence and statements of interpretation. There are two main reasons for this. First, we ourselves did not have personal command over the more detailed original sources—though, for example, we have read a good many anthropological field monographs—and could have mastered such sources only for a small part of the field. Second, that order of detail would have been relatively meaningless to most of our readers and would have severely increased the difficulty of producing a selection which might be compatible with our limitations of space.

The criteria for selection were first, probable validity as judged by an article's reputation among specialists in its field and, secondly, its bearing on the theoretical, largely sociological, problems we have had in mind and attempted to state, though in very condensed form, in Chapter 2 of *Societies*. Especially in this Reader, finally, we have used still another supplementary criterion for selection, which is an extension of the criterion of theoretical significance. This is that we have either emphasized only one aspect of the society in question, or given to one or two aspects what many would regard as disproportionate emphasis, in order to highlight institutions which seem most important in comparative perspective. Thus on ancient Egypt, three selections dealing with the articulation of religion and kingship may seem disproportionate. There are, we feel, two justifications for this emphasis. First for ancient Egypt documentary sources on economic and social organization are not nearly as plentiful or adequate for theoretical purposes as is evidence, from inscriptions, papyri and sculpture and architecture, for the integration of monarchy with its religious meanings. Furthermore, on theoretical grounds, we consider this to be the "keystone of the arch" of Egyptian society and culture and the primary focus of its distinctiveness.

Another even more striking case is our inclusion of only one selection on ancient Israel, and this on specifically religious themes, namely Martin Buber's discussion of the prophetic complex known as "Deutero-Isaiah." Including this has meant neglect of such classical summaries of the social and political organization of Israel as Max Weber presented in his *Ancient Judaism.* In the context of severely limited space, our justification is that the *historic* significance of Israel did not lie mainly in its patterns of socio-political organization but in its primarily religious culture, however interdependent the two. The Buber selection discusses with admirable succinctness and clarity a particularly crucial stage in the development of the main religious themes through which Israel profoundly influenced subsequent cultural development and social organization.

The theoretical scheme to which we have related source materials in both books is of course the one to which we subscribe, in the sense that it is one with which we have long worked and which we find especially useful in trying to understand the patterns of development and change of human society and culture. We do not pretend to include "all possible points of view"—an aim which would necessitate an "anthology" based on a sampling of such points of view. Neither, do we claim a monopoly of legitimate intellectual insight. We hope we have been reasonably sensitive to other points of view than our own. At one level they are indefinitely many; and "impartiality" would result in a formless eclecticism. On another level, however, there has been a notable recent intellectual movement which emphasizes not only social change—which any evolutionary perspective as distinguished from "cross-sectional" comparative methods alone, inherently does—but also change through conflict. Further, there is again a "neo-Marxist" tendency to emphasize the "material" factors, especially in the structuring of conflicts. The sense in which these "material" factors are conceived to be decisive is not always clear.

The older socialist–communist concern of Marxism seems, however, to have been altered, as perhaps best evidenced by the conspicuous lack of interest of most neo-Marxists in the more technical economic theory of Marx himself or his successors in that tradition. Since the "economic factor" was held to be crucial in the earlier Marxian tradition, relative lack of interest in its theoretical understanding clearly seems to be a symptom of intellectual change. We suspect that these issues, e.g., as to the relative predominance of the "forces of production" and of the "superstructure," or in the somewhat more generalized version, the German contrast between *Realfaktoren* and *Idealfaktoren,* are no longer so clear-cut as they seemed to be a generation ago. However, the significance of these issues to the historical background of the social sciences, and of course their presumptive future, has been very much in our minds.

We have not attempted any general analytical discussion of these issues in *Societies,* the present Reader, or my second book *The System of Modern Societies,* the sequel to *Societies.* In all three cases it seemed better to attempt a straightforward organization, presentation, and interpretation of material in terms of our own theoretical scheme. Our avoidance of any claim to a monopoly of intellectual legitimacy in the discussion of the very vital subject-matter of these works, is linked to our conviction that, as in other scientific fields, competent command of empirical evidence, and correspondingly competent analysis and theoretical interpretation will in the long run lead to the resolution of most of the controversies which, at a given moment, seem so acute as to be intellectually insoluble. Clearly the Reader is in one sense the most objective of the three publications, namely in the sense that the authors/editors— remembering that Mr. Lidz had a very important hand in both the books formally "authored" by myself—have injected their more particular points of view only through their selections of readings and of course through the introductory materials.

This Reader includes in addition to this very general introduction, introductions to each of the main sections, the content of which follows the organization of *Societies.* These, attempting to explain the problems and the rationale for the selections and some designation of what they contribute, have been written by Lidz, but of course responsibility for their assertions is shared by both editors.

Finally, a few words may be said about the bearing of some of the materials presented both in the Reader and in *Societies* on our conception of some of the essentials of the pattern of societal evolution, and less fully on some aspects of its process. The decisive problems arise in the last two sections of both books, where we are concerned with "historic civilizations" and the "seedbed societies." Of the four "historic" categories of Empire with which we have dealt, the Roman Empire, as contrasted with the Chinese, Indian, and Islamic cases, proved to be the socio-cultural soil in which the next main stage of societal evolution, the step to "modernity" took root. It is our view, however, that, out of its own resources, Roman society did not have the potential for bringing about such a development, but required what metaphorically we may call "fertilization" from the cultures generated in what we have called the "seedbed" societies of Israel and Greece. Through inclusion of their original territorial bases and through diffusion of their cultures in Roman-controlled areas, both of these were thoroughly "included" in the later Roman system.

In our view this rather special combination of circumstances was the main basis of differentiation between the Roman and the other three historic Empires. It seems that, at the critical level in the interpenetration of society and culture, the other three all lacked the universalistic patterning of institutions that made Roman society "fertile soil" for these cultural "seeds." This universalistic structure was most fully embodied in Roman Law, especially the *jus gentium,* as described by Sohm in Chapter Nineteen. By contrast the legal systems of the Chinese, Indian, and Islamic Empires were much more particularistic. Of course universalistic elements were present in all three of the cultures, but they were not nearly so fully institutionalized at the level we have come to think of as "legal."

This combination of highly special cultural elements, which in very important ways complemented each other, was essential, but to continue the metaphor, a long period of "gestation" in fact ensued, and probably had to, before an outline of a new evolutionary phase, quite different from *any* of the historic societies, began to emerge. The story of its emergence and development is the main theme of *The System of Modern Societies*. The fully developed "seed" from which this development occurred came from a special "integration" of the two components in Christianity, namely Hebrew and Greek elements, without which Christianity makes no cultural sense whatever.

It seems reasonable to us to argue that "modernity" emerged in the *West*— which meant not the Roman Empire as a whole, but its Western, predominantly Latin, half,—not only because of the greater universalism of Roman institutions, especially law, but also because of the relative absence or weakness, in the other three cases, of cultural "seeds," or the fact they could not "take root." Both the Israelitic and the Greek traditions were certainly relevant to Islam, as was the later Christian tradition. With respect to the Israelitic component, we may say that anything like its diffusion within the Roman Empire was precluded by its close kinship to Islam: The later Islamic movement was under severe pressure to "contain" any specific Hebrew elements in order to protect the integrity of the prophetic tradition in its own version. Similarly, Greek patterns of rationality were precluded from diffusing in Islamic Empires by the monolithic political control at the top, which was fused with a religious tradition of a quite different cultural type from the Greek. Furthermore, the very fact of the political establishment of Islam meant that there could not be a process of proselytizing either Greek or Christian elements independently of the main political, though not legal structure, as happened in the Roman Empire for Judaism, Hellenism, and Christianity. There is a major difference between a group with a strong and distinctive cultural tradition whose adherents control the main territorial political system and, on the other hand, one that is "tolerated" within a political system controlled by groups with cultural commitments "alien" to them. The latter was the situation for both Jews and Greeks within the Roman Empire, for Greeks especially in the Western half. Given the very close affinity in cultural type between Israel and Islam, it is thus probably the fact of Islamic political control which, in spite of the involvement of Islam with almost the whole of the predominantly Hellenistic territory and later many important Christian territories and groups, in the paramount politico-cultural echelons of Islamic Empire in the Middle East, explains why the "Western" cultural heritage, most especially its Greek component, was repudiated, as crystallized in the writings of Al Ghazzali.

The other two primary historic "culture areas," China and India, were out of reach of the Israelitic and Greek components. We would, however, like to suggest here that there have been indigenous movements in the Orient which probably stood in a relation to the "classical" Chinese and Indian societies somewhat comparable to that of Judaism, Hellenism, and Christianity to the Roman structure. The two most plausible candidates for such cultural roles seem to us to be first, and until recently by far paramount, Buddhism which, it will be remembered, has been forced into a "diaspora" relative to its home ground in India, but has prospered mightily in the "diaspora." The second candidate seems to be that element of Japanese tradition which in a religious reference can be called Shinto.

It may well be an index of the Western parochialism of our thinking that, though we have paid special attention to the role of the "insignificant" societies of Israel and Greece, only in the sequel to *Societies* has any reference been made to Japan which, on a background of Roman-type diffusion of Chinese culture and institutions, also brought together Buddhistic influences and its own indigenous Shinto tradition.[1]

We stick to our judgment in the *System* book, foreshadowed in *Societies,* that the origins of what we and many others, notably Max Weber, have called modern society are broadly as we have stated them, and they are predominantly "Western." If, however, there is, as is already adumbrated by some, to be a "post-modern" society, we suggest that the non-Western components we have outlined—namely the Chinese (rather than Hindu) "neo-Roman" base, and the "seed" components from Buddhism and Shinto—will prove to be essential.

At the same time we suspect that a primary condition of the emergence of a new either Oriental-led or certainly Oriental-included phase of socio-cultural evolution will be the adequate integration of these Oriental components with the heritage of predominantly Western origin. We further suspect that one of the most important current vehicles of this integration is Marxism, but in its greatly modified version, via not only Lenin, but also Mao. One major symptom of this modification is that the symbolic "savior" is no longer the industrial proletariat, but on the one hand peasant masses, on the other "undeveloped" societies. The other vehicle is Western "liberalism" mediated above all through American influence.

This is not the place to attempt to follow out the complex ramifications of the perspective just outlined. We conclude by pointing out two "morals" which seem to be involved. The first concerns returning to the question of the relative importance of "factors" in social development or change, the rationale of why we are "Weberians"[2] rather than "Marxians." This lies in our conviction that, not only, as Weber himself set forth in masterly fashion, are the basic *differentiating* factors in socio-cultural evolution much more "ideal" or cultural than they are "material," but that this is also true of the considerations which must be analyzed to explain such integrative processes

---

1 Robert N. Bellah. *Tokugawa Religion.* (Glencoe, Ill.: The Free Press, 1957.)

2 In a slightly different reference, less concerned with the patterning of social evolution we are more "Durkheimians" than "Weberians." Cf. Talcott Parsons, "On Building Social System Theory: A Personal History," *Daedalus* (Fall 1970), pp. 826–81.

as the emergence of Christianity from the combination of Judaic and Greek cultural elements, with the establishment of a church on the social "soil" of Roman society, or the relation of Buddhism to the non-Indian societies into which it spread, and the more obscure possible significance of Shinto outside Japan.

This is essentially to say that with Weber we think the main outline of social structure is more nearly uniform at certain general evolutionary stages, taking into account size of population and territory and factors of that order, than are the principal cultural movements with their sometimes much smaller-scale societal "bearers." For example, in the "historic" societies we very generally find a predominantly peasant base with relatively little urbanization, an upper class with a heavy dependence on control of land and the people on the land, and a monarchial institution which both symbolized the "glory" of the political system, and controlled a more or less highly developed civil, military, and often to a considerable extent also religious "bureaucratic" system.[3] We frankly do not see how the distinctiveness of the socio-cultural development of the West can be explained on Marxian premises, which is to say a distinctiveness at the level of the "material" factors, comparing the Western Roman Empire with China, India, and the Middle East. On the "Weberian" premises we have utilized, however, we think a quite intelligible account has been given. We believe this view to be consistent with many important developments in general science since Marx and Weber wrote, especially that of "cybernetic" points of view, the emphasis on "information" and the maturing of related fields such as linguistics.

This leads over to the second "moral." In the Introduction to the new book on *The System of Modern Societies* I stressed the importance to the social evolutionist of the problem of continuity between his own concern with systems of human action, and the organic level of the study of living systems, in particular societies and cultural systems. Even since that Introduction was drafted evidence for this continuity has been immensely strengthened. Thus the great advance in the understanding of the processes of genetic inheritance at the microbiological levels, has involved a theoretical framework in which codes analogous to those of language and performing cybernetic and information-processing functions have been found to be central.[4] Somewhat similar theoretical models have been gaining in prominence in the study of the central nervous system since the days of Claude Bernard and W. B. Cannon, in non-neural macrobiological physiology.

We feel that this development does not confront the social sciences in which we work with a "reductionist" pressure to consider only the "real" fundamentals of the "physical" aspects of the organic on the one hand, the "material" aspects of the processes of human action on the other. What has been emerging is quite different, namely a picture of an evolved and evolving system of living

---

[3] S. N. Eisenstadt, *The Political Systems of Empires.* (New York: The Free Press of Glencoe, 1963.)

[4] James D. Watson, *The Molecular Biology of the Gene,* 2nd ed. (New York: W. A. Benjamin Co., 1970.)

6 general introduction

systems which are coming to be understandable in terms of theoretical models which seem to be in important respects "isomorphic" throughout the whole range, something which has only very recently begun to be at all widely appreciated. We hope that our three small volumes, designed as condensed summary discussions at the socio-cultural end of this evolutionary continuity will constitute a contribution to the impressive integration in thought about the nature of the world of life which has been occurring for more than a generation now.

Part 1

introductory
readings

The readings in Part 1 provide a general introduction to the evolutionary perspectives that have guided the selection and organization of the materials presented in this volume. Each of the three selections addresses a different but very central aspect of the theoretical foundations of contemporary research upon and knowledge of social evolution. The essay by A. Irving Hallowell is concerned with the emergence of systems of social action organized upon cultural-symbolic levels of communication as part of the broader developmental process by which the human species evolved from "lower" primates. It demonstrates the essential continuity between biological evolution and the processes of socio-cultural change that justifies—indeed, requires—the incorporation of evolutionary perspectives into sociological theory. Robert N. Bellah discusses the religious dimensions of the social and cultural aspects of human evolution, dimensions which seem to impart the controlling guidance that holds particular societies to their characteristic paths of development. Bellah organizes his discussion about a typology of the principal stages through which religious systems have evolved. Much of the importance of his article derives from the ways in which he adapts general evolutionary concepts to the analysis of change in social and cultural systems. There is a strong possibility that his typology of stages, perhaps with some modification, can fruitfully be generalized to deal with the evolution of other principal aspects of socio-cultural systems. The essay by Talcott Parsons analyzes social change from a perspective that is quite different from but complementary to Bellah's treatment of broad stages of development. Parsons presents a relatively systematic analysis of the various forces that enter into the processes by which societies change from particular states or conditions into others, i.e., of the factors of the detailed changes which cumulatively comprise social evolution. He places special emphasis upon the dynamic nature of the mutually adaptive relations that obtain between social systems and their environments and among various specific components of social systems, a perspective that encourages the analysis of change in terms that articulate with both evolutionary concepts and analytical sociological theory.

Hallowell organizes his discussion about an hypothetical construct he calls the protocultural phase in the evolutionary emergence of humankind and human society. This phase is conceived as a crucial watershed in which early hominids, adding characteristics such as bipedal locomotion, tool-using and making, a larger brain, some language abilities, greater learning capacity, and more flexible social organization to elements of the biological, psychological, and social inheritances of earlier primates, attained the enhanced adaptiveness that established the distinctive line of evolution that has led to contemporary man. Hallowell notes several characteristics of the social life of most primate species that seem to have comprised critical prior conditions for the emergence of protocultural man, for example, the territorial nature of the band groupings, the highly communicative, "social" nature of the individual, the prominence of social ranking or stratification in the group organization, and the comparatively long period of infant dependency. The distinctive flexibility and variability characteristic of fully human society are interpreted as arising from the evolutionary extension of the developments that crystallized the protocultural system. Thus, psychological systems having the intelligence to manipulate symbolic codes and the capacity to internalize personality structure through participation in social roles, as well as cultural systems consisting of patterns of belief, especially of values, which allow action to be oriented on the level of meaning, are treated as the primary environments of human social systems. It is through constant interaction with these environments that social systems have evolved their basic human characteristics (and vice versa). Social systems containing a plurality of differentiated and specialized social roles that are structured, through institutions, on the normative grounds of "oughtness" seem to provide the only mode of integrating processes of social action that is sufficiently flexible to bring together effectively the outputs of cultural and human psychological systems. No other mode could structure social interaction that is meaningfully oriented or regulate the role-related motivations of the personalities of individual actors. If all processes of human action may be analyzed in terms of "intelligent" behavioral systems, personality systems, normative social systems, and cultural systems, it is because of their evolved status as irreducible aspects of human adaptation.

Bellah writes from the Weberian perspective of concern with religion as a cultural and institutional mechanism which develops and maintains the patterns of meaning and evaluation that provide the highest-level and most general guidance for the development and organization of society. Religious evolution is of special interest, in part because any substantial change in such a regulatory mechanism is apt to generate more massive alterations in the other principal sectors of society, but more basically because the evolutionary levels of whole societies and civilizations are fundamentally delimited by the regulatory capacities of their religions. Evolution of the religious regulatory mechanism is defined as increase in its differentiation and complexity that enhances its capacity to control its action environments. Abstracting beyond many mixed and interstitial cases and allowing for change that is evolutionarily regressive, Bellah arrays five principal types of religion in sequence according to their respective adaptive capacities.

For Bellah as for Weber, the critical turning point in religious evolution came with the rise of religions of the third type, the historic or world or salvation religions. These religions broke through the mythical cosmologies of the less evolved religions and oriented themselves in terms of philosophically rationalized conceptions of transcendental orders that stand over, against, and above the worldly cosmos. Religious individuals and committed collectivities then came to focus their ultimate concerns not in worldly interests or entanglements, but in the transcendent principles, standards, and evaluative implications. Special religious elites emerged to develop and preserve the doctrines concerned with the transcendent order. Generally, these elites came to monopolize contact with the transcendent and to control the mediation of salvation to individuals and collectivities in other statuses in society. Their control over the philosophically rationalized sectors of culture and over the channelling of salvation and charisma tended over the long run to exert strong pressures toward the rationalization of practically all sectors of social organization.

Compared with historic religions, the most primitive religions contain extremely little capacity to exert rationalizing pressure upon social organization. Even the most generalized elements of their sacred orders link directly into the social structure, providing particularistic sacralization of quite specific social arrangements—for example, in the way that totems and totemic orders sanctify the principal solidary units and the relations among them. The dramatic message of primitive myth seems to be that social life cannot legitimately be organized in any fashion other than that particularized in its symbolism. Archaic religions exhibit much greater regulatory flexibility and diversity than primitive religions, but lack the capacity of historic systems for systematic rationalization. Archaic mythical beings, or at least principal ones, are distant, majestic figures who stand above and generally command the human realm. Ritual involves less an entrance into the mythical realm itself, as in primitive religion, than an effort to gain the favors of the powerful gods through sacrifice, supplication, and declaration of subservience. By claiming to have received special recognition from the gods, advantaged groups are sometimes able to consolidate diffusely upper-class positions and gain control over privileged concentrations of prestige, authority, and economic resources. The introduction of such religiously legitimated class stratification generally involves important extensions in the size and complexity of society.

The modern types of religion, which have their origins in the Reformation, are founded upon reconstructions of the historic conceptions of the transcendent order and of its relations with the world. Early modern religion increased the generalization of the concept of transcendental order, setting it off more radically from and restructuring its tensions with the world. True and certain knowledge of the transcendent—for example, of God's will—became in principle unattainable for the merely human. No human institution could be believed to control the channelling of saving grace or legitimating charisma into society in the historic sense. Each individual had to confront the transcendent in the hope for grace as an autonomous, responsible conscience. The religious ideal was no longer an escape from the world to protect the purity of commitment to transcendent principles, but rather the perfection of the individual as an active agency for establishing transcendent principles in the world itself. Accommodations could not be made with worldly conditions, for the evils of the world were to be vanquished. As a sizable tradition of scholarship has demonstrated, the resulting religious impetus toward the transformation and rationalization of the social order played a very great role in the rise of modern society. With considerable caution, Bellah interprets certain elements in the current religious scene in the West as being indicative of the emergence of a new stage in religious evolution. Perhaps the most important of these elements is an apparent undermining of the hierarchical dualism between otherworld and world in favor of a symbol system that interrelates the two orders more flexibly. There has also been a decline in the concern with and assertion of dogma, perhaps offset by a personalization of belief and of participation in religious action. The long-run evolutionary consequences of the rise of this type of religion probably lie predominantly in the future.

Parsons outlines a general approach to the analysis of structural change of social systems within the framework of equilibrium theory. By structural change, he refers specifically to alteration in the normative institutions which control the interactive processes of social systems. This general conception of structural change encompasses great variation in regard to the type of institution that may undergo change and the consequences for the system of changes in institutions differently located within it. Parsons argues that the processes of structural change are always initiated by prior alterations at some boundary of the system involved, whether a boundary with another social system, another subsystem of action, or some aspect of the physical environment. Such boundary change will consist specifically in an imbalance between the inputs and outputs of the system that cannot be reversed or otherwise compensated for by the system's equilibrating mechanisms, for the most part in the so-called mechanisms of social control. The imbalance will have the effect of setting up a strain in the system by causing it to fail in some degree to fulfill the particular requirements of its adequate functioning. In proportion to the severity of the strain placed upon the system by the continuing, uncontrolled imbalance, attempts will be made to find alternative institutional arrangements that can lessen the strain by allowing for more adequate fulfillment of the system's functional needs—a matter somewhat complicated by the probability that the system's needs will be somewhat altered by the institutionalization of a new structure. The consequences of searching out and testing potential structures, which may be considered the sociological counterpart of variation in biological evolution, depend upon what combination of a number of factors develops. The outcome may vary from functional "failure" and collapse of the system to a state of continued structural indeterminacy or anomie, to the reestablishment of the old structure, to the establishment of a specific new replacement structure, to the more or less general reorganization of the system about either more complex or simpler structures. Parsons presents an analysis of the typical conditions under which factors will combine into a stable outcome that constitutes an evolutionary advance in the sense of an enhancement in the general capacities of the system to perform its characteristic functions. In this case, the structure that has been the focus for strain becomes differentiated into two or more structures which are more highly specialized in their functioning. The new structures must then be integrated into the broader system, serviced by resources (i.e., inputs) adapted to their new requirements, and legitimated by the more general values of the system.

the protocultural foundations
of human adaptation

one

A. IRVING HALLOWELL

...With the discovery of new types of early hominids (small brained but bipedal in locomotion), the accumulation of observations on the social behavior of nonhominid primates in their natural state, the development of psychoanalytic theories, culture and personality studies, and the conceptualization of the nature of culture provided by twentieth-century cultural anthropologists, we now have a more fruitful point of departure for enlarging the boundaries of evolutionary thinking beyond a morphological frame of reference. What appears to be indicated is a conjunctive approach to problems of hominid evolution in which relevant data from various specialized disciplines can be integrated and major categories of variables defined in the general framework of behavioral evolution.

Whether we consider hominid evolution in an ecological, a social, a psychological, or a linguistic frame of reference, behavior is the unifying center to which we must constantly return at any adaptive level. As we proceed to new levels, we must consider novel integrations of determinants brought about by potentialities for behavioral adaptations that did not previously exist. In the evolutionary process, differential behavior patterns provide major clues to significant variables. The social behavior characteristic of the mode of cultural adaptation that eventually became the most distinctive feature of hominid development could not have arisen *de novo*. It must have complex roots in the evolutionary process. It could not have emerged suddenly as a saltatory configuration. Unique as a cultural mode of adjustment appears to be when observed in *Homo sapiens,* there are behavioral continuities as well as discontinuities to be observed when man is considered in the total setting of his primate heritage. In ...a previous publication I suggested that the level of development represented by cultural adaptation can be focused more sharply in evolutionary perspective if we hypothecate a *protocultural* phase in hominid evolution and attempt to define its characteristic features. This earlier stage in development, deductively conceived, should embody some of the necessary, but not all of the sufficient, conditions for a fully developed human level of existence. On the one hand,

Reprinted from Sherwood L. Washburn, ed., *Social Life of Early Man* (Chicago, 1961), pp. 236–53, by permission of the publisher and of the author. Copyright 1961 by Aldine Publishing Co.; Viking Fund Publication in Anthropology no. 31.

it must have constituted a behavioral link between early hominids and other primates. On the other hand, it must have provided a preadaptive stage necessary for the later full-blown mode of cultural adaptation with which we are familiar in *Homo sapiens* by direct observation and experience.

What are the earmarks of a protocultural stage, and how may we identify them? We can best proceed, it seems to me, by selecting very broad categories for the purpose of comparing man with other hominids and infrahominid primates that, in addition to being relevant to all species, likewise bring into focus behavioral dimensions in which changes must have occurred in the course of the evolutionary process. What the selective pressures may have been that initiated such changes is not our present concern. The categories chosen here for brief discussion are: (1) social behavior and social structure, (2) ecological relations, (3) modes of communication and their properties, and (4) psychological capacities and organization. Observed behavioral similarities and differences, when considered with reference to the evolutionary process, indicate continuities and discontinuities in such behavioral categories and suggest some of the crucial features that, in combination, distinguish a protocultural phase in hominid evolution from a later and more fully realized level of cultural adaptation.

Social Behavior and Social Structure

Perhaps the major clue to the basic continuity that links the Hominidae to the other primate groups, and thus makes comparisons of similarities and differences in this category of behavioral evolution significant, is the fact we are dealing with gregarious animals. Whatever the ultimate determinants of sociality in the primates may be shown to be, all forms of cultural adaptation, as we know them in their fully developed stage, are based on some system of social action. But systems of social action are not unique in man. They also occur in infrahuman primates, and, structurally varied as they may be in different species, they constitute, nevertheless, a generic and characteristic mode of adaptation. Consequently, we may infer that social structure long antedated any form of cultural superstructure that, when eventually built into an organized system of social action in the course of hominid evolution, established the foundation of a new level of social living with the inherent potentialities that led to the emergence of various types of socio*cultural* systems. Cultural adaptation, then, is a mode of social existence deeply rooted in the behavioral evolution of the primates, where systems of social action were an ancient and typical feature of primate life. More detailed analysis shows basic similarities, as well as differences, in mating patterns and principles of organization that are meaningful in evolutionary perspective.

Mating patterns, of course, have suggested the closest human analogies. We see these analogies in types of mateship and in the range of their variation. Since lar gibbons, for example, live in groups that consist of one male and one female and their young, we have a close analogy to the "nuclear family" in man, which likewise represents a monogamous type of mateship. Some biological writers have applied the term "family" exclusively to this kind of primate social unit, despite the fact that in anthropological writing the term "family" is never limited to the nuclear family. The gibbon type of mateship, in which the sexual drive of the male appears to be low, would seem to be a limiting case in the total range of social units found among infrahuman primates and without evolutionary implications. In *Homo sapiens* we find two types of polygamous mateships, polygyny and polyandry, and social structures based on these are ordinarily called "families." Relatively rare in man in an institutionalized form, polyandrous mateships appear to be absent in infrahuman primates. On the other hand, polygynous mateships are common in both monkeys and apes. In the chimpanzee and gorilla this type of mateship seems to furnish the basis for independent social groups. In some monkeys, as, for instance, the baboon, "harems" occur as subgroups within the larger "troops" or "bands" found in these animals. Monogamous mateships, on the other hand, do not occur in groups of larger size because females in heat mate with more than one male.

Past attempts to establish any regular evolutionary sequence of mateship within *Homo sapiens* have failed, as well as have attempts to link any particular type of mateship in the nonhominid primates with early man. Perhaps it might be better to recognize that, since there are only a limited number of possibilities in mateships, it is not surprising to find them recurring at both the nonhominid and hominid levels of evolutionary development in the primates and in social units of varying size and composition. Whatever form they take, all these mateships serve the same reproductive ends. Their importance lies in this constancy in biological function rather than in any direct relation that can be shown to the evolution of group organization. They all lie close to biologically rooted central tendencies and continuities in behavioral evolution that link *Homo sapiens* to his

precursors. For what we find as the common social core of all but the lowest primate groups, despite their variation, is the continuous association of adults of both sexes with their offspring during the portion of the latter's life cycle that covers the period from birth to the threshold of maturity. This core pattern of associated individuals, when considered with reference to their interrelated roles, is linked with the fact that basic functions are involved, that is, the procreation, protection, and nurture of offspring—born singly, relatively helpless at birth, and dependent for a period thereafter. Variations in mateship or size of group may occur without affecting these functions. In addition, the sex needs of adults and the food needs of all members of the group can be taken care of. The role of the female in relation to her young does not seem to vary widely, nor does the behavior of infants and juveniles. The protective role of the male in relation to infants and juveniles is similar in gibbon and howler, even though the young of the group in the latter genus are not all his own offspring, and the actual biological relationship between these two species is remote. Among monkeys and apes the adult males never provide food for juveniles or females. After being weaned, the juveniles always forage for themselves. Whether we call nonhominid primate groups "families," "clans," "troops," or "bands," their basic social composition can be expressed by the same general formula: X males $+ X$ females $+ X$ infants $+ X$ juveniles.

Whatever the mating types or size of early hominid groups may have been, their social composition must have conformed to this fundamental pattern. This generic type of social structure, associated with territorialism, must have persisted throughout the extremely long temporal period during which major morphological changes occurred in the species of the primate order, including those that ultimately differentiated the Hominidae from the Pongidae and later hominids from earlier ones. Underlying it, physiologically, was the type of ovarian cycle characteristic of practically all the primates. In contrast to some mammalian species, in which females have only one oestrus period a year, primate females, along with those of a limited number of other mammalian species, are characterized by successive oestrus cycles in the course of a year. Breeding is not seasonal but continuous.

The evolutionary significance of the social organization of primate groups cannot be fully appreciated, however, without considering behavioral patterns other than those directly connected with reproduction. For the structuralization of infrahuman societies is by no means a simple function of differential roles determined by sex and age. Of central importance in many of the groups so far investigated is the existence of interindividual behavior influences by an order of social ranking in the group, a dominance gradient. Males are, quite generally, dominant over females, and the females associated with them may sometimes outrank other females. While it appears that in different species the "slope" of the dominance gradient varies considerably, some kind of rank order occurs. This factor in the operation of the social structure is important because it reduces aggression between males, determines priorities to mates and food, influences the spatial disposition of individuals within the group, affects the socialization of group habits, and may determine the relations of groups adjacent to one another. Nevertheless, the ranking position of individuals is not fully determined once and for all; an individual's role in the dominance hierarchy may change. There are psychological factors that must be taken into account.

Enough has been said to indicate that in evolutionary perspective a necessary locus and an indispensable condition for a cultural system is an organized system of social action in which social behavior is patterned by role differentiation. Role differentiation in the nonhominid primates, in other gregarious animals, and in man exemplifies a basic principle in the organization of social relations, whether the determinants be innate or learned or a combination of both. A social structure, therefore, can be identified as one of the characteristic features of a protocultural stage in hominid evolution. Once this is recognized, I believe that the emergence of a cultural system is made intelligible if we assume that any adaptive genetic changes that took place inevitably became of vital importance to the social order. The interplay and cumulative effects of changes of all sorts must have been fed back into the system of social action that prevailed and led to modifications in its operation. Cultural adaptation, indeed, may be viewed as the culmination of *social* evolution in the primates. It could not have occurred if there had not been changes in ecological relations, psychological capacities, and codes of communication that directly affected both the behavior of individuals and the social structure. Overemphasis sometimes has been given to the brain as such, in relation to the development of culture. We now know that it was bipedal locomotion rather than brain size that gave initial morphological impetus to the hominid radiation. While no one would wish to minimize the importance of the later expansion of the brain in behavioral evolution, cause-and-effect relations are oversimplified if we do not take into account the continuing social context of behavior, the potentialities for change in the patterns of inter-individual relations and, consequently, in the attributes of the social order considered as an evolving system. Whatever new potentialities may be attributed to the acquisition of additional neurones in the brain, and their organization, the resulting behavior must have become functionally manifest in a system of social action already in existence.

Ecological Relations

A cultural level of adaptation, in addition to requiring a preadaptive base in a system of social action, also required an environmental setting in which ecological relations at a protocultural stage provided the foundation for later developments. Whatever part arboreal adaptation may played in the earlier evolution of the primates, including the development of distinctive psychological capacities and behavorial patterns, it is difficult, if not impossible, to imagine an arboreal niche as the basic ecological matrix of the hominid line of evolution that eventuated in a cultural mode of adaptation. It was terrestrial living that provided the ecological framework of this development and, when the necessary psychological capacities, experience, and technological traditions had been developed, enabled the hominids to accelerate the behavioral differences between themselves and other primates by exploiting the resources of their environment through knowledge of it and a succession of discoveries and inventions.

Even if capacities for *tool-using* were present in arboreal primates, how could the properties of stone have been discovered, exploited, and developed through shaping techniques into the lithic industries of a *tool-making* tradition by creatures who spent relatively little time on the ground? How could fire have become of importance in the life of primates confined to an arboreal niche? It was terrestrial living that provided the opportunity for the discovery of new food resources and made possible the shift to a carnivorous diet and the cooking of food, which ultimately led, through a scavenging stage perhaps, to the hunting of large mammals. If an upright posture with bipedal locomotion be taken as crucial generic features in hominid structural and behavioral differentiation, the terrestrial adaptation that accompanied them led to radical changes in the ecological relations of evolving hominids as compared with their primate forebears and the arboreally adapted monkeys and pongids. Motor functions already present, like grasping, were freed for new uses, and the discriminatory functions of binocular stereoscopic vision facilitated new developments in tactile skills, in manual dexterity, and probably in visual imagery, which ultimately became increasingly mediated through the more complex level of cortical organization made possible by the expansion of the brain. A new ecological niche provided the opportunity for the exercise, at a new level of behavioral organization, of behavioral potentialities already present, as well as for the development of new behavioral patterns. From an ecological point of view, a terrestrial habitat was a necessary setting for the protocultural stage in hominid adaptation that established the behavioral foundation for subsequent cultural adaptation.

One of the most characteristic features of the adaptation of infrahuman primates is territoriality. The locus of the social structures already discussed is a bounded area defined by the spatial range of the daily activities of members of each group. Ecologically, territoriality is the means by which the dispersal of the total primate population of a given region is spatially ordered and the independence of these breeding and nurturing groups maintained as distinguishable social units. Ordinarily, members of the different groups in a given region do not freely mix, nor do adults of different groups interbreed. The strong avoidance behavior that prevails between different groups is complemented by the factors that promote in-group integration. Territoriality, as observed among living primates is, therefore, a fundamental ecological adaptation that, at the same time, functions as a barrier to social integration of a higher order and to more complex social composition and role differentiation.

If we assume that territoriality persisted among the earliest hominids, some interesting questions arise. What was the size and range of these groups, and at what point in hominid development and under what conditions were groups of a higher order of complexity formed? For in men of the historic period, at least, we always find types of social organization that transcend in composition and role differentiation, if not always in size, what we find at the infrahuman primate level. The later, more evolved, forms of social organization incorporate the nuclear family, as well as other types of family structure, in a larger whole that includes individuals of all ages, as well as both sexes, and three or more generations. At this level, of course, sexual differentiation of roles in the performance of economic tasks has emerged, a phenomenon unknown in the nonhominid primates. We can only assume that, in the course of hominid evolution, factors must have come into play that made possible the functional integration of groups with radically different social composition and role differentiation from those that existed at the earliest stage of hominid development. At the same time it also became possible to transcend, through the development of new patterns of ecological relationships, the older form of ecological adaptation that formerly prevailed. Although social organization and ecological adjustment of the kind just mentioned must have considerable historical depth, for which there is some archeological as well as ethnographical evidence among hunting and gathering peoples, one must associate such developments with euhominids, who already had arrived at a cultural level of adaptation. As Sahlins has said:

Primate territorial relations are altered by the development of culture in the human species. Territoriality among hunters and gatherers is never exclusive, and group membership is apt to shift and change according to the variability of food resources in space and time. Savage society is open, and corresponding to ecological variations, there are degrees of openness.[1]

At an earlier protocultural stage the size, composition, structure, and behavioral range of social groups was determined by the same basic factors of ecological adaptation generally characteristic of nonhominid primates. At the same time, behavior was limited by psychological factors that made it impossible for systems of social action of a higher order to

---

[1] Marshall D. Sahlins, "The Social Life of Monkeys, Apes, and Primitive Man," in J. N. Spuhler, ed., *The Evolution of Man's Capacity for Culture* (Detroit; Wayne State University Press, 1959), p. 58.

arise. Washburn and Avis point out:
The acquisition of hunting habits must
have been accompanied by a great en-
largement of territory, since the source
of food was now more erratic and
mobile.... Whether early man scavenged
from the kills of the big carnivores, followed herds looking for a chance to kill,
drove game, or followed a wounded animal, his range of operations must have
been greatly increased over that of arboreal apes. The world view of the early
human carnivore must have been very
different from that of his vegetarian
cousins. The interests of the latter could
be satisfied in a small area, and other
animals were of little moment except for
the few which threatened attack. But the
desire for meat leads animals to know a
wider range and to learn the habits of
many animals. Human territorial habits
and psychology are fundamentally different from those of apes and monkeys....
This carnivorous psychology was fully
formed by the middle Pleistocene and
it may have had its beginnings in the
depredations of the Australopithecines.[2]

**Modes of Communication and Their
Properties**

The prevailing sensory modes of
communication among primates are
visual and acoustic. Both appear to be
extremely important. Schultz speaks
of the intricate "silent vocabulary" of
the nonhominid primate.

Crouching down, presenting buttocks,
extending hands in pronation, exposing
teeth partly or fully, raising eyebrows,
protruding lips, shaking branches, pound-
ing chest, dancing in one place, etc., all
are actions full of definite meaning....
[Although] the long lists of different
postures, gestures, and facial movements
characteristic of monkeys and apes have
not yet been compiled,...any careful

observer realizes that they represent an
intricate "silent vocabulary" of great aid
in social intercourse.

In the perfectly adapted arboreal life of
monkeys and apes the limited variety
of sounds, together with the great variety
of meaningful gestures and facial expressions, is fully adequate for all social life
within such close contact as permits
seeing and hearing these detailed means
of communication.[3]

The utterance of sounds, Schultz says,
is "the essence of primate life..., the
simian primates are by far the noisiest
of all mammals." In species that have
been closely investigated, like the
howling monkeys of Panama and the
lar gibbon, differentiated vocalizations
have been shown to have functional
significance in the social coordination
of the individuals belonging to a
group. Schultz says:

[The primatologist] regards *language* not
as the result of something radically new
and exclusively human, but rather as a
quantitative perfection of the highly specialized development of man's central
nervous control of the anatomical speech
apparatus in the larynx, tongue, and lips,
the latter being as good in an ape as in
man.... As soon as the early hominids
had ventured into open spaces, had begun to use and even make tools, and had
co-operated in hunting, the total variety
of all means of expression needed additions, which could come only from an
increase in sounds, since the comparatively little changed anatomy had already
been fully used for all possible gestures,
etc.... Gestures have always persisted in
human evolution, but they have become
overshadowed by an infinitely greater
variety of sounds in increasing numbers
of combinations.[4]

Oakley and others have suggested
that early hominids may have de-

2 S. L. Washburn and Virginia Avis,
"Evolution and Human Behavior," in Ann
Roe and G. G. Simpson, eds., *Behaviour
and Evolution* (New Haven: Yale University Press, 1958), p. 434.

3 A. H. Schultz, "Social Behavior and
Early Man," in S. L. Washburn, ed.,
Social Life of Early Man (Chicago: Aldine
Publishing Co., 1961).
4 *Ibid.*

pended primarily on gestures "mainly of mouth and hands, accompanied by cries and grunts to attract attention" and that speech may have been a comparatively late development.[5] If so, a nonhominid mode of communication would have persisted in the protocultural phase of hominid evolution. Unfortunately, this interpretation must remain speculative. It is difficult to imagine...how a fully developed cultural mode of adaptation could operate without speech. However, if one of the necessary conditions for the functioning of a typically human system of communication is a speech community, an organized social system is as necessary for human language as it is for a cultural mode of adaptation. This condition was present even at the nonhominid level. So what we can discern in primate evolution is a behavioral plateau that provided the necessary context, but, at first, not all the sufficient conditions for either speech or culture.

Hockett has...pointed out that "part of the problem of differentiating man from the other animals is the problem of describing how human language differs from any kind of communicative behavior carried on by nonhuman or prehuman species. Until we have done this, we cannot know how much it means to assert that only man has the power of speech."[6] He has approached the problem by identifying seven "key properties" of the speech of *Homo sapiens* and comparing them with the available data on nonhuman systems of communication, discovering that there was considerable over-lapping in the properties selected, although

they did "not recur, as a whole set, in any known nonhuman communicative system."[7] This suggested that the combination of properties that characterize speech, "those design-features...which seem to be of crucial importance in making it possible for language to do what it does,"[8] did not arise full blown. Hockett argues that this assemblage of properties, considered with reference to man's lineage, "could not have emerged in just any temporal sequence. Some of them either unquestionably or with high likelihood imply the prior existence of some of the others."[9] Consequently, he is led to suggest a tentative evolutionary reconstruction. Since one of the key properties of a human system of communication is "cultural transmission," a property absent in the communication systems of primates and other animals, this factor becomes highly significant chronologically and, I think, has wider implications than those developed by Hockett, who suggests, in effect, that, although learning and the social transmission of habits, or what he calls "culture of a rather thin sort" may have existed at a very early stage in the development of the higher primates, the associated system of communication that prevailed may have operated without "cultural transmission."[10] The significance of the fact that these earlier

---

[5] Kenneth P. Oakley, "A Definition of Man," *Science News,* No. 20 (1951), p. 75.

[6] Charles F. Hockett, *A Course in Modern Linguistics* (New York: Macmillan, 1958), p. 570.

[7] *Ibid.,* p. 574.

[8] Charles F. Hockett, "'Animal Languages' and Human Language," in Spuhler, *Evolution of Man's Capacity,* p. 32.

[9] Charles F. Hockett, *Modern Linguistics,* p. 581.

[10] Hockett, "'Animal Languages,'" says: "A behavior pattern is transmitted culturally if it is not only learned but *taught,* and if the teaching behavior, whatever it may be, is also learned rather than genetically determined." Cf. *Modern Linguistics,* pp. 578–80. Teaching and learned teaching behavior, of course, re-

codes of communication did not function through learning and social transmission lies in the limitations this imposed upon the systems of social action developed in nonhominid and, perhaps, the earliest hominid groups. At the same time, these codes of communication, operating through the same sensory modes that appear at a later level may be considered prerequisite for the evolutionary development of a communication system characterized by the total assemblage of properties discussed by Hockett.

This kind of evolutionary inquiry is, of course, a far cry from earlier approaches, particularly those that began by concentrating on the problem of "primitive" languages spoken by *Homo sapiens*. Hockett's approach does permit us to have a fresh look at speech in greater evolutionary depth. And by direct observation we know that, whereas some of the great apes have been able to acquire a "thin sort" of human culture when closely associated with members of our species, they do not have the capacity to acquire and use our distinctive form of symbolic communication, even when systematically motivated. There seems little reason to doubt that in the course of behavorial evolution psychological capacities of crucial importance lay back of the ultimate emergence among the hominids of a characteristic system of linguistic communication. While this system shared some "design features" with that of nonhominid primates, capacities that transcended those of the other primates permitted the development and integration of novel features. These, in turn, resulted in the functional potentialities of speech as we know it in *Homo sapiens*.

Psychological Capacities and Organization

Far down the evolutionary scale we have evidence that indicates that some activities of animals may originate, or be changed, through experience and affect subsequent behavior. When such responses cannot be reduced to innate determinants, or maturational processes, they are ordinarily referred to as "learned," although the conceptualization is loose. Harlow maintains that "there is no evidence that any sharp break ever appeared in the evolutionary development of the learning process" while, at the same time, "it is quite clear that evolution has resulted in the development of animals of progressively greater potentialities for learning and for solving problems of increasing complexity."[11] My principal concern here is with the relevance of learning to the question of a protocultural platform in hominid evolution. While, as Nissen once said, "experience will not make a man out of a monkey," nevertheless, the extent to which learning is an integral part of the systems of social action, ecological relations, and modes of communication in monkeys and apes is relevant for an understanding of hominid evolution in an inclusive evolutionary perspective. What needs particular emphasis is what is learned and what is not, and the fact that what is individually learned by one animal may directly influence the behavior of other animals. It is not learning as such that requires consideration as a diagnostic characteristic of a protocultural stage. What is significant is that the part that learn-

---

quire a level of psychological organization far higher than that observed in any nonhominid primate.

[11] Harry F. Harlow, "The Evolution of Learning," in Roe and Simpson, *Behavior and Evolution*, pp. 288, 289.

ing plays in the life history and social relations of the nonhominid primates closely parallels, at so many points, the part that it plays in human socio-cultural systems.

Beach, for example, says: "Descriptions of mother-infant relations in monkeys and chimpanzee leave no doubt as to the importance of learning in the filial responses of immature primates. The infant learns to obey gestures and vocal communications given by the mother and derives considerable advantage from her tuition and guidance."[12] Socialization of the young, moreover, is an important factor in the formation and maintenance of infrahuman primate groups, as Carpenter pointed out long ago. And Collias, considering socialization in the wider perspective of behavioral evolution, points out: "In both insect and vertebrate societies, maintenance of cooperative relations depends to a large extent on socialization of the young. Among vertebrates, this trend reaches its climax in the primates."[13] The formation of dominance gradients likewise involves learning, even in lower mammals, and the phenomenon of territoriality in the primates also requires learning. It seems reasonable to assume, therefore, that the intimate relations between learning, social structure, and ecological adaptation, so fundamental in the functioning of culture, were well established in the nonhominid primates prior to the anatomical changes that led to both erect posture and the expansion of the brain.

---

12 Frank A. Beach, "Instinctive Behavior: Reproductive Activities," in S. S. Stevens, ed., *Handbook of Experimental Psychology* (New York: Wiley, 1951), p. 426.
13 N. E. Collias, "Social Life and the Individual among Vertebrate Animals," *Annals, New York Academy of Science,* Vol. 50: 1087.

Even more important, perhaps, is that fact that, at this same stage in both monkeys and apes, learned habits might not only be acquired by individuals of various ages but also could be transmitted through social interaction to other individuals in the group. The most striking cases have been reported by observers who have been studying *Macaca fuscata* at the Japanese Monkey Center. These primates have been lured from their forest habitat into open feeding places, where, among other things, they have been offered new foods. Systematic observation has shown that newly acquired food habits, such as eating candies, become quite readily socialized. Imanishi points out, moreover, that young macaques acquire the candy-eating habit more quickly than do the adults and that some mothers learned to eat candies from their offspring, rather than the other way round. It has likewise been observed that the spread of a new food habit may be directly related to the dominance gradient that is a central feature of their social structure. Adult females of high rank were observed to imitate the wheat-eating of a dominant male very quickly, and the habit was passed on to their offspring. Females of lower rank, in a more peripheral position in the group, only later acquired the habit from their offspring, who, in turn, had picked it up through association with their playmates. The rate of transmission was extremely rapid in this case, the entire process occurring within two days. In another instance, a young female initiated the habit of washing sweet potatoes before eating them. This habit, having been transmitted to her playmates, as well as to her mother, was slowly transmitted to a number of groups during the next three years. The same class of phenomenon in the anthropoid apes is illustrated by nest-building in chimpanzee and the transmission of the technique of working the drinking fountain at Orange Park, which champanzees learned from each other.

In the past, the social transmission of acquired behavior patterns has sometimes been stressed as one of the distinctive characteristics of culture. But in the light of our present knowledge of primate behavior it is better to consider it as one of the conditions necessary for cultural adaptation rather than as the distinguishing feature of it. Social transmission of acquired behavior patterns is, rather, a prerequisite of culture and an earmark of an earlier protocultural behavior plateau. The fact that even some animals other than primates may learn from one another or that some chimpanzees in social interaction with members of our species have acquired "culture traits," is no indication that a full-fledged level of cultural adaptation has been reached in these species. It only confounds the conceptualization and the investigation of hominid evolution if the term "culture" is applied, without qualification, to the phenomena of social transmission of simple habits in infrahuman species. J. P. Scott, for example, writes:

The more the capacities for learning and for variable organization of behavior are present, the more it is possible for an animal to learn from its parents and pass the information along to the next generation. As we accumulate greater knowledge of natural animal behavior, we find more and more evidence that many animals possess the rudiments of this new ability, which we can call cultural inheritance. The migration trails of mountain sheep and the learned fears of wild birds are two of many examples. . . . At the present time all our evidence indicates that cultural inheritance exists only in quite simple form in animals other than man, but future research may show that it is more common and complex than we now suspect.[14]

While it is true that a variety of gregarious animals possess the *rudiments* of an ability to be influenced by the behavior of other individuals of their species, the part this ability plays in their total life history and social relations is what needs precise analysis. In phylogenetic perspective it is only in the primates that capacities and conditions arose which led to the transcendence of a rudimentary stage. And at this stage the primates are distinguished from other animals by a higher capacity for observational learning. Munn concludes that: "it is only in monkeys and apes that anything clearly approximating such observational learning can be demonstrated and even at this level the problems solved by imitation are relatively simple."[15] If we use the term culture to refer to different levels of behavioral evolution, our vocabulary fails to discriminate the quantitative and qualitative differences between cultural adaptation in man and the very rudimentary "cultural" manifestations found in infrahuman animals, to say nothing of possible differences between primates and nonprimates. Dobzhansky, in a brief discussion of the "Rudiments of Cultural Transmission among Animals," has pointed out one essential difference between a protocultural and a cultural level of behavior, although he does not analyze specific cases in detail and his chief citations refer to birds rather than to primates. He says:

In animals the individuals of one generation transmit to those of the next what

---

¹⁴ J. P. Scott, *Animal Behavior* (Chicago: University of Chicago Press, 1958), p. 237.

¹⁵ Norman L. Munn, *The Evolution and Growth of Human Behavior* (Boston: Houghton Mifflin, 1955).

they themselves learned from their parents—not more and not less. Every generation learns the same thing which its parents have learned. In only very few instances the evidence is conclusive that the learned behavior can be modified or added to and that the modifications and additions are transmitted to subsequent generations.[16]

Simple conditioning and possibly observational learning account for these facts. The greater capacity for observational learning in primates also accounts for the socialization of nest-building habits in chimpanzee and the spread of the habit of washing sweet potatoes observed in the macaque group already referred to. But, so long as social transmission was dependent on capacities for observational learning, this fact limited the kind of acquired habits or innovations that could become significant in the adaptation of the group. Intervening factors were required before quantitative and qualitative differences in the kind of innovations possible at this level could be modified or changed and become effective through other mechanisms of socialization. It is difficult, for example, to imagine how the manufacture of tools, and the development of tool-making traditions could have arisen at a protocultural stage at which the mechanism of social transmission was exclusively observational learning and at which communication was mediated through signs rather than through any form of symbolic representation. Washburn and Avis, moreover, have expressed the opinion that tool-using may require

much less brain than does speech and might have started as soon as the hands

were freed from locomotor functions. Oral traditions essential for complicated human society probably were not possible with less than 700 or 800 cc. of brain [as contrasted with a range of about 450 to 600 cc. in the Australopithecines], and there is no likelihood that elaborate traditions of tool making are possible at lesser capacities, although simple pebble tools might well be.[17]

Among other things, too, tool-making must have involved a whole series of discoveries and the accumulation of information necessary in a discriminating search for and selection of lithic materials with particular properties, in addition to the development and application of skilled methods of chipping. Even if we assume that there must have been successive stages in the development of tool-making traditions, these cannot be envisaged in a social and psychological vacuum, so that questions about a capacity for temporal orientation toward the future, the existence of property rights, as well as the kind of communication system to be assumed are relevant to the problem. It has often been said, for example, that a fully developed tool-making tradition is difficult to conceive in the absence of speech. It becomes all the more significant, then, that, despite the part that learning plays in the life of living primates at a protocultural level, they can be negatively characterized by the fact that no code of communication exists with the assemblage of properties appearing in speech and that whatever sublinguistic codes prevail appear to be transmitted genetically rather than through learning. We also know that chimpanzees cannot be taught to speak, despite the fact that, when closely associated with members of

---

16 T. Dobzhansky, *Evolution, Genetics, and Man* (New York: Wiley, 1955), pp. 340–41.

17 Washburn and Avis, "Evolution and Human Behavior," p. 432.

our species, it is possible for them to acquire many human habits through learning. Whatever inferences we make about the transition from a protocultural stage to a level of cultural adaptation, we must consider what habits were socially transmitted and what were not. And, quite aside from the properties of any code of communication, the question of its social transmittal must be taken into account.

Thus, while we may say that in the course of hominid evolution all the characteristic features of a protocultural stage were incorporated at a subsequent level of cultural adaptation, at the same time we must account for the differences observed. Here, organic changes, considered as intervening factors, must be taken into account. At the protocultural stage the psychological capacities of the actors determined the limiting framework of social and ecological adaptation. Although we cannot now observe the behavioral characteristics of the protohominids themselves, subsequent hominid developments in social structure, ecological relations, and modes of communication can hardly be dissociated from the known organic changes in the central nervous system after prior morphological changes in posture and locomotion have distinguished the hominid radiation. Account must be taken also of the sociopsychological effects produced by biological factors that prolonged dependency of the young, delayed reproduction, and increased the life span in an already well-advanced hominid whose psychological functioning was, at the same time, being greatly enhanced and restructured. All the distinctive features of a protocultural stage were being raised to a new level of sociopsychological integration through the increasing part that cortical processes came to play.

In time, this new level of psychological organization affected every aspect of the earlier mode of protocultural adaptation. It led to the transformation of provincial social structures, through a change in their underlying dynamics, into the more inclusive, complex, and diversified socio*cultural* systems of the euhominids. At this more evolved stage a normative orientation became an inherent and distinctive feature of these systems of social action. Psychological factors became paramount in the functioning of these systems because the socially sanctioned values that characterized them were linked with the cognitive processes, motivations, and need satisfactions of individuals through the formation of a new and distinctive type of personality organization molded in the socialization process. What was learned in this process, beginning in infancy, not only included habits, roles, and adjustment to a physical environment, but also speech and a sense of values that pervaded every phase of personal adjustment and behavior. Conduct was evaluated in relation to socially sanctioned ethical standards. Food and material objects were not merely possessed; possession was regulated by a system of property rights. Skills and techniques used in the manufacture of material objects were also appraised in relation to recognized standards. Knowledge and beliefs were judged true or false, and art forms and linguistic expression were brought within the sphere of a normative orientation. All sociocultural systems became infused with appraisals that involved cognitive, appreciative, and moral values. If the total ramifications of the normative orientation of human societies are taken into account, we have a major clue to the kind of radical psychological transformation that must have occurred in hominid evolution and a measure of its depth and significance for an understanding of the dynamics of a cultural mode of adaptation as compared with what we find at a protocultural level.

Psychologically, a normatively oriented social order requires a capacity for self-objectification on the part of the individual actors. This makes possible self-identification over time, and an appraisal of ones' own personal conduct and that of others in a common framework of socially transmitted and sanctioned values. Without the capacity for a psychological level of organization that permits the exercise of these and other functions, the social system could not function at the level of normative orientation nor could moral responsibility for conduct exist. Learning remains important, of course, but it operates at a higher level of sociopsychological integration than was possible at a protocultural level. The relations between needs, motivation, socially recognized goals, and learning are more complex because cortical processes have become increasingly important. It is impossible to attribute an equivalent level of psychological functioning to the earliest hominids.

What occurred in the psychological dimension of hominid evolution was the development of a human personality structure in which the capacity for self-awareness, based on ego functions, became of central importance. The functioning of ego processes contributed new qualities to the psychological adjustment of individuals in the socialization process. Ego functions became integral factors in determining responses to the outer world in the interests of inner needs, particularly when delay or postponement of action is required. They became intimately connected with such cognitive processes as attention, perception, thinking, and judgment. Con-

sidered in evolutionary perspective, ego may be said to be the major "psychological organ" that structurally differentiates the most highly evolved members of the Hominidae from infrahuman primates. At the same time, there is some evidence that suggests that rudimentary ego functions may be present in some of the higher apes, so it is possible that equivalent functions may have been present in the early hominids.

In ontogenetic development, as observed in *Homo sapiens,* ego processes can be identified in the first half-year of life, but a fully developed sense of self-awareness represents a psychological level of functional integration that is only manifest later. The initial development of the ego process does not appear to be dependent upon the prior existence of speech or culture, whereas self-awareness, on the other hand, requires socialization, a normative orientation, and the manipulation of what I have called extrinsic forms of symbolization. In other words, self-awareness is an integral psychological factor in cultural adaptation itself. It is rooted not only in ego functions but also in an already existent psychological capacity to abstract significant bits from the flow of experience and to represent their content in a meaningful form of expression extrinsic to the experience itself. This capacity to *project and objectify* significant aspects of experience may be contrasted with the evidence for *intrinsic* symbolic processes that occur in nonhominid primates and even lower mammals, that is, central processes that function as substitutes for, or representatives of, sensory cues or events that are not present in the immediate perceptual field. In the evolved hominid, processes of this kind can become socially significant by objectification in a variety of extrinsic symbolic forms.

In nonhominid primates, on the other hand, only outward behavior in its concrete forms can become meaningful through perception. And the response, as has been indicated, may be observational learning. But what is privately sensed, imaged, "conceptualized," or "thought" cannot be responded to without an overt sign that represents it, but is, at the same time, extrinsic to the experience itself. In the evolved hominid, extrinsic symbolic forms, functioning through vocal, graphic, plastic, or gestural media, make it possible for groups of human beings to participate in a common world of meanings and values that is no longer confined to the perception of outward behavior alone or to concrete objects or events immediately given in perception. Both art and speech exploit this novel capacity for extrinsic symbolization. The artists of the Upper Paleolithic were capable of invoking intrinsic symbolic processes (memory images of animals), abstracting significant features, and representing these animals in a graphic form. In principle, the same capacity, expressed in arbitrary sound clusters that have no iconic relation to the objects and events represented, is one of the characteristics that distinguishes speech from infrahuman forms of communication in which signs, without symbolic value, are found.

The capacity for individual and social adaptation through the integral functioning of intrinsic symbolic processes and extrinsic symbolic forms enabled an evolving hominid to enlarge and transform his world and to become, at the same time, an object to himself. Means now became available whereby inwardly as well as outwardly directed references to an individual's own experience and that of others, and to objects and events in his world other than self, could find common ground through symbolic mediation. The immediate, local, and time-and-space-bound world of other primates who could not deal effectively with objects and events outside the field of direct perception was transcended. Speech, through the use of kinship terms, made it possible, among other things, for an individual to symbolize, and thus objectify himself, in systems of social action. And, as Professor Grace A. De Laguna has pointed out, becoming an object to one's self "carries with it the awareness of other persons not only as *objects,* but as *fellow-subjects.* An 'other' person is not only 'him' *of* whom I speak, but you *to* whom I speak and in turn an 'I' who speaks to me." As a consequence of self-objectification, sociocultural systems could function through the commonly shared value orientations of *persons,* self-conscious individuals in contrast to the societies of nonhominid and early hominid primates, where ego-centered processes, even though they existed in a rudimentary form, had not yet become salient at the psychological level of self-awareness. In fact, when viewed from the standpoint of this peculiarity of man, culture may be said to be an elaborated and socially transmitted system of meanings and values that, in an animal capable of self-awareness, implemented a type of adaptation that made the roles of the human being intelligible to himself, with reference both to an articulated universe and to his fellow men.

In anthropological writing prior to the culture and personality movement, the connection between learning and culture remained vague because it had not been carefully analyzed in relation to the development of personality structure, cognitive orientation, motivation, etc. The fact had been overlooked that the only way in which a sociocultural system can be perpetuated is through the characteristic psychological structuralization of individuals in an organized system of social action. In the perspective of hominid evolution it is significant that the foundation for this later development was laid at the protocultural level, where learning was also intimately linked with the functioning of social structures, dominance gradients, and with the social transmission of habits. But at this protocultural stage what was learned was greatly restricted by the psychological capacities of the nonhominids. In *Homo sapiens,* on the other hand, we see the quantitative maximization of learning that, because of expanded psychological capacities, has led to qualitatively distinctive consequences. Among other things, we find cognitive processes raised to a higher level of functioning by means of symbolic forms, which can be manipulated creatively through reflective thought and experience. Cultural modes of adaptation, or certain aspects of them, learned and transmitted as they may be, can be objectified, thought about, analyzed, judged, and even remodeled. Man has never been completely enslaved by this traditional cultural heritage. The great novelty, then, in the behavioral evolution of the primates was not simply the development of a cultural mode of adaptation as such. It was, rather, the psychological restructuralization that, occurring in a primate where a system of organized social action already was present, not only made possible a more advanced level of social existence but laid the foundation for subsequent cultural readjustment and change. The psychological basis of culture does not lie only in a capacity for highly complex forms of learning and personality organization. What should not be overlooked is the potentiality that exists for transcending what is learned—a capacity for innovation, creativity, reorganization, and change in sociocultural systems themselves.

religious evolution

two

ROBERT N. BELLAH

"Time in its aging course teaches all things."

—Aeschylus: *Prometheus Bound*

Though one can name precursors as far back as Herodotus, the systematically scientific study of religion begins only in the second half of the 19th century. According to Chantepie de la Saussaye, the two preconditions for this emergence were that religion had become by the time of Hegel the object of comprehensive philosophical speculation and that history by the time of Buckle had been enlarged to include the history of civilization and culture in general.[1] In its early phases,

Reprinted from the *American Sociological Review,* 29 (June 1964): 358–74, by permission of The American Sociological Association and the author.

Part of this paper was given as an open lecture at the University of Chicago on October 16, 1963. Many of the ideas in the paper were worked out in presentations to a seminar on social evolution which I gave together with Talcott Parsons and S. N. Eisenstadt at Harvard University in the spring of 1963. I wish to acknowledge the criticisms received from Professors Parsons and Eisenstadt and the students in the seminar as well as the comments of Parsons on this manuscript.

---

[1] Chantepie de la Saussaye, *Manuel d'Histoire des Religions,* French translation directed by H. Hubert and I. Levy, Paris: Colin, 1904, author's introduction.

partly under the influence of Darwinism, the science of religion was dominated by an evolutionary tendency already implicit in Hegelian philosophy and early 19th century historiography. The grandfathers of modern sociology, Comte and Spencer, contributed to the strongly evolutionary approach to the study of religion as, with many reservations, did Durkheim and Weber.

But by the third decade of the 20th century the evolutionary wave was in full retreat both in the general field of science of religion and in the sociology of religion in particular. Of course, this was only one aspect of the general retreat of evolutionary thought in social science, but nowhere did the retreat go further nor the intensity of the opposition to evolution go deeper than in the field of religion. An attempt to explain the vicissitudes of evolutionary conceptions in the field of religion would be an interesting study in the sociology of knowledge but beyond the scope of this brief paper. Here I can only say that I hope that the present attempt to apply the evolutionary idea to religion evidences a serious appreciation of both 19th century evolutionary theories and 20th century criticisms of them.

Evolution at any system level I define as a process of increasing differentiation and complexity of organization which endows the organism, social system or whatever the unit in question may be, with greater capacity to adapt to its environment so that it is in some sense more autonomous relative to its environment than were its less complex ancestors. I do not assume that evolution is inevitable, irreversible or must follow any single particular course. Nor do I assume that simpler forms cannot prosper and survive alongside more complex forms. What I mean by evolution, then, is nothing metaphysical but the simple empirical generalization that more complex forms develop from less complex forms and that the properties and possibilities of more complex forms differ from those of less complex forms.

A brief handy definition of religion is considerably more difficult than a definition of evolution. An attempt at an adequate definition would, as Clifford Geertz has...demonstrated, take a paper in itself for adequate explanation.[2] So, for limited purposes only, let me define religion as a set of symbolic forms and acts which relate man to the ultimate conditions of his existence. The purpose of this definition is to indicate exactly what I claim has evolved. It is not the ultimate conditions, nor, in traditional language, God that has evolved, nor is it man in the broadest sense of *homo religiosus*. I am inclined to agree with Eliade when he holds that primitive man is as fully religious as man at any stage of existence, though I am not ready to go along with him when he implies *more* fully.[3]

Neither religious man nor the structure of man's ultimate religious situation evolves, then, but rather religion as symbol system. Erich Voegelin, who I suspect shares Eliade's basic philosophical position, speaks of a development from compact to differentiated symbolization.[4] Everything already exists in some sense in the religious symbol system of the most primitive man; it would be hard to find anything later that is not "foreshadowed" there, as for example, the monotheistic God is foreshadowed in the high gods of some primitive peoples. Yet just as obviously the two cannot be equated. Not only in their idea of God but in many other ways the monotheistic religions of Judaism, Christianity and Islam involve a much more differentiated symbolization of, and produce a much more complex relation to, the ultimate conditions of human existence than do primitive religions. At least the existence of that kind of difference is the thesis I wish to develop. I hope it is clear that there are a number of other possible meanings of the term "religious evolution" with which I am not concerned. I hope it is also clear that a complex and differentiated religious symbolization is not therefore a better or a truer or a more beautiful one than a compact religious symbolization. I am not a relativist and I do think judgments of value can reasonably be made between religions, societies or personalities. But the axis of that judgment is not provided by social evolution and if progress is used in an essentially ethical sense, then I for one will not speak of religious progress.

Having defined the ground rules under which I am operating let me now step back from the subject of religious evolution and look first at a few of the massive facts of human

---

2 Clifford Geertz, "Religion as a Cultural System," unpublished, 1963.

3 Mircea Eliade, *Patterns in Comparative Religion,* New York: Sheed and Ward, 1958, pp. 459–65.

4 Erich Voegelin, *Order and History,* Vol. I: *Israel and Revelation,* Baton Rouge: Louisiana State University Press, 1956, p. 5.

religious history. The first of these facts is the emergence in the first millenium B.C. all across the Old World, at least in centers of high culture, of the phenomenon of religious rejection of the world characterized by an extremely negative evaluation of man and society and the exaltation of another realm of reality as alone true and infinitely valuable. This theme emerges in Greece through a long development into Plato's classic formulation in the Phaedo that the body is the tomb or prison of the soul and that only by disentanglement from the body and all things worldly can the soul unify itself with the unimaginably different world of the divine. A very different formulation is found in Israel, but there too the world is profoundly devalued in the face of the transcendent God with whom alone is there any refuge or comfort. In India we find perhaps the most radical of all versions of world rejection, culminating in the great image of the Buddha, that the world is a burning house and man's urgent need is a way to escape from it. In China, Taoist ascetics urged the transvaluation of all the accepted values and withdrawal from human society, which they condemned as unnatural and perverse.

Nor was this a brief or passing phenomenon. For over 2000 years great pulses of world rejection spread over the civilized world. The *Qur'an* compares this present world to vegetation after rain, whose growth rejoices the unbeliever, but it quickly withers away and becomes as straw.[5] Men prefer life in the present world but the life to come is infinitely superior—it alone is everlasting.[6] Even in Japan, usually so innocently world accepting, Shōtoku Taishi declared that the world is a lie and only the Buddha is true, and in the Kamakura period the conviction that the world is hell led to orgies of religious suicide by seekers after Amida's paradise.[7] And it is hardly necessary to quote Revelations or Augustine for comparable Christian sentiments. I do not deny that there are profound differences among these various rejections of the world; Max Weber has written a great essay on the different directions of world rejection and their consequences for human action.[8] But for the moment I want to concentrate on the fact that they were all in some sense rejections and that world rejection is characteristic of a long and important period of religious history. I want to insist on this fact because I want to contrast it with an equally striking fact—namely the virtual absence of world rejection in primitive religions, in religion prior to the first millenium B.C., and in the modern world.[9]

Primitive religions are on the whole oriented to a single cosmos—they know nothing of a wholly different world relative to which the actual world is utterly devoid of value. They are concerned with the maintenance

---

[5] *Qur'an* 57, 19–20.

[6] *Qur'an* 87, 16–17.

[7] On these developments see Ienaga Saburo, *Nihon Shisōshi ni okeru Hitei no Ronri no Hattatsu* (The Development of the Logic of Negation in the History of Japanese Thought), Tokyo: 1940.

[8] Max Weber, "Religious Rejections of the World and Their Directions," in Hans H. Gerth and C. Wright Mills (eds.), *From Max Weber*, New York: Oxford University Press, 1946.

[9] One might argue that the much discussed modern phenomenon of alienation is the same as world rejection. The concept of alienation has too many uses to receive full discussion here, but it usually implies estrangement from or rejection of only selected aspects of the empirical world. In the contemporary world a really radical alienation from the whole of empirical reality would be discussed more in terms of psychosis than religion.

of personal, social and cosmic harmony and with attaining specific goods—rain, harvest, children, health—as men have always been. But the overriding goal of salvation that dominates the world rejecting religions is almost absent in primitive religion, and life after death tends to be a shadowy semi-existence in some vaguely designated place in the single world.

World rejection is no more characteristic of the modern world than it is of primitive religion. Not only in the United States but through much of Asia there is at the moment something of a religious revival, but nowhere is this associated with a great new outburst of world rejection. In Asia apologists, even for religions with a long tradition of world rejection, are much more interested in showing the compatibility of their religions with the developing modern world than in totally rejecting it. And it is hardly necessary to point out that the American religious revival stems from motives quite opposite to world rejection.

One could attempt to account for this sequence of presence and absence of world rejection as a dominant religious theme without ever raising the issue of religious evolution, but I think I can account for these and many other facts of the historical development of religion in terms of a scheme of religious evolution. An extended rationale for the scheme and its broad empirical application must await publication in book form. Here all I can attempt is a very condensed overview.

The scheme is based on several presuppositions, the most basic of which I have already referred to: namely, that religious symbolization of what Geertz calls "the general order of existence"[10] tends to change over time,

at least in some instances, in the direction of more differentiated, comprehensive, and in Weber's sense, more rationalized formulations. A second assumption is that conceptions of religious action, of the nature of the religious actor, of religious organization and of the place of religion in the society tend to change in ways systematically related to the changes in symbolization. A third assumption is that these several changes in the sphere of religion, which constitute what I mean by religious evolution, are related to a variety of other dimensions of change in other social spheres which define the general process of sociocultural evolution.

Now, for heuristic purposes at least, it is also useful to assume a series of stages which may be regarded as relatively stable crystallizations of roughly the same order of complexity along a number of different dimensions. I shall use five stages which, for want of better terminology, I shall call primitive, archaic, historic, early modern and modern.[11] These stages are ideal types derived from a theoretical formulation of the most generally observable historical regularities; they are meant to have a temporal reference but only in a very general sense.

Of course the scheme itself is not intended as an adequate description of historical reality. Particular lines of religious development cannot simply be forced into the terms of the scheme. In reality there may be compromise formations involving elements from two stages which I have for theoretical reasons discriminated;

---

10 Geertz, *op. cit.*

11 These stages are actually derived from an attempt to develop a general schema of sociocultural evolution during the seminar in which I participated, together with Talcott Parsons and S. N. Eisenstadt. This paper must, however, be strictly limited to religious evolution, which is in itself sufficiently complex without going into still broader issues.

earlier stages may, as I have already suggested, strikingly foreshadow later developments; and more developed may regress to less developed stages. And of course no stage is ever completely abandoned; all earlier stages continue to coexist with and often within later ones. So what I shall present is not intended as a procrustean bed into which the facts of history are to be forced but a theoretical construction against which historical facts may be illuminated. The logic is much the same as that involved in conceptualizing stages of the life cycle in personality development.

Primitive Religion

Before turning to the specific features of primitive religion let us go back to the definition of religion as a set of symbolic forms and acts relating man to the ultimate conditions of his existence. Lienhardt, in his book on Dinka religion, spells out this process of symbolization in a most interesting way.

I have suggested that the Powers may be understood as images corresponding to complex and various combinations of Dinka experience which are contingent upon their particular social and physical environment. For the Dinka they are the grounds of those experiences; in our analysis we have shown them to be grounded in them, for to a European the experiences are more readily understood than the Powers, and the existence of the latter cannot be posited as a condition of the former. Without these Powers or images or an alternative to them there would be for the Dinka no differentiation between experience of the self and of the world which acts upon it. Suffering, for example, could be merely "lived" or endured. With the imaging of the grounds of suffering in a particular Power, the Dinka can grasp its nature intellectually in a way which

satisfies them, and thus to some extent transcend and dominate it in this act of knowledge. With this knowledge, this separation of a subject and an object in experience, there arises for them also the possibility of creating a form of experience they desire, and of freeing themselves symbolically from what they must otherwise passively endure.[12]

If we take this as a description of religious symbolization in general, and I think we can, then it is clear that in terms of the conception of evolution used here the existence of even the simplest religion is an evolutionary advance. Animals or pre-religious men could only "passively endure" suffering or other limitations imposed by the conditions of their existence, but religious man can to some extent "transcend and dominate" them through his capacity for symbolization and thus attain a degree of freedom relative to his environment that was not previously possible.[13]

Now though Lienhardt points out that the Dinka religious images make possible a "differentiation between experience of the self and of the world which acts upon it" he also points out earlier that the Dinka lack anything closely resembling our conception of the " 'mind,' as mediating and, as it were, storing up the experiences

---

[12] Godfrey Lienhardt, *Divinity and Experience,* London: Oxford University Press, 1961, p. 170.

[13] One might argue that it was language and not religion that gave man the capacity to dominate his environment symbolically, but this seems to be a false distinction. It is very unlikely that language came into existence "first" and that men then "thought up" religion. Rather we would suppose that religion in the sense of this paper was from the beginning a major element in the *content* of linguistic symbolization. Clearly the relations between language and religion are very important and require much more systematic investigation.

of the self."[14] In fact, aspects of what we would attribute to the self are "imaged" among the divine Powers. Again if Lienhardt is describing something rather general, and I think there is every reason to believe he is, then religious symbolization relating man to the ultimate conditions of his existence is also involved in relating him to himself and in symbolizing his own identity.[15]

Granted then that religious symbolization is concerned with imaging the ultimate conditions of existence, whether external or internal, we should examine at each stage the kind of symbol system involved, the kind of religious action it stimulates, the kind of social organization in which this religious action occurs and the implications for social action in general that the religious action contains.

Marcel Mauss, criticizing the heterogeneous sources from which Lévy-Bruhl had constructed the notion of primitive thought, suggested that the word primitive be restricted to Australia, which was the only major culture area largely unaffected by the neolithic.[16] That was in 1923. In 1935 Lévy-Bruhl, heeding Mauss's stricture, published a book called *La Mythologie Primitive* in which the data are drawn almost exclusively from Australia and immediately adjacent islands.[17] While Lévy-Bruhl finds material similar to

his Australian data in all parts of the world, nowhere else does he find it in as pure a form. The differences between the Australian material and that of other areas are so great that Lévy-Bruhl is tempted to disagree with Durkheim that Australian religion is an elementary form of religion and term it rather "pre-religion,"[18] a temptation which for reasons already indicated I would firmly reject. At any rate, W. E. H. Stanner, by far the most brilliant interpreter of Australian religion in recent years, goes far to confirm the main lines of Lévy-Bruhl's position, without committing himself on the more broadly controversial aspects of the assertions of either Mauss or Lévy-Bruhl (indeed without so much as mentioning them). My description of a primitive stage of religion is a theoretical abstraction, but it is heavily indebted to the work of Lévy-Bruhl and Stanner for its main features.[19]

The *religious symbol system* at the primitive level is characterized by Lévy-Bruhl as *"le monde mythique,"* and Stanner directly translates the

---

the structure of primitive thought, in his introduction to the English translation of Robert Hertz, *Death and the Right Hand,* New York: Free Press, 1960, p. 24. These are the only two volumes of Lévy-Bruhl on primitive thought that have not been translated into English.

18 *La Mythologie Primitive,* p. 217.

19 Of Stanner's publications the most relevant are a series of articles published under the general title "On Aboriginal Religion" in *Oceania* 30 to 33 (1959–1963), and "The Dreaming" in T. A. G. Hungerford (ed.), *Australian Signpost,* Melbourne: Cheshire, 1956, and reprinted in William Lessa and Evon Z. Vogt, editors, *Reader in Comparative Religion,* Evanston, Ill.: Row, Peterson, 1958. (References to "The Dreaming" are to Lessa and Vogt volume.) Outside the Australian culture area, the new world provides the most examples of the type of religion I call primitive. Navaho religion, for example, conforms closely to the type.

---

14 Lienhardt, *op. cit.,* p. 149.

15 This notion was first clearly expressed to me in conversation and in unpublished writings by Eli Sagan.

16 In his discussion of Lévy-Bruhl's thesis on primitive mentality, reported in *Bulletin de la Société française de Philosophie,* Seance du 15 Febrier 1923, 23e année (1923), p. 26.

17 Lucien Lévy-Bruhl, *La Mythologie Primitive,* Paris: Alcan, 1935. This volume and Lévy-Bruhl's last volume, *L'Experience Mystique et les Symboles Chez les Primitifs,* Paris: Alcan, 1938, were recently praised by Evans-Pritchard as unsurpassed in "depth and insight" among studies of

Australians' own word for it as "the Dreaming." The Dreaming is a time out of time, or in Stanner's words, "everywhen," inhabited by ancestral figures, some human, some animal.[20] Though they are often of heroic proportions and have capacities beyond those of ordinary men as well as being the progenitors and creators of many particular things in the world, they are not gods, for they do not control the world and are not worshipped.[21]

Two main features of this mythical world of primitive religion are important for the purposes of the present theoretical scheme. The first is the very high degree to which the mythical world is related to the detailed features of the actual world. Not only is every clan and local group defined in terms of the ancestral progenitors and the mythical events of settlement, but virtually every mountain, rock and tree is explained in terms of the actions of mythical beings. All human action is prefigured in the Dreaming, including crimes and folly, so that actual existence and the paradigmatic myths are related in the most intimate possible way. The second main feature, not unrelated to the extreme particularity of the mythical material, is the fluidity of its organization. Lienhardt, though describing a religion of a somewhat different type, catches the essentially free-associational nature of primitive myth when he says, "We meet here the typical lack of precise definition of the Dinka when they speak of divini-

ties. As Garang, which is the name of the first man, is sometimes associated with the first man and sometimes said to be quite different, so Deng may in some sense be associated with anyone called Deng, and the Dinka connect or do not connect usages of the same name in different contexts according to their individual lights and to what they consider appropriate at any given moment."[22] The fluid structure of the myth is almost consciously indicated by the Australians in their use of the word Dreaming: this is not purely metaphorical, for as Ronald Berndt has shown in a careful study, men do actually have a propensity to dream during the periods of cult performance. Through the dreams they reshape the cult symbolism for private psychic ends and what is even more interesting, dreams may actually lead to a reinterpretation in myth which in turn causes a ritual innovation.[23] Both the particularity and the fluidity, then, help account for the hovering closeness of the world of myth to the actual world. A sense of gap, that things are not all they might be, is there but it is hardly experienced as tragic and is indeed on the verge of being comic.[24]

Primitive *religious action* is characterized not, as we have said, by worship, nor, as we shall see, by sacrifice, but by identification, "participation," acting-out. Just as the primitive symbol system is myth *par excellence,* so primitive religious action is ritual *par excellence.* In the ritual the participants become identified with the mythical beings they represent. The mythical beings are not addressed or propitiated or beseeched.

---

20 "The Dreaming," p. 514.

21 This is a controversial point. For extensive bibliography see Eliade, *op. cit.,* p. 112. Eliade tends to accept the notion of high gods in Australia but Stanner says of the two figures most often cited as high gods: "Not even by straining can one see in such culture heroes as Baiame and Darumulum the true hint of a Yahveh, jealous, omiscient and omnipotent" ("The Dreaming," p. 518).

22 *Op. cit.,* p. 91.

23 Ronald Berndt, *Kunapipi,* Melbourne: Cheshire, 1951, pp. 71–84.

24 Stanner: "On Aboriginal Religion I," *Oceania,* 30 (December, 1959), p. 126; Lienhardt, *op. cit.,* p. 53.

The distance between man and mythical being, which was at best slight, disappears altogether in the moment of ritual when everywhen becomes now. There are no priests and no congregation, no mediating representative roles and no spectators. All present are involved in the ritual action itself and have become one with the myth.

The underlying structure of ritual, which in Australia always has themes related to initiation, is remarkably similar to that of sacrifice. The four basic movements of the ritual as analyzed by Stanner are offering, destruction, transformation, and return-communion.[25] Through acting out the mistakes and sufferings of the paradigmatic mythical hero, the new initiates come to terms symbolically with, again in Stanner's words, the "immemorial misdirection" of human life. Their former innocence is destroyed and they are transformed into new identities now more able to "assent to life, as it is, without morbidity."[26] In a sense the whole gamut of the spiritual life is already visible in the Australian ritual. Yet the symbolism is so compact that there is almost no element of choice, will or responsibility. The religious life is as given and as fixed as the routines of daily living.

_____

25 "On Aboriginal Religion I," p. 118. The Navaho ritual system is based on the same principles and also stresses the initiation theme. See Katherine Spencer, *Mythology and Values: An Analysis of Navaho Chantway Myths,* Philadelphia: American Folklore Society, 1957. A very similar four act structure has been discerned in the Christian eucharist by Dom Gregory Dix in *The Shape of the Liturgy,* Westminster: Dacre Press, 1943.

26 "On Aboriginal Religion II," *Oceania,* 30 (June, 1960), p. 278. Of ritual Stanner says, "Personality may almost be seen to change under one's eyes." "On Aboriginal Religion I," *op. cit.,* p. 126.

At the primitive level *religious organization* as a separate social structure does not exist. Church and society are one. Religious roles tend to be fused with other roles, and differentiations along lines of age, sex and kin group are important. While women are not as excluded from the religious life as male ethnographers once believed, their ritual life is to some degree separate and focused on particularly feminine life crises.[27] In most primitive societies age is an important criterion for leadership in the ceremonial life. Ceremonies are often handed down in particular moieties and clans, as is only natural when the myths are so largely concerned with ancestors. Specialized shamans or medicine men are found in some tribes but are not a necessary feature of primitive religion.

As for the *social implications* of primitive religion, Durkheim's analysis seems still to be largely acceptable.[28] The ritual life does reinforce the solidarity of the society and serves to induct the young into the norms of tribal behavior. We should not forget the innovative aspects of primitive religion, that particular myths and ceremonies are in a process of constant revision and alteration, and that in the face of severe historic crisis rather remarkable reformulations of primitive material can be made.[29] Yet on the whole the religious life is the strongest reinforcement of the basic tenet of Australian philosophy, namely that life, as Stanner puts it, is a "one possibility thing." The

_____

27 Catherine Berine Berndt, *Women's Changing Ceremonies in Northern Australia,* Paris: Herman, 1950.

28 Emile Durkheim, *The Elementary Forms of the Religious Life,* Glencoe, Ill.: The Free Press, 1947.

29 Anthony Wallace, "Revitalization Movements," *American Anthropologist,* 58 (April, 1956), pp. 264–79.

very fluidity and flexibility of primitive religion is a barrier to radical innovation. Primitive religion gives little leverage from which to change the world.

Archaic Religion

For purposes of the present conceptual scheme, as I have indicated, I am using primitive religion in an unusually restricted sense. Much that is usually classified as primitive religion would fall in my second category, archaic religion, which includes the religious systems of much of Africa and Polynesia and some of the New World, as well as the earliest religious systems of the ancient Middle East, India and China. The characteristic feature of archaic religion is the emergence of true cult with the complex of gods, priests, worship, sacrifice and in some cases divine or priestly kingship. The myth and ritual complex characteristic of primitive religion continues within the structure of archaic religion, but it is systematized and elaborated in new ways.

In the archaic *religious symbol system* mythical beings are much more definitely characterized. Instead of being great paradigmatic figures with whom men in ritual identify but with whom they do not really interact, the mythical beings are more objectified, conceived as actively and sometimes willfully controlling the natural and human world, and as beings with whom men must deal in a definite and purposive way—in a word they have become gods. Relations among the gods are a matter of considerable speculation and systematization, so that definite principles of organization, especially hierarchies of control, are established. The basic world view is still, like the primitives,' monistic. There is still only one world with gods dominating particular parts of it, especially important being the high gods of the heavenly regions whose vision, knowledge and power may be conceived as very extensive indeed.[30] But though the world is one it is far more differentiated, especially in a hierarchical way, than was the monistic world view of the primitives: archaic religions tend to elaborate a vast cosmology in which all things divine and natural have a place. Much of the particularity and fluidity characteristic of primitive myth is still to be found in archaic religious thinking. But where priestly roles have become well established a relatively stable symbolic structure may be worked out and transmitted over an extended period of time. Especially where at least craft literacy[31] has been attained, the mythical tradition may become the object of critical reflection and innovative speculation which can lead to new developments beyond the nature of archaic religion.

Archaic *religious action* takes the form of cult in which the distinction between men as subjects and gods as objects is much more definite than in primitive religion. Because the division is sharper the need for a communication system through which gods and men can interact is much more acute. Worship and especially sacrifice are precisely such communication systems, as Henri Hubert and Marcel Mauss so brilliantly established in their great essay on sacrifice.[32] There

[30] Raffaele Pettazzoni, *The All-Knowing God,* London: Methuen, 1956.

[31] By "craft literacy" I mean the situation in which literacy is limited to specially trained scribes and is not a capacity generally shared by the upper-status group. For an interesting discussion of the development of literacy in ancient Greece see Eric Havelock, *Preface to Plato,* Cambridge: Harvard University Press, 1963.

[32] Henri Hubert and Marcel Mauss, "Essai sur la nature et la fonction du Sacrifice," *L'Annee Sociologique,* 2 (1899).

is no space here for a technical analysis of the sacrificial process[33]; suffice it to say that a double identification of priest and victim with both gods and men effects a transformation of motives comparable to that referred to in the discussion of primitive religious action. The main difference is that instead of a relatively passive identification in an all-encompassing ritual action, the sacrificial process, no matter how stereotyped, permits the human communicants a greater element of intentionality and entails more uncertainty relative to the divine response. Through this more differentiated form of religious action a new degree of freedom as well, perhaps, as an increased burden of anxiety enters the relations between man and the ultimate conditions of his existence.

Archaic *religious organization* is still by and large merged with other social structures, but the proliferation of functionally and hierarchically differentiated groups leads to a multiplication of cults, since every group in archaic society tends to have its cultic aspect. The emergence of a two-class system, itself related to the increasing density of population made possible by agriculture, has its religious aspect. The upper-status group, which tends to monopolize political and military power, usually claims a superior religious status as well. Noble families are proud of their divine descent and often have special priestly functions. The divine king who is the chief link between his people and the gods is only the extreme case of the general tendency of archaic societies. Specialized priesthoods attached to cult centers may differentiate out but are

usually kept subordinate to the political elite, which at this stage never completely divests itself of religious leadership. Occasionally priesthoods at cult centers located interstitially relative to political units—for example, Delphi in ancient Greece—may come to exercise a certain independence.

The most significant limitation on archaic religious organization is the failure to develop differentiated religious collectivities including adherents as well as priests. The cult centers provide facilities for sacrifice and worship to an essentially transient clientele which is not itself organized as a collectivity, even though the priesthood itself may be rather tightly organized. The appearance of mystery cults and related religious confraternities in the ancient world is usually related to a reorganization of the religious symbol and action systems which indicates a transition to the next main type of religious structure.

The *social implications* of archaic religion are to some extent similar to those of primitive religion. The individual and his society are seen as merged in a natural-divine cosmos. Traditional social structures and social practices are considered to be grounded in the divinely instituted cosmic order and there is little tension between religious demand and social conformity. Indeed, social conformity is at every point reinforced with religious sanction. Nevertheless the very notion of well characterized gods acting over against men with a certain freedom introduces an element of openness that is less apparent at the primitive level. The struggle between rival groups may be interpreted as the struggle between rival deities or as a deity's change of favor from one group to another. Through the problems posed by religious rationalization of political change new modes of

---

[33] Two outstanding recent empirical studies are E. E. Evans-Pritchard, *Nuer Religion,* London: Oxford, 1956, esp. chs. 8 through 11, and Godfrey Lienhardt, *op. cit.,* esp. chs. 7 and 8.

religious thinking may open up. This is clearly an important aspect of the early history of Israel, and it occurred in many other cases as well. The Greek preoccupation with the relation of the gods to the events of the Trojan War gave rise to a continuous deepening of religious thought from Homer to Euripides. In ancient China the attempt of the Chou to rationalize their conquest of the Shang led to an entirely new conception of the relation between human merit and divine favor. The breakdown of internal order led to messianic expectations of the coming of a savior king in such distant areas as Egypt on the one hand and Chou-period China on the other. These are but a few of the ways in which the problems of maintaining archaic religious symbolization in increasingly complex societies drove toward solutions that began to place the archaic pattern itself in jeopardy.

Historic Religion

The next stage in this theoretical scheme is called historic simply because the religions included are all relatively recent; they emerged in societies that were more or less literate and so have fallen chiefly under the discipline of history rather than that of archaeology or ethnography. The criterion that distinguishes the historic religions from the archaic is that the historic religions are all in some sense transcendental. The cosmological monism of the earlier stage is now more or less completely broken through and an entirely different realm of universal reality, having for religious man the highest value, is proclaimed. The discovery of an entirely different realm of religious reality seems to imply a derogation of the value of the given empirical cosmos: at any rate the world rejection discussed above is, in this stage for

the first time, a general characteristic of the religious system.

The *symbol systems* of the historic religions differ greatly among themselves but share the element of transcendentalism which sets them off from the archaic religions; in this sense they are all dualistic. The strong emphasis on hierarchical ordering characteristic of archaic religions continues to be stressed in most of the historic religions. Not only is the supernatural realm "above" this world in terms of both value and control but both the supernatural and earthly worlds are themselves organized in terms of a religiously legitimated hierarchy. For the masses, at least, the new dualism is above all expressed in the difference between this world and the life after death. Religious concern, focused on this life in primitive and archaic religions, now tends to focus on life in the other realm, which may be either infinitely superior or, under certain circumstances, with the emergence of various conceptions of hell, infinitely worse. Under these circumstances the religious goal of salvation (or enlightenment, release and so forth) is for the first time the central religious preoccupation.

In one sense historic religions represent a great "demythologization" relative to archaic religions. The notion of the one God who has neither court nor relatives, who has no myth himself and who is the sole creator and ruler of the universe, the notion of self subsistent being, or of release from the cycle of birth and rebirth, are all enormous simplifications of the ramified cosmologies of archaic religions. Yet all the historic religions have, to use Voegelin's term, mortgages imposed on them by the historical circumstances of their origin. All of them contain, in suspension as it were, elements of archaic cosmology alongside their transcendental assertions. Nonetheless, relative to earlier forms the historic religions are all universalistic. From the point of view of these religions a man is no longer defined chiefly in terms of what tribe or clan he comes from or what particular god he serves but rather as a being capable of salvation. That is to say that it is for the first time possible to conceive of man as such.

Religious action in the historic religions is thus above all action necessary for salvation. Even where elements of ritual and sacrifice remain prominent they take on a new significance. In primitive ritual the individual is put in harmony with the natural divine cosmos. His mistakes are overcome through symbolization as part of the total pattern. Through sacrifice archaic man can make up for his failures to fulfill his obligations to men or gods. He can atone for particular acts of unfaithfulness. But historic religion convicts man of a basic flaw far more serious than those conceived of by earlier religions. According to Buddhism, man's very nature is greed and anger from which he must seek a total escape. For the Hebrew prophets, man's sin is not particular wicked deeds but his profound heedlessness of God, and only a turn to complete obedience will be acceptable to the Lord. For Muhammad the *kafir* is not, as we usually translate, the "unbeliever" but rather the ungrateful man who is careless of the divine compassion. For him, only Islam, willing submission to the will of God, can bring salvation.

The identity diffusion characteristic of both primitive and archaic religions is radically challenged by the historic religious symbolization, which leads for the first time to a clearly structured conception of the self. Devaluation of the empirical world and the empirical self highlights the conception of a responsible self, a core self or a true self, deeper than the flux of everyday experience, facing a reality over against itself, a reality which has a consistency belied by the fluctuations of mere sensory impressions.[34] Primitive man can only accept the world in its manifold givenness. Archaic man can through sacrifice fulfill his religious obligations and attain peace with the gods. But the historic religions promise man for the first time that he can understand the fundamental structure of reality and through salvation participate actively in it. The opportunity is far greater than before but so is the risk of failure.

Perhaps partly because of the profound risks involved the ideal of the religious life in the historic religions tends to be one of separation from the world. Even when, as in the case of Judaism and Islam, the religion enjoins types of worldly participation that are considered unacceptable or at least doubtful in some other historic religions, the devout are still set apart from ordinary worldings by the massive collections of rules and obligations to which they must adhere. The early Christian solution, which, unlike the Buddhist, did allow the full possibility of salvation to the layman, nevertheless in its notion of a special

---

34 Buddhism, with its doctrine of the ultimate non-existence of the self, seems to be an exception to this generalization, but for practical and ethical purposes, at least, a distinction between the true self and the empirical self is made by all schools of Buddhism. Some schools of Mahayana Buddhism give a metaphysical basis to a notion of "basic self" or "great self" as opposed to the merely selfish self caught up in transience and desire. Further it would seem that *nirvana,* defined negatively so as rigorously to exclude any possibility of transience or change, serves fundamentally as an identity symbol. Of course the social and psychological consequences of this kind of identity symbol are very different from those following from other types of identity symbolization.

state of religious perfection idealized religious withdrawal from the world. In fact the standard for lay piety tended to be closeness of approximation to the life of the religious.

Historic religion is associated with the emergence of differentiated religious collectivities as the chief characteristic of its *religious organization*. The profound dualism with respect to the conception of reality is also expressed in the social realm. The single religio-political hierarchy of archaic society tends to split into two at least partially independent hierarchies, one political and one religious. Together with the notion of a transcendent realm beyond the natural cosmos comes a new religious elite that claims direct relation to the transmundane world. Even though notions of divine kingship linger on for a very long time in various compromise forms, it is no longer possible for a divine king to monopolize religious leadership. With the emergence of a religious elite alongside the political one the problem of legitimizing political power enters a new phase. Legitimation now rests upon a delicate belance of forces between the political and religious leadership. But the differentiation between religious and political that exists most clearly at the level of leadership tends also to be pushed down into the masses so that the roles of believer and subject become distinct. Even where, as in the case of Islam, this distinction was not supported by religious norms, it was soon recognized as an actuality.

The emergence of the historic religions is part of a general shift from the two-class system of the archaic period to the four-class system characteristic of all the great historic civilizations up to modern times: a political-military elite, a cultural-religious elite, a rural lower-status group (peasantry) and an urban lower-status group (merchants and artisans). Closely associated with the new religious developments was the growth of literacy among the elite groups and in the upper segments of the urban lower class. Other social changes, such as the growth in the market resulting from the first widespread use of coinage, the development of bureaucracy and law as well as new levels of urbanization, are less directly associated with religion but are part of the same great transformation that got underway in the first millenium B.C. The distinction between religious and political elites applies to some extent to the two great lower strata. From the point of view of the historic religions the peasantry long remained relatively intractable and were often considered religiously second-class citizens, their predilection for cosmological symbolization rendering them always to some degree religiously suspect. The notion of the peasant as truly religious is a fairly modern idea. On the contrary it was the townsman who was much more likely to be numbered among the devout, and Max Weber has pointed out the great fecundity of the urban middle strata in religious innovations throughout the several great historical traditions.[35] Such groups developed new symbolizations that sometimes threatened the structure of the historic religions in their early form, and in the one case where a new stage of religious symbolization was finally achieved they made important contributions.

The *social implications* of the historic religions are implicit in the remarks on religious organization. The differentiation of a religious elite brought a new level of tension and a new possibility of conflict and

____

[35] Max Weber, *The Sociology of Religion,* Boston: Beacon, 1963, pp. 95–98, etc.

change onto the social scene. Whether the confrontation was between Israelite prophet and king, Islamic ulama and sultan, Christian pope and emperor or even between Confucian scholar-official and his ruler, it implied that political acts could be judged in terms of standards that the political authorities could not finally control. The degree to which these confrontations had serious social consequences of course depended on the degree to which the religious group was structurally independent and could exert real pressure. S. N. Eisenstadt has made a comprehensive survey of these differences[36]; for our purposes it is enough to note that they were nowhere entirely absent. Religion, then, provided the ideology and social cohesion for many rebellions and reform movements in the historic civilizations, and consequently played a more dynamic and especially a more purposive role in social change than had previously been possible. On the other hand, we should not forget that in most of the historic civilizations for long periods of time religion performed the functions we have noted from the beginning: legitimation and reinforcement of the existing social order.

Early Modern Religion

In all previous stages the ideal type was based on a variety of actual cases. Now for the first time it derives from a single case or at best a congeries of related cases, namely, the Protestant Reformation. The defining characteristic of early modern religion is the collapse of the hierarchical structur-

ing of both this and the other world. The dualism of the historic religions remains as a feature of early modern religion but takes on a new significance in the context of more direct confrontation between the two worlds. Under the new circumstances salvation is not to be found in any kind of withdrawal from the world but in the midst of worldly activities. Of course elements of this existed in the historic religions from the beginning, but on the whole the historic religions as institutionalized had offered a mediated salvation. Either conformity to religious law, or participation in a sacramental system or performance of mystical exercises was necessary for salvation. All of these to some extent involved a turning away from the world. Further, in the religious two-class systems characteristic of the institutionalized historic religions the upper-status groups, the Christian monks or Sufi shaykhs or Buddhist ascetics, could through their pure acts and personal charisma store up a fund of grace that could then be shared with the less worthy. In this way too salvation was mediated rather than immediate. What the Reformation did was in principle, with the usual reservations and mortgages to the past, break through the whole mediated system of salvation and declare salvation potentially available to any man no matter what his station or calling might be.

Since immediate salvation seems implicit in all the historic religions it is not surprising that similar reform movements exist in other traditions, notably Shinran Shonin's version of Pure Land Buddhism but also certain tendencies in Islam, Buddhism, Taoism and Confucianism. But the Protestant Reformation is the only attempt that was successfully institutionalized. In the case of Taoism and Confucianism the mortgage of archaic

<hr>

36 S. N. Eisenstadt, "Religious Organizations and Political Process in Centralized Empires," *Journal of Asian Studies,* 21 (May, 1962), pp. 271–294, and also his *The Political Systems of Empires,* New York: Free Press, 1963.

symbolization was so heavy that what seemed a new breakthrough easily became regressive. In the other cases, notably in the case of the Jōdo Shin-shū, the radical implications were not sustained and a religion of mediated salvation soon reasserted itself. Religious movements of early modern type may be emerging in a number of the great traditions today, perhaps even in the Vatican Council, and there are also secular movements with features strongly analogous to what I call early modern religion. But all of these tendencies are too uncertain to rely on in constructing an ideal type.

Early modern *religious symbolism* concentrates on the direct relation between the individual and transcendent reality. A great deal of the cosmological baggage of medieval Christianity is dropped as superstition. The fundamentally ritualist interpretation of the sacrament of the Eucharist as a re-enactment of the paradigmatic sacrifice is replaced with the antiritualist interpretation of the Eucharist as a commemoration of a once-and-for-all historical event. Even though in one sense the world is more devalued in early Protestantism than in medieval Christianity, since the reformers re-emphasized the radical separation between divine and human, still by proclaiming the world as the theater of God's glory and the place wherein to fulfill his command, the Reformation reinforced positive autonomous action in the world instead of a relatively passive acceptance of it.

Religious action was now conceived to be identical with the whole of life. Special ascetic and devotional practices were dropped as well as the monastic roles that specialized in them and instead the service of God became a total demand in every walk of life. The stress was on faith, an internal quality of the person, rather than on particular acts clearly marked "religious." In this respect the process of identity unification that I have designated as a central feature of the historic religions advanced still further. The complex requirements for the attainment of salvation in the historic religions, though ideally they encouraged identity unification, could themselves become a new form of identity diffusion, as Luther and Shinran were aware. Assertion of the capacity for faith as an already received gift made it possible to undercut that difficulty. It also made it necessary to accept the ambiguity of human ethical life and the fact that salvation comes in spite of sin, not in its absolute absence. With the acceptance of the world not as it is but as a valid arena in which to work out the divine command, and with the acceptance of the self as capable of faith in spite of sin, the Reformation made it possible to turn away from world rejection in a way not possible in the historic religions. All of this was possible, however, only within the structure of a rigid orthodoxy and a tight though voluntaristic religious group.

I have already noted that early modern religion abandoned hierarchy as an essential dimension of its religious symbol system.[37] It did the same in its *religious organization*. Not only did it reject papal authority, but it

---

[37] God, of course, remains hierarchically superior to man, but the complex stratified structure of which purgatory, saints, angels, and so on, are elements is eliminated. Also, the strong reassertion of covenant thinking brought a kind of formal equality into the God-man relation without eliminating the element of hierarchy. Strictly speaking then, early modern (and modern) religion does not abandon the idea of hierarchy as such, but retains it in a much more flexible form, relative to particular contexts, and closely related to new emphases on equality. What is abandoned is rather a single overarching hierarchy, summed up in the symbol of the great chain of being.

also rejected the old form of the religious distinction between two levels of relative religious perfection. This was replaced with a new kind of religious two-class system: the division between elect and reprobates. The new form differed from the old one in that the elect were really a vanguard group in the fulfillment of the divine plan rather than a qualitative religious elite. The political implications of Protestantism had much to do with the overthrow of the old conception of hierarchy in the secular field as well. Where Calvinistic Protestantism was powerful, hereditary aristocracy and kingship were either greatly weakened or abandoned. In fact the Reformation is part of the general process of social change in which the four-class system of peasant societies began to break up in Europe. Especially in the Anglo-Saxon world, Protestantism greatly contributed to its replacement by a more flexible multi-centered mode of social organization based more on contract and voluntary association. Both church and state lost some of the reified significance they had in medieval times and later on the continent. The roles of church member and citizen were but two among several. Both church and state had their delimited spheres of authority, but with the full institutionalization of the common law neither had a right to dominate each other or the whole of society. Nonetheless, the church acted for a long time as a sort of cultural and ethical holding company, and many developments in philosophy, literature and social welfare took their initiative from clerical or church groups.[38]

The *social implications* of the Protestant Reformation are among the more debated subjects of contemporary social science. Lacking space to defend my assertions, let me simply say that I stand with Weber, Merton, *et al.*, in attributing very great significance to the Reformation, especially in its Calvinistic wing, in a whole series of developments from economics to science, from education to law. Whereas in most of the historic civilizations religion stands as virtually the only stable challenger to the dominance of the political elite, in the emerging early modern society religious impulses give rise to a variety of institutional structures, from the beginning or very soon becoming fully secular, which stand beside and to some extent compete with and limit the state. The direct religious response to political and moral problems does not disappear but the impact of religious orientations on society is also mediated by a variety of worldly institutions in which religious values have been expressed. Weber's critics, frequently assuming a pre-modern model of the relation between religion and society, have often failed to understand the subtle interconnections he was tracing. But the contrast with the historic stage, when pressures toward social change in the direction of value realization were sporadic and often utopian, is decisive.

In the early modern stage for the first time pressures to social change in the direction of greater realization

---

[38] Of course, important developments in modern culture stemming from the recovery of Classical art and philosophy in the Rennaissance took place outside the main stream of religious development. However, the deep interrelations between religious and secular components of the Rennaissance should not be overlooked. Certainly the clergy in the Anglo-Saxon world were among the foremost guardians of the Classical tradition in literature and thought. The most tangible expression of this was the close relation of higher education to the church, a relation which was not seriously weakened until the late 19th century in America.

of religious values are actually institutionalized as part of the structure of the society itself. The self-revising social order expressed in a voluntaristic and democratic society can be seen as just such an outcome. The earliest phase of this development, especially the several examples of Calvinist commonwealths, was voluntaristic only within the elect vanguard group and otherwise was often illiberal and even dictatorial. The transition toward a more completely democratic society was complex and subject to many blockages. Close analogies to the early modern situation occur in many of the contemporary developing countries, which are trying for the first time to construct social systems with a built-in tendency to change in the direction of greater value realization. The leadership of these countries varies widely between several kinds of vanguard revolutionary movements with distinctly illiberal proclivities to elites committed to the implementation of a later, more democratic, model of Western political society.

Modern Religion

I am not sure whether in the long run what I call early modern religion will appear as a stage with the same degree of distinctness as the others I have distinguished or whether it will appear only as a transitional phase, but I am reasonably sure that, even though we must speak from the midst of it, the modern situation represents a stage of religious development in many ways profoundly different from that of historic religion. The central feature of the change is the collapse of the dualism that was so crucial to all the historic religions.

It is difficult to speak of a *modern religious symbol system*. It is indeed an open question whether there can be a religious symbol system analogous to any of the preceding ones in the modern situation, which is characterized by a deepening analysis of the very nature of symbolization itself. At the highest intellectual level I would trace the fundamental break with traditional historic symbolization to the work of Kant. By revealing the problematic nature of the traditional metaphysical basis of all the religions and by indicating that it is not so much a question of two worlds as it is of as many worlds as there are modes of apprehending them, he placed the whole religious problem in a new light. However simple the immediate result of his grounding religion in the structure of ethical life rather than in a metaphysics claiming cognitive adequacy, it nonetheless pointed decisively in the direction that modern religion would go. The entire modern analysis of religion, including much of the most important recent theology, though rejecting Kant's narrowly rational ethics, has been forced to ground religion in the structure of the human situation itself. In this respect the present paper is a symptom of the modern religious situation as well as an analysis of it. In the world view that has emerged from the tremendous intellectual advances of the last two centuries there is simply no room for a hierarchic dualistic religious symbol system of the classical historic type. This is not to be interpreted as a return to primitive monism: it is not that a single world has replaced a double one but that an infinitely multiplex one has replaced the simple duplex structure. It is not that life has become again a "one possibility thing" but that it has become an infinite possibility thing. The analysis of modern man as secular, materialistic, dehumanized and in the deepest sense areligious seems to me fundamentally misguided, for such a judgment is based on standards that cannot adequately gauge the modern temper.

Though it is central to the problems of modern religion, space forbids a review of the development of the modern analysis of religion on its scholarly and scientific side. I shall confine myself to some brief comments on directions of development within Protestant theology. In many respects Schleiermacher is the key figure in early 19th century theology who saw the deeper implications of the Kantian breakthrough. The development of "liberal theology" in the later 19th century, partly on the basis of Schleiermacher's beginnings, tended to fall back into Kant's overly rational limitations. Against this, Barth's reassertion of the power of the traditional symbolism was bound to produce a vigorous response, but unfortunately, due to Barth's own profound ambiguity on the ultimate status of dogma, the consequences were in part simply a regressive reassertion of the adequacy of the early modern theological formulation. By the middle of the 20th century, however, the deeper implications of Schleiermacher's attempt were being developed in various ways by such diverse figures as Tillich, Bultmann and Bonhoeffer.[39] Tillich's assertion of "ecstatic naturalism," Bultmann's program of "demythologization" and Bonhoeffer's search for a "religionless Christianity," though they cannot be simply equated with each other are efforts to come to terms with the modern situation. Even on the Catholic side

the situation is beginning to be recognized.

Interesting enough, indications of the same general search for an entirely new mode of religious symbolization, though mostly confined to the Protestant West, also appear in that most developed of the non-Western countries, Japan. Uchimura Kanzō's non-church Christianity was a relatively early indication of a search for new directions and is being developed even further today. Even more interesting perhaps is the emergence of a similar development out of the Jōdo Shinshū tradition, at least in the person of Ienaga Saburo.[40] This example indeed suggests that highly "modern" implications exist in more than one stand of Mahayana Buddhism and perhaps several of the other great traditions as well. Although in my opinion these implications were never developed sufficiently to dominate a historical epoch as they did in the West in the last two centuries, they may well prove decisive in the future of these religions.

So far what I have been saying applies mainly to intellectuals, but at least some evidence indicates that changes are also occurring at the level of mass religiosity.[41] Behind the 96 per cent of Americans who claim to

____

39 Paul Tillich, *The Courage to Be,* New Haven: Yale, 1952; Karl Jaspers and Rudolf Bultmann, *Myth and Christianity,* New York: Noonday, 1958; Dietrich Bonhoeffer, *Letters and Papers from Prison,* London: SCM Press, 1954. Numerous other works of these theologians could be cited.

____

40 Robert N. Bellah, "Ienaga Saburo and the Search for Meaning in Modern Japan," in Marius Jansen (ed.), *Japanese Attitudes toward Modernization,* Princeton: Princeton University Press, 1965.

41 There are a few scattered studies such as Gordon Allport, James Gillespie and Jacqueline Young, "The Religion of the Post-War College Student," *The Journal of Psychology,* 25 (January, 1948), pp. 3–33, but the subject does not lend itself well to investigation via questionnaires and brief interviews. Richard V. McCann in his Harvard doctoral dissertation, "The Nature and Varieties of Religious Change," 1955, utilized a much subtler approach involving depth inter-

believe in God[42] there are many instances of a massive reinterpretation that leaves Tillich, Bultmann and Bonhoeffer far behind. In fact, for many churchgoers the obligation of doctrinal orthodoxy sits lightly indeed, and the idea that all creedal statements must receive a personal reinterpretation is widely accepted. The dualistic world view certainly persists in the minds of many of the devout, but just as surely many others have developed elaborate and often pseudo-scientific rationalizations to bring their faith in its experienced validity into some kind of cognitive harmony with the 20th century world. The wave of popular response that some of the newer theology seems to be eliciting is another indication that not only the intellectuals find themselves in a new religious situation.[43]

To concentrate on the church in a discussion of the modern religious situation is already misleading, for it is precisely the characteristic of the new situation that the great problem of religion as I have defined it, the symbolization of man's relation to the ultimate conditions of his existence, is no longer the monopoly of any groups explicitly labeled religious. However much the development of

Western Christianity may have led up to and in a sense created the modern religious situation, it just as obviously is no longer in control of it. Not only has any obligation of doctrinal orthodoxy been abandoned by the leading edge of modern culture, but every fixed position has become open to question in the process of making sense out of man and his situation. This involves a profounder commitment to the process I have been calling religious symbolization than ever before. The historic religions discovered the self; the early modern religion found a doctrinal basis on which to accept the self in all its empirical ambiguity; modern religion is beginning to understand the laws of the self's own existence and so to help man take responsibility for his own fate.

This statement is not intended to imply a simple liberal optimism, for the modern analysis of man has also disclosed the depths of the limitations imposed by man's situation. Nevertheless, the fundamental symbolization of modern man and his situation is that of a dynamic multi-dimensional self capable, within limits, of continual self-transformation and capable, again within limits, of remaking the world including the very symbolic forms with which he deals with it, even the forms that state the unalterable conditions of his own existence. Such a statement should not be taken to mean that I expect, even less that I advocate, some ghastly religion of social science. Rather I expect traditional religious symbolism to be maintained and developed in new directions, but with growing awareness that it is symbolism and that man in the last analysis is responsible for the choice of his symbolism. Naturally, continuation of the symbolization characteristic of earlier stages without

---

viewing and discovered a great deal of innovative reinterpretation in people from all walks of life. Unfortunately lack of control of sampling makes it impossible to generalize his results.

[42] Will Herberg, *Protestant, Catholic, Jew,* Garden City: Doubleday, 1955, p. 72.

[43] Bishop J. A. T. Robinson's, *Honest to God,* Philadelphia: Westminster, 1963, which states in straightforward language the positions of some of the recent Protestant theologians mentioned above, has sold (by November, 1963) over 300,000 copies in England and over 71,000 in the United States with another 50,000 on order, and this in the first few months after, publication. (Reported in *Christianity and Crisis,* 23 (November 11, 1963), p. 201).

any reinterpretation is to be expected among many in the modern world, just as it has occurred in every previous period.

Religious action in the modern period is, I think, clearly a continuation of tendencies already evident in the early modern stage. Now less than ever can man's search for meaning be confined to the church. But with the collapse of a clearly defined doctrinal orthodoxy and a religiously supported objective system of moral standards, religious action in the world becomes more demanding than ever. The search for adequate standards of action, which is at the same time a search for personal maturity and social relevance, is in itself the heart of the modern quest for salvation, if I may divest that word of its dualistic associations. How the specifically religious bodies are to adjust their time honored practices of worship and devotion to modern conditions is of growing concern in religious circles. Such diverse movements as the liturgical revival, pastoral psychology and renewed emphasis on social action are all efforts to meet the present need. Few of these trends have gotten much beyond the experimental but we can expect the experiments to continue.

In the modern situation as I have defined it, one might almost be tempted to see in Thomas Paine's "My mind is my church," or Thomas Jefferson's "I am a sect myself" the typical expression of *religious organization* in the near future. Nonetheless it seems unlikely that collective symbolization of the great inescapabilities of life will soon disappear. Of course the "free intellectual" will continue to exist as he has for millenia but such a solution can hardly be very general. Private voluntary religious association in the West achieved full legitimation for the first time in the early modern situation, but in the early stages especially, discipline and control within these groups was very intense. The tendency in more recent periods has been to continue the basic pattern but with a much more open and flexible pattern of membership. In accord with general trends I have already discussed, standards of doctrinal orthodoxy and attempts to enforce moral purity have largely been dropped. The assumption in most of the major Protestant denominations is that the church member can be considered responsible for himself. This trend seems likely to continue, with an increasingly fluid type of organization in which many special purpose sub-groups form and disband. Rather than interpreting these trends as significant of indifference and secularization, I see in them the increasing acceptance of the notion that each individual must work out his own ultimate solutions and that the most the church can do is provide him a favourable environment for doing so, without imposing on him a prefabricated set of answers.[44] And it will be increasingly realized that answers to religious questions can validly be sought in various spheres of "secular" art and thought.

Here I can only suggest what I take to be the main *social implication* of the modern religious situation. Early modern society, to a considerable degree under religious pressure, developed, as we have seen, the notion of a self-revising social system in the form of a democratic society. But at least in the early phase of that development social flexibility was balanced

---

[44] The great Protestant stress on thinking for oneself in matters of religion is documented in Gerhard Lenski, *The Religious Factor*, Garden City: Doubleday, 1961, pp. 270–273.

against doctrinal (Protestant ortho-doxy) and characterological (Puritan personality) rigidities. In a sense those rigidities were necessary to allow the flexibility to emerge in the social system, but it is the chief characteristic of the more recent modern phase that culture and personality themselves have come to be viewed as endlessly revisable. This has been character-ized as a collapse of meaning and a failure of moral standards. No doubt the possibilities for pathological dis-tortion in the modern situation are enormous. It remains to be seen whether the freedom modern society implies at the cultural and personality as well as the social level can be stably institutionalized in large-scale socie-ties. Yet the very situation that has been characterized as one of the col-lapse of meaning and the failure of moral standards can also, and I would argue more fruitfully, be viewed as one offering unprecedented oppor-tunities for creative innovation in every sphere of human action.

Conclusion

The schematic presentation of the stages of religious evolution just con-cluded is based on the proposition that at each stage the freedom of personality and society has increased relative to the environing conditions. Freedom has increased because at each successive stage the relation of man to the conditions of his existence has been conceived as more complex, more open and more subject to change and development. The distinction be-tween conditions that are really ulti-mate and those that are alterable be-comes increasingly clear though never complete. Of course this scheme of religious evolution has implied at al-most every point a general theory of social evolution, which has had to remain largely implicit.

Let me suggest in closing, as a modest effort at empirical testing, how the evolutionary scheme may help to explain the facts of alternat-ing world acceptance and rejection which were noted near the beginning of the paper. I have argued that the world acceptance of the primitive and archaic levels is largely to be ex-plained as the only possible response to a reality that invades the self to such an extent that the symbolizations of self and world are only very par-tially separate. The great wave of world rejection of the historic reli-gions I have interpreted as a major advance in what Lienhardt calls "the differentiation between experience of the self and of the world which acts upon it." Only by withdrawing cathexis from the myriad objects of empirical reality could consciousness of a centered self in relation to an encompassing reality emerge. Early modern religion made it possible to maintain the centered self without denying the multifold empirical reality and so made world rejection in the classical sense unnecessary. In the modern phase knowledge of the laws of the formation of the self, as well as much more about the structure of the world, has opened up almost un-limited new directions of exploration and development. World rejection marks the beginning of a clear objec-tification of the social order and sharp criticism of it. In the earlier world-accepting phases religious conceptions and social order were so fused that it was almost impossible to criticize the latter from the point of view of the former. In the later phases the pos-sibility of remaking the world to con-form to value demands has served in a very different way to mute the extremes of world rejection. The world acceptance of the last two stages is shown in this analysis to have a profoundly different significance from that of the first two.

Construction of a wide-ranging evolutionary scheme like the one presented in this paper is an extremely risky enterprise. Nevertheless such efforts are justifiable if, by throwing light on perplexing developmental problems they contribute to modern man's efforts at self-interpretation.

the problem of
structural change

three

TALCOTT PARSONS

. . . The process of structural change may be considered the obverse of equilibrating process; the distinction is made in terms of boundary-maintenance. Boundary implies both that there is a difference of state between phenomena internal and external to the system; and that the type of process tending to maintain that difference of state is different from the type tending to break it down. In applying this concept to social systems, one must remember that their essential boundaries are those vis-à-vis personalities, organisms, and cultural systems, and not those directly vis-à-vis the physical environment.

A boundary is thus conceived as a kind of watershed. The control resources of the system are adequate for its maintenance up to a well-defined set of points in one direction: beyond that set of points, there is a tendency for a *cumulative* process of change to begin, producing states progressively

farther from the institutionalized patterns. The metaphor of the watershed, however, fails to demonstrate the complexity of the series of control levels and, hence, of the boundaries of subsystems within larger systems. The mechanisms discussed earlier are involved in the dynamic aspects of such a hierarchical series of subboundaries; if a subboundary is broken, resources within the larger system counteract the implicit tendency to structural change. This is most dramatically shown in the capacity of social control mechanisms, in a narrow sense, to reverse cumulative processes of deviance. The conception of the nature of the difference between processes of equilibration and processes of structural change seems inherent in the conception of a social system as a cybernetic system of control over behavior.

As observed, structural change in subsystems is an inevitable part of equilibrating process in larger systems. The individual's life-span is so short that concrete role-units in any social system of societal scope must, through socialization, continually undergo structural change. Closely bound to this is a low-order collectivity like the nuclear family. Though the institutional norms defining "the family" in a society or a social sector may remain stable over long periods, *the family* is

"

never a collectivity; and real families are continually being established by marriages, passing through the "family cycle," and, eventually, disappearing, with the parents' death and the children's dispersion. Similar considerations apply to other types of societal subsystems.

Within this frame of reference, the problem of structural change can be considered under three headings, as follows: (1) the sources of tendencies toward change; (2) the impact of these tendencies on the affected structural components, and the possible consequences; and (3) possible generalizations about trends and patterns of change.

The Sources of Structural Change

The potential sources of structural change are exogenous and endogenous—usually in combination. The foregoing discussion has stressed the instability of the relations between any system of action and its situation, because this is important for defining the concepts of goal and the political function. We were emphasizing *relation,* and a relation's internal sources of instability may derive from external tendencies to change.

Exogenous Sources of Change
The exogenous sources of social structural change consist in endogenous tendencies to change in the organisms, personalities, and cultural systems articulated with the social systems in question. Among such sources are those operating through genetic changes in the constituent human organisms and changes in the distribution of genetic components within populations, which have an impact on behavior as it affects social role-performance, including the social system's capacities for socialization. Changes in the physical environment are mediated most directly either through the organism—e.g., through perception— or through appropriate aspects of the cultural system—e.g., technological knowledge.

One particularly important source of exogenous change is a change originating in other social systems. For the politically organized society, the most important are other politically organized societies. To consider change in this context, it is essential to treat the society of reference as a unit in a more inclusive social system. Even when the system's level of integration is relatively low and chronic conflicts between its subunits continually threaten to break into war, *some* element of more or less institutionalized order always governs their interrelations—otherwise, a concept like "diplomacy" would be meaningless. Of course, exogenous cultural borrowing and diffusion are mediated through interrelations among societies.

Endogenous Sources: "Strains"
The most general, commonly used term for an endogenous tendency to change is "strain." *Strain* here refers to a condition in the *relation* between two or more structured units (i.e., subsystems of the system) that constitutes a tendency or pressure toward changing that relation to one incompatible with the equilibrium of the relevant part of the system. If the strain becomes great enough, the mechanisms of control will not be able to maintain that conformity to relevant normative expectations necessary to avoid the breakdown of the structure. A strain is a tendency to disequilibrium in the input-output balance between two or more units of the system.

Strains can be relieved in various ways. For the system's stability, the ideal way is resolution—i.e., restoring full conformity with normative expectations, as in complete recovery from motivated illness. A second relieving mechanism is arrestation or isolation —full conformity is not restored, but some accommodation is made by which less than normal performance by the deficient units is accepted, and other units carry the resulting burden. However, it may be extremely difficult to detect a unit's failure to attain full potentiality, as in the case of handicap contrasted with illness. Completely eliminating the unit from social function is the limiting case here.

Strain may also be relieved by change in the structure itself. Since we have emphasized strain in the *relations* of units (instability internal to the unit itself would be analyzed at the next lower level of system reference), structural change must be defined as alteration in the normative culture defining the expectations governing that relation—thus, at the systemic level, comprising all units standing in strained relations. The total empirical process may also involve change in the structure of typical units; but the essential reference is to *relational pattern.* For example, chronic instability in a typical kind of market might lead to a change in the norms governing that market; but if bargaining units change their tactics in the direction of conforming with the old norms, this would not constitute *structural* change of *this* system. In line with the general concepts of inertia and of the hierarchy of controls, we may say that endogenous change occurs only when the lower-order mechanisms of control fail to contain the factors of strain.

Factors in Change

In introducing our discussion of the factors in structural change, we must establish the essential point that the conception of a system of interdependent variables, on the one hand, and of units or parts, on the other,

by its nature implies that there is no necessary order of teleological significance in the sources of change. This applies particularly to such old controversies as economic or interest explanations *versus* explanations in terms of ideas or values. This problem is logically parallel to the problem of the relations between heredity and environment. Of a set of "factors," *any or all may be sources of change,* whose nature will depend on the ways an initial impetus is propagated through the system by...types of dynamic process....

To avoid implying a formless eclecticism we must add two other points. First, careful theoretical identifications must be made of the nature of the factors to which an impetus to structural change is imputed. Many factors prominent in the history of social thought are, according to the theory of social systems, exogenous— including factors of geographical environment and biological heredity, and outstanding personalities, as "great men," who are never conceived of simply as products of their societies. This category of exogenous factors also includes cultural explanations, as those in terms of religious ideas. Furthermore, these different exogenous sources are not alike in the nature of their impact on the social system.

Among these exogenous sources of change is the size of the population of any social system. Perhaps the most important relevant discussion of this was Durkheim's, in the *Division of Labor,* where he speaks of the relations between "material" and "dynamic" density. Populations are partially resultants of the processes of social systems, but their size is in turn a determinant.

The second, related point concerns the implications of the hierarchy of control in social systems. It may be difficult to define magnitude of impact; however, given approximate equality of magnitude, the probability of producing structural change is greater in proportion to the position in the order of control at which the impact of its principal disturbing influence occurs. This principle is based on the assumption that stable systems have mechanisms which can absorb considerable internal strains, and thus endogenous or exogenous variabilities impinging at lower levels in the hierarchy of control may be neutralized before extending structural changes to higher levels. It follows that the crucial focus of the problem of change lies in the stability of the value system.

The analytical problems in this area are by no means simple. Difficulties arise because of the complex ways in which societies are composed of interpenetrating subsystems, and because of the ways in which the exogenous factors impinge somehow on every role, collectivity norm, and subvalue. Thus the collectivity component of social structure has been placed, in general analytical terms, only third in the general control hierarchy. Yet every society must be organized as a whole on the collectivity level, integrating goal-attainment, integrative, and pattern-maintenance functions. Hence an important change in the leadership composition of the over-all societal collectivity *may* have a far greater impact on the norms and values of the society generally than would a value change in lower-order subsystems. Hence a naïve use of the formula, the higher in the control hierarchy the greater the impact, is not recommended.

The Impact of the Forces of Change

Our approach to the problem of impact has already been fore-shadowed. Disturbance may result from deficient or excessive input at a given point in the system. The generalization about the disturbing effects of excess is a direct corollary of the concept of equilibrium; it seems contrary often to common sense, but it has been clearly validated for many cases in social interaction. One of the best known cases is the Keynesian point about the relation between over-saving and unemployment; another is Durkheim's generalization about the positive relation between increasing economic prosperity and rates of suicide; a third would be the pathogenic effect of maternal overprotection on a developing child. The point is crucial for present purposes, because, in any important boundary relation of a society, the stability of both systems is a function of a *balancing* of rates of input and output which go *both* ways. This consideration also clearly applies to both exogenous and endogenous sources of change.

Impact will vary as a function of at least five ranges of variation in the nature of the impinging process, as described below: (1) the magnitude of the disturbance—not an absolute quantity, but magnitude of *change* from previous customary input-output rates, which have become accommodated to the system's conditions of equilibrium. (2) The proportion of units in the system at the relevant levels that are affected. (3) The strategic character of the unit's functional contribution to the system—e.g., the sudden death of 50 per cent of the unskilled workers would not have the same impact as the death of 50 per cent of the highest 10 per cent of political leaders. (4) The incidence of the disturbance on analytically distinguishable components of the system's structure. Given the strategic significance of a structural unit, roles are most readily replaceable or reparable, subcollectivities less so, norms even less so, and value-commitments least. The reverse order holds for exposure to the impact of change; the conditions of individuals' role-performances are most exposed and therefore most likely to "give," whereas value-commitments are least exposed because they are neither function- nor situation-specific. Finally, (5) there is the degree of resistance by the relevant parts of the system to the impact of forces of change—i.e., the level of effectiveness of the mechanisms of control. A relatively large disturbance may not lead to major change in a very stable system; a much smaller disturbance may lead to drastic change in an unstable system. Stability is variable both quantitatively and qualitatively.

Empirically, forces making for change seldom operate neatly according to discrete analytical categories; their impact is diffused. Thus the Cold War's impact on American society operates primarily on two levels. One is by its effect on national security—primarily a political problem. Since the United States can no longer rely on a stable European power system for its security, as it did through the nineteenth century, the Cold War is the immediate cause for maintaining a large military establishment and attempting to foster the rapid development of military technology—with all the repercussions that this essentially new peacetime situation has throughout the society. The Cold War also has an important impact at the level of commitments to values and the most generalized level of norms. Without this "challenge of communism"—not just the challenge of a strong military power, but a challenge to the *legitimacy* of the "American way"—the current situation would be far less disturbing.

These two components are empir-ically associated. But they are analyt-ically distinguishable, and their pro-portionate importance may vary, in the same case over time as well as in different cases. A comparably seri-ous military threat to national secu-rity, unaccompanied by the ideological factor, would be much less disturbing at present to the United States, be-cause internal changes in American society have produced factors of in-stability at integrative levels that were not previously so acute. Our problem in really accepting our universalistic values, for example, is clearly shown in the present segregation-desegrega-tion issue. A major development of societal political responsibility, as a function of both internal development and changed international position, is necessary. Without special sensitivities to the symbolic reverberations of "communism"—independent of "real-istic" dangers—a phenomenon like McCarthyism would be incomprehen-sible.

Analytical discrimination of factors within the framework of empirical variation makes more precision about matters of impact possible. Thus tech-nological processes concerning the physical environment have quite a different significance from problems of the motivational commitments of individuals and collective subunits to functional performance in the system. For example, in America there has allegedly been a major shift recently in this respect—in Riesman's terms, from "inner-directed" to "other-directed"; in Kluckhohn's, a "decline of the Protestant Ethic." Both inter-pretations suggest a retreat from oc-cupational contributions into the sphere of private preoccupations. Though discussions of such problems are often couched in the terminology of values, this problem belongs more at the level of motivation to functional contribution. Whether or not a change in the societal value-system underlies this at a higher level of control is an analytically distinguishable part of the empirical problems.

By present definition, a change in the structure of a social system is a change in its normative culture. At the most general level, it is a change in the paramount value system. From this level through the series of differentiation, segmentation, and specification, it involves changes in the normative culture of subsystems, of progressively lower order, that are increasingly specific with reference to function in the larger system and to situation. Through specification we arrive eventually at the *role* level and, with this, at the psychological motivation of the individual. It is my thesis that *any* major disturbance will occasion widespread disturbances in individuals' motivations at the role level, and under the requisite conditions will lead to structural changes at least there. But it does not follow either from the presence of widespread symptoms of disturbance, or from important structural changes in such motivational patterning, that the structure of the system at all levels—especially in the paramount value system—has changed.

In considering the general problem of impact, we must remember that every structurally distinguished subsystem of a society is both complex and never fully integrated. Moreover, the structural components are interlarded in all the different subsystems; yet even minimal integration requires some measure of consistency between values and norms both at the higher and lower levels of specification and across the lines of functional differentiation. Such considerations help account for the facts that many processes of change occur simultaneously at several levels, and that influences are propagated through the levels of control in the system from one to another.

An important example is presented by underdeveloped societies at the present time. If we take economic development, in the sense of industrialization, as the focal content of the process, the two primary foci of the impact of inputs are political and cultural, in the value-sense; they are not, in the usual analytical sense, economic. Both focus primarily on the relations of underdeveloped societies to economically advanced societies.

The great stirring which has been going on focuses first on national independence and power, as evidenced by the acute sensitivity to the negative symbol of "imperialism." This political preoccupation's effect then seems to be propagated in two directions: to economic development as *instrumental* to political power (and as a symbol of collective achievement); and to the *functional* value-systems associated with political power and economic productivity. The highest-level values will still be carefully *contrasted* with those of the societies serving as models of political and economic development. Another important symbolic expression of this is the common imputation of materialism to Western societies, whereas it is alleged that India, for example, can somehow have all the advantages of high industrialization without being infected with the materialistic values of the Western world. Further—contrary to the explicit content of Marxian ideology—it is often alleged that communism, because collectivistic, is less materialistic than so-called "capitalism," though communist societies have been marked by a far more exclusive dedication to economic development than *any* capitalistic society. The essential point here is the tendency to maintain the highest-level values while permitting major changes in the next level of value-specification, i.e., that of the primary functional subsystem.

It is difficult to see how, in the longer run, this can fail to engender major strains; however, there is a twofold proximate ideological defense, namely, the instrumental character of political and economic development, and the bridging of the implicit conflict by symbols like "socialism." The important point analytically is that, without at least two different orders of input beyond normal levels, impetus for major change is unlikely to occur. One order is the *real* political inferiority, symbolized as "colonial dependency," of the disturbed society. The other is the existence, in the social environment, of a *model* of instrumentally appropriate reorganization, whose partial functional values can be adopted, initially allegedly without disturbing the highest-level values of the system.[1]

Types of Process of Structural Change

Finally, we must attempt to determine whether any important generalizations can be made about the types of process of change found at the structural level. The phenomena of the institutionalization of normative culture imply internalization in the personality structures of constituent personalities, which in turn implies

that institutionalization is embedded in the non-rational layers of motivational organization. It is not accessible to change simply through the presentation, to an actor, of rational advantages in the external definition of the situation.

In social structure, the relation of normative culture to personality is expressed by the fundamental distinction between two types of integrative mechanism in the social system—those allocative mechanisms, operating through media like money and power, that affect the balance of advantages and disadvantages in the situation of an acting unit; and those which, like integrative communication, operate through affecting the motivational state of the unit, concerning the definition of what he wants and not how he can get it.

Only when strain impinges on and involves this level of the system of behavioral control can structural change in the present sense become possible. Once it has occurred, the question is whether the impetus to change goes "over the watershed" or, under the countervailing impact of the mechanisms of social control, falls back again.

In either case, strain at this level is manifested by a series of symptoms of disturbance showing the psychological marks of irrationality. These will be organized along the major axes of hope and fear, of "wishful thinking" and "anxiety" showing unrealistic trends in *both* respects. Psychologically, this goes back to the ambivalent structure of motivation to deviance already mentioned.

The directions of this positive-negative polarization are defined in terms of the structural possibilities of deviance. The most important variables are the polarizations between activity and passivity, between compulsive alienation and compulsive con-

---

[1] Naturally in the total picture, specifically economic factors of production are also necessary inputs, from other societies or from other "systems" operating in the territory of the society, like motivation, capital, etc. But because of the relation to the hierarchical structure of social systems, the inputs of political urgency and functional value-commitment are far more critical in what Rostow calls the "take-off" phenomenon than is the availability of adequate factors of production in the strictly economic sense.

formity, that yield the types of rebelliousness, withdrawal, "ritualism," and compulsive performance. In other words, there will be fantasies of utopian ideal future states, of idealized past states, of security in a status quo from which sources of disturbance could conveniently be banished, and of eliminating sources of disturbance directly within the framework of the old structure. There will be corresponding foci of anxiety.

These motivational components are common to all symptoms of disturbance in the institutionalization of social structures. The symbols to which they become attached will depend on the appropriate system references and situations. At the societal level, it is not difficult to detect the utopian element in "communism," in the sense of an alleged actual type of society; or, on the other side, a complete "free enterprise" system. The socially regressive idealization of an unrealistically conceived past appears in such symbols as the simple, unspoiled "Americanism" of the McCarthyites, or in the *Volksgemeinschaft* of German Romantics (particularly in its most extreme version, Naziism). Such symbols as "imperialism," "capitalism," and "communism" are foci of irrational anxiety and aggression.

Another symbolic content is found where the focus of disturbance is a different order of social system. "Authoritarianism" and "conformity" are good examples of anxiety-laden symbols widely current in our society. Some of the irrational symbols in this context have functions in social systems analogous to those of the personality's mechanisms of defense. The equivalents of diplacement and projection are found in the imputation of the sources of disturbance to exogenous systems—particularly similar systems—when much of the motivation really arises from internal strain. Indeed, displacement and/or projection on *personalities* of the products of strain in social systems cause much of the attributing of ill-will to, e.g., "ruling circles."

Symptoms of disturbance, with the kind of structure just sketched, are common to processes which do and do not result in structural change. Whether or not the change occurs depends on the *balance* between the strength of the disturbing forces and the kinds of reception they meet—i.e., the balance between acts motivated by response to disturbance and the sanctions that they stimulate in both endogenous and exogenous agencies. This statement is not a tautology if these conceptions are given content through definition of the nature of the performances and sanctions, and of the strategic significance of content for the equilibrium of the system.

Structural change is possible only when a certain level of strain on institutionalized structure is reached. Such strain may be propagated from technological, economic, and political levels; but the fact that a system is faced with severe problems on those levels is never *by itself* a sufficient explanation of structural change. It is necessary to trace the repercussions of these strains on the higher levels of the control system.

Even when the institutional level is reached, severity of strain is never alone an adequate explanation of change. Structural change is only one possible outcome of strain. Other results are the resolution of the strain, through mechanisms of control, that leaves the old structure intact; and the isolation of disturbing forces, at the cost of some impairment of the system's functioning—and, of course, radical dissolution of the system.

Besides the generalized strength-weakness balance of the disturbances and controls respectively, the most important factors favoring structural change are the following: (1) Adequate mechanisms for overcoming the inevitable resistances of institutionalized structural patterns (vested interests) to abandonment. Overwhelming force or political coercion may impose very severe strains, but, in the absence of such mechanisms, they lead only to active or passive resistance, even though the resistance is realistically hopeless. Endogenously, the balance between positive and negative components in the symptoms of disturbance is the primary factor. For example, if the negative side outweighs the positive, anxiety and aggression will block new institutionalization. (2) Among the positive reactions, there must be combinations with adequate constructive possibilities. The component of alienation must be strong enough to motivate detachment from the older patterns, but not so closely connected with other negative components that it motivates only destructive behavior. On the other hand, too great passivity would motivate only withdrawal. (3) A model, from exogenous sources or endogenously produced, of the pattern to be newly institutionalized is necessary. In socializing the child, the parents, older peers, teachers, and others serve as "role-models" whose personalities and actions embody the patterns of value and norms which the child is expected to internalize; without such adequate models, the internalization would be impossible. (4) The pattern of sanctions evoked by behavior in the transitional phases must selectively reward action conforming with the new model (and must not reward action in terms of the old pattern), and must be sufficiently consistent over a period to bring about the coinciding of the values of units and their self-interest that is the hallmark of institutionalization.

The socialization of the child actually constitutes a process of structural change in one set of structural components of social systems, namely, the role-patterns of the individual— indeed, much of the foregoing paradigm has been derived from this source. These considerations may then be extended to the next level: the corollary of the proposition that the child internalizes new roles in the process of socialization is that the social systems in which this process occurs, e.g., the mother-child system and the nuclear family, must undergo processes of structural change. Thus, the nuclear family with one infant is, structurally speaking, not the same system as that with two adolescent children and one latency-period child, though in another perspective it may still be the same family.

For a more general sociological analysis, however, it may be better to illustrate by two types of process of structural change close to the societal level, in one of which the "model" is predominantly endogenous to the system, in the other, exogenous. The first is the case usually referred to as "structural differentiation" affecting the level of primary functional subsystems; the second, the case involving change in the value-system at the societal level.

The Differentiation of Occupational from Kinship Roles

In the above discussion, reference has often been made to the relative "functional diffuseness" of many social structures. The process of functional differentiation is one of the fundamental types of social change, and has evolutionary aspects and implications. In its bearing on the type of system, it involves more than increasing complexity—e.g., the fact that flexible disposability of resources depends on such differentiation. This dependence requires higher-order mechanisms of integration, substituting the more specialized processes of control associated with markets, power systems, etc., for control through embeddedness in diffuse structures.

Perhaps the best example is the differentiation of occupational roles, in the ideal sense already discussed, from embeddedness in kinship structures which have enjoyed ascribed claims to the functional equivalents of such services. On the role-structure level, the change means that what has been one role of an individual in a single kinship collectivity (which may, however, be internally differentiated) becomes differentiated into two roles in two distinct collectivities, the kinship group and the employing organization.

The first prerequisite of change is disengagement from the preceding pattern. In other words, some order of relative deprivation becomes attached to following the old way. The impingement of the deprivation is on the individual and on the kinship collectivity. The impingement may take such forms as deterioration of previously assumed market conditions, or of the availability of new opportunities which cannot be utilized within the old structural framework. Such severe and prolonged relative deprivation would eventually give rise to symptoms of disturbance of the sort discussed.

In order to prevent the overwhelming consolidation of the negative components of the reactions to disturbance, there must be an adequate range of institutionalized permissiveness and support, in addition to the imposition of deprivations for following the old pattern. There should not be too great immediate pressure for abandoning the old ways precipitately and totally. In the Industrial Revolution in England, this institutionalized permissiveness, as Smelser shows, comprised considerable remaining realistic opportunity in the old domestic pattern of industrial organization, compromise organizational patterns whereby whole families were hired by the cotton mills as units, and considerable "romantic" ideological support for the value of the old ways.

A positive model for the new patterning of work contribution must be demonstrated, first on the immediately relevant organizational level— e.g., factories are organized and jobs made available which offer advantages, i.e., various components of reward, including but not confined to money wages, to the worker and his household. But one crucial problem concerns the ways in which this new model can be made legitimate in terms of the relevant values.

As Smelser shows, it was very important in the British case that the structural changes in the role-organization of the labor force of the late eighteenth century were preceded, and for some time accompanied, by a marked revival in precisely the geographical section and population groups involved, of the Puritan religion. According to the famous Weber hypothesis, Puritanism has legitimized both profit-making and more broadly effective contribution to instrumental function in society. More immediately, the main justification of the factory system was its greater productive effectiveness. In the typical working-class household, there was promise of both realistic opportunity to organize work in a new way, and legitimation of that way in terms of a firmly institutionalized religious tradition. A steady pattern of sanctions operated to reinforce the change, whose most tangible aspect was the steady increase of real wages, largely derived from the productivity of the new industry.[2]

The outcome of the process was the incorporation of a very large new group of the working-class labor force into the factory system, in fully differentiated occupational roles, with the concomitant loss of most of the function of family economic production. Working in factory premises, for an individual wage and under factory rather than kinship discipline, was a main structural feature of the outcome. Smelser makes it clear that this was not a simple matter of attracting workers by better wages than could be offered elsewhere—it was only possible through a major restructuring of the institutional structure of the working-class kinship system.

For the larger system, the part played by the *endogenous* sources of the model components of the process was particularly important. It is not necessary to question the common belief that the immediate impetus came from mechanical inventions. Implementing this impetus at levels bearing on the structure of occupational roles, however, was mainly the work of entrepreneurs—some of whom, like Arkwright, were also the inventors. But the legitimation of the new opportunities could be derived by *specification,* in the light of the new opportunities, of an already firmly institutionalized value-system. The essential point is that enhanced economic productivity was defined as good, in a way justifying the major distubances of institutional structures at lower levels necessary for taking advantage of the greater opportunities. The legitimation of profit-making is only part of a larger complex, whose focus is on the valuation of productivity.

The distinction between the process of structural differentiation and that involving the value-system of a society is relative. In complex societies, processes of differentiation are continually going on at relatively low levels of specification and high levels of structural segmentation. The differentiation of occupational roles from embeddedness in kinship should, however, be placed among the very important processes having repercussions in the society extending far beyond their immediate locations. It is clearly a function of great extension in the division of labor and, consequently, in the extent of markets. It makes salient a whole series of new problems with respect to the institution of contract and the conditions of employment—including the beginnings of large-scale union organization and collective bargaining, and various other questions about the status of the working classes. When a process occurs of the magnitude of the rise of the cotton textile industry until about 1840—*magnitude* not only absolutely but in terms of its place in the total economy of Great Britain—it constitutes a major change in the structure of the society. It is not surprising that the disturbances associated with it included much agitation in national

---

[2] A tragic case of the misfiring of such a process of change, illustrating the importance of the balance of these factors, was the case of the hand-loom weavers. The original impetus for greatly increased productivity came in spinning. The resulting greatly increased supply of yarn put pressure on the weaving branch. But in the absence of usable inventions—which came later—and of other aspects of reorganization in this field, the main result was an enormous quantitative expansion of the weaving trade on the *old* basis of social structure. When the power loom took over, the unrestructured weaving trade was left high and dry. It is not surprising that this group was the main center of disturbance in North England in that period. . . .

politics and noticeable "effervescence" in religion. At the same time, the change did not involve introducing a new value system at the national level—i.e., the fundamentals of Puritan orientation and its place in British national values had been settled in the sixteenth and seventeenth centuries.

Change in the Social Value System

At the highest normative level, two main types of structural change may be distinguished. The first, already described, is the one where the principal model component comes from outside the society. This has been true of the contemporary underdeveloped areas, as outlined. To some degree, it was true of all the post-British cases of industrialization, including the American.

The American case went farthest in accepting the British model of free enterprise, though with some important qualifications. This can be attributed first to the fact that the value system deriving mainly from the ethic of ascetic Protestantism had been strongly institutionalized in this country by the early nineteenth century; furthermore, the basic structural position of religion had been settled by the adoption of the Constitutional separation of church and state that paved the way for denominational pluralism. The British model, therefore, posed no serious problem of value-orientation; the American case was considerably closer to a pure culture of the ascetic branch of Protestantism most involved in industrialization than was the British. The problem in our case was primarily the process of structural differentiation. Many religious movements, especially revivalist ones, played an important part on the fringes of the spread of industrialization. These have been essentially similar to Methodism in the north of England in the later eighteenth century.

This is probably one of the major causes of the relatively small role of political agency in the American case, though political agency played a greater part in such fields as the subsidizing of railway-building in America than in Britain. Essentially, there was no very serious problem of gaining general acceptance of the functional values necessary for industrialization, as there was in underdeveloped areas or even in most Continental European countries. It is probably not entirely fortuitous that both Japan and the Soviet Union, although very different, became industrialized under very heavy governmental pressure; in both cases, the ideological justification of the requisite value-commitments played a particularly important part. In Japan, the nationalistic connotations of aspects of the Shinto religious tradition were particularly important. In the Soviet case, the revolutionary force of the Communist movement was grafted onto a Russian social structure that had always emphasized the priority of the state over private interests—far more strongly than in most Western countries. The Party functioned as the primary agency of ideological indoctrination which, under the utopian conception of communism, has inculcated the values necessary for high commitment to economic productivity—values which seem to have been relatively weak in pre-Revolutionary Russia.

The combination of practical urgency and the absence of the functional-level value commitment constitutes a major reason that, for the underdeveloped countries, governmental agency and the importance of the ideological symbol of "socialism" play such an important role in industrialization. Even the rigid authoritarianism of Communist organizational practices occasions far less resistance in these circumstances, since there is both the factor of urgency, to an extent which we do not feel, and, perhaps even more important, the necessity of counterbalancing, in the inevitable ambivalent structure, the profound resistance to value change.[3]

The second main type of societal value-change is that occurring when the cultural model cannot be supplied from a socially exogenous source, but must, so far as the social system reference is concerned, be evolved from within the society. This is the situation to which Max Weber's famous category of charismatic innovation applies. The focus of the change must be in the cultural system's religious aspects. It must concern alterations in the definition of the meaning of the life of the individual in society and of the character of the society itself.

In the process of development, a cultural change which could change values at a societal level would arise, through some complex process involving the interaction and interdependence of social and cultural systems. Considerations such as those reviewed by Weber in [his discussion of] classes, status groups and religion . . . would be highly relevant in so far as they concern society. The whole system of action, and the action-exogenous environment impinging upon it, is also relevant to this problem. The special role of the charismatic personality may involve problems specific to personality theory and not reduci-

______

[3] The most conspicuous example of a failure to overcome this resistance, very probably because of the failure to provide the necessary permissiveness and support to ease the process of relinquishment of old values, is probably the case of the Russian peasantry. Agriculture is clearly the main sore spot of Soviet productivity, and this seems to go back to the violently coercive procedures adopted in the collectivization program.

ble either to sociological or cultural terms.

The obverse is the process of institutionalizing new religious values. The first question arising concerns the specification of the values from the cultural to the social system level, that is, defining of the implications of the cultural premises for the *kind of society* considered desirable. The second basic problem concerns the processes by which, once such a set of societal values is available, the strategically most important elements in the population may be motivationally committed to them. In other words, these elements must be socialized in the new definition of the situation if they are to exert the leverage necessary for extending the institutionalization of the values to all the important levels of specification and areas of differentiated function in the society.

A few points may be mentioned that are pertinent. The bearers of the new values must somehow become established in such a way that they cannot be reabsorbed in the older system. Religious or semi-religious movements, churches, etc., must be structurally independent of the paramount politically organized collectivity. Once consolidated, however, the institutionalization of new values in the secular society is possible only when these bearers can acquire a fundamental influence over the leadership elements of the paramount political system, through conversion of these elements, through infiltration, or through revolution. In early medieval Europe, the Church was the main locus of the values which later underlay the activism of modern Western society. The religious orders were the main locus of the values' growth and consolidation. If the Church and its orders had merely been a part of the political organization, this would not have occurred. In the great period from Gregory VII to Innocent III, the Church was able to impose much more of its values on a reluctant political laity than it otherwise could have. This did not happen without a good deal of direct interpenetration of political and religious leadership; but the basic principle of differentiation of church and state, though under considerable strain, was not abandoned.

Part 2

primitive
societies

Just as the vast majority of biological species are relatively simple forms of life, most societies that have taken part in the course of human existence have been of the primitive type. Among contemporary primitive societies of which we have reliable anthropological studies, to say nothing of the prehistoric societies about which our knowledge remains unfortunately limited, there is immense variation—indeed, the variation is so great that precise generalization about them has proven extremely difficult. As compared with societies exemplifying any of the other evolutionary types, however, primitive societies may be treated as simple in basic structure. That is, they are characterized by relatively diffuse structures which are interrelated minimally through differentiation and functional specialization. In Durkheim's analysis, they have comparatively little division of labor and are integrated on the basis of mechanical solidarity. Nevertheless, primitive societies do exhibit all the fundamental elements of complexity that are characteristic of the human condition itself. Action within them is oriented in terms of the complex symbolic structures of culture, roles are performed in ways that vary with the motivations and convictions of individual personalities, high levels of skill and intelligence are required to execute and co-ordinate the myriad tasks of social life, and the functional exigencies confronting their social systems must be managed on the changeable and conflict-prone bases of structures of normative institutions. Thus, anthropological evidence has long ago forced evolutionary theory to abandon the judgment that primitive societies are simple in anything but a comparative sense.

Each of our readings on primitive society deals principally with one of the four primary aspects of the functioning of a society, namely the religious and culture-maintaining, the integrative or solidarity-generating, the political, and the economic aspects. In this respect, the essays have been selected for their excellence in demonstrating how well adapted various structures in primitive society may be for the performance of the primary societal functions, as well as how complicated may become the networks of social relationships regulated by the basic institutional structures of even a "simple" society. At the same time, each reading analyzes a society from a different one of the world's primitive "culture areas"—respectively, from Aboriginal Australia, South Asia, the American Pacific Northwest, and Central Africa. Thus, relative to the brevity imposed by the present format, it is hoped that the selections in Part 2 will present something of a comprehensive overview of the kinds of interesting institutional arrangements that modern anthropological studies have been reporting from primitive societies.

Even in the absence of general ethnographic accounts which would make careful and detailed comparison possible, the reader will notice many indications of important structural variation among the four societies analyzed in the readings. Certain of the differences are criterial for analytical judgments of level or stage of evolution. The Australian Aborigines and the Purum exemplify a type of society which may—the judgment involves much theoretical projection—lie close to the minimal levels of differentiation and complexity compatible with the sustenance of human culture and social existence. The Coast Salish and the Bemba, however, although preliterate and hence primitive in the present typology, seem to belong to a more differentiated type of society. Despite much fusion among structures fulfilling different functional requirements, societies of this more advanced type are characterized by a better articulated world view and set of religious beliefs accompanied by a more highly organized cult system, more durable and inclusive structures of societal solidarity based upon a class system of stratification, a more centralized and hierarchized authority structure, and more flexible institutions regulating the production and circulation of economic resources. Some "advanced" primitive societies might be categorized as archaic in the schema proposed by Bellah in Part 1.

W. E. H. Stanner's essay on the totemism of the Australian Aborigines has special sociological interest in that it brings the findings of much modern research to the analysis of the systems that Durkheim (and after him, Bellah) considered to be "the elementary forms of religion" *par excellence*. Stanner shows that the core of Aboriginal religion consists of the ramified, loosely organized constructions of beliefs about the Dream Time, the sacred order of instituted realities that together comprise the "given condition of life." Myths of happenings in the realm of the Dream Time reveal and dramatize the fundamental religious and moral meanings of the significant elements of the Aboriginal environment (places, animal species, weather conditions, etc.) and socio-cultural order (customs, rites, social groupings, etc.). Things that are given a place or role or justification in the Dream Time by the myths are thereby sacralized; and the Dream Time itself, taken as a vaguely unified order of the truly meaningful realities, serves to sacralize the underlying design of the world in all of its modalities as experienced by believing Aborigines. The rites associated with the principal myths enable participants to experience dramatic engagement in the sacred Dream Time events directly, thereby in a sense sacralizing themselves and their actions and committing themselves with great emotional intensity to the ways of living ordained in the Dream Time.

The totems themselves are intrinsically spiritual—complex symbols that demark the main points of meaning in the Dream Time order of reality, the major parts of life about which the mythical stories are constructed. They represent constitutive memberships in the Dream Time, but also in the groups and personal statuses institutionalized in Aboriginal society. Hence, they provide sacred grounding or legitimation on a thoroughly particularistic basis for the collectivities and important roles in the society. At the same time, the totems establish that only specific patterns of relationships among collectivities and among members of society are within the realm of moral possibility. Even though the central role in society of clans and lineages and of loyalties to them is what the totems affirm most clearly and directly, the entire social structure is ordained totemistically. It is to this mode of relation between cultural construction and social institution, which incorporates no cultural awareness of legitimate alternatives, that Stanner refers when he says that for Aboriginal totemists social life is a "one possibility" thing.

Modern social anthropology has concentrated more study on systems of kinship and marriage than on any other aspect of the functioning of primitive societies. In part, this has been due to the formidable problems, both theoretical and empirical, of understanding the complexities of particular kinship systems and of placing kinship studies upon a sound comparative basis. However, a more basic reason has probably been the sheer importance of kinship and affinal relations to the institutional structuring of solidarity in primitive societies. In societies like the Australian Aborigines or the Purum and in some more advanced primitive systems, the societal community is largely constituted by an affinal collectivity, i.e., its general boundaries and internal lines of division or cleavage are set through the relationships obtaining among intermarrying kin groups. Moreover, given the functional diffuseness of primitive societies, the ties of kinship and affinity which comprise the core institutional matrix of societal integration tend to become principal structures in the organization of pattern maintenance, politics, and economic action as well.

Rodney Needham's discussion of Purum kinship and marriage shows how a simple institutional mechanism, termed prescriptive marriage, serves to generate a very complex network of ties among the descent groups, clans, and villages of the society. Under Purum rules of prescriptive marriage, there are particular groups from which the men of any given descent group must choose their wives and different groups from which they must find husbands for their female kin. The entire marriage system may be visualized as a complex set of cross-cutting and interlocking cycles through which women are circulated from descent group to descent group in stable patterns. Since the cycles interrelate descent groups among different villages and since the clans consisting of mutually exogamous descent groups are generally represented in each village, solidary ties are also established on a territorial basis.

Standing at the institutional crux of the prescriptive marriage system, the relationships of wife-giving to wife-taking groups are critical to the solidarity of Purum society. Needham shows them to be strongly asymmetrical in status terms, the wife-giving groups always having a particularistic higher standing (but not generally higher prestige since all groups stand below their own wife-givers). Wife-taking families continually owe their wife-givers a long series of prescribed gifts and services in compensation for their wives. The affinal relationships are very heavily ritualized, the dependence of the wife-taking families—and hence the importance of solidary affinal ties—being strongly symbolized. Indeed, Needham shows that the wife-giver to wife-taker relationship comprises a fundamental theme in the dyadic categoreal scheme of Purum cosmology, thereby taking on the status of a basic dimension of the order of the universe for the Purum.

Studies of primitive economies have, since Marcel Mauss's *The Gift*, attended carefully to a dynamic that may seem familiar after review of Needham's materials, namely the interdependencies that arise from the giving of gifts, the obligation of the gift-recipient to the gift-giver, and the generation or reaffirmation of basic solidary ties. Mauss noted that gifts are generally made in the expectation that they are to be reciprocated in some way. Hence, the receiving of a gift involves an acceptance of an obligation to the gift-giver on the part of the recipient. The trust involved not only in giving a gift and relying upon the recipient to make an appropriate reciprocation, but also in accepting the responsibility of having to meet an obligation to the gift-giver particularly, presumes solidarity or potential for solidarity in the relationship. The presentation and reciprocation of gifts will test a solidary relationship, for the solidarity may be broken, reinforced, or expanded, depending on events. However, the expectations of either party can be secured only insofar as gift exchanges are grounded in firmly solidary relationships. In societies where the absence or primitivity of economic markets and monetary systems requires that resource circulation take the form of the exchange of gifts among social units, economic relationships cannot be sharply divorced from the principal integrative structures of the society. The greater the value of the resources being circulated— and the value might be more symbolic or ritual than strictly economic—the more exchange relationships would require grounding in diffuse and reliable solidarity. Thus, Mauss argued that the patterns through which a primitive society circulates resources tend to be determined less by the direct play of economic interests than by the principal structures of solidarity, and that gift circulation inherently has important integrative significance, in that it tests relationships of solidarity critical to the organization of the society. Indeed, many ritual gift exchanges function not to realize economic purposes but to provide regularized, secure opportunities to solidify relationships of importance to societal integration.

Reexamining the institutions of potlatch which comprised important case material for Mauss, Wayne Suttles advances our understanding of the ways in which gift circulation, in drawing upon the integrative capacities of a primitive society, can enhance and stabilize the essentially economic adaptation of the society to its environment. Among the Coast Salish, cycles of gift exchange are started when kin groups living in a particular locality have been able to collect food beyond their own requirements. They may then present their food surpluses to affines living in other localities and obtain, in return, more durable but less necessary items of wealth, usually blankets. The more durable items can at a later time be reexchanged for food. In a sense, the durables represent necessities of life "banked" with affinal groups against times of local famine. Sizable holdings of such wealth greatly enhance the economic security of a local group, for they constitute means of obligating their affines to give them food. At the same time, they comprise evidence of having extended necessities of life to affinal groups in exchange for objects of merely ceremonial significance. So long as the productive system is not broken down by concomitant famines in the different ecological zones occupied by the various local groups, the system of exchange and "banking" constitutes a flexible mechanism by which each local group can secure its own economic future while perhaps also aiding its affines.

However, the solidarity of affinal ties could be endangered if particular groups were to accumulate too much wealth, for their claims upon the food collected by their affines might threaten the latter's livelihood or willingness to meet exchange obligations. Against this possibility, the potlatch, a ritual in which a group purposefully burns at least some of its wealth, comprises an important equilibrating mechanism. In a potlatch, a group destroys its claims against other groups for food, thereby both redistributing the wealth in the society and improving the economic security of other groups. Such cancelling of claims is regarded as highly honorable, so that the performer of a big potlatch receives much prestige, including greater privilege to assert political leadership. Indeed, the rewards of enhanced status serve as an institutional sanction motivating group leaders to organize potlatches.

Audrey I. Richards presents a general account of the political system of the African Bemba, a large tribe with a simple class system of stratification and a well institutionalized hierarchy of authority. She shows how the Bemba have been able to combine a rather dispersed system of settlement with power arrangements that achieve much centralization of control.

At the base of the Bemba power hierarchy, village headmen provide leadership and supervision for the collective activities, especially ritual ones, of small settlements of about thirty to fifty huts. The headmen hold their positions by the favor and under the control of district chiefs or subchiefs. The chiefs rule their districts from central capitals, where they provide ritual leadership, preside over courts, settle political disputes, supervise their tribute labor, and manage the gardens which feed their courts. In performing these functions, they are advised and assisted by varying numbers of officials, elders, and favorites. Above the chiefs and at the peak of the power hierarchy stands the paramount chief, who has the largest and most elaborate court and who holds the ultimate authority.

At all levels of authority, kinship ties interpenetrate very thoroughly with the controls over power. All of the chiefdoms are filled by male relatives of the paramount chief, with closer relatives holding the more important positions and members of distant, localized branches of the royal family receiving subchiefdoms. The total body of relatives of the paramount chief hold statuses of generalized privilege, and hence comprise a clearly bounded upper class in a two class system. The privileges of the upper class, but especially the right to hold office, are legitimated in terms of religious beliefs about chiefly kinship with the sacred tribal ancestors. All offices are gained by descent, but as Richards shows, through flexible rules that encompass a range of kinship ties, ensure fairly regular successions from lower to higher offices, and allow officials to be selected partly for ability. At the same time, the hereditary rights to office of a chief's principal subordinates and advisors, as well as the ritual elements of their duties, enable them to exercise fairly effective checks on his powers.

religion, totemism, and symbolism

four

W. E. H. STANNER

I shall sketch as briefly as possible the positive character of [Aboriginal] religion as we now understand it. (1) The Aborigines thought the world full of signs to men; they transformed the signs into assurances of mystical providence; and they conceived life's design as fixed by a founding drama. (2) At its best the religion put a high worth on the human person, both as flesh and as spirit. (3) It magnified the value of life by making its conservation and renewal into a cult. (4) It acknowledged the material domain as being under spiritual authority. (5) Religious practice included a discipline to subdue egotistical man to a sacred, continuing purpose. (6) Religious belief expressed a philosophy of assent to life's terms. (7) The major cults inculcated a sense of mystery through the use of symbolisms pointing to ultimate or metaphysical realities which were known by their signs. Each proposition rests on well-established facts, which have often been recorded and left, uninterpreted, as mere "custom." To deny them what seem their plain

Reprinted from Ronald M. Berndt and Catherine H. Berndt, eds., *Aboriginal Man in Australia* (Sydney: Angus and Robertson, 1965), pp. 213–21, 225–35, by permission of the publisher and of the author.

implications is now unjustifiable. I shall discuss each of the main statements in turn. It will then be clear, I hope, that what prevented their earlier recognition were the unexamined assumptions of scholars who were either not interested in religion as such, or had too narrow a conception of it, or misunderstood their task.

1.   The Aborigines' positive knowledge has been well appreciated, especially that involved in their techniques of subsistence and in their manipulation of the segmentary forms of social organization. In those fields of life they were masterfully confident. What may be called their religious confidence has been left rather understated. They lived as though sure of their power, through ritual observances, to sustain their being in a world which, though grounded on mystery, had no real problem of futurity. The nomadic life of hunting and foraging must have had its fair share, perhaps more, of vicissitudes. But their religion had a notably strong theurgic component which expressed itself everywhere in the continent, at least, in all the regions about which we have good knowledge, in the conception of a great founding drama. That drama was marked by a climax in which everything—including man, and his

whole condition of life—came to be as it is. Form, style, and function became determinate. Consequently, the types of tension between past, present, and future that characterize so many systems of religion were entirely absent from theirs. The given condition of life was one in which the typical preoccupations of many other religious faiths could have had no function. A full understanding of the Aboriginal view of life and the world requires a careful study of the whole body of doctrine about the Dream Time (*altjira, bugari*), which is the common but not universal way of referring to the time of the founding drama. It has not yet been appraised at all adequately. But it represents an immense store of meanings, variably drawn on by different cult-groups, yet evidently never fully explored or used by any of them because subtle (and probably important) variations occurred in different regions. The religious tone was certainly affected. In Cape York Ursula McConnel found that many myths dealing with the founding drama had a quality of "self-dedication"; in the Northern Territory the quality seemed to me rather that of "sad finality." Those were not wholly subjective impressions. One would expect that, within a continent of so many contrasting environments, many qualitative differences would occur. Had there been a higher rate of social change in Aboriginal life than was evidently the case, many elements which were subliminal would probably have developed. A foundation existed for a systematic belief in gods and for institutions of priesthood, prayer, and sacrifice. Once observers were able to cease identifying religion with theism, a perception of those foundations drew them on to many false attributions. That error in turn has to be rectified. The central problem of study is to stay within the actual evidence but at the same time to draw from it the legitimate religious implications. Widely, two complementary emphases stood out in the doctrine of the Dream Time: the fixation or instituting of things in an enduring form, and the simultaneous endowment of all things—including man, and his condition of life—with their good and/or bad properties. The central meaning was clear. Men were to live always under that foundation.

When the myths about the drama of the Dream Time are studied with care it becomes clear that the Aborigines had taken, indeed, had gone far beyond, the longest and most difficult step toward the formation of a truly religious outlook. They had found in the world about them what they took to be signs of intent toward men, and they had transformed those signs into *assurances* of life under mystical nurture. Their symbolic observances toward the signs, in rites of several kinds, were in essence acts of faith toward the ground of that assurance.

It is not yet possible to bring together under that principle all the ritualized cults of which we have heard, but those that fit within the trilogy suggested many years ago by A. P. Elkin—historical rites, initiation rites, and "increase" rites (*talu, intichiuma*) intended to maintain and renew the life of natural species—appeared in some sense to recapitulate some feature or aspect of the founding drama. One could doubtless speak of "imitation" and thus cast all the ritual into the mould of "magic," but that really will not do. The aetiology is obviously too profound. If the word "religion" means, as its probable etymology suggests, two dispositions in man—to ponder on the foundations of human life in history, and to unite or reconcile oneself with the design incorporated in those foundations—then the Aborigines were a very religious-minded people. The motive of their strong sense of religious duty and the purpose of their rites become more understandable if approached from that viewpoint. So do the intellectual, emotional, psychological, and social components of their religious thought and life. *If* life has a mystical foundation, and *if* its design was fixed once-for-all, what else should rational men do but maintain and renew that design? Most anthropologists familiar with the Aborigines would testify to their apparent inability to grasp that life can have any other rationale as satisfying and conclusive as that on which their religion is founded.

If one can judge from contemporary and recent Aboriginal life, what must have fascinated them—it still does—was the apparent evidence of *design* in the world; design in the sense of pattern, shape, form, structure; *given* design that seemed to them to point to *intent*. It would be tedious to list the facts of that kind of which they take sharp note, but the proofs that they always did so are contained in their language categories. It is to those facts, not to the imaginary phenomena with which Herbert Spencer, Tylor, and Frazer made so much play, that a theorist of the origins of Aboriginal religion should turn. Pattern, shape, form, and structure, occurring in what we call "nature," constituted for them a world of signs to men. Part of their religion seems to be like a return of equivalent or compensatory signs to the mysterious domain whence they came. There cannot have been many primitive rites which so strongly suggested a conscious attempt by men to bind themselves to the design in things they saw about them, and to the enduring plan of life as they experienced it.

2. The worth attached to the person was shown in a striking manner by the high ritualization of the life-cycle of males. Always a particular person, or a very small group of equivalent persons, was thus honoured; and the community, not a clique or set, paid the honour. Each individual, at his due times, was brought to the first place in public life. For days or weeks he was made the focus of elaborate efforts of the imaginative and material arts. The effect was to dignify and in some sense sanctify each person so honoured. One is impelled to conclude that the rites had a plain meaning: *man is of value in himself and for others*. The relative value of initiates at such times was the highest that society could contrive for them. The meaning "man has value" was also implied by the respect for totems, totem-places, and insignia and emblems standing for persons; by the restraints against the use of names, or other extensions of personality such as shadows and tracks, in a dangerous or disrespectful way; by the undemonstrative care of the sick, blind, halt, and mentally afflicted; and by the dutiful obsequies to the body, the spirit/soul/ghost/shade, and the social memory of the dead. Such acts, attitudes, and beliefs are deeply inconsonant with a low valuation of human life and personality. One could not rightly say that in themselves they amounted to a religious view of man. But there was a further fact that, added to them, warrants such a conclusion. In several parts of Aboriginal Australia one met the fundamental belief that great guardian-spirits (Baiame, Kunmanggur) existed—whether as ancestral or as self-subsistent beings—to "look after" living men. Elsewhere, lesser spirits did so. The conception thus deepens: man is of value in himself and for others, and *there are spirits* *who care*. That, by any test, is a religious view of man. But the generalization must be given its true measure in the light of certain negative facts. The religious valuation was qualified by a secular valuation both within, and especially between, clans and tribes. The worth of infants and the very old was notoriously held of small account: in desperate circumstances, both were left to die. On occasions, individuals acted toward others with intense cruelty, disregard, and selfishness within small kin-groups and, outside—except in respect of close cognates and affines—without restraint other than that induced by fear of consequences. Almost universally, the valuation of women was low in respect of their personal as distinct from their functional worth. They were usually held in low regard ritually, too, but not always in all circumstances. Their blood-making and child-giving powers were thought both mysterious and dangerous, but there was nothing elevated in their sex or marriage. It may be suggested that those negative facts were the products of pragmatic, egotistic, and politic conditions, the concomitants of any religious system in practice. Aboriginal religion was not alone in being infiltrated and, in some respects, made part-prisoner by ex·pediency, power, and vested interest. But all that only qualified Aboriginal man's dignity. It flawed, but did not destroy, the estate into which he came in the Dream Time.

3. What I have called the "magnification of life" was shown by the intense, one could almost say obsessive, preoccupation with the signs, symbols, means, portents, tokens, and evidences of vitality. The whole religious corpus vibrated with an expressed aspiration for life, abundant life. Vitality, fertility and growth; the conservation, production, protection, and rescue of life: themes such as these seem to have been widely implicit and, in some notable regional cases, quite explicit. Vitalistic things obtruded throughout the myths and rites— water, blood, fat, hair, excrements; the sex organs, semen, sexuality in all its phases, the quickening in the womb; child-spirits, mystical impregnation and reincarnation; the development of the body from birth to death; the transitions of the human spirit from before organic assumption until after physical dissolution; apparently animated phenomena such as green leaves, rain and the seasons, lightning, whirlwinds, shooting stars and the heavenly bodies; or things of unexplained origin, unusual appearance and giant size. Poor descriptions of rites, and bad or over-literal translations of myths, have often left such stresses latent or obscure. But the careful studies by Warner, Elkin, and R. M. and C. H. Berndt in Arnhem Land, by E. A. Worms more widely, and the skilful linguistic work by A. Capell and T. G. H. Strehlow, to choose a few examples only, make clear what must have been commonly the case. The known evidence suggests that Aboriginal religion was probably one of the least materialminded, and most life-minded, of any of which we have knowledge. It may not have "magnified goodness," as Bacon said of Christianity, but it did magnify life.

4. The overrule of the material dimension by spiritual authority was not complete. By "spiritual authority" I mean the rule of all invisible potencies, however imagined, that were believed to have effects on men's lives, effects not possible by unaided means in the hands of ordinary men. We have evidence that the *whole* of materiality was not thought to be influenced in that way, so that runaway

doctrines of animatism and animism are unjustified. No *one* spirit or potency had authority over *all* the materiality that was so influenced. Not all spirits were thought of as man-like; some were supposed to have quasi-animal forms, or even to be indescribable. Of those that were man-like only some were thought ancestral; others were considered to be "self-finding" (self-existent, self-subsistent). But there were many things in the environment that were just things, themselves only and no more, without import, standing for nothing. And the authority of spirits and other potencies, as understood by the Aborigines, was only vaguely a moral-ethical authority. Those reservations having been stated, one really need point only to *two* well-known classes of fact to justify the main proposition, though of course many more could be cited. The first is the class of beliefs concerning the impregnation of women by pre-existing child-spirits that *act under their own volition*. The second is the class of beliefs concerning the dependence of men on a *potential* of life (for example, of humans, animals, and plants) *pre-existing* in totem-places. Men could—should—help the child-spirits to do their work, and could—indeed, must—ritually facilitate the release of the potential. But they did not create that store and without it were helpless. The *manifestation* of life on a visible, material plane was thus a spiritual function. So was the power of humans to *subsist* on that plane. Those postulates were fundamental to Aboriginal social existence as a form of being-as-it-is. (The question whether we are dealing with "magic" or "religion" does not arise in the case of the first set of beliefs and, in the second, concerns only the mode of releasing the potential.)

5. The myths contain much of the "human-all-too-human" character of man. A certain image of *original* man emerges as though with two faces, one well drawn, the other less so. The first face has on it the marks of egotism, always wayward and self-willed, sometimes wanton: greed, envy, bad faith, anger, selfishness, pride, disobedience, and the like are common themes in the myths. To complete the features of the other (let us think of it for the time being as *one* face, though we will probably find many when the matter is studied with care) one has to do things: elicit the conventions of understanding within which the myths were told and heard, and interpret the climax of each myth. Both are dangerous procedures since it is easy to slip beyond the evidence. Many myths, one cannot say all, had a homiletic effect; perhaps the Aborigines drew a moral lesson from them; but to all appearances a strong, explicit religious ethic was absent, probably for the same reasons that a religious creed was absent. Three vital preconditions were missing—a tradition of intellectual detachment; a class of interpreters who had the prerogative or duty to codify principle; and a challenge that would have forced morals and beliefs to find anatomies.

All this made the moral aspect of the religion rather amorphous, although what was there was consistent. But a study of the ritual practices now suggests a possible need to modify that rather unfavourable judgment. Until recently, to know how to investigate the problem more adequately seemed peculiarly difficult. But it now appears possible to compare fruitfully two things that did not seem comparable—the structural anatomies of myths and rites. Many myths reveal a mounting of incidents to a crisis or culmination that exhibits a cluster of meanings with a distinct moral quality. The initiatory rites all rose to a tense crisis that brought about, or was supposed to bring about, a physical-moral-spiritual change in the initiates. The two types of crisis appear to have been symbolic paramorphs. In myth, an imagined crisis was dealt with by a spoken imagery. In rite, an actual crisis was dealt with by a gestural-visual imagery. In such cases the myths, although a sort of allegorical poesy, may have served as the implicit moral "theory" of the rites. How far that approach will stand up to test, and how far the morphological likenesses can be traced through the symbolic systems, remain to be seen. It is too soon to say certainly that the funerary rites contained the same symbolic pattern, or one comparable, or whether all variants of the trilogy studied so formatively by Elkin did so. But even a partial success in demonstrating that that was the case will reinforce what we already know. All the evidence collected since Collins's time establishes that the rites of initiation existed as *disciplines*. They both *fashioned* uncompleted man, and *transformed* him into a being of higher worth.

The moral and mystical content of the rites varied regionally. It may have varied too over time as one cult replaced or mixed with another. But the canon of the rites was invariable: to subdue refractory, unfinished personalities to a purpose held to be sacred and timeless. They put on the body, mentality, and social personality of initiates ineffaceable signs designating stages in the socialization of man. It is a plausible hypothesis that the outward signs were thought of as having inward counterparts; that the rites were held to put on initiates a moral-spiritual mark as well. The crude vehicles of that purpose—tooth-avulsion, depilation, scarification, circumcision, subincision—have been stumbling-blocks of European understanding. It is most necessary here to look beyond the symbol to the symbolized. But it is also necessary to take more account of the experiential and creative aspects of Aboriginal religion. The convention followed for so long that the study of a religion is to be equated with the study of its beliefs and actions (myths and rites) is plainly too restrictive. Aboriginal religion drew on a human experience of life, and had a creative purpose in life. The four categories of experience, belief, action, and purpose were coordinate. If any is neglected a study may be *about* religion but not *of* it.

6. There were no Aboriginal philosophers and one can thus speak of "philosophy" only metaphorically. But there is ground for saying that they lived—and therefore thought—by axioms, which were "objective" in that they related to a supposed nature of man and condition of human life. Myths presented the axioms in an intuitive-contemplative aspect. Rites presented them in a passionist-activist aspect. No Aboriginal put the axioms into words but the existence and efficacy of anything—including intuitional awarenesses and insights—do not depend on someone's formal affirmation of them in words. Myths would not be stories, and rites would not have an invariant structure, if axioms could not subsist by other than formalized means. I shall not try to do more than state what I believe to have been the principle of Aboriginal philosophy in the metaphorical sense. I propose to call it a principle of assent to the disclosed terms of life. Anthropologists who have worked with Aborigines commonly note that a supposed past— the whole doctrine of the Dream Time—was said to, and to all appear-

ances did, weigh on the present with overmastering authority. But as far as one can tell, the human response to that situation was not tragic, pessimistic, fatalistic or even quietistic on the one hand, or rebellious and complaining on the other. I have remarked elsewhere that the Aborigines seemed either to have stopped short of, or gone beyond, a true quarrel with the terms of life. They appeared to assent to a reality-as-it-is-and-must-be. Hence, I suggest, three things: the "human-all-too-human" quality postulated as true of men and life's condition in the Dream Time; the constancy of the ritual motive to memorialize the culminating events of that mythical time; and the absence from religious thought and practice of any life-compensatory themes. But within that larger equipoise they evidently sought to make the physical and social life-process of man a process of moral development as well.

Any such construction must take into account a number of facts which, though not new, are now coming into better perspective among anthropologists. There is no doubt that cultural influences, including religious influences, coming from beyond the continent (especially but not only to Arnhem Land—and thence, who knows how far?) had powerful effects before European settlement. It is also certain that the dynamic of development within Australia was higher, and diffused its products more widely, than was once supposed. Thirdly, cults recently and now under study give some evidence—as yet indirect, but to my mind very suggestive—of a process of religious discovery. Conceivably, all those things were causally connected. That possibility remains to be investigated. But taking, as far as one can at this stage, a continental view, it is difficult to resist a conclusion that both the religious and the social cultures were in a dynamic state when Europeans came. We shall undoubtedly learn much more by deeper analyses of the surviving regional cults, no less in their steady phases than in the fervour of their rise and the possible degenerations of their fall. One may end with a question. If the philosophy was one of assent, why the *creative* effort of *new* cult?

7. In several respects the known cults suggest a classification with the mystery-religions. With remarkable theatrical skill, they used mystagogy to inculcate an attitude—an *archaist* attitude—to things of *this* world. Whether the cultists taught or learnt anything of moral or spiritual significance is perhaps open to doubt. The fact may be, as Aristotle said of the Greek mysteries, that "the initiated do not learn anything so much as feel certain emotions and are put in a certain frame of mind." Most anthropologists who have seen the cults practised would agree that there were probably deep effects on both mind and personality. But the ritual symbolisms were also treasured for their own sakes. In some sense, the Aborigines may have been imprisoned by them through the aesthetic pleasure of taking part. One need not hesitate to speak of "mystical participation" in the sense of taking part in evocative dramas having to do with mysteries. But any suggestion of mere traditionalism or mindless automatism would be wrong. Effort, treasure, and enthusiasm were spent far too freely.

.   .   .

Religion is necessarily both individual *and* collective, personal *and* social, sacred *and* secular. Let me therefore raise, and dismiss briefly, a matter on which anthropologists would probably not speak with one voice. I refer to the social aspect of totems. The supposition that there is a causal connection between totems and social organization is in my opinion erroneous. I have not found that Aboriginal men are, say, brothers because they are of the same totem. They are of the same totem because they are brothers. A man does not marry a woman because she is of a different totem. The difference of totem makes marriage permissible for other reasons. Two strangers who discover they are of the same totem may treat each other as class-brothers, if there is no great difference of age, and if there is, then as father-son or grandfather-grandson. But the totem is a sufficient condition, not a determinant, of any such relationship. It is a sign of unity between things or persons *unified by something else*. The "something else" is one or more of a possibly vast set of significations of that totem. There are many possible symbolizations of the ground and cause of unity. One of the most common is the symbolic complex "one flesh—one spirit—one country—one Dreaming." Much of the anthropological record may need re-examination with such cautions in mind, but probably no great harm results from using, as a manner of speaking, such phrases as "totemic clans" or "totemic groups," provided it is realized that they are sign-bearing groups, explaining their unity by the signs, but deriving their structural and functional organizations quite differently. But I would think that Radcliffe-Brown said perhaps all that is necessary in pointing out that the "social aspect" of Totemism is really the organization of the clan (or other such group). To say so in no way diminishes the interest or importance of enquiry into the conditions in which this or that totemic feature or complex—thing, locality, emblematic

or mimetic design, secret lore, track or path, dance, song, cult—are in fact associated with combinations or groups of people having one or more such features in common; in other words, the conditions in which totemic features are socialized.

A totem is in the first place a thing; an entity, an event, or a condition—what I have called an existent. Virtually anything perceivable can serve: plants and animals of all kinds—anything in the entire floral and faunal realms; wind, rain, storms, thunder, lightning, stars, sun, moon and clouds —anything of heaven; tools and weapons, food and cosmetics, fire and smoke, mist and spume, fresh water and salt—anything of earth; the human exuviae and genitals—almost anything of the human body. In listing the totems of sets of people who compose clans, moieties, and tribes an anthropologist may think at first that he is recording mere utilities. That impression does not long survive. Totemic significance goes far beyond utility. Sexual desire, cold weather, sweethearts, vomiting, runaway wives, mothers' milk, and innumerable pests have all been recorded as totems. A part of an object can serve—the handle of a spear-thrower, or the bowels of an animal; so can a disease— diarrhoea or colds; so can flood-wrack swirling down a river, or tide-marks on a beach. Living persons evidently cannot be totems, but a mythical person can be—for example, the Warramunga "laughing boy" who is supposed never to have died. Things without any particular significance for the Aborigines—gold, precious stones —are passed over. But so too are some objects of symbolic worth—the Milky Way, or the glans penis. The rationale of any tribal selection is not really clear. Probably it is irreducibly arbitrary. We do not know. All we can do is deduce it. But, clearly, a set of totems is not just a set: it is something more; yet it is less than a fully systematic catalogue. But as far as we know it never exhausts the perceivable world of any tribe. It roughs out a significant world within what is perceived.

The fact, existence, or presence of any totem is, among other things, a sign to the Aborigines of any given region. Many such signs are widely inter-tribal, a few universal. Each sign appears to signify a marvel that has credit among them as having happened in the long ago, the Dream Time or Dreaming, concerning which a myth or a set of myths purports to give evidence, sometimes contradictory evidence. Under study, the marvels reveal themselves as more cosmological than cosmogonical. That is, they have less to do with the setting up of the world than with the instituting of relevances within it; in other words, with the instituting of a moral-rational order. No marvel is a datum: it is a theorem from a ground on which the marvel stands. The totems are a perennial reminder and a token of the marvels and the ensuing instituted order. It is in that sense that they can be said to be signs—declarative, indicative, signs presenting contemporary, immediate, and visible reminders of cosmological marvels of the past. There is no evidence of conflict in Aboriginal minds between the fact that totems may be mundane utilities or disutilities, may have no workaday significance at all or may have high symbolic worth and, at one and the same time, are also signs signifying remote, marvellous events full of supernal importance for all men.

It would be at best incautious and probably inexact to describe them as "natural" signs. Some of them are certainly that in part to the Aborigines: universally, lightning is a sign of danger; fire, of security/danger. But the word "natural" is apt to mislead until the idea "nature" is stripped of all European associations and clad in the dress of Aboriginal ideas. The idea of a sign is thoroughly Aboriginal. Anthropological testimony on the point is overwhelming. The verbal concept may be lacking (though roundabout phrases with that meaning are common). But most of the choir and furniture of heaven and earth are regarded by the Aborigines as a vast sign-system. Anyone who, understandingly, has moved in the Australian bush with Aboriginal associates becomes aware of the fact. He moves, not in a landscape, but in a humanized realm saturated with significations. Here "something happened"; there "something portends." Aborigines, seeing the signs, defer to the significations; and, watching others do so, seem to understand why. Insofar as they have any idea of "nature"—the essential form, content and quality of things—their nearest equivalent appears to be what ensued from the ordering marvels of the Dream Time. All things *now* significant for men, *then* took on their values, positive, negative, or neutral. All *exponents* became the *constants* they now are. Until then, all had been somewhat *indeterminate;* after then, all became *determinate*. Those categories of understanding are contemporary, as they must be: the underlying eschatological conception is thoroughly Aboriginal.

The import of totems will be misunderstood if the basic sign-character is not appreciated. A proper grasp of what may be called the totemic sign-function will help to remove much of the intellectualistic falsity that has come to be associated with Totemism. In that function there are three elements: (i) living men, (ii) signs (the totems and totem-places), and (iii) the significations or sign-objects (the marvels). The signifying of the marvels to living men is the function of the signs. In particular tribes history may have obliterated some of the significations. In such cases the Aborigines say frankly that they do not know what to make of certain totems. (The false shame taught by Europeans has the same effect: some Aborigines now deny the possession of sexual totems.) Yet other totems may have retained only a cryptic significance. More hover somewhere between the cryptic and the implicit. But the unknown or the dubious are a minority. The majority are still vested with high certainty. "Yes," the Aborigines say, "we know that Dreaming; we cannot let it go." It is that class which led Elkin to describe Australia as an "ideal laboratory" for the study of totemic symbolism.

The indicative, declarative—that is, the presentational—aspect of totems as signs is overlaid by abstract and discursive symbolism. A failure to grasp how abstract and discursive the symbolism is has had much to do with the confusions reigning since McLennan's day. There is no quick way of sorting out the confusions, and it would be too time-consuming to follow them through, stage by stage. But it is possible to give a clearer view of essentials.

Tylor was doubly wrong in thinking a totem a "species-deity." The Aborigines do not divinize any entity. They lack any clear idea of the nature of a species, though they have a magnificent eye for the visible facts of speciation and variegation. But a totem is not a species or variety or class as such. Nor is it any particular member of them.

Aboriginal thought is possibly best expressed by saying that all and any members of a species, variety, or class are "the" totem without respect to space or time. Not *this* eaglehawk or *that* crow, but all and any eaglehawks or crows that were, are, or might be. One can but acknowledge the difficulties in that statement. A European, thinking with European concepts and using European words, must do what he can to phrase and grasp the Aboriginal conception. Is "totem" then a true universal? That seems to force an alien intellectualism on Aboriginal mentality. The matter may be put another way. Except for the class of personal ("individual") totems, when a particular totem is cited it is as though it were the cardinal number of all the family of sets associated with that number. In this aspect a totem is *an abstract symbol for the possible membership, over all space and time, of the sets of people symbolized by it—the dead, the living, the unborn.* The whole family of sets is "listed" or "mapped" under the abstract symbol and brought into a many-to-one correspondence with it. Any particular instance of a totem at a place or point of time is, in the symbolic sense, an image of the whole indefinite family of sets. A thoughtful Aboriginal once said to me: "There are Honey People all over the world." Totems, then, may be associated only with primitive peoples but there is no primitivity in Aboriginal totemic thought and imagery. Properly regarded, it is a feat implying considerable intellect. The power of symbolism is what truly marks off the Aborigines from "the beasts that perish," with whom the Reverend Mr. Lang identified them.

To say that Aborigines "have" or "possess" totems is wrong. They themselves do not speak—and probably do not think—of the relation in that way. European language makes problems here also. The nearest one can come to Aboriginal thought is to say that a totem is *of* a person, a sort of property of his spiritual, physical and social constitution. Even that is not clear enough. Body, spirit, name, shadow, track, *and* totem and its sacred place are all within the one system. . . .

As far as present knowledge goes, no productive or solicitous act by a person can obtain for him a totem. The Aborigines may speak of being "given" a totem by father, mother's brother, or some other relative, but they do not mean this literally. What really happens is that the totem is ascribed to them in consequence of one or both of two conditions—a sort of revelation or divination, and a sort of genetic-historic imperative. The revelation is usually some kind of dramatic incident at or about the time of conception, quickening, or birth; or a dream or act of augury; or a like transcendental event irrupting on and into the earthy dimension. Whatever it may be, it is taken as a declarative and efficacious sign—in certain cases made *as an act of will* by a pre-existing spiritual agent which assumes the totemic form for the occasion—that the totem should be what is thus revealed. That is the way, for example, in which the so-called "individual" or "personal" totems are often made known and then ascribed. The class is difficult to separate in some cases from what have been called "conceptional" totems, but the distinction is one on which it would be imprudent to enlarge here. A person's other totems are made known by public inference —a socially and religiously imperative inference—from the totems of relatives, such as the father, mother, mother's brother, or mother's father. (The regional variations are too complex to risk summarizing.) In a sense, a totem is inherited, but not in the true sense of inheritance. Totemic

*dis*inheritance is not really possible. (When totems are ascribed patrilineally, the children of men who marry wrongly have been said to "lose" the paternal totems, but the evidence is difficult to interpret with certainty.) There are rules, both religious and secular, governing acquisition, so that a person's totem could be said to be a matter of right, but public ascription and agreement (disputes do arise) both seem necessary conditions. Those conditions may be settled before a person's birth (and thus be, really, predictions about facts yet to eventuate) or after birth, as late even as initiation (and thus be judgments after historical facts which have now been given certainty). But once there has been such a settlement the idea of losing, or abandoning, the ascribed totem seems to appear to the Aborigines inconceivable—like denying self-identity, or shedding an intrinsic property of the social person. [My own experience includes one instance only of a man's abandoning ("killing") his totem: he had declared publicly his intention never to go back to his clan-country.] To sum up: the connection between totem and person is irreversible and perpetual, with a fourfold-character: historical, mystical, substantial, and essential. So "totem" is an abstract and discursive symbol for all that too.

Totems are often associated with places marked by striking or unusual physical features. A hill, a rocky outcrop, a deep pool, or something of the kind, is accepted too as a sign left by the mythical participants in a marvel supposed to have occurred there. Such places are to be approached and treated with a formality ranging from respect to reverence. In certain cases they may be made the scenes of "rites of increase." These are rites to maintain and renew, or conserve and produce the totem. The sites have credit as being its "home" or "beginning place." (Regional doctrines vary so greatly that each of those statements needs qualification for groups of tribes, even for particular tribes. Much mischief has resulted from the supposition that all Aborigines in all important respects resemble the Aranda, Kamilaroi, Kurnai, and Murngin.) Every anthropological study has recorded totems without place-ties (but, within the limits already mentioned, scarcely any without a place in mythical space-time). Even when sites are known, not all are named, or thought important, or treated with formality, or made the scenes of rites. Such variations, coupled with the type varieties and regional varieties, make most clear a truth that must be stated often and firmly: not even in Australia is there a something to be called Totemism in the sense of an invariant complex of beliefs, customs, and groups. If not there, then probably not anywhere. Aboriginal Australia appears to be made up of regions in which beliefs about, acts toward, or associations with this or that feature of a totemic collocation are intensified to the point of cult. The locality aspect is one such feature, but not the only one. The fourfold relation between totem and person seems most elaborated in connection with ritualized cults of commemoration, celebration, conservation, and production at known and hallowed places.

Scholars familiar with the Aborigines have usually had one impressive experience in common: to be taken by Aboriginal friends to places in the wilds and there shown something—tree, rocky outcrop, cranny, pool—with formality, pride and love. Conversations follow rather like this: "There is my Dreaming [place]. My father showed me this place when I was a little boy. His father showed him." Perhaps a child stands near by, all eyes and ears. Here is tradition being made continuous, as in the past, by overlapping life-spans. What had his father said? "He said: 'Your Dreaming is there; you want to look after this place; you don't want to let it go [forget, be careless about it]; it is from the first [totemist] man.'" The historical link is thus made: from the now-old to the still-young; from the living to the anciently dead; from very first true man to next true man; from the oldest time to the here-and-now. (Down with a crash come the needless postulates of a racial and a collective unconscious.) What did the father do there? "He used to come here every year with the old men, the wise men; they used to do something here [hit, rub, break off pieces, brush with green leaves, sing]; that way they made the [totem] come on, come back, jump up, spread out." *How* did that happen? *What* is it that is in the place? "We do not know. *Something* is there. Like my spirit [soul, shadow, invisible counterpart]; like my brother [father, father's father, mate, friend, helper]; like my Dreaming [naming the totem entity]." Will he think more? What else did his father say? That there was something in the Dreaming-place? The dark eyes turn and look intent, puzzled, searching. "My father did not say. He said this: "My boy, look! Your Dreaming is there; it is a big thing; you never let it go [pass it by]; all Dreamings [totem entities] come from there; your spirit is there." Does the white man now understand? The blackfellow, earnest, friendly, makes a last effort. "Old man, you listen! Something is there; we do not know what; *something*." There is a struggle to find words, and perhaps a lapse into English. "Like engine, like power, plenty of power; it does hard-work; it *pushes*." (Perhaps now the anthropologist begins to understand; to fit his own abstract, discursive symbol-structures to that understanding.) The historical link—a sequence of named men—has been asserted. The mystical link—of belief, trust and faith in mysterious, powerful unknowns—has been proclaimed. The continuous substantial link—"my brother," "my father," "my mate"—has been avowed in one of the many forms in which voice is given to the idea of a corporeal connection between man, totem, and spirit-home. There has been a statement of the most familiar claim of all, that of the essential link: "My spirit is there"; "I myself am there"; "I came from there."

.   .   .   .

Except that it contains an additional element, the symbol-function is identical with the sign-function. It thus has four elements: (i) living men (totemists) serving as the interpreters of (ii) signs (totems and totem-places), by using (iii) vehicles that form and express affective conceptions of (iv) sign-objects, which are the significations of the Dream Time marvels. By studying the additional element, (iii), one may hope to interpret the imagery of Aboriginal religious thought and practice. An understanding of the vehicles and the correlated conceptions and aspirations is the only means of going beyond the symbol to the symbolized.

The raw materials of study are of large range. They include: (a) conventionalized movements that mark out in space geometric designs (lines, curves, circles, spirals, zigzags); (b) postures, stances, gestures, and facial expressions; (c) silences, laughter, wailing, expletives, cries, invocations, instructions, and commands; (d) chants and songs; (e) stories, tales and myths; (f) mimes and dances; (g) many uses and products of the plastic and graphic arts to make abstract and representational designs; and (h) a host of stylized acts—the whole repertory of theatrical forms, the making and use of fire, the drawing and pouring of human blood, spraying with water and spittle, the use of semen and other exuviae, covering and revealing objects, laying on of hands, etc., etc.—all to be seen performed within ritualized processes or described in the associated myths. All may be classed as vehicles, or symbolizing means, or symbolisms. They form the content and provide the formulary of liturgical rites (by liturgical I mean reverent work in duty to sacred things).

The vehicles or symbolisms are not themselves the symbols. For reasons of convenience one may often wish to refer to any of the elements in (a) to (h) as being "a symbol," but the usage is inaccurate and may be confusing. It seems better to mean by symbol the patterns, structures, and designs that connect arrangements or systems of vehicles or their elements. For example, in certain initiatory rites a blood-smeared bullroarer is thrust between the loins of young men. Blood, bullroarer, and loins are all symbolic of something else, but the significations may vary with context. In this case, evidently it is the pattern or structure or arrangement of the whole act that is "the symbol." But what is symbolized by it is not revealed directly, or necessarily, in the immediacy of the act itself. While it would bring a great illumination to analyse Aboriginal ritual practice in terms of all the vehicles or symbolisms listed in (a) to (h), one must remember that to do so still leaves one in a half-way house. One studies symbolisms for the sake of the symbols, and the symbols for the sake of the symbolized. The things to which the symbols point are metaphysical objects, in patterns, structures and designs that, in religious study, are the true subjects of enquiry. In Aboriginal religions they form a highly involuted complex which Anthropology is only beginning to break down. Whether such objects are "real" is a question for philosophy, not for Anthropology. It is sufficient that the Aborigines use symbols to conceptualize and express them, or features or aspects of them, in perceivable or inferrable ways. The symbols, by pointing to, stand for; by standing for, they represent; by representing, they objectify; by objectifying, they betoken ultimate or metaphysical things, which they thus mediate to living men by means of images. The vehicles conveying the images attract to themselves the sentiments, thoughts, and acts properly due to what they ultimately designate. The vehicles are not themselves "the religion," though they have sometimes been confounded with it because of a failure to distinguish symbols from what is symbolized. They are but the husk around a kernel; means of symbolizing something else; tools or instruments that help to form and, through associated acts, express demands of action consonant with the things, values, and aspirations which are symbolized. The symbol-function may thus be stated as the betokening or mediation to living men of all the signs, metaphysical realities, and demands of action of the Dream Time by means of conceptual-expressive devices of symbolism.

.   .   .   .

One of the two greatest difficulties of study arises from the fact that in any region a number of separable systems of symbolism—no doubt one or more for each class of vehicles—present themselves to observation *together*. One meets each instance in a certain *historical* state. The separable systems are *already* formed into a *system of systems*. That is, there are *n* systems *integrated* into a complex compound rite or myth developed over an unknown, perhaps a very long, period of time. One also encounters at a given place what, in a region some distance away, may have been yesterday's cult and, in another region, tomorrow's mixing with a still older cult. (The Kunapipi cult of North Australia seems to be an example.) In those circumstances the approaches I have suggested—a discrimination between the sign and the symbol-functions, an ever-present awareness that one is studying the symbol for the sake of the symbolized, and a lively sense of the historical development that may lie behind the cults—could yield rewarding results. The other main difficulty is to know to construct the metaphysic of life that invests, though in a cryptic fashion, these elaborate arrangements. But the study of rites, myths, and all the "languages of the mind," is really auxiliary to that end *if one's purpose is to understand the religion*. Obviously, one has to go beyond the spoken images of myth, the acted images of rite, and the graven or painted images of art. The data of symbolism are a means of working back to the theorems of life implicit in the liturgical and mythical charters. All the symbolism defers to the ontology there started. At the core is a concern with *man's* being. So far Anthropology has failed in that task. It is a profoundly puzzling matter to establish the vision of life and the demands of action that so strange a metaphysic imposes on the living Aborigines. In a few cases an ancestral spirit is credited with having laid down something tantamount to commands, but mostly one hears nothing of explicit moral imperatives. The Aborigines say only that they "follow up the Dreaming."

To some extent they seem to do so. But to state the quality and law of the fact is a baffling problem. To "follow up the Dreaming" (a metaphor of following a track) appears not quite a duty, whether light or burdensome; not quite a voluntary act yet not involuntary; not quite a deliberate preference over possible alternatives...perhaps that brings the truth nearer: the Aborigines appear to have visualized *no* alternative as really possible. The Dream Time was a ground of consummation. The doctrine of the Dreaming is a sort of eschatology, a doctrine of final things which were also first things.

analysis of
purum kinship ties

five

RODNEY NEEDHAM

The Purum are an "Old Kuki" tribe of Manipur, on the eastern border of India. They are of Mongoloid physical stock, and speak a Tibeto-Burman language. In 1932, i.e., in the period from which our information mostly comes, they numbered 303 individuals. They are divided among four villages: there are no non-Purum in these villages, and there are no Purum in other villages. Marriage is permissible with the Chawte, another Old Kuki tribe with whom the Purum claim a common historical origin, but no cases are reported.

The villages are politically autonomous, each governed by its own council. There is no indigenous centralized government or judiciary. The villages are linked, however, in the first place, by the fact that every clan except one (and this also in the past) is represented in every village. We cannot assert on the evidence available that the villages are related to each other as villages on this basis; but local descent groups in different villages are related by common clanship, and

since the component groups are so related it may well be that the villages are politically related also within the descent system.

There are five named, exogamous patrilineal clans, which are further distinguished by personal names traditionally proper to each clan, and by possessing separate sections within each village burial ground. Four of the clans are subdivided into named lineages. The names of these descent groups, and their distribution throughout the three villages for which such information is available, are shown in Table 1. Mnemonic letters are appended to the names of the clans and villages, and the lineages are numbered; so that in the following analysis M_3, for example, will stand for Rim-ke-lek lineage of Marrim clan. One lineage of Thao clan (viz., Teyu) died out in 1924, but is retained in the table because it has a place in the argument.

The descent groups are systematically related by ties of prescriptive alliance. The prescribed marriage is with the "mother's brother's daughter," while marriage with the "father's sister's daughter" is strictly forbidden. The rule, however, does not enjoin marriage with the individual matrilateral first cousin, but also covers marriage with a woman from the clan of the mother's brother, i.e., with

"

TABLE 1   **Purum Descent Groups**

Clan	Lineage	Village		
		Khulen (Kh)	Tampak (Ta)	Chumbang (Chu)
Kheyang (K)	1. Julhung	+	+	+
	2. Aihung		+	+
Makan (Mk)	1. Kankung	+	+	+
	2. Makan-te	+		
Marrim (M)	1. Rimphunchong	+		
	2. Rimkung	+		
	3. Rim-ke-lek		+	
	4. Pilling		+	+
Parpa (P)		+	+	+
Thao (T)			+	
	1. Thao-kung			
	2. Thao-run	+		
	3. Teyu			
	4. Rangshai	+		

a woman who does not stand in any particular degree of genealogical relationship. The actual marriage is contracted by a three-year period of bride-service, after which residence is patrilocal.

.   .   .   .

The relationships of affinity are not merely ties between individuals or families. Descent groups, whether localized or dispersed, are also related as groups by ties of prescriptive alliance. A descent group may take wives by traditional claim from certain groups but not from others; women are transferred obligatorily in one "direction," and there can be no direct exchange. The total society is divided by the Purum themselves into: (1) lineally related descent groups, (2) wife-giving groups, (3) wife-taking groups; and the fundamental cycle of alliance is exhibited by the specific statement that a wife-taking group may be identical with a wife-giving group of one's own wife-givers.

Members of these three major categories, each of which may comprise one or more descent groups in relation to any particular descent group, are terminologically related in the same way as individuals are related in particular affinal relationships. All the men of a wife-giving group are *pu,* a term of which one of the genealogical specifications is "mother's brother"; and all the men of Ego's generation and below in a wife-taking group are *tu,* one of the specifications of which is "sister's son." Within Ego's own generation all the women of any wife-giving group are *nau(nu),* one of the genealogical specifications of which is "mother's brother's daughter"; and all those of a wife-taking group are *tu(nu),* one of the specifications of which is "father's sister's daughter."

Purum society thus exhibits the structural categories and relations of a social system based on prescribed marriage with the "mother's brother's daughter." We may now examine the individual marriages which actually take place and which maintain this system. The information is perfectly clear on the vital point that marriage is not necessarily or even usually with the matrilateral first cousin, but with a classificatory matrilateral cross-cousin. Analysis of the 54 marriages recorded from three villages (Khulen,

Tampak, and Changninglong) shows that no fewer than 26 (48.1 per cent) are with women of clans other than that of the mother (Table 2). This means that at least this proportion of marriages in this record could not possibly have been with the daughter of the maternal uncle. Furthermore, the proportion is cetainly higher, for it is not possible to distinguish in the evidence marriages with the first cousin from marriages with a classificatory relative of the same category in the mother's clan.

. . .

Let us proceed to an examination of the relations between groups established and maintained by such marriages. In Table 3 is presented a scheme of alliances between all the component descent groups of Purum society. The groups of reference constitute the center column; the arrows show the direction of transfer of women. Wife-givers are on the left, wife-takers on the right; so that, e.g., K_1 takes wives from Mk_2, from M_2, etc., and gives wives to Mk_1, to M_1, and to M_3. . . . For any man in K_1, every woman in his own genealogical level in every one of the wife-giving groups, viz., Mk_2, M_2, M_4, P, T_1, T_2, T_3, and T_4 is a "mother's brother's daughter." Furthermore, each of these alliance groups may comprise a number of local alliance groups: e.g., the local representatives of Parpa clan in the three villages of Khulen, Tampak, and Changninglong.

If a man is going to visit "the mother's brother" often, as Homans and Schneider say he does, he is going to do an awful lot of walking.[1] But

[1] George C. Homans and David M. Schneider, *Marriage, Authority, and Final Causes* (New York: The Free Press, 1955.)

TABLE 2   **Marriages Outside the Mother's Clan**

		Clan of Wife					Outside
	K	Mk	M	P	T	Total	Mother's Clan
Clan of Mother							
K	3				2	5	2
Mk		3		1		4	1
M	6		6	2		14	8
P		5	2	5	3	15	10
T		1	2	2	11	16	5
Totals						54	26

TABLE 3   **Scheme of Alliances**

$$Mk_2, M_2, M_4, P, T_1, T_2, T_3, T_4 \rightarrow \quad K_1 \rightarrow Mk_1, M_1, M_3$$
$$Mk_1, Mk_2, M_2, P, T_1, T_4 \rightarrow \quad K_2 \rightarrow M_1, M_3, M_4$$
$$K_1, M_2, P \rightarrow Mk_1 \rightarrow K_2, M_1, M_3, M_4, T_1, T_2, T_3, T_4$$
$$K_1, M_1, M_2, M_3, M_4, P \rightarrow Mk_2 \rightarrow K_2, T_1, T_2 \, T_3 \, T_4$$
$$K_1, K_2, Mk_1 \rightarrow \quad M_1 \rightarrow Mk_2, P$$
$$T_1, T_2, T_3 \rightarrow \quad M_2 \rightarrow K_1, K_2, Mk_1, Mk_2, P$$
$$K_1, K_2, Mk_1, T_1, T_2, T_3, T_4 \rightarrow \quad M_3 \rightarrow Mk_2, P$$
$$K_2, Mk_1, T_1, T_2, T_3 \rightarrow \quad M_4 \rightarrow K_1, Mk_2, P$$
$$M_1, M_2, M_3, M_4 \rightarrow \quad P \rightarrow K_1, K_2, Mk_1, Mk_2, T_1, T_2$$
$$Mk_1, Mk_2, P \rightarrow \quad T_1 \rightarrow K_1, K_2, M_2, M_3, M_4$$
$$Mk_1, Mk_2, P \rightarrow \quad T_2 \rightarrow K_1, M_2, M_3, M_4,$$
$$Mk_1, Mk_2 \rightarrow \quad T_3 \rightarrow K_1, M_2, M_3, M_4$$
$$Mk_1, Mk_2 \rightarrow \quad T_4 \rightarrow K_1, K_2, M_3$$

why ever should he? Because, Homans and Schneider tell us, he is "fond" of the mother's brother. To be fond of roughly a third of all the men of his father's generation in the total society seems a promiscuous lavishing of sentiment, but suppose he is? Well, then, we are told, "he will tend to get fond of the daughter." But this, similarly, means being fond of something like one-third of all the women in his own generation, a very expansive affection. Anyway, he is held to have a "sentimental claim" to all these young women, marriage with any one of this large class will be "sentimentally appropriate"—and this implausible tale is the real explanation of the rule of marriage.

The facts so far examined are damaging enough to Homans and Schneider's argument, but we have hardly begun to see the complexity of the social and symbolic systems associated with the rule of marriage. . . . A defining feature of a system with a matrilateral prescription is the "cycle" of women linking the descent groups into a system, the *"échange généralisé"* of Lévi-Strauss. In the model this is a single cycle; but, as we should expect, the factual situation which this so simply represents is very much more complex. From Table 3 we can determine what degree of correspondence there is between the features of the model and those of social reality. There are a large number of cycles to be discerned in it, of which Table 4 gives twenty examples. There are many others to be extracted from the scheme of alliances, but these are ample to show the large number and the complexity of the affinal ties linking a small number of intermarrying descent groups. Complex though this representation is, it is nevertheless an abstraction from a still more complex reality in terms of local groups. The relation K_1–Mk_1 is a simple relationship between two distinct, named descent groups; but it has to be remembered —if we are to appreciate more exactly what happens in terms of people on the ground—that K_1 comprises three local descent groups, one in each of the villages in Table 1, and that Mk_1 also comprises three territorially separate groups. An analysis of alliance cycles as they in fact link such local groups—which is what a political

TABLE 4   **Examples of Alliance Cycles**

1. K_1—M_1—Mk_2—K_2—M_3—P—(K_1)
2. K_1—M_1—Mk_2—K_2—M_4—(K_1)
3. K_1—M_1—Mk_2—K_2—M_4—P—(K_1)
4. K_1—M_1—Mk_2—T_1—(K_1)
5. K_1—M_3—Mk_2—K_2—M_1—P—(K_1)
6. K_1—M_3—Mk_2—K_2—M_4—(K_1)
7. K_1—M_3—Mk_2—T_1—(K_1)
8. K_1—Mk_1—M_1—Mk_2—K_2—M_3—P—(K_1)
9. K_1—Mk_1—M_1—P—(K_1)
10. K_1—Mk_1—M_1—Mk_2—K_2—M_3—P—(K_1)
11. K_1—Mk_1—M_1—Mk_2—T_1—(K_1)
12. K_1—MK_1—M_3—P—(K_1)
13. K_1—Mk_1—M_4—(K_1)
14. K_1—Mk_2—T_1—(K_1)
15. K_2—M_1—Mk_2—(K_2)
16. K_2—M_1—P—(K_2)
17. M_1—P—Mk_1—(M_1)
18. M_2—Mk_1—T_1—(M_2)
19. M_2—Mk_2—T_1—(M_2)
20. M_3—P—Mk_1—(M_3)

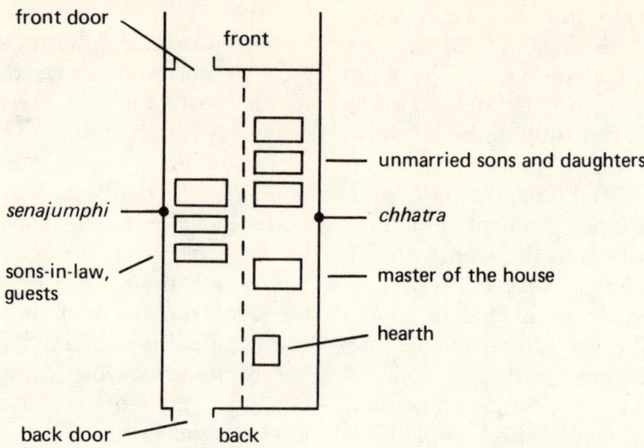

Figure 1. Plan of Purum House

study of Purum society would ultimately involve—would therefore be far more complex than the situation as I have analyzed it here. . . .

The reference to a political study brings us finally to the relationships established between villages by the alliances between their component local descent groups. These can be seen from Table 5. Out of the fifty-four marriages recorded, eleven (20.3 per cent) have taken place between villages. That is, the autonomous political units of Purum society are also related by the alliances between descent groups which are fundamental to social life.

In sum, so far as the social order is concerned, the same tripartite categorization orders relations between individuals, between descent groups, and between the component local descent groups of the village, and creates ties between the politically independent villages.

• • •

Whatever its analytical and empirical complications, a society based on matrilateral alliance is fundamentally a very simple and clearly defined system. It is therefore the more feasible to determine, through a consideration of its symbolic usages, whether or not there are more abstract structural principles underlying both social relations of the sorts we have examined above and other aspects of its culture

TABLE 5 Intervillage Marriages

		Married into			Total Marriages	Women Married out of Village
	→	Kh	Ta	Cha		
Women from						
Kh		30	3	1	34	4
Ta		6	10		16	6
Cha		1		3	4	1
Totals					54	11

which are not obviously connected with them. What we seek is in fact (so far as the literature allows) the "total structure" of Purum society. The ethnography on this particular instance of the system is not the most revealing in this respect, but it is possible to glimpse, chiefly in the symbolism of ritual, certain structural features which are radical to Purum society.

A convenient and characteristic point at which to start is the house and its divisions (Fig. 1). This is divided lengthwise into two named parts: *phumlil* on the right (looking from a position inside at the back) and *ningan* on the left. The "master of the house" has his bed in the *phumlil* half, near a special post called *chhatra,* and his unmarried sons and daughters sleep near him on the same side. Future sons-in-law (men who live in the house while fulfilling their bride-service) and other young men who pass the nights there as guests (courting the unmarried daughters) sleep in the *ningan* half, near a post called *senajumphi.* At night the *phumlil* is taboo to those outsiders who sleep in the *ningan,* and even married daughters of the house sleep in the *ningan* when they visit their parents' home. The two posts *chhatra* and *senajumphi,* associated respectively with *phumlil* and *ningan,* are of ritual importance. When the house is built they are erected in a fixed order: first *chhatra,* then *senajumphi;* and the stringers which rest on them are also put up in the same order. This order, this ascription of primacy, seems to accord with a difference in status which evidently exists between the two sides of the house, for without doubt the master of the house is of superior status to the sons-in-law who labor for him and to casual young guests. *Phumlil,* we may infer, is superior to *ningan,* and *chhatra* is superior to *senajumphi.* The front

door is in what I have designated the "left" (*ningan*) side of the house, and so is the back door. These facts may also be regarded as consistent with the inferred inferior character of this side of the house. The hearth, on the other hand, is in *phumlil:* we know what importance this usually possesses, and we shall see that it is ritually important among the Purum. We may see in this sum of conventional dispositions a division of the house into private and public, family and outsiders, kin and affines, all subsumed under the general characters of superior (*phumlil*) and inferior (*ningan*). Related to this scheme is the probability that the back is superior to the front of the house. In the same way as the stringers are placed right (*phumlil*) first, left (*ningan*) second, so the cross-beam at the back is traditionally set in place first and then the crossbeam at the front. This in turn is consistent with the facts that the house-owner's bed, the hearth, and the altar of the house-god are all in the back part of the house. These circumstances also confirm the ascription of the designations "right" and "left."

Another context in which the opposition of right and left is seen is the sacrifice of a fowl to the god of the house or the clan. The position of the legs of the bird at the time of death augurs the future of the sacrificers: if the right leg is on top of the left, it augurs well; but if the left is on top of the right it augurs ill. Here, then, right is auspicious, left inauspicious: i.e., right is superior to left. I think it is significant, too, that a sacrificial animal (pig or buffalo) is speared in the right side. This differentiation of value is confirmed by another situation, which clinches the argument with a further correlation. At the name-giving ceremony for a child of either sex, augury is sought in the same way in order to ascertain the child's future. In the case of a boy, a cock is strangled by the priest; and here also if the right is on top of the left leg it is regarded as a good omen, while the reverse forebodes evil. This we readily understand, but now the ritual opposition of right and left is reversed, in a feminine context. In the case of a girl, the ceremony is performed with a hen; and it is if the left leg is on top of the right that the augury is good, while the right on the left forebodes ill. We need not be surprised at this contextual reversal of the symbolism of the legs, nor does it controvert the inference about the general significance of right and left. As we shall see later, it introduces a scheme of oppositions wider than the opposition of the sides, and with which this particular instance of differential interpretation is entirely consistent. The interesting matter at this point is that male is associated with right and female with left.

This brings us back to the divisions of the house. Now *phumlil* is the "masculine" side, associated with the master of the house and with the resident males who are stationary while the women circulate. *Ningan* is certainly the "feminine" side, for the word also denotes all the women of the house, without distinction of generation, after they have been married out of the family and their clan. That is, it denotes women who have been transferred to wife-taking groups. Significantly, as we have seen, daughters who have married out sleep in the *ningan* half when they visit their parents, not in the *phumlil;* so that their status in the alliance system is marked even by the place where they have now to sleep in the house where they were born. This confirms, too, the association of kin with the *phumlil* side, affines with the *ningan* side of the house.

We may now introduce the term *maksa,* which most prominently denotes the husbands of the father's sister, the sister, and the daughter. There is of course the distinct term *rang* for father's sister's husband, while males of the succeeding generations are in any case denoted by the one term *tu;* but the term *maksa* is evidently not redundant. It denotes, not simply members of wife-taking categories, but individual men with whom alliances (by the cession of women to them) have actually been contracted.

The *maksa* are of supreme social and ritual importance to their wife-givers. At a certain prestige-feast it is the *maksa* of the celebrant who ceremonially kills the ox on his behalf, spearing it (significantly) in the right side. At the agricultural festival of Shanghong, each of the village officials performs a rite in connection with the rice and provides rice beer for the villagers; and it is the *maksa* who prepares the beer. At the installation feast of a village official, it is his *maksa* who distributes the rice beer. It is the *maksa* who is in charge of building a new house, not the house-owner; who prepares the rice beer for the feast of formal entry; who ceremonially kindles the first fire in it (cf. the observation above on the symbolic importance of the hearth); and who kills the animals for the feast.

An important ceremony in a child's life—that, in fact, at which his social life begins—is the first hair-cutting, by which he is ritually separated from the ancestral spirits and brought into membership of the lineage group. Rice beer and curried pork are offered to the ancestors, and it is the *maksa* and the *ningan* (their wives) who prepare the offerings. A pig is killed by the *maksa* and is then placed on the veranda with its head pointing east. Not only is the beer made by the *ningan,* but they must fetch the water for it themselves. This means that a *ningan* cannot be helped by women of her natal clan, for whose members the beer is made and to whose ancestors it is offered. The stipulation marks ritually the wife's complete severance from her natal group—she is so assimilated into her husband's group that when she dies she is buried in the cemetery of his clan—and maintains the symbolic separation of the alliance groups. At the feast the *maksa* and *ningan* sit apart from the elders and adult men of the child's descent group, with the young men, women, and children.

At the end of the period of bride-service it is the *maksa* who go to the house of the groom's father, kill a pig provided by him, and prepare a special sort of curry. This they take to the bride's house, with *ningan* bearing containers of rice beer. This party which goes out to bring back the married couple, to transfer the woman physically and finally from her natal group into that with which her marriage creates an alliance, consists of only *maksa* and *ningan* of the husband's group. No member of the clan of the groom's father can go, or can share the presents of meat and beer made at the feast in the house of the bride's father. These items are taboo to the bride and groom themselves, and to all female members who belong by birth to the bride's clan. The *maksa* and *ningan* bring the wife to the house of her husband's father.

At a burial the *maksa* are equally important. They wash the body of their "wife's father," and dress it; one of them spears a pig, and they prepare rice beer. The *ningan* may also bring rice beer with them: this is drunk by the village officials and other guests, but rice beer and other comestibles belonging to the house of the deceased cannot be touched. The *maksa* dig the grave, and four of them carry the corpse to the clan burial ground and bury it. Everything at the funeral is in the hands of the

maksa: lineal relatives of the deceased take no part.

It is thus evident that in practically every event and institution of both individual and social importance the *maksa*—the actual wife-takers—are not only ritually important but are indispensable. A Purum cannot be socially born, or be married, he cannot make a new house, or assume an office, or approach the gods, he cannot even die, without the aid of his wife-takers.

Let us now look at material prestations and at the extent of their significance. Rice beer and pig-meat are movable economic valuables which are highly prized by the Purum and appear in a variety of contexts. The common character of these contexts, the apparent significance of the transfer of these articles, leads to the inference that we have here symbolic usages which are characteristic of this type of society.

Beer is typically given as an offering to gods and ancestral spirits: viz., at the invocation of a certain deity on entering a new house, the assumption of office by a village official, the ceremony devoted to the deity of the gates, and the invocation of the ancestral spirits at the hair-cutting ceremony. Pigs are sacrificed to gods and ancestral spirits: viz., to secure release from diseases which particular deities are believed to cause, at the election of the village headman, at the worship of the deity of the gates, at the harvest "thank-offering," to the ancestral spirits at the hair-cutting ceremony, and at the invocation of the forest deity. Whatever else may be symbolized, it is clear that in these cases beer and pigs are prestations from inferiors to superiors.

With the general character of these items established, we may look at the social relationships in which they also figure. Pigs and rice beer are always given by village officials when they are elected to office; fixed numbers and quantities are given for a village feast by the elected person according to the grade of the position. When a man is honored with a certain feast, he gives three pigs and twenty pots of beer. The set numbers and quantities indicate some symbolic element, but there is no certain evidence in the literature of what the significance may be. But other situations are quite clear. When a man enters his novitiate to become a "medicine-man" he presents his prospective teacher with beer and asks formally for instruction; and when he becomes a master he makes a formal presentation to his teacher of a number of prescribed articles, first among which is rice beer. He shows "respect" to his teacher, and on the latter's death he presents rice beer to his household. Here there is certainly the expression of deference, a prestation from an inferior to a superior.

Fines are the only forms of punishment for delicts and are always levied in beer and pigs. There are other forms of valuables, including cash, with which compensation could be made and economic deprivation inflicted, but beer and pigs are the only permitted forms. In economic terms, the rice with which the beer is made would be an almost equally punitive fine, but it is the beer that has to be given. It is not completely explanatory that pigs and rice are prominent economic valuables in an agricultural society of this sort: the invariant form of the fine and the ban on economic equivalents point to a symbolic significance, which is evidently that of expressing submission, the recognition of inferior status, by a symbolic prestation to a superior.

This leads us to what is structurally the most important context, the relationship between affines. A man wishing to marry his son to a certain girl takes a present of rice beer to the girl's father, begging him not to be "angry," and if the latter agrees to the proposal he drinks it. Here there is a double significance: that of the character of the present; and the fact that it is the wife-taker who pays the visit, humbly acknowledges his inferiority, and makes the proposal which the other may refuse. We know already that at the wedding rice beer is taken from the groom's father and given to the wife's father, together with a pig-meat curry.

Wife-takers, then, give rice beer and pig-meat to their wife-givers, just as do mortals to the gods. There is no indication anywhere in the literature that the reverse might be possible. We have already seen that wife-takers are inferior to wife-givers, and in this transfer of symbolic goods we see this status difference expressed.

We have also seen that, structurally speaking, there is a cycle of women, these supreme "movable valuables" being communicated in one "direction." Opposed to this cycle there is now a cycle of rice beer and pigs going in the opposite direction. That is, there is a division of economic goods (or those which are accorded symbolic significance) into "masculine" and "feminine" goods in contrary cycles. In matrilateral alliance the masculine goods circulate in the opposite direction to that of the women, and feminine goods in the same direction as the women. If we take the rice beer and meat to be masculine goods, what are the Purum equivalents of feminine goods other than the women themselves? There is unfortunately little evidence about gift exchange, but the important fact is clearly stated that when a woman is sent to her husband's house she takes with her one or more of the following articles: cloth, a brass plate, a carrying-basket, a storage-basket for valuables, a chopper, a brass cup, and a loom. If we may assume that the chopper is a domestic utensil proper to a woman's use (the monograph tells us that women use choppers in clearing land, and that it is they who collect firewood), it is satisfyingly clear that all these articles can be regarded as feminine goods and appropriate to the feminine cycle of prestations. Most significantly, we must note the presence of two items —cloth and the loom—which in better-known Indonesian systems of matrilateral alliance are pre-eminently feminine goods.

This division into two classes of goods is not merely a rational extension of the sexual division of labor, for Purum women cultivate and harvest the rice, raise pigs, and manufacture both cloth and beer, i.e., goods which belong to both classes. The goods and their cycles are conventionally opposed in a symbolism which is far wider and more significant, ritually and socially, than the particularities of any one institution or field of activity.

We may now return to the interpretation of the role of the *maksa*. We have seen that there are highly important chains of unilateral transfers of women and goods, which we have called cycles. In one direction there is structurally a circulation of women and certain associated goods in a "feminine cycle," and in the opposite direction there is a circulation of certain other goods in a "masculine cycle." But the importance of the valuables in the masculine cycle must seem rather trivial when compared with the value of women. In fact, however, this cycle includes other values, so that there is more of a "balance" than at first appears. Purum bride-service lasts three years, and we may picture as part of the masculine cycle three-year "units" of masculine labor circulating as prestations in exactly the same way as the more tangible masculine goods. Not

only this, but there is a more vital type of prestation—the indispensable ritual services rendered by wife-takers to wife-givers. We may perhaps see, then, in these opposed cycles and classes a balance between two sorts of values each vital to the total society. If the wife-takers depend on their wife-givers for women and the continuance of their lines, so in a similar fashion wife-givers depend utterly on their wife-takers (*maksa*) for indispensable aid in all the major events of life.

Thus the system is not characterized by the one cycle of the initial model, consisting of a unidirectional circulation of women, important though this is, but by a reciprocal opposition of two cycles, masculine and feminine. There may seem a contradiction in the fact that the superior wife-givers transmit feminine goods, while the inferior wife-takers transmit masculine goods, but I am sure there is not. Wife-takers in other such societies are characterized by the type of goods they receive, and it is they who are associated with the feminine cycle, not the group from which feminine goods issue. Generalizing, we may say that a prestation must be appropriate to the character and status of the receiver, and that a group is associated with those goods which are given to it. Masculine goods are therefore proper to wife-givers, and feminine goods to wife-takers: wife-givers are associated in this way with the (superior) masculine cycle, and wife-takers with the (inferior) feminine cycle.

But this opposition is itself part of a dualistic system of symbolic classification in which pairs of opposite but complementary terms are analogically related as in the scheme in Table 6. To begin with, the oppositions are listed seriatim as they have been elicited in the exposition of the relevant facts; but I have added a num-

Left	Right
Ningan division	*Phumlil* division
Front	Back
Affines	Kin
Public	Private
Strangers	Family
Wife-takers (*tu, maksa*)	Wife-givers (*pu*)
Inferior	Superior
Female	Male
Below	Above
Inauspicious	Auspicious
Feminine goods	Masculine goods
women	pigs, buffaloes
cloth	rice beer
loom	ritual services
domestic articles	labor (bride-service)
Mortals	Gods, ancestral spirits
Sun	Moon
Earth	Sky
(North)	South
West	East
Bad death	Good death
Even	Odd
Death	Life
Profane	Sacred
Sexual activity	Sexual abstinence
Forest	Village
Famine	Prosperity
Evil spirits, ghosts	Beneficent spirits

ber of others which I have not demonstrated. Since I have shown the principles and the pervasive nature of the classification in the major institutions of Purum society, it does not seem necessary to continue the demonstration in this place down to the last particular.

We see here, as elsewhere with prescriptive alliance, a mode of classification by which things, individuals, groups, qualities, values, spatial notions, and other ideas of the most disparate kinds are identically ordered within one system of relations. In particular. I would draw attention to the remarkable concordance and interconnection of social and symbolic structure. In spite of the fact that structurally there must be three cyclically related lines in the alliance system, the basic scheme of Purum society is not triadic but dyadic. Any given alliance group is wife-taker and therefore inferior to another, but it is also wife-giver and therefore superior to another group in a different context. That is, alliance status is not absolute but relative. The distinction to be appreciated is that between the triadic *system* and its component dyadic *relation*. It is through this mode of relation that the social order concords with the symbolic order.

But in fact, though one may use these distinctive designations for convenience of description and analysis, what one is really dealing with in such a society as this is a classification, a system of categories, which orders both social life and the cosmos. That is, Purum social organization is ideologically part of a cosmological conceptual order and is governed identically by its ruling ideas.

affinal ties, subsistence, and prestige among the coast salish

six

WAYNE SUTTLES

The nature of Northwest Coast social stratification and the nature of the institution most initimately related to it, the potlatch, are problems of widely recognized importance. Yet attempts at solving these problems have not been wholly satisfactory. Generalizations about social stratification have been betrayed by failure to give sufficient weight to all of the difference in social structure that existed among the various Northwest Coast tribes. Explanations of the potlatch have been only partial ones, finding its function in the expression of the individual's drive for high status or in the fulfillment of society's need for solidarity. Relating these functions to man's other requirements for survival has often been inhibited by an assumption that the satisfaction of alimentary needs through the food quest and the satisfaction of psychological needs through the manipulation of wealth form two separate systems, the "subsistence economy" and the "prestige economy." Or if a relationship between the two is hy-

Reprinted from the *American Anthropologist* (1960): 296–305, by permission. [Some terminological translations omitted]

pothesized, the hypothesis usually makes the "prestige economy" dependent upon the "subsistence economy"; it is assumed that a rich habitat provides an abundance of food which in turn supports the prestige economy which in turn maintains social stratification. I believe, however, that it is more reasonable to assume that, for a population to have survived in a given environment for any length of time, its subsistence activities and prestige-gaining activities are likely to form a single integrated system by which that population has adapted to its environment. I will try to show how this may be true of one group of Northwest Coast tribes, the Coast Salish of Southern Georgia Strait and the Strait of Juan de Fuca, and in particular I will try to show that in the socio-economic system of these tribes a role of crucial importance was played by the ties established through inter-community marriage.

Native social organization in this area was characterized by a seeming looseness. Kinship was reckoned bilaterally. Residence was usually, but not always, patrilocal. The nuclear families of brothers, cousins, and brothers-in-law formed extended families, occupying great cedar-plank houses and claiming rights to certain

"

local resources and to certain inherited privileges. One or more such extended families formed a village or community. The community was linked through ties of marriage and kinship with other communities and these with still others to form a social network with no very clear boundaries. Groups of villages like the Lummi and Cowichan were linked by common dialect and traditions as "tribes" but in recent generations these village groupings were certainly not separate "societies."

Within most communities there seem to have been three distinct social classes—a majority identified as "high class," a somewhat smaller group identified as "low class," and a still smaller group of slaves. The slaves lived in the households of the upper class; the lower class often occupied separate houses in its own section of the community or in a location sufficiently separate so that it might be regarded as a lower class community subservient to an upper class group. In native theory the lower class consisted of people who "had lost their history," that is, people who had no claim to the most productive resources of the area and no claim to recognized inherited privileges, and who furthermore "had no advice," that is, they had no private knowledge and no moral training.

For the upper class the most proper and usual sort of marriage was one arranged between families of similar social standing in different communities. The arrangements usually included preliminary negotiations by members of the prospective groom's family, a vigil kept by the young man at the girl's house, and an exchange of property between the two families. This exchange was the wedding itself. It was held in the bride's house. The groom's family brought wealth for the bride's family; the bride's family gave wealth, perhaps nearly an equal amount, to the groom's family; and the bride's father also gave, if possible, an inherited privilege or privileges, such as a name or the right to use a rattle or mask, to the couple for their child or children. After the wedding the couple usually went to live with the groom's family. The two families could continue to exchange property as long as the marriage endured. And the marriage might be made to endure longer than the life of one party to it, for if one or the other died the family of the deceased might provide another spouse for the survivor.

The kinship terms seem to indicate something of the nature of these relationships. The terms for blood kin form a system in some respects like the English, bilateral with lineal and collateral kin distinguished in parents' and children's generations, the most important difference being that the sibling terms distinguish older and younger siblings and are extended to cousins to distinguish senior from junior lines of descent.

But the affinal terms form an entirely different system. For the relationships indicated by the English terms "father-in-law," "mother-in-law," "son-in-law," "daughter-in-law," "brother-in-law," "sister-in-law," there are four native terms: *sk^wítəw* (spouse's parent, wife's brother), *scəwtɛ́t* (child's spouse, man's sister's husband), *smɛ́təx^wtən* (man's sister-in-law, woman's brother-in-law), *sx^wʔɛ́ləx* (woman's sister-in-law). Thus the affinal terms, quite unlike the consanguineal terms, may lump persons of different generations and distinguish by sex of speaker. The English affinal terms form a structure that mirrors that formed by the consanguineal terms; the native affinal terms form an entirely different sort of structure. The key to this structure seems to be that it shows the "direction of the marriage," that is, the direction of the movement of women as wives, and it shows the possibility of secondary affinal marriage. A man calls by the term *skʷítəw* his wife's father and brother, that is, the men from whom he received her, and he is called *scəwtɛ́t* by them. And conversely he uses the term *scəwtɛ́t* for his sister's husband and daughter's husbands, that is, the men who have received women from him, and they of course call him *skʷítəw*. Siblings-in law of the opposite sex, that is, men and women who might marry through the operation of the levirate or sororate, call each other *smɛ́təxʷtən*. Sisters-in-law call each other *sxʷʔeləx*, which means literally "one who functions as sister." If a spouse dies, his or her relatives are all called by a single term *c̄ɛ́yʔɛ* by the widow or widower. To marry one's *c̄ɛ́yʔɛ* is called *c̄ɛ́yʔɛm*. If this is done the former terms are again used.

The most important remaining affinal kinship term is *skʷə́lwəs*, child's spouse's parent. Since there is no usual English term for *skʷəlwəs*, I propose to use a term of my own, "co-parent-in-law." This relationship is one of the most important in the whole social system. Co-parents-in-law are people linked by the marriage of their children. These are the people who exchange wealth at the wedding and who may continue to make exchanges as long as the marriage lasts. After the death of one party to the marriage they become *ctxɛ́ɛm* (those who weep together") until the marriage is reconstituted.

According to informants from several tribes in the area, a man could at any time take food to a co-parent-in-law and expect to receive wealth in return. To make such a trip was called *íst* (literally "to paddle") or *təwɛ́n* in Straits, *ʔə́xəl* or *kʷəlwəsɛ́ɛn*

in Halkomelem. The person taking food invited members of his community to help him take it; these people were called *šq̉áʔwəl*. The person or family receiving the food then invited members of their own community to share the food in a feast. At this time they hired a speaker to "pay the paddles" and to "thank" the co-parent-in-law. To "pay the paddles" meant to pay each of the *šq̉áʔwəl* who had helped bring the food, and also to make payments for the canoes themselves, the paddles, and even the bailers. The Swinomish, Lummi, and Katzie seem to have spoken of "paying" the co-parent-in-law for the food, using the verb (in Halkomelem) *nə́wnəc*, "to pay for something bought." A Lummi informant stated that on Vancouver Island people did not pay their co-parents-in-law. My Musqueam informants likewise stated that they and the Cowichan did not pay for the food. But then they explained that you had to "thank" your co-parents-in-law. The Vancouver Island people still do this—at Cowichan "you ought to thank them with between ten and twenty dollars." The difference then is only in the terms used. Everywhere one can take food and expect to receive wealth.

This sort of exchange is not confined to co-parents-in-law; it may take place between father-in-law and son-in-law or between brothers-in-law, or between cousins in different communities as well. But informants usually speak of the exchange first in relation to co-parents-in-law, probably because this is the relationship of the two families who have established the tie through marrying their children to one another and who begin the series of exchanges. Exchanges between other relatives are, I believe, simply the continuation of exchanges begun by co-parents-in-law.

Several informants indicated that

the exchanges of food and wealth between affinals could become competitive. The amount of wealth extracted from an in-law could be increased by increasing the amount of food taken and by increasing the number of fellow villagers invited to help take it. But if the amount of wealth required were very great, the recipient of the food might "pay for it with a song," that is to say, he might sing an inherited song or (perhaps only among the Klallam) a spirit song bestowed by a wealth spirit. If the recipient of the food had such a song which he might sing at this time as additional payment, the bringer of the food might then feel obliged to thank him for this performance with a gift of wealth, or to treat him in the same fashion when the situation was reversed.

Two things must be made clear. First, this sort of exchange between affinals is not simply a repayment of the bride price or a balancing out of the exchanges that took place at the wedding. Historically it may be derived from this, or in individual cases it may begin with this, but families seem to have continued and developed the series of exchanges long after the original connection was established. Second, this sort of exchange is not to be confused with the potlatch. The potlatch is an occasion when the host or hosts invite members of other communities to the host community to receive gifts of wealth to validate changes of status and exercise of inherited privileges. The sponsor may be an individual, but it seems that more often a number of persons in the host community pooled their occasions for the validation of claims to high (or at least new) status and invited guests at the same time so that the community as a whole served as host.

As I said earlier, I believe the exchange between affinals that I have just described plays an important part in the native socio-economic system. First, it is an important link in the relationship between food, wealth, and high status, a relationship that has not been very thoroughly explored for any Northwest Coast society.

Among the Coast Salish of the area I am describing food and high status are directly related. High status comes from sharing food. The variety of native subsistence techniques and property rights, together with individual differences in skill (generally interpreted in native ideology as resulting from differences in supernatural support), made for considerable differences in productivity. And, of course, the man who produced more than others was honored. A man was expected to share food with his close relatives and house-mates. Certain types of food, such as sea mammals, were usually shared at feasts at which someone from each family was served and given a portion called *mə́q̓aθ* to take home. And, as I have indicated, a man used food brought by his co-parents-in-law for a feast for his own people, so that having productive affinals meant being a food provider yourself—as long as you could thank your affinals properly for their gifts.

People also shared food with neighbors and relatives from other communities by sharing access to their techniques and/or resources. One conjugal family working alone had the instruments for and equal access to most types of resources within the territory of its community. But some of the most productive techniques required the cooperation of several persons. Moreover, access to some of the most productive sites was restricted by property rights. Not all, but the best camas beds, fern beds, wapato ponds, and clam beds were owned by extended families with control exercised by individuals. Most duck net sites were so owned; deer-net sites were not, but the investment of material and labor in the nets was such that only a few hunters had them, and the same was probably true of seal nets. Weirs and traps for salmon seem usually to have been built by a whole community, perhaps under the direction of the head of an extended family, but with no distinction in access. However, the houses standing at the weir sites, which were necessary for smoking the catch, were owned by individuals or extended families. Some other types of fishing were more restricted by property rights. The sturgeon traps of the Musqueam belonged to extended families. The reef-net locations of the Straits tribes (Lummi, Saanich, Songish,) were owned by individuals. But in one way or another access was shared, both within the community and among communities. The director of a Musqueam sturgeon trap might give permission to members of other extended families to help take fish from it for a share. The owner of a Straits reef-net location might "hire" a crew from members of other extended families or even other communities. Some Cowichans fished in the summer on reef nets belonging to Saanich and some of the Saanich, who had no important stream in their territory, went to the Cowichan River for the fall runs of fish caught at weirs. The Katzie were hosts to people from up and down the Fraser when it was time to take wapato from their ponds or pick berries on their bogs.

High status also comes from directing food production. Perhaps every kind of joint enterprise had a director in the owner of the gear or the "owner" of the site. The actual degree of control given to an individual probably varied with the complexity of the process and the responsibility required of him. The Straits reef net was a complex device that had to be carefully made and skillfully operated; the reef-net location was always said to be "owned" by one man or at most two brothers, who evidently had considerable authority over it. On the other hand, the Musqueam sturgeon trap was simply a kind of tidal pound from which fish could be easily drawn out at low tide; members of the extended family that had built the trap were its "owners" and were free to come and take fish at any time without consulting the director—it being expected they would share the fish; while the only responsibility of the director was to see that the trap was repaired once a year and to give permission to nonmembers to participate in the taking of fish. But even the Katzie wapato ponds and berry bogs had an "owner" who gave permission to outsiders to collect there. Thus, for some subsistence techniques there may be technical reasons for control by a director while for others there are not. But with such widespread sharing of access to resources, there are surely social reasons why there may be an "owner" even when technical reasons are minimal, simply in order to show outsiders that *somebody's* permission had to be asked.

The potlatch very likely played an important part within this system of sharing access to resources. By potlatching, a group established its status vis-à-vis other groups, in effect saying "we are an extended family (or a village of several extended families) with title to such-and-such a territory having such-and-such resources." And when a leading member assumed a name that harked back to the beginning of the world when the ancestors of the group first appeared on the spot, this not only demonstrated the validity of the group's title but perhaps also announced in effect "this is the man in charge of our resources." But could not any sort of spectacle serve the same ends? It seems to me that these functions are not sufficient to explain that feature which is most typical of the potlatch—the lavish giving of wealth.

The relationship between wealth and high status is quite clear. As in other Northwest Coast societies, by giving wealth at a potlatch a man validates a claim to noble descent and inherited privilege and thus converts wealth into high status. It might be argued then that the relationship of wealth and high status only parallels that of food and high status, but the argument is convincing only if food and wealth are unrelated.

Food and wealth are indeed separate categories of goods in native culture. "Wealth" consisted of blankets, shell ornaments, fine baskets, hide shirts, bows and arrows, canoes, slaves—items of varying utility but all relatively imperishable. Blankets were the most important such item, especially since they could be ripped apart and the wool rewoven time after time. Food was not classed as "wealth." Nor was it treated as wealth. There is some evidence that food was seen as a gift from the supernatural; *xé'xɛ sítən*, "holy food," a Semiahmoo informant called it. It should be given freely, he felt, and could not be refused. Food was evidently not freely exchanged with wealth. A person in need of food might ask to buy some from another household in his community, offering wealth for it, but food was not generally offered for sale.

Food and wealth were *indirectly* related in one important way. A man who could produce more food could release some of the members of his household from food-producing activ-ities and let them produce wealth and he could attract more food-producing and wealth-producing persons to his household as wives for himself (poly-gyny being permitted) and for his sons, brothers, and nephews, and as sons-in-law (residence with wife's family being permitted). Thus food could be indirectly converted into wealth. But of course a larger household means more mouths to feed at all times and conditions of production must have set limits to the size of a household.

And finally, as described above, food could be taken to affinal relatives and wealth received in return. This then appears to have been the most important mechanism for *directly* converting food into wealth. The relationship of food, wealth, and high status is complete. They all form a single system.

Thus the first thing I want to point out about the food-for-wealth exchange between affinals is its importance within the total system of food, wealth, and high status. The second is that through it the total system is an adaptive one.

The environmental setting of native culture was characterized by four significant features: 1) *variety of types of food,* including sprouts, roots, berries, shellfish, fishes, waterfowl, land and sea mammals; 2) *local variation* in the occurrence of these types, due to irregular shore lines, broken topography differences between fresh and salt water, local differences in temperature and precipitation; 3) *seasonal variation,* especially in vegetable foods and in an adromous fishes; 4) *fluctuation from year to year,* in part due to the regular cycles of the different populations of fish, in part to less predictable change, as in weather.

The first three of these four environmental features are no doubt closely related to the clearly patterned yearly round of subsistence activities. In the spring the different families occupying the sections of a big house left the community, perhaps separately, to spend a good part of the year moving from place to place accumulating stores of food. But this food quest was not at all a random movement. People knew quite well where and when they were likely to find what food and so they generally exploited a certain place at a certain time for a certain thing. Their choice was determined largely by the first three of the environmental features just mentioned, together with technological and social factors suggested earlier. But the fourth of the environmental features, fluctuation from year to year, must have demanded versatility and adaptability. While these environmental features were characteristic even of the small territory identified with each community, they were of course of greater significance for the whole area under consideration. The rather pronounced differences in resources among communities, plus year-to-year fluctuation in quantities, must have put a premium on intercommunity cooperation.

The sharing of access to resources was a form of intercommunity cooperation that must have made for greater efficiency in the exploitation of the environment. But this form of cooperation was probably one that required some planning, as when a Saanich reef-net captain hired Cowichan net pullers or when a Musqueam family decided to visit their Katzie relatives at wapato harvesting time, and worked out best for predictable differences in resources. But the availability of food was clearly not always predictable; there were temporary unforeseen shortages and surpluses. Under all of these conditions any mechanism by which members of one community could "bank" a temporary surplus of some particular item of diet with members of another community would be advantageous. The exchange between affinals was such a mechanism. If one community had a sudden oversupply of, say, herring, its members could take canoeloads to their various co-parents-in-law, receive mountain-goat wool blankets in exchange, with which they might later "thank" their co-parents-in-law for gifts of camas bulbs or dried sturgeon. Wealth then was credit for food received. Wealth was a part of this adaptive system.

Looking now at that most famous institution, the potlatch, I find that *within this total socio-economic system,* its most important function is to be found neither in the expression of the individual's drive for high status nor in the fulfillment of the society's need for solidarity, neither in competition nor in cooperation, but simply in the redistribution of wealth. Wealth has been accumulated by various means—producing it within one's own household, receiving it for services, receiving it as gifts validating the status of donors at previous potlatches, and receiving it in thanks for food taken to one's in-laws in other communities. Since wealth is indirectly or directly obtainable through food, then inequalities in food production will be translated into inequalities in wealth. If one community over a period of several years were to produce more food than its neighbors, it might come to have a greater part of the society's wealth. Under such circumstances the less productive communities might become unable to give wealth back in exchange for further gifts of food from the more productive one. If amassing wealth were an end in itself the process of sharing surplus food might thus break down. But wealth, in the native view, is only a means to high status achieved through the giving of it. And so the community that has converted its surplus food into weath and now has a surplus of wealth gets rid of its wealth by giving it away at a potlatch. And this, though the participants need not be conscious of it, by "restoring the purchasing power" of the other communities, enables the whole process to continue. The potlatchers have converted their surplus wealth into high status. High status in turn enables the potlatchers to establish wider ties, make better marriages with more distant villages, and thus extend the process farther.

This interpretation of the potlatch among this particular group of tribes suggests that it serves as a regulating mechanism within the total socio-economic system. The drive to attain high status emerges from this interpretation as a prerequisite to the sorts of behavior that keep the system operating. Satisfying this drive is a "function" of the potlatch only in a secondary or instrumental sense (i.e. it serves an end that is only a means to another end); by satisfying the individual potlatcher's and the community's drive to attain high status, the potlatch provides the rewards necessary to keep others striving to rise. The drive for high status is itself a part of the total system. Since it is necessary to the system, we may assume that values stimulating and supporting it have developed at the expense of values inhibiting it. Some of the values stimulating and supporting the drive to attain high status are seen in native ethical theory, which insists that knowledge of good behavior is the monopoly of the "good" families and that the lower class are "without advice" (i.e. without properly enculturated values), and some are seen in native supernaturalism, which insists that success in any practical activity is achieved with supernatural support and thus gives the seeker for supernatural power both the confidence and the incentive to succeed in the practical. These values are given to the individual early in life and are reaffirmed until the end. They provide a constant stimulation to the drive for high status, which finds its greatest satisfaction in the potlatch.

But the drive to attain high status is clearly not the explanation of the potlatch. Nor is the production of surplus. Nor the cooperation achieved by the potlatching community. The potlatch is a part of a larger socio-economic system that enables the whole social network, consisting of a number of communities, to maintain a high level of food production and to equalize its food consumption both within and among communities. The system is thus adaptive in an environment characterized by the features indicated before—spatial and temporal variation and fluctuation in the availability of resources. Values, drives, surpluses, competition, and cooperation—all of these may be as much effects as causes. The whole has probably developed through a process of variation and selection, within the limitations of environment and cultural means, that can be best described by the term "cultural evolution."

the political system
of the bemba tribe

seven

AUDREY I. RICHARDS

Kinship

The Bemba are a matrilineal tribe practising matrilocal marriage. Descent is reckoned through the mother and a man is legally identified with a group of relatives composed of his maternal grandmother and her brothers and sisters, his mother and her brothers and sisters, and his own brothers and sisters. His membership of this group determines his succession to different offices and his status in the community, although in a matrilocal society it only occasionally determines his residence. He also belongs to a wider descent group, the clan (*umukoa*, plur. *imikoa*) which is also traced in the woman's line. Each *umukoa* is distinguished by the name of an animal, plant, or natural phenomenon, such as rain. It has a legend of origin usually describing the split-off of the clan ancestors from the original lineage group, and an honori-

Reprinted from M. Fortes and E. E. Evans-Pritchard, eds., *African Political Systems* (London: Oxford University Press, under the auspices of the International African Institute, 1940), pp. 87–101, 103–12, by permission of the publisher and of the author. Dr. Richards has very kindly contributed some improvements to the original text expressly for the present reprinting. [Some footnotes omitted]

fic title or form of greeting. Clans are in effect exogamous, since a man may not marry a woman he calls "mother," "sister," or "daughter," and these terms are extended to the limits of clan membership on the maternal side. Through his clan affiliation, a man traces his descent, rank—if he belongs to the royal clan—rights to succeed to certain offices, such as hereditary councillorship, and claims to his relatives' help and hospitality.

Some clans have a higher status than others, according to whether their original ancestors arrived in the country as part of the following of the first Citimukulu, or alternatively, split off as a separate descent group later. Thus the crocodile clan (*Bena nandu*) is the *umukoa* of the first immigrant chief and stands highest in status (cf. "Rank"), while various others, such as the fish clan, millet clan, etc., are said to be of similar antiquity. The hereditary councillors described later belong to these clans. All the *imikoa* are paired with opposite clans that perform reciprocal ritual duties for each other, but this form of social grouping does not seem to affect the political organization at all at the present day.

Within the clan, smaller lineage groups are recognized. These have no distinct name; though the Bemba often refer to them as "houses" (*amaianda,* sing. *inanda*) of the same clan. Such a house consists of the direct descendants of one particular ancestress traced back to three or four generations—five at the most. Within this smaller descent group, succession to office is usually limited, and chieftainships tend to become hereditary within three or four generations in such lines. Social replacement of one man for another, either as an heir, an officiant in a religious ceremony, in fulfilment of a marriage contract (in the case of a woman), or in compensation for blood guilt in the old days, tends and tended to take place within the "house" and not the clan, though members of the *umukoa* do replace each other if there is no one more nearly related within the *inanda* to do so.

It is the smaller descent-group which is important in considering the influence of the ancestral spirits (*imipashi,* sing. *umupashi*) over the living, either as affecting the welfare of their descendants in general or as entering the wombs of pregnant women of that descent-group to act as guardian spirits to the children as yet unborn.

Apart from the descent-group that determines his status, there is the body of kinsmen with whom a Bemba co-operates actively in daily life. These are the people with whom he may choose to live, and who gather together at any important event in his life, such as marriage, the birth of a child, illness, or a death. This group is known by a distinct term, the *ulupwa.* It has a bilateral basis, since it is composed of the near relatives on both sides of the family and also relatives in law. The balance between the powers of the maternal and paternal relatives is a very even one in Bemba society, in spite of the legal emphasis on the matrilineal side, and the ties uniting the members of the *ulupwa* are very strong. Though it is more usual to live with kinsmen on the matrilineal side, the grandfather or the mother's brother, yet a man may choose to live with his father's people by preference, and they play an important part at all the great ceremonial occasions in his life. The strength of the bilateral *ulupwa* is in fact one of the distinguishing features of the Bemba kinship system as compared with the strongly patrilineal societies of South Africa to my mind. It affects the political system in two ways. First, it allows for a much greater variety in the composition of the village, and more possibilities of change in its membership; and, secondly, we find in the case of the chief's relatives that the *ulupwa* of a ruler is an important unit in the whole political machine. A ruler's sons receive positions and office as well as his heirs, the maternal nephews; and his father's relatives and those related to him by marriage are also favoured, so that his grip over the country is a strong one.

Local Grouping

The local unit in Bemba society is the village (*umushi,* plur. *imishi*). It contains on an average thirty to fifty huts, and is a kinship unit first and foremost. A village comes into being when a middle-aged or elderly man has acquired a big enough following of relatives to justify his applying to the chief for permission to set up a community on his own. He usually builds near other relatives, but land is so plentiful that it is perfectly possible for him to settle almost where he pleases within the chief's domain. The core of the village consists in the first place of the headman's own matrilocal family group, i.e. his married daughters with their husbands and children, and probably members of his matrilineal descent-group, i.e. his sisters and their children. Polygamy is rare. A chief will have a number of wives, say ten to fifteen, but commoners do not often have more than one.

A successful headman will be able to attract more distant relatives to him, both on the patrilineal and matrilineal side. On his death he may be succeeded by his heir, and such a local community may continue in existence with frequent changes in its composition, for two, three, or even more generations. Indeed, the village of the hereditary officials of the paramount chief (*bakabilo*), remain permanently fixed in one village. Thus in every district there are a number of new villages brought into existence by the chief's favour (*ukupokelafye kuli mfumu*) and therefore specially dependent on his support. These include communities newly gathered together by commoner headmen, as described, as well as existing villagers which have been given, with or without the inhabitants' goodwill, to a relative of the chief. Besides these new headmanships, there are those founded in the chief's predecessors' reigns and described as such, and on the whole less dependent on the present ruler. The proportion of new to old villages in Citimukulu's district in 1933 was as follows:

On 160 villages: *percent*

New villages	28
Villages with one previous holder of the headmanship	16
Villages with two previous holders of the headmanship	10
Villages with three or more holders of the headmanship	40
Villages constituted from remnants of two old villages	6

The skill with which he allots headmanships, and the positions in which he places his own relatives, contribute greatly to a chief's power.

In spite of the provisions for inheritance of headmanships, the Bemba village is an impermanent community from many points of view. It moves every four or five years, in keeping with the practice of shifting cultivation, and is liable to disruption at the death of an important member or at any loss of popularity by the headman. The plentiful supply of land and the many alternative possibilities of kinship grouping provide ample opportunities for a man to change from one village to another if he pleases, and in any case he is almost bound to live in a series of communities during his lifetime, e.g. the village of his birth, that to which he moves when he marries, any other village he may go to when he acquires the right to move his wife and family from her people's care, and lastly, in some cases, a community of which he may acquire the headmanship through succession to his maternal uncle. Hence, although a man's companions and fellow workers are those of his *umushi* and he speaks with some affection of the village of his birth or of his mother's people (*icifulo*), yet the bonds of kinship are much stronger than those of the impermanent local group. A Bemba is a member of a *ulupwa* and may move as he pleases to live with any of the relatives composing it, and he is the subject of a chief and may obtain permission to live in any part of the latter's territory, but his ties to a given locality are not necessarily strong.

A chief's village (*umusumba*) is very much larger than that of a commoner. Inhabitants of the capital are composed of relatives of the chief, his followers, and also a number of families which moved there originally to win royal favour and have become accustomed to court life.[1] Since a

---

[1] The phrase *"umwino musumba"* ("inhabitant of the capital") is used to indicate a "chief's man" or a person of specially polished manners and knowledge of affairs.

chief's reputation depends largely on the size of his capital, and his councillors, courtiers, and administrative officers were drawn largely from his villagers, the *umusumba* is an important unit in the political machine. The late Nkula's village had about 400 huts when I visited it in 1931, that of the Citimukulu 150 in 1938. The capitals of pre-European days were evidently very much larger. These communities were divided into sections (*ifitente,* sing. *icitente*) and though nowadays there are nine *ifitente* at the paramount's village, there were formerly thirty to forty, according to native accounts.

The whole Bemba territory is divided into districts (*ifyalo,* sing. *icalo*). The *icalo* is a geographical unit with a fixed boundary and a name dating from historical times, e.g., the district of the Citimukulu is known as Lubemba, the country of the Bemba, and that of Mwamba, Ituna. These districts are territories originally allotted to members of the royal family, but once so divided they have never been sub-divided to provide smaller chieftainships for a new generation of princes as has happened in some parts of South Africa.

But the *icalo* is also a political unit. It is the district ruled over by a chief with a fixed title—the name of the first ruler to be appointed over each particular strip of land, always a close relative of one of the earlier Citimukulus. There are several types of chief, the paramount, who has his own *icalo,* as well as being overlord of the whole Bemba territory; the territorial chiefs, five or more in number, who have under them sub-chiefs who may rule over very small tracts of country or, rather, over a few villages.

Each of these chiefs is known by the same title *mfumu* and each *icalo* is a more or less self-contained unit, a replica of the social structure of the other. Each capital has its own court, however small. Each chief has rights over the labour of his own villages. They work for him only and not for the paramount as happens among the Zulu, Swazi and other tribes with the regiment system. The *icalo* is also a ritual unit. At each capital are the sacred relics (*babenye*) of the first holders of the chiefly title and their ancestral spirits are thought to act as tutelary deities of the district, and are worshipped at the *umusumba,* at village shrines, and old hut sites throughout the country, and are also commonly supposed to act as guardian spirits to children born within the *icalo*. Naturally the ritual and political organization of the paramount's capital is more elaborate than that of his inferiors, but even the smallest sub-chief maintains his miniature court and tries to ape the state of those above him while the bigger territorial chiefs sometimes rivalled the power of the Citimukulu in the old days.

The territorial chieftanships are arranged in order of precedence, according to their nearness to the centre of the country—Lubemba—and the antiquity of their office. The most important of these chiefdoms—the Mwambaship, the Nkulaship, the Nkolemfumuship, and the Mpepoship—are held by the nearest relatives of the Citimukulu, his brothers and maternal nephews. Bemba say that the one should succeed to the other in seniority. However, this rule of succession from chieftanship to chieftanship has often been broken in fact. Thus the present Citimukulu, Kanyanta, has acted in turn as the Nkolemfumu, and the Mwamba before succeeding to the paramountcy. On the other hand, the sub-chieftainships have tended to become concentrated in local branches of the royal family, and the paramount's strong grip over the country and his intimate knowledge of affairs at the courts of his fellow chiefs is certainly weaker in these outlying districts than in the case of chiefdoms ruled by his close relatives.

To the commoner, membership of an *icalo* means his allegiance to the chief of that territory. He will describe himself as an inhabitant of a district, such as *Icinga*, i.e. *mwine Icinga* or, alternatively, as the subject of its chief, Nkula, i.e. *mwine Nkula,* and both terms are synonymous. He may move from village to village within the *icalo,* but he remains his chief's man. The latter, in his turn, reckons his assets, not in terms of the size of his territory or its natural resources, but rather by the number of his people and in particular the villages he has under his rule.

Rank

Rank is acknowledged in Bemba society. It is based on kinship, real or fictitious, with the chief. All members of the royal crocodile clan (*Bena nandu*) are entitled to special respect, precedence on ritual and social occasions, and sometimes to claims on the people's services. The potential heirs of a chief within his own branch of the family—that is to say, his brothers, maternal nephews, or maternal grandsons—are treated with particular deference. The former two categories are described as chiefs and addressed by the title *mfumu,* while the latter, only slightly lower in status, are referred to by a special name *beshikulu ba mfumu* ("grandchildren of the chiefs") and have their own ritual and social prerogatives.

Women of the royal line, the mothers, sisters, maternal nieces, and granddaughters of the chiefs are called *banamfumu* and are treated with much the same deference as are the men of the family. The "mother" of the paramount (who is not always his actual mother) is highly honoured, succeeds to a fixed title—the *Candamukulu*—takes part in tribal councils, and has several villages of her own. The sisters of chiefs are privileged persons, protected and supported by their royal brothers, and usually granted one or more villages to rule. They are above the law in matters of sex morality, and a princess is allowed to have as many lovers as she pleases, provided she produces many children as potential heirs to the throne.

Not only members of the royal clan, but also persons who merely belong to the *ulupwa* of the chief, can claim high rank, i.e. his relatives on his paternal side, and his own sons. Some fathers of chiefs were nobodies and were quickly forgotten, but some have been famous men, honoured by their sons when the latter succeeded to the throne. The children of chiefs, though not members of his clan, and therefore not heirs, are also entitled to special privileges, and the *bana hamfumu* ('children of the chief') form a class of their own. They are brought up at the court, where they are treated in many ways more favourably than the heirs themselves and are able to claim headmanships and even chieftainships.[2] Even the half-brothers of chiefs, through other fathers (*bakaulu*), have rights to special treatment at court.

Added to this, already numerous class of royal personages are the descendants of close relatives of dead chiefs. Roughly speaking, any person who can claim to be maternal nephew, grandson, or son of a chief is succeeded by a man who continues to hold the same rank by the

____

[2] A few chieftainships are definitely handed on to "sons of chiefs" instead of to "chiefs," e.g., the Makassaship, the Lucembeship, or the Munkongeship.

ukupyanika system described on p. 114. He is then addressed as "chief" or "son of chief." The descendants of royal princesses are also entitled to honour, as well as those of wives of chiefs and even consorts of princesses. It will be seen, therefore, that the royal rank is a very large one. Any one who can possibly claim connexion of any sort with any chief, dead or living, does so, although the perquisites of rank are in most cases honour only and the possible favours of the chief, rather than any material assets. Every one outside the royal clan, or *ulupwa,* is an *umupabi,* or "ordinary person," and in old days there was a slave class below—men and women captured in battle or enslaved to their own people for some crime. These individuals were known as *bashya.* The term is now used as an opprobrious epithet especially for foreigners—often assumed to have been enslaved by the Bemba formerly. Slavery itself no longer exists.

Other Principles of Social Grouping

Age is not a principle of social grouping among the Bemba. Precedence is reckoned on the basis of seniority, as in most Bantu societies, and there are special terms used to describe the different stages of life, suckling, infant, child, adolescent, unmarried, married, old etc. But there are no regiments based on age, as in South and parts of East Africa, and the boys initiation ceremonies so often found associated with such institutions do not exist among this group of the Central Bantu.

There are no occupational groups, with the exception of certain specialist fishing communities on the banks of the big rivers, and in the old days there were specialist hunters of big game. Secret societies, such as the *ubutwa,* which is common among neighbouring tribes over the Congo border, and has been adopted by the Bisa of the swamps, do not seem to have been introduced among the Bemba.

To conclude, Bemba society is as yet undifferentiated to any large extent. The tribe is an outgrowth of a lineage-group which has occupied its present territory for 200 to 300 years, and has remained more or less homogeneous. The original kinship structure is still apparent. All the social groups to which a man belongs are ultimately based on kinship—whether it is his household village or descent group, and there are no other forms of association such as age-sets to cut across this original grouping by descent. Rank consists of membership of the clan of the first immigrants to enter the land.

Economic Background

The Bemba are an agricultural people like most of the Central Bantu group to which they belong. They keep no cattle. Tsetse-fly at present prevents their keeping stock over most of the country, but in any case they seem to have no pastoral traditions, whatever they may have had formerly. Thus they have no means of storing wealth as have the Southern Bantu. Their marriage contracts are fulfilled by service and not by the passage of cattle. In the old days military glory and the extraction of tribute from conquered peoples seems to have been the dominant ambition of the Bemba chiefs, and their wealth consisted in the size of their following and the amount of service they were able to command. This fact profoundly influences their position at the present day.

The soil of most of this district is poor and it has not attracted white settlement. The staple crop is finger millet, while some kafir corn, a little maize, legumes, and pumpkins are also grown. The people practise shifting cultivation of a primitive type, and the plentiful supply of land and the lack of any localized natural resources which might attract the inhabitants to settle in one area rather than another all affect the political system. As has been shown, they decrease the strength of local ties as against political or kinship affiliations, and they account for the fact that the power to distribute land is not an important prerogative of leadership in distinction to conditions in most Southern Bantu tribes.

Hunting and fishing contribute a small share of the food-supply only. Organized marketing does not exist, and under modern conditions no cash crop has been found for this area. This fact, together with the absence of opportunities for local employment, forces the adult male population to look for work outside the tribal area, with resultant effects, as will be seen, on the political system of the tribe.

·   ·   ·

Bases of Authority

The positions of leadership in Bemba society consist of the following offices: (*a*) *territorial rulers* (chiefs and headmen); (*b*) *administrative officers and councillors;* (*c*) *priests, guardians of sacred shrines, and magic specialists with economic functions;* (*d*) *army leaders* in the old days. Succession to all these offices is based on descent in nearly every case. Chieftainships were limited to one clan, as we have seen; some of the councillorships (i.e. the *bakabilo*) are confined to a few of the older clans; and headmanships, though they may be won through the chiefs' favour, tend to become hereditary in their turn. All priestly offices are hereditary without exception, as is natural where an ancestral cult of this type is prac-

tised. Magico-economic specialists, particularly those in charge of fishing villages, usually acquire their powers by descent also, as do some of the doctors and diviners (*nanga*). In each case the supernatural powers almost invariably correlated with political authority in this area are conferred by a rite, of great complexity, in the case of the succession of a chief, known as *ukupyanika*. For these reasons it is essential to study the dogma of descent by which these powers are believed to be transferred from one generation to another, and the legal rules of succession by which status and office are passed from one man to another.

The Dogma of Descent

By dogma of descent I mean, first, those theories of procreation which express a people's beliefs as to the physical contribution of the father and mother to the formation of the child, and hence the traditional conception of the physical continuity between one generation and the next; and next their beliefs as to the influence of the dead members of each social group over the living, and hence the social identification of a man with the line of his dead ancestors.

Among the Bemba it is believed that a child is made from the blood of a woman which she is able to transmit to her male and female children. A man can possess this blood in his veins, but cannot pass it on to his children, who belong to a different clan. Physiological paternity is recognized. Children are often described as being like their fathers, and are expected to give the latter affection and respect although they have no legal obligations to them under the matrilineal system. "We take our fathers presents because they begot us," they say. But it is nevertheless the physical continuity of the mother's line of ancestors which is the basis of legal identification with her descent group. A royal princess might even produce an heir by a slave father in the old days without lowering her child's prestige. The relationship between brother and sister, which is a very close one, legally and ritually, is based on the fact that the two were born from one womb, and in the case of the royal family it appears to be equally strong when the two are children of different fathers. These theories of procreation account, not only for the matrilineal descent of the Bemba, on which succession to chieftainship is based, but also for the rank accorded to the royal princesses as mothers of chiefs, and the headmanships and other positions of authority given them.

The Bemba dogma as to the influence of the dead over the living is also of the utmost importance as a basis for political authority. The spirit of a dead man (*umupashi,* plur. *imipashi*) is thought to survive as a guardian presence associated with the land or village site formerly inhabited, and as a spiritual protector of different individuals born in the same lineage group and called by the same name. The *imipashi* of dead chiefs become tutelary deities of the land they ruled over, and responsible for its fertility and the welfare of its inhabitants. They can be approached by the successor to the chieftainship at various sacred spots in the territory and at the sacred relic shrines (*babenye*) in his own village. A chief is said to be powerful because he "has great *imipashi*!" It is for this reason he is described as the *umwine calo,* "owner of the land," and it is important to note that in every case the most important *imipashi* and the most sacred relics are those of the first chiefs to enter the land, or the first occupants of a chieftainship.

This dogma as to the influence of the dead over the living inhabitants of a district, or the members of a descent group, is very similar to the general Bantu pattern. But the Bemba belief in the social identification between the dead man and his appointed successor seems to me to be particularly complete. It is the basis of the belief as to the supernatural influence exerted by the chief in his own person as distinct from his direct approach to the spirits in prayer. When a man or woman dies, his or her social personality must be immediately perpetuated by a successor who passes through a special ritual (*ukupyanika*) and thus acquires the name, the symbols of succession (a bow for a man and a girdle for the woman), and the *umupashi* of the dead man. By this social identification, a man assumes the latter's position in the kinship-group, uses the same kinship terms and, in the case of a chief, it is almost impossible to tell when a man is describing incidents which took place in his own life or those of an ancestor two or three generations dead. So important is this social perpetuation of the dead considered that immediately after a death, before the successor has finally been appointed, a small boy or girl, usually a maternal grandchild, is chosen to inherit the name of the deceased temporarily (*ukunwa menshi,* "to drink the water"). He or she is given some small piece of the latter's property and thereafter addressed as grandfather or grandmother, or whatever the right kinship term may be.

In the same way, a chief, once he has succeeded to the name, the spirit, and the sacred relics of his predecessor, has magic influence over the productive capacity of his whole territory. His ill health or death, his pleasure or displeasure, his blessings or curses, can affect the prosperity of the people, and even his sex life reacts on the state of the community.[3] For a chief to break a sex taboo is an act which may cause calamity to the whole people, and the rites by which he is purified after sexual contacts form one of the most important elements in the politico-religious ceremonial requiring the participation of thirty or forty hereditary officials (*bakabilo*) in the case of the paramount. Conversely, legitimate sex intercourse, especially as prescribed on certain ritual occasions, may actually be a health-giving influence. Any headman has a certain degree of supernatural influence in his own village as the successor to his predecessor's *umupashi*, but a chief has considerably more. For all these reasons, ritual precautions guard the sacred person of a chief. Special taboos must be kept to preserve the ritual purity of the ruler's sacred fire, and his sacred food, and to protect his person and that of the sacred relics from the contagion of illness, death, or sex defilement.

The ritual by which a successor to the chieftainship is converted from an ordinary individual to a ruler with almost divine powers, has a good deal of political importance. It confers authority on the priests—in this case hereditary officials (*bakabilo*) who carry it out—and gives them, as we shall see, considerable power to check the chief himself. The complete ritual by which the *umupashi* of a dead ruler is liberated to guard the land he governed, and the new heir is in-

stalled, is too complex to describe here and now. Briefly speaking, it consists of the desiccation of the body during a period of a year, from one kafir-corn harvest to the next; its burial in a special grove (with human sacrifices in the old days); and the building of a shrine on the site of the deserted capital. To make the new chief, *bakabilo* must preside at the installation of a new great wife, arrange for the sexual purification of the royal pair, and the lighting of their new sacred fire.[4] They must hand over to the heir the heirlooms (*babenye*) of which they have been in charge during the interregnum, and must finally found a new village and build again the sacred huts in which the relics are to be kept. Such a ceremonial may take eighteen months to two years and the participation of all the *bakabilo* and hereditary buriers (*bafingo*) in the case of the paramount; a lesser time and very many fewer priestly dignitaries in the case of the territorial chiefs. The secrecy and awe surrounding these ceremonies is, I believe, one of the ways by which the people's reverence for their chiefs is maintained.

Legal Rules of Descent and Succession

Against this background of beliefs as to the continuity between one generation and another, the nature of descent and succession is defined exactly by legal rule. Descent in the royal family is reckoned to the time of first occupation of the country, and twenty-five to thirty Citimukulus are remembered. In the case of a territorial chief, the line of ancestors is not so long, and most are described as having been "born in the country."

---

[3] There are rumours that chiefs were throttled by their hereditary councillors when they were obviously sick unto death, for fear they took "the land" into the grave with them. This information was sent me by Mr. T. Fox-Pitt after I had left the country and was afterwards checked by Mr. Godfrey Wilson. In fact it is probable that in the old days the Bemba chiefs would fall under Frazer's definition of a "divine king."

[4] Hence the importance of the great wife of the chief (*umukolo ua calo*) in the political life of the tribe and the belief that her behaviour also influences the welfare of the land.

Most of the names honoured are those of men but some are those of women, and it seems that the first ancestress to inhabit a new chiefdom, or one who was a mother of numerous powerful sons and was thus able to found a new branch, could claim to be so respected.[5] But it is to the men holders of titles that most shrines are built.

The hereditary officials (*bakabilo*) also trace their descent to the first arrival for the most part, and tell stories which account for their right to the ritual offices they hold to-day, e.g. the *bafingo* who now bury the chief, claim to be the descendants of those who buried the first Citimukulus when on the march. This reckoning of descent to a definite epoch in history very clearly remembered is of service in maintaining the myth of absolute continuity of the chiefly lines. In actual fact, the present Citimukulu is a descendant of one Cileshye, who seized the throne from the occupier, Cincinta, only four generations back. This branch of usurpers is able to claim descent from the first Citimukulu all the same. The first ancestors are remembered very accurately and their sacred relics kept. The ensuing vagueness in the chain seems to be of no account.

In most types of succession whether to the name and spirit of a dead man or to his office, there are usually two or three potential heirs, and although there are certain rules of priority, it is practically never the case that there is one child known as heir to the chieftainship from birth and brought up as such, as occurs in those South African tribes in which the eldest son of the great wife must always succeed. A Bemba chief, or commoner, is succeeded by his brothers in order of age, next by his sister's children, and, failing them, by his maternal grandsons. Difficulties arise when there is a choice between an older classificatory "brother," not a sibling, but possibly a mother's sister's son, or an even more distant "brother" still, and a young man, a maternal nephew who is the child of the deceased's own sister, with whom, as we have seen, his ties are very close. Here the principles of primogeniture conflict with that of propinquity of kinship, in the case of a branch of a family that has been in existence for three or four generations, and it is probable that in these cases the nearest heir is appointed unless he is manifestly unsuitable, when the more distant "brother" or "maternal nephew" is selected. I never heard of a regent being appointed for a young man as is commonly done in those Bantu tribes where the heir to the throne is known from his time of birth.

The situation is more complicated in the case of succession to chieftainships, since through the custom of inheriting one big territorial chieftainship after another within the paramount's immediate family, it is claimed, though it is not always the fact, that, e.g., the holder of the Mwambaship succeeds to the Citimukuluship, whatever the priority of kinship. This claim was put forward in the last succession dispute (1925) and is commonly supported by Government officials who naturally prefer a fixed system of succession to the discussion of rival candidates' rights that seems to have been the older procedure. There is also a tendency becoming more and more evident for

---

5 e.g. Bwalya Cabala, the first ancestress said to have been fetched from Lubaland by her brothers when the latter had occupied what is now Bembaland; or the Nakasafye, grandmother of the present Nkula, who is described as having started a new line, and was evidently a woman of great character as well as the mother of many sons.

certain of these bigger chieftainships to be confined to sub-branches of the main royal line, as distinct from sub-chieftainships which are nearly always given to descendants of local branches of the crocodile clan (e.g. the Mwabaship). This constant growth and separation of different sub-lines or houses of the royal clan seems to have been continuous in the past.

•   •   •

Functions and Prerogatives of Leadership

The functions of the territorial heads, i.e. chiefs and headmen, seem to be derived from two sources—the position of the leader as head of a kinship group and his role as the representative of a line of dead ancestors in a particular district. In the case of a headman, these two aspects are indistinguishable, while the latter predominates where a chief is concerned.

The Headman

Bemba headmen are described as looking after, keeping, or actually "herding the people" (*ukuteka bantu*). As senior kinsman of most of the villagers, a headman is responsible for the discipline of the children and young people; he hears cases informally and directs some economic activities. There are few activities carried out by the whole community in common except fishing and hunting, but besides organizing these latter pursuits a good headman initiates each new agricultural process and encourages and criticizes the younger men and women. Land is not often a matter of dispute in this area. The headman does not allot individual plots, but listens to cases should any arise. He is said to "feed his people" and actually does so if they are in need, besides dispensing hospitality to strangers.

The head of the village acts as its ritual head. In the old days, he put up one village shrine to his own ancestors and one or more others to the dead chiefs of the land. This is still done in out-of-the-way parts of the country and in most places, I think, prayers are offered to these tutelary deities, whether shrines are built to them or no. The headman, like the chief, also influences the life of the community through his own person. He must "warm the bush" (*ukukafye mpanga*) by an act of ritual intercourse with his wife before the huts of a new village are occupied. He blesses seeds for sowing, axes for tree-cutting, and first-fruits. His fire stands for the life of the community as a whole and must be ritually lighted when occasion demands. He presides over the special divination rites connected with village activities, such as the founding of a new community or the death of a member, and blesses new babies or individuals who are sick.

In the political hierarchy, the headman has his definite place. No Bemba may cultivate land except as a member of a village group, and the headman is responsible for organizing the supply of tribute and labour which must be paid to a chief by the community as a whole. He accompanies his villagers to court when they have cases to present and often speaks for them. He transmits the orders of a chief to his people and nowadays those of the Government. His prerogatives are few in number. As head of a kinship-group, he can command personal service from his younger relatives and should be able to exact one day's work from his people on the first day of tree-cutting and sowing. He is always given tribute of beer or meat. But probably, apart from these few economic privileges, the Bemba headman values most his position of authority, his small following, and the favour of his chief.

The sanctions for his authority nowadays are mainly his popularity, together with the strength of kinship feeling, and the belief of the Bemba that it is dangerous to allow an older relative to die injured. His supernatural powers were a source of strength in the old days, but to a very small extent now, and it must be admitted that the forces which keep a village together are not very strong. It is a constant fear to a headman that his people will melt away.

The Chief

The functions of the different types of chief differ only in degree. All are said to look after their people, to "work the land," and, with reference to their supernatural powers, to "spit blessings over the land" (*ukufunga mate*). Their political duties consist in the administration of their capitals and also of their territories as a whole. A large *umusumba* means plenty of coming and going, enough workers for joint enterprises, a large panel of advisers for court cases, many messengers to keep in touch with the surrounding villages—in short, the possibility of keeping the tribal machine running. To maintain and even augment such a community by his popularity and his reputation for generosity is one of the chief's important political tasks. He has also to keep contact with the people widely dispersed over his *icalo* and to appoint new headmen, amalgamate old villages, and decide as to the selection of heirs to old titles. On his success in these last duties the integration of his people as a political unit largely depends.

As a judicial authority, the chief presides over his court with advisers selected from his village, and in the old days he alone could hear charges of witchcraft and, in the case of the greater territorial chiefs, put the accused to the poison ordeal (*mwafi*). In the economic sphere, he initiates agricultural activities by performing the customary ceremony before each begins; he makes big gardens with the aid of tribute labour from which he is able to fill large granaries and thus find the wherewithal to feed his following; he controls directly certain fishing and hunting enterprises: and he criticizes and directs the gardening work of his own villagers.

The ritual duties of a chief consist in the observation of the taboos for the protection of his own person and the safety of the sacred relics at his disposal, and the carrying out of a number of rites for the sake of his whole *icalo*—in the case of the paramount, for the whole tribe. These last consist of economic rites, tree-cutting, sowing, and first-fruit ceremonies, those performed in case of national calamity, and for success in war in the old days. He was formerly bound to protect the people from witches and used to employ a special doctor at his court to destroy, by burning, the bodies of those found guilty of this offence.

In the old days the chief organized military expeditions, although he did not necessarily take part in the fighting. As one chief put it, "If we were killed, the whole *icalo* would fall to pieces." The ruler had certain military captains in his following, could call up men to fight, direct their operations from afar, and arrange for the performance of war magic for success before battle and for purification from the stain of blood after it.

The prerogatives of a chief consist in rights over the labour of his people, who are required to do a few days' tribute labour each year and to answer sudden calls for help if made;

and also claims to tribute in kind, usually paid in the form of an annual present of beer and/or grain, and portions of animals killed in the hunt. It is through this tribute that he is able to pay his advisers, servants, labourers—and soldiers in the old days. Formerly, he maintained rights to certain monopolies, such as ivory tusks, salt from the big inland deposits at Mpika, and guns and cloth traded from Arabs. Slaves or booty captured by the army were brought to him, and he had a number of his own people enslaved for various offences. Besides these economic prerogatives, he commanded great, one might almost say abject deference, and had the satisfaction of seeing his following grow, his authority increased, and his power over life and death over his subjects recognized.

The sanctions for a chief's authority are numerous, and they were still greater in the old days. The most important of these has already been described as the people's belief in their rulers descent from a long line of ancestors and the supernatural powers thought to be so conferred. Besides this, a reputation for generosity and a system by which advancement could only be attained through royal favour naturally bound people to him. Much of his power also rested in the old days on force. A chief practised savage mutilations on those who offended him, injured his interests, laughed at him or members of his family, or stole his wives. A number of these mutilated men and women still survive in Bemba country to-day. Command over the army and over the supply of guns also lay in the chief's hands and there is no doubt that the greatness of the *Bena rjandu* rested to a large extent on fear. The people explain that the royal family were named after the crocodile because "they are like crocodiles that seize hold of the common people and tear them to bits with their teeth."

The Machinery of Government

Within each district there are a series of officials, messengers, etc., who carry out the activities of government and the different forms of ritual on which the chief's power depends. Some of these are personal followers of the chief promoted by him for their special loyalty (e.g. the *bafilolo, basano*), while others are hereditary officials who are more independent of their ruler's favour (e.g. *bafilolo* and *bafingo*). All these different dignitaries can be classed under various functional heads, i.e.:

Administrative

These include the executive officials in charge of business in the *umusumba* and those responsible for carrying out the chief's orders in the *icalo* at large. Within the capital the most important are the heads of divisions (*bafilolo*), who are appointed from among the chief's personal friends. These are charged with keeping the peace of the village, organizing the tribute labour from the capital, allotting land for cultivation, which is often necessary in the bigger settlements, arranging hospitality for visitors—an important task at the capital —and acting as a panel of advisers on all occasions (cf. "Judicial," below). Besides these elder men, there are at the *umusumba* a number of courtiers and in the old days young men (*bakalume ba mfumu*). Young boys, often members of the royal clan, were, and still occasionally are, sent to court to be educated there, and some families remain as courtiers for several generations apparently. All these act as messengers, attendants, and in the old days took duty as executioners.

As regards the country at large, the main difficulty was keeping in touch with the scattered villages. The Bemba have no general meeting like the *pitso* of the Sotho peoples or the *libandla* of the Nguni. For the chief's orders to be conveyed to his villages, messengers have to go to and fro. Other officers are required to recruit the tribute labourers and to demand beer or produce for the chief, and to apprehend criminals. Since some villages are sixty miles or so from the capital, an enormous amount of time is spent in coming and going in this way and even with the introduction of the bicycle a great many messengers of one sort or another are still required. In the old days courtiers and younger relatives of the chief acted in this capacity. Nowadays they have anything from four to twelve uniformed messengers, *kapasus,* and for the rest they go short of service.

Military

There was no general military organization in this tribe, but attached to each big court were one or two captains (*bashika*). Some of these were hereditary, with ritual functions connected with war magic, and others appointed at the chief's will. They now act as specially trusted messengers.

Judicial

There is no fixed composition to a Bemba court, although its procedure is laid down by custom. At a small chief's court, the elderly men of the village attend, while the *bafilolo* act as advisers at the big *imisumba*. Cases go on appeal from sub-chief to chief, chief to paramount, and in the event of a case of extreme difficulty presenting itself, the Citimukulu can summon from their villages some of his hereditary priests or councillors, the *bakabilo* (cf. below). Witnesses are brought by each party to a case and are marshalled by the *bafilolo*. The senior man present claps as each point is made to mark the recognition of the court, and the chief himself finally sums up and gives judgement. The advisers speak when asked a point of precedent or law, and influence the chief's final decision by black looks or alternatively enthusiastic clappings of the hand.

Advisory

There is no council or meeting of all the adult men of the tribe for special occasions, as among many Southern Bantu. Sub-chiefs have a panel of village elders and relatives to advise them, while the biggest territorial chiefs have hereditary officials who combine political and judicial with ritual functions. In the case of the paramount, these officials—the *bakabilo*—number between thirty-five and forty and form an advisory council on special matters of State. The *bakabilo* have been described as having descent as long as that of the chief himself in many cases and possess sacred relics in their own rights. The power of these relics is so strong that the Citimukulu is not permitted to pass through their villages for fear that one chieftainship should harm the other. *Bakabilo* are immune from tribute, wore special feather head-dresses in the old days, and even now claim special respect equal to that given to a chief when travelling about the country. They call themselves *Fwe Babemba* ("We, the Babemba"), may not leave the central territory (Lubemba) for long, must be buried within the royal district, and keep sex taboos similar to those of the chiefs. They succeed by a special accession ceremony and are buried according to particular rites. They are divided into groups according to the order of their ancestors' arrival in the country, and each has a special office based on the privileges of his original ancestor, e.g. the care of the royal drum, the right to sit on a stool in the chief's presence, or the duty to call him in the morning by clapping outside his door.

The main duties of the *bakabilo* in native eyes are ritual, as has been described. They are in charge of the ceremonies at the sacred relic shrines and take possession of the *babenye* when the chief dies. They alone can purify the chief from the defilement of sex intercourse so that he is able to enter his relic shrine and perform the necessary rites there. They are in complete charge of the accession ceremonies of the paramount and the bigger territorial chiefs, and some of their number are described as *bafingo,* or hereditary buriers of the chief. Besides this, each individual *mukabilo* has his own small ritual duty or privilege, such as lighting the sacred fire, or forging the blade of the hoe that is to dig the foundations of the new capital.

Besides their priestly duties, the *bakabilo* acted as regents at the death or absence of the chief, and any question of succession or other matter of tribal importance is placed before the *bakabilo,* and the big ceremonies I witnessed at the chief's capital were all made occasions of such discussions. The procedure is complex, but an effective method of deliberation. The paramount sends two special hereditary messengers, also *bakabilo,* to place the matter before the council. The senior members speak and if a difficulty arises they refer the matter to the head priest of the land, the Cimba, who sits apart with his own following, and gives decisions on matters of tribal precedent or suggests rewording decisions to be carried to the chief. Some of the discussion is carried on in archaic *cibemba.*

The importance of the *bakabilo's* council is the check it holds over the paramount's power. These are hereditary officials and therefore cannot be removed at will. Two or three of the *bakabilo* have been chased out of the country in the past for overweening pride, according to tradition, and the Cimba was removed from office in 1934, but only after the tribe had suffered for many years from the results of a species of megalomania to which he seemed to be subject. Otherwise the *bakabilo* are immune from the chief's anger and exert a salutary influence over him by refusing to perform the ritual functions that are necessary to the chief's state.[6]

Other advisory officials consist of the near relatives of the chief himself. These do not attend discussions as to succession to chieftainships, but are constantly informed of the progress of affairs. The paramount's mother and the Makassa (the eldest "son of the chief") play an important part in this way. In the past senior members of the royal family seem to have intervened occasionally when some chief was behaving too outrageously, as, for instance, in the case of a sub-chief, Fyanifyani, apparently attacked by a sort of bloodlust. This man was removed from his office, according to history.

In brief, the Bemba system of government is not a democratic one in our sense of the word. The elder commoner has fewer rights to speak on tribal matters than have the Zulu, Swazi, or even some of the Sotho peoples. The affairs of the *icalo* are in the hands of a body of hereditary

---

6 During 1934 I found the paramount living in grass huts. He was unable to build his new village because the *bakabilo,* indignant at his behavior, refused to perform the foundation ceremony for the new community.

councillors whose offices and most of whose deliberations are secret. But I was impressed by the sense of tribal welfare which these *bakabilo* showed, and they were quite able to discuss and shrewdly adapt some old tribal precedent to modern conditions. Their strength, as regards tribal government at the present day, is their *esprit de corps* and sense of responsibility; their weakness, the fact that in the eyes of the people and the Government their function is mainly a ritual one.

The Integration of the Tribe

The integration of the tribe depends chiefly on the sentiment of tribal cohesion and loyalty to the paramount, and the means by which the activities of the different districts are brought under one control in this widely dispersed group. The dogmas of kinship have been shown again and again to be the basis of tribal feeling and of the allegiance given to the territorial and paramount chiefs. In other Bantu tribes there is some tribe-wide organization such as the Nguni regiment system, that seems to act as an integrating force. There are also forms of public ceremonial at which all the adult men of the tribe are gathered, or all the warrior classes. The first-fruit ceremonies of the Swazi or of the Zulu in the old days are an example. The big tribal councils of most of the African peoples described as being attended by "every one" and in reality very large meetings, must also act as occasions when the loyalty of the tribe is fostered. Among the Bemba much of the tribal ritual is secret, as has been shown, and the advisory council is composed of what might be called an aristocratic caste. If the *bakabilo* meet in sitting on the open ground in the capital, as I have seen happen, they use archaic language on purpose, so that the common people cannot understand. It is no occasion for high-flown oratory or any of the demagogue's arts. On the other hand, the Bemba chiefs were formerly considered very nearly divine, and the belief in their supernatural powers is still strong enough to integrate the tribe. The sacredness of the royal ceremonial largely depends on its secrecy and the fact that only persons of the right descent can take their part in the ritual. The ordinary people do not attend the ceremonies except in the case of some inhabitants of the capital, but they value their secret nature and speak contemptuously of the Bisa and neighbouring tribes with less complex rites. The number of the *bakabilo*, each scattered through the chief's *icalo* and each with his own ritual function, sometimes secret from his own fellows, also adds to the strength of the whole ceremonial system. Each is insistent that *his* part is absolutely essential to the welfare of the tribe, and his own village is convinced to that effect, too. Another integrating factor is the belief in royal descent and presence in the society of such a large number of men and women who claim chiefly rank. These are dispersed all over the country, generally in charge of villages, and they naturally support the chiefs from whom they derive their power.

As regards the activities of the different *ifyalo*, it has been seen that these are self-contained units and there is no regular provision for regular meetings of *icalo* heads. They are linked by the overlordship of the paramount, who acts as judge of their court of appeal, and the different tiny states are bound together because of the close relationship between their different chiefs. Messengers constantly go from one court to another to in-quire after family matters, the children of one chief are sent to be brought up at the capital of another, the chiefs themselves take office first in one *icalo* and then another, and even the Citimukulu takes no important step, ritual or political, without consulting his "brothers," the big territorial heads.

But here again ritual is one of the big integrating forces. The Citimukulu can initiate a series of sacrifices (*ulupepo lukalamba*), which start at his relic houses and spread to all the shrines throughout the land. The *bakabilo* are sent from Lubemba to bury any of the bigger territorial chiefs who die in their distant *ifyalo* and to install the new heir. The paramount prays for rain on the rare occasions when it is required, on behalf of the whole tribe. Thus for ritual purposes, in spite of the quarrels and jealousies between different lines of the royal family, the whole Bemba country can be said to act as a whole and to be conscious of its unity. If the paramount chief were to turn Christian before the political institutions of this tribe have been considerably adapted, tribal cohesion would, I think, be very much weakened, whether temporarily or permanently.

Part 3

archaic
societies

Societies that have developed to a fully archaic level of evolution differ from advanced primitive societies in a number of important respects. They tend to be larger in territory and population, to contain urban concentrations of population which serve, usually quite diffusely but often with notable differentiation, as economic, political, prestige, and religious centers of societal life; to have very extensive networks for the circulation and mobilization of economic resources, including regular markets for trade in agricultural and handicraft products and provision for the extension of mercantile credit; a patrimonial and/or feudal system of authority with the administrative means to aggregate monumental amounts of wealth and especially labor services; a societal community differentiated into a plurality of classes with markedly distinct life-styles and regulated by a written and formally promulgated code of laws; and a religion based upon a ramified set of priest-administered cults and a grandiose cosmology elaborated in myths by literate priest-intellectuals.

Archaic societies have not been nearly so numerous as have primitive societies. However, they have emerged independently at a considerable number of times and places, for example, in Egypt, Mesopotamia, Persia, India, North and South China, Japan, Mexico, and Peru, to mention what are perhaps the principal instances. In each of these cases, once the archaic stage of civilization was attained, a plurality of separate societies developed—through the influence of one society on peoples surrounding it or through the breakdown of a central society—and entered into complex, diffuse interrelations of crossfertilization, competition, and conflict. The prototypical case of intense interstimulation was Mesopotamia, where the political boundaries, economic ties, and religious influences shifted constantly in the relations among the hundreds of city-states as larger Empires emerged and then declined, bringing about changes in the location, potency, and patterning of the influential centers of civilization. Archaic societies have also emerged on the fringes and under the influence of the major historic civilizations, for example, the Tibetan and Indo-Chinese states in the areas between India and China.

Max Weber's famous discussion of traditional authority, our first reading, has been the preeminent classic source of contemporary understanding of the organization and dynamics of archaic societies. Although Weber's analysis covers a broad range of pre-modern cases, from primitive to historic, the central type of patrimonialism is probably best exemplified by the more sizable archaic empires.

Traditional authority is legitimated through belief in the sanctity of the given institutional order of society and distribution of powers, and exercized through the personal prerogatives of status of the rulers and their retainers. The latter are not "officials" who operate within legally delimited spheres of competence that are organized into a rational bureaucracy, for they hold their powers as personal rights and privileges. They gain their authority either through traditional ties of special loyalty to the chief, which generally contain at least elements of ascription to their kinship groups, or through acceptance of the purely personal favor of the chief, e.g., in vassalage.

The major political sources of variation among patrimonial systems are the degree and extent to which the ruler or chief is able to appropriate powers, develop and control an administrative staff, and obtain dependable flows of the resources necessary for centralized administration. In traditional beliefs in the sanctity of local authorities, in attachment to local groups or the privileges of local nobility, and in ascriptive control of resources in localities, archaic societies contain forces of very diverse sorts that oppose patrimonial centralization. Weber's discussion of the problems of support of the administrative staff indicates some of the ways in which these forces can come together to affect the ruler's power. For example, if the retainers gain hereditary control of fiefs so that they do not rely very directly upon the ruler for their support, they may become autonomous local leaders legitimated in their independence from central authority and cease functioning as agents of effective commands of the ruler. When the ruler can retain control over the benefices granted to the staff for support, he is better able to prevent his retainers from becoming foci for the crystallization of autonomous power.

The remainder of the readings on archaic societies concentrate on the ancient Egyptian and Mesopotamian empires. These are probably the most intensively studied and best understood archaic civilizations. Moreover, they offer a striking and fascinating contrast: Egyptian society emphasized pattern maintenance and political functioning and was structured in a rather rigidly hierarchical fashion about the central institution of its kingship, while Mesopotamian society emphasized economic and integrative functioning and was structured, much less stably, on the principle of rather legalistic association of relatively autonomous social units. Cutting across their basic differences, however, we will see that both Egypt and Mesopotamia attained very full elaboration of the archaic pattern of civilization.

The first unification of Egypt was associated with the emergence of a more centralized and effective system of rule promulgated from a new capital in Memphis. Henri Frankfort demonstrates that the keystone of the new system was the Memphite Theology, which mythically elaborated a variety of traditional religious themes into a constitutive symbolism that portrayed the unified Empire and its rule by the pharoah as central components of the entire order of the cosmos. Frankfort emphasizes the pharoah's being given the status of a principal god, Horus, who inherited his rule of Egypt from his divine father, Osiris. The mystical ritual of succession, in dramatizing the following of Osiris by Horus as a central act in the timeless order of all existence, relativized the changes of history to the continuity of an overweening principle and provided a basis of security for the affairs of men. As Horus, the pharoah ensured through his rule that human society would remain regulated in the harmonious fashion ordained by the gods in their acts of creation. His actions had the status of divine measures taken to preserve the sacred order or of elements of the sacred order itself, and hence stood majestically above the merely human acts of others. His rule alone could ensure that the gods would provide for the welfare of the people.

William Edgerton's piece provides a brief account of the patrimonial authority structure in the Old Kingdom of the Memphite Theology, as well as of its later breakdown into feudalism. Although the majestic figure of the pharoah monopolized the highest levels of authority in the Old Kingdom and alone could provide public leadership on the most important matters of policy and law, his leadership was nevertheless largely ceremonial. The routine oversight of the sizable administrative staff was controlled by a vizier. From the collection of taxes, the profits of the state mercantile monopolies, the produce of royal domains, and the work of corvée labor, extensive resources were mobilized for the support of the central administrative apparatus. Almost all principal functionaries derived their rights to authority from kinship with the pharoah, ties which also could be used to control their activities. This was especially important for the cases of the nomarchs (governors of the territories), who had more autonomous control over local resources. The feudalistic decline of central authority resulted from a vicious process in which benefices and fiefs became heritable, the central administration became impoverished, and power gravitated to the increasingly autonomous nomarchs.

Given the commitment of Egyptian society to a centralized order, feudalism was bound to bring extensive economic and political dislocation and much social turmoil. However, as John A. Wilson shows, it also engendered a profound religious bewilderment and moral malaise. Perhaps the key factor in this deep reaction was the obvious upset in the pharoah's grandiose cosmic role, which intensely disturbed the people's sense of spiritual welfare and security.

Frankfort's discussion of Mesopotamian kingship and religion emphasizes many fundamental contrasts with the Egyptian pattern. Mesopotamian theology revolved not about an harmonious and eternally stable cosmic order but about a tumultuous assembly of gods engaged in jealous bickering and political conflict. Marduk, the king of gods, was depicted as having won his right to head the divine assembly in war. Human kings did not have divine status nor could they participate in the divine assembly. Rather, their rights to rule stemmed from their having been chosen the favorites of the leading gods associated with their city-states or empires. In ritual, public proclamation, and policy-setting, the kings strongly and constantly emphasized the signs of their being favored by the gods, for the divine favor was in principle transferable to others. The gods were not greatly restricted by rules of inheritance in bestowing their favors, so that succession to the throne was often complicated by conflict among cempeting claimants and interregna became anxious times of potential internal war. Moreover, the state without a designated ruler was believed to be deprived of the divine welfare which a "chosen" king could secure. Thus, the king was believed to fulfill a divine function or carry a divine burden on behalf of the public weal, even though his actions were thoroughly mortal. A central part of this divine burden was the obligation to provide legal justice and welfare for the subjects over whom the gods had placed the king. Nevertheless, the king's law was not, like that of the Egyptian pharoah, part of a divine cosmic order, but an essentially mortal effort to regulate the changing, often volatile, forces of society.

The readings by Sabatino Moscati, H. W. F. Saggs, and G. R. Driver and J. C. Miles in Chapter Twelve indicate the great importance, quite distinctive among archaic societies, the Mesopotamian states placed upon specifically legal regulation of social statuses and activities and upon judicial administration. The famous Babylonian code of Hammurapi is only one among many different Mesopotamian codes which have now been recovered. Apparently, these codes were comprised less of laws in our modern sense than of model judicial decisions to which the king, as the highest authority, wished to give his imprimatur as standards of justice. The codes were not intended as closed "systems" of law but as surveys of ways in which justice might be served in relation to a variety of critical problems. Matters of welfare raised by changing economic conditions received much attention in all of the codes, indicating that the economy was sufficiently market-oriented to generate major social problems in times of marked expansion or recession. Indeed, the law regulating rights in property, contractual arrangements, the fixing of prices and wages, and the extension and repayment of loans was highly elaborated and formalized, especially after Hammurapi. All of the Mesopotamian codes gave legal sanction to the existence of three separate classes, namely patricians, plebians, and slaves. For example, the punishment for criminal acts varied not only with the nature of the act but also with the class of the offender and of the person offended. Justice was administered through a system of public courts organized on a number of levels. Lower courts were generally comprised of peers and elders, but the higher courts were conducted by groups of judges who were literate and had professional training in the law. There were rights of appeal that could bring access to the court of the king and to his responsibility to the gods to assure that the laws were justly made and administered. As Driver and Miles show, however, it is not clear how judgments of the courts were generally executed, whether by the king's army or by the aggrieved parties' own actions as witnessed by the court.

traditional authority

eight

MAX WEBER

A system of imperative co-ordination will be called "traditional" if legitimacy is claimed for it and believed in on the basis of the sanctity of the order and the attendant powers of control as they have been handed down from the past, "have always existed." The person or persons exercising authority are designated according to traditionally transmitted rules. The object of obedience is the personal authority of the individual which he enjoys by virtue of his traditional status. The organized group exercising authority is, in the simplest case, primarily based on relations of personal loyalty, cultivated through a common process of education. The person exercising authority is not a "superior," but a personal "chief."

His administrative staff does not consist primarily of officials, but of personal retainers. Those subject to authority are not "members" of an association, but are either his traditional "comrades" or his "subjects." What determines the relations of the administrative staff to the chief is not the impersonal obligation of office, but personal loyalty to the chief.

Obedience is not owed to enacted rules, but to the person who occupies a position of authority by tradition or who has been chosen for such a position on a traditional basis. His commands are legitimized in one of two ways: (a) partly in terms of traditions which themselves directly determine the content of the command and the objects and extent of authority. In so far as this is true, to overstep the traditional limitations would endanger his traditional status by undermining acceptance of his legitimacy. (b) In part, it is a matter of the chief's free personal decision, in that tradition leaves a certain sphere open for this. This sphere of traditional prerogative rests primarily on the fact that the obligations of obedience on the basis of personal loyalty are essentially unlimited.[1] There is thus a double sphere: on the one hand, of action which is bound to specific tradition; on the other hand, of that which is free of any specific rules.

In the latter sphere, the chief is free to confer "grace" on the basis of his personal pleasure or displeasure, his personal likes and dislikes, quite

Reprinted from *The Theory of Social and Economic Organization* (New York: The Macmillan Company, 1947), pp. 341–58, by permission. Copyright 1947 by Talcott Parsons. [Some footnotes omitted]

---

[1] This does not seem to be a very happy formulation of the essential point. It is not necessary that the authority of a person in such a position, such as the head of a household, should be unlimited. It is rather that its extent is unspecified. It is generally limited by higher obligations, but the burden of proof rests upon the person on whom an obligation is laid that there is such a conflicting higher obligation.—[ED.]

arbitrarily, particularly in return for gifts which often become a source of regular income. So far as his action follows principles at all, these are principles of substantive ethical common sense, of justice, or of utilitarian expediency. They are not, however, as in the case of legal authority, formal principles. The exercise of authority is normally oriented to the question of what the chief and his administrative staff will normally permit, in view of the traditional obedience of the subjects and what will or will not arouse their resistance. When resistance occurs, it is directed against the person of the chief or of a member of his staff. The accusation is that he has failed to observe the traditional limits of his authority. Opposition is not directed against the system as such.

It is impossible in the pure type of traditional authority for law or administrative rules to be deliberately created by legislation. What is actually new is thus claimed to have always been in force but only recently to have become known through the wisdom of the promulgator. The only documents which can play a part in the orientation of legal administration are the documents of tradition; namely, precedents.

A traditional chief exercises authority with or without an administrative staff. The typical administrative staff is recruited from one or more of the following sources:

(*a*) From persons who are already related to the chief by traditional ties of personal loyalty. This will be called "patrimonial" recruitment. Such persons may be kinsmen, slaves, dependents who are officers of the household, clients, coloni, or freedmen.

(*b*) It may be recruited from other sources on an "extra-patrimonial" basis. This category includes people in a relation of purely personal loyalty, such as all sorts of "favorites," people standing in a relation of fealty to their chief—"vassals"—and, finally, those who have of their own free will entered into a relation of personal loyalty as officials.

In traditionalistic organizations, it is very common for the most important posts to be filled with members of a ruling family or clan.

In patrimonial administrations, it is common for slaves or freedmen to rise even to the highest positions. It has not been uncommon even for Grand Viziers to have been at one time slaves.

The typical household officials have been the following: the senechal, the marshal (once in charge of horses), the chamberlain, the carver, the steward, who was the head of the service personnel and possibly even of the vassals. These are to be found everywhere in Europe. In the Orient, in addition, the head eunuch, who was in charge of the harem, has been particularly important. In the African kingdoms, the executioner is often included. Universally, the body physician, the astrologer, and various others have been common.

In China and in Egypt, the principal source of recruitment for patrimonial officials lay in the clientele of the king. Armies of coloni have been known throughout the Orient and were typical of the Roman nobility. Even in modern times, in the Mohammedan world, armies of slaves have existed.

The regime of "favorites" is characteristic of every patrimonial system and has often been the occasion for "traditionalistic" revolutions.

The status of "vassal" will be dealt with separately.

Bureaucracy has first developed in patrimonial states with a body of officials recruited from extra-patrimonial sources; but, as will be shown presently, these "officials" have originally been personal followers of their chief.

In the pure type of traditional authority, the following features of a bureaucratic administrative staff are absent: (a) a clearly defined sphere of competence subject to impersonal rules, (b) a rational ordering of relations of superiority and inferiority, (c) a regular system of appointment and promotion on the basis of free contract, (d) technical training as a regular requirement, (e) fixed salaries, in the type case paid in money.

In place of a well-defined impersonal sphere of competence, there is a shifting series of tasks and powers commissioned and granted by a chief through his arbitrary decision of the moment. They then tend to become permanent and are often traditionally stereotyped. An important influence is exerted by competition for sources of income and advantage which are at the disposal of the persons acting on behalf of the chief or of the chief himself. It is often in the first instance through these interests that definite functional spheres are first marked off and, with them, genuine administrative organs.

In the first instance, those with permanent functions are household officials of the chief. Their functions outside the administration of the household itself are often in fields of activity which bear a relatively superficial analogy to their household function, or even which have originated in a completely arbitrary act of the chief, and have later become traditionally stereotyped. In addition to household officers, there have existed primarily only persons with *ad hoc* specific commissions.

The absence of clear spheres of competence is clearly evident from a perusal of the list of the titles of officials in any of the Ancient Oriental states. With rare exceptions, it is impossible to associate with these titles a set of functions rationally delimited in the modern Western sense which has remained stable over a considerable period.

The process of defining permanent functions in terms of competition among and compromise between interests seeking favours, income, and other forms of advantage is especially clearly evident in the Middle Ages. This phenomenon has had very important consequences. The interests in fees of the powerful Royal courts and of the powerful legal profession in England was largely responsible, partly for breaking the influence of Roman and Canon law, partly for limiting it. Existing irrational divisions of official functions have frequently in all periods been stereotyped by the existence of an established set of rights to fees and perquisites.

In contrast to the rational hierarchy of authority in the bureaucratic system, the question who shall decide a matter—which of his officials or the chief himself—or who shall deal with complaints, is, in a traditional regime, treated in one of two ways. (1) Traditionally, on the basis of the authority of particular received legal norms or precedents. (2) Entirely on the basis of the arbitrary decision of the chief. Whenever he intervenes personally, all others give way to him.

In Germanic law, apart from the traditionalistic system of adherence to precedent, there is a principle which is derived from the arbitrary power of the political chief; namely, that in the presence of the chief himself the jurisdiction of any court is suspended. This principle has the same source as the *jus avocandi,* in the arbitrary grace of a monarch and its modern derivative, chamber justice. A court rendering judgment in terms of precedents was in the Middle Ages very often the agency which declared and interpreted the law and was thus the principal source from which the law of a locality was taken.

As opposed to the bureaucratic system of free appointment, household officials and favorites are very often recruited on a purely patrimonial basis from among the slaves or serfs of the chief. If, on the other hand, the recruitment has been extra-patrimonial, they have tended to be holders of benefices which he has granted as an act of grace without being bound by any formal rules. A fundamental change in this situation is first brought about by the rise of free vassals and the filling of offices by a contract of fealty. Since, however, such relations of fealty have been by no means primarily determined by considerations of objective function, this has not altered the situation with respect to definite spheres of competence or clearly determined hierarchical relationships. Except under certain circumstances when the administrative staff is organized on a basis of praebends, there is such a thing as "promotion" only according to the arbitrary grace of the chief.

Rational technical training as a basic qualification for office is scarcely to be found at all among household officials or the favorites of a chief. Where there is even a beginning of technical training for appointees, regardless of what it consists in, this fact everywhere makes for a fundamental change in the development of administrative practice.

For many offices a certain amount of empirical training has been necessary from very early times. This is particularly true of the "art" of reading and writing which was originally truly an art with a high scarcity value. This has often, most strikingly in China, had a decisive influence on the whole development of culture through the mode of life of persons with a literary education. Among other things, it has eliminated the recruiting of officials from intra-patrimonial sources and has thus limited the power of the chief by making him dependent on a definite social group.

In place of regular salaries, household officials and favorites are usually supported and equipped in the household of the chief and from his personal stores. Generally, their exclusion from the lord's own table means the creation of benefices, at first usually benefices in kind. It is easy for these to become traditionally stereotyped in amount and kind. Along with the elements supported by benefices or in place of them, there are various agencies commissioned by the lord outside his own household, as well as various fees which are due him. The latter are often collected without any regular rate or scale, being agreed upon from case to case with those seeking favors.

Gerontocracy, Patriarchalism, and Patrimonialism

1. The most primitive types of traditional authority are the cases where a personal administrative staff of the chief is absent. These are "gerontocracy" and "patriarchalism."

The term "gerontocracy" is applied to a situation where so far as imperative control is exercised in the group at all it is in the hands of "elders"— which originally was understood literally as the eldest in actual years, who are the most familiar with the sacred traditions of a group. This is common in groups which are not primarily of an economic or kinship character. "Patriarchalism" is the situation where, within a group, which is usually organized on both an economic and a kinship basis, as a household, authority is exercised by a particular individual who is designated by a definite rule of inheritance. It is not uncommon for gerontocracy and patriarchalism to be found side by side. The decisive characteristic of both is the conception which is held by those subject to the authority of either type that this authority, though its exercise is a private prerogative of the person or persons involved, is in fact pre-eminently an authority on behalf of the group as a whole. It must, therefore, be exercised in the interests of the members and is thus not freely appropriated by the incumbent. In order that this shall be maintained, it is crucial that in both these cases there is a complete absence of an administrative staff over which the individual in authority has personal control. He is hence still to a large extent dependent on the willingness of the group members to respect his authority, since he has no machinery to enforce it. Those subject to authority are hence still members of the group and not "subjects." But their membership exists by tradition and not by virtue of legislation or a deliberate act of adherence. Obedience is owed to the person of the chief, not to any established rule. But it is owed to the chief only by virtue of his traditional status. He is thus on his part strictly bound by tradition.

The different types of gerontocracy will be discussed later. Primary patriarchalism is related to it in that the authority of the patriarch carries strict obligations to obedience only within his own household. Apart from this, as in the case of the Arabian Sheik, it has only an exemplary character, similar to charismatic authority. He is able to influence people only by example, by advice, or by other non-compulsory means.

2. With the development of a purely personal administrative staff, especially a military force under the control of the chief, traditional authority tends to develop into "patrimonialism." Where absolute authority is maximized, it may be called "Sultanism."

The "members" are now treated as "subjects." An authority of the chief which was previously treated principally as exercised on behalf of the members, now becomes his personal authority, which he appropriates in the same way as he would any ordinary object of possession. He is also entitled to exploit it, in principle, like any economic advantage—to sell it, to pledge it as security, or to divide it by inheritance. The primary external support of patrimonial authority is a staff of slaves, coloni, or conscripted subjects, or, in order to enlist its members' self-interest in opposition to the subjects as far as possible, of mercenary bodyguards and armies. By the use of these instruments of force the chief tends to broaden the range of his arbitrary power which is free of traditional restrictions and to put himself in a position to grant grace and favors at the expense of the traditional limitations typical of patriarchal and gerontocratic structures. Where authority is primarily oriented to tradition but in its exercise makes the claim of full personal powers, it will be called "patrimonial" authority. Where patrimonial authority lays primary stress on the sphere of arbitrary will free of traditional limitations, it will be called "Sultanism." The transition is definitely continuous. Both are distinguished from primary patriarchalism by the presence of a personal administrative staff.

Sometimes even Sultanism appears superficially to be completely bound by tradition, but this is never in fact the case. The non-traditional element is not, however, rationalized in impersonal terms; but consists only in an extreme development of the sphere of arbitrary will and grace. It is this which distinguishes it from every form of rational authority.

3. When, in a system of patrimonial authority, particular powers and the corresponding economic advantages have become appropriated, this will be called "decentralized" authority. As in all similar cases appropriation may take the following forms:

Appropriation may be carried out by an organized group or by a category of persons distinguished by particular characteristics. It may, on the other hand, be carried out by individuals, for life, on a hereditary basis, or as free property.

Decentralized authority thus involves, on the one hand, limitations on the chief's power of free selection of his administrative staff because positions or governing powers have been appropriated. Thus they may be limited to the members of a corporate group or of a group occupying a particular social status.

In addition, on the other hand, there may be appropriation by the individual members of the administrative staff. This may involve appropriation of positions, which will generally include that of the economic advantages associated with them, appropriation of the non-human means of administration, and appropriation of governing powers.

Those holding an appropriated status may have originated historically from the members of an administrative staff which was not previously an independent class. Or, before the appropriation, they may not have belonged to the staff.

Where governing powers are appropriated by members of an independent group, the costs of administration are met from the incumbent's own means, which are not distinguishable from his personal property. Persons exercising military command or members of this type of army provide their own equipment and may even recruit units of the army on their own responsibility. It is also possible that the provision of means of administration and of the administrative staff can be made the object of a profit-making enterprise which exploits access to payments from the stores or the treasury of the chief. This was the principal mode of organization of the mercenary armies in the sixteenth and seventeenth centuries in Europe. Where appropriation by independent groups is complete, all the powers of government are divided between the chief and the different branches of the administrative staff, each on the basis of his own personal rights. It is also, however, possible for these rights to be regulated by special decrees of the chief or special compromises with the holders of appropriated rights. The first type is illustrated by the court offices of a realm when they have become appropriated as fiefs; the second, by landlords who, by virtue of their privileged position or by usurpation, have appropriated powers of government. The former is apt to be merely a legalization of the latter.

Appropriation by an individual may rest on leasing, on pledging as security, on sale, or on privileges—which may in turn be personal, hereditary, or freely appropriated—may be unconditional, or may be subject to performance of certain functions. Such a privilege may be purchased in return for services or granted for compliance with the chief's authority, or it may constitute merely the formal recognition of actual usurpation of powers.

Appropriation by an organized group or by those occupying a particular social status is usually a consequence of a compromise between the chief and his administrative staff or between him and an organized social group. It may leave the chief relatively free in his selection of individuals, or it may lay down rigid rules for the selection of incumbents.

Appropriation, finally, may rest on a process of education or apprenticeships. It will be necessary to devote a special discussion to this case.

1. In the cases of gerontocracy and patriarchalism, so far as there are clear ideas on the subject at all, the means of administration are generally appropriated by the corporate group as a whole or by the household of the individual who carries out the governing functions. The administrative functions are performed "on behalf" of the group as a whole. Appropriation by the chief personally is a phenomenon of patrimonialism. It may vary enormously in degree to the extreme cases of a claim to full proprietorship of the land and to the status of master over subjects treated as slaves. Appropriation by particular social groups generally means the appropriation of at least a part of the means of administration by the members of the administrative staff. In the case of pure patrimonialism, there is complete separation of the functionary from the means of carrying out his function. But exactly the opposite is true of decentralized patrimonialism. The person exercising governing powers has personal control of the means of administration—if not all, at least of an important part of them. This was true of the feudal knight, who provided his own equipment, and of the count, who by virtue of holding his fief took the court fees and other perquisites for himself and met his obligations to his superior lord from his own means, in which these appropriated sources of income over which he had full control were included. Similarly, the Indian *jagirdar,* who provided and equipped a military unit from the proceeds of his tax benefices, was in complete possession of the means of administration. On the other hand, a colonel who recruited a mercenary regiment on his own account, but received certain payments from the royal exchequer and paid his deficit either by curtailing the service or from booty or requisitions, was only partly in possession of the means of administration and was subject to certain regulations. On the other hand, the Pharaoh, who organized armies of slaves or coloni, put his clients in command of them, and clothed, fed, and equipped them from his own storehouses, was acting as a patrimonial chief in full personal control of the means of administration. It is not always the formal mode of organization which is most decisive. The Mamelukes were formally slaves recruited by the purchases of their owner. In fact, however, they monopolized the powers of government as completely as any feudal class has ever monopolized fiefs.

There are examples of land appropriated in fief by a closed corporate group without any individual appropriation. This occurs where the land is granted to individuals quite freely by chiefs so long as they are members of the group, as well as subject to regulations specifying qualifications. Thus, military or possibly ritual qualifications have been required of the candidates, whereas, on the other hand, once these are given, close blood relations have had priority. The situation is similar in the case of artisans attached to a court or to guilds or of peasants whose services have been attached for military or administrative purposes.

2. Appropriation by lease, especially tax farming, by pledging as security, or by sale, have been found in the Western World, but also in the Orient and in India. In Antiquity, it was not uncommon for priesthoods to be sold at auction. In the case of leasing, the aim has been partly a practical financial one to meet stringencies caused especially by the costs of war. It has partly, also, been a matter of the technique of financing, to insure a stable money income available for budgetary uses. Pledging as security and sale have generally arisen from financial necessities. This is true of the Papal States as well as others. Appropriation by pledging played a significant role in France as late as the eighteenth century in filling judicial posts in the *Parlements*. The appropriation of officers' commissions by regulated purchase continued in the British army well into the nineteenth century. Privileges, as a sanction of usurpation, as a reward, or as an incentive for political services, were common in the European Middle Ages, as well as elsewhere.

Modes of Support of the Patrimonial Retainer

The patrimonial retainer may receive his support in any of the following ways: (a) by maintenance at the table and in the household of his chief; (b) by allowances from the stores of goods or money of his chief, usually primarily allowances in kind; (c) by rights of use of land in return for services; (d) by the appropriation of property income, fees, or taxes; (e) by fiefs.

So far as in an amount or within a scope which is traditionally stereotyped, they are granted to individuals and thereby appropriated, but not made hereditary, the forms (b) to (d), inclusive, will be called "benefices." When an administrative staff, according to its fundamental principle of organization, is supported in this form, it will be said to be based on "praebends." In such a situation it is possible to maintain a system of promotion on a basis of seniority or of

particular objectively determined achievements. And it is also possible to require a certain social status as a criterion of eligibility and to make use of the corresponding sense of honour of a distinctive social group.

A set of appropriated governing powers will be called a "fief" if it is granted primarily to particular qualified individuals by a contract and if the reciprocal rights and duties involved are primarily oriented to conventional standards of the honour, particularly in a military connexion, of a distinctive social group. The situation where an administrative staff exists which is primarily supported by fiefs, will be called "feudalism."

The transition between fiefs and military benefices is so gradual that at times they are almost indistinguishable.

In cases (d) and (e), sometimes also in (c), the individual who has appropriated governing powers pays the cost of his administrative function, and possibly also of equipment, from the proceeds of his benefice or fief. In that case his own position of authority over the subject may take on a patrimonial character and thus become hereditary, and capable of division by inheritance.

1. The earliest form of support for royal retainers, household officials, priests and other types of patrimonial followers has been their participation at the table and in the household of the chief or their support by allowances arbitrarily paid out from the stores. The "men's house," which is the oldest form of professional military organization and will have to be dealt with below, very often has the character of communistic consumption. Separation from the table of the chief or of the temple or cathedral and the substitution of allowances or the use of land for this direct mode of support has by no means always been regarded with approval. It has, however, been the usual consequence of the establishment of independent families. Allowances in kind granted to temple priests and officials who have left the chief's household constituted the original form of support of officials throughout the Near East and have also existed in China, India, and to a large extent in the Western World. The use of land in return for military services is found throughout the Orient from very ancient times and also in Medieval Germany as a means of providing for household officials, officers of the court and other functionaries. The sources of income of the Turkish *spahis,* of the Japanese *samurai,* and of various other types of Oriental retainers and knights are, in the present terminology, "benefices" and not "fiefs," as will be pointed out later. In some cases they have been derived from the rents of certain land; in others, from the tax income of certain districts. In the latter case, they have not necessarily been combined with appropriation of governmental powers in the same district; but this has, however, been the general tendency. The concept of the fief can be further developed only in relation to that of the state. Its object may be land under a patrimonial system, or it may be any one of various kinds of claims to property income and fees.

2. The appropriation of property income and rights to fees and the proceeds of taxes in the form of benefices and fiefs of all sorts is widely distributed. It became an independent form of organization in a highly developed fashion in India in particular. The usual arrangement was the granting of rights to these sources of income in return for the provision of military contingents and the payment of administrative costs.

Decentralized Patrimonial Authority

In patrimonial systems generally, and particularly in those of the decentralized type, all governmental authority and the corresponding economic rights tend to be treated as privately appropriated economic advantages. This does not, of course, mean that they cannot be qualitatively differentiated. This is true particularly in that some of them are appropriated in a form subject to special regulations. Furthermore, the appropriation of judicial and military powers tends to be treated as a legal basis for a privileged class position of those appropriating them, as compared to the appropriation of purely economic advantages having to do with the income from domains, from taxes, or other sources. Within the latter category, again, there tends to be a differentiation of those which are primarily patrimonial from those which are primarily extra-patrimonial or fiscal in the mode of appropriation. For the present terminological purposes the decisive fact is that, regardless of content, governing powers and the associated advantages are treated as private rights.

Von Below is quite right in emphasizing strongly that it was especially the appropriation of judicial authority which was made the basis of special treatment and a source of privileged class status. Indeed it is not possible to prove that the medieval political organization had either a purely patrimonial or a purely feudal character. Nevertheless, so far as judicial authority and other rights of a purely political origin are treated as private rights, it is for present purposes terminologically correct to speak of patrimonial authority. This concept itself, as is well known, has been most consistently developed by Haller in his *Restauration der Staatswissenschaften.* Historically there has never been a purely patrimonial state in the sense of one corresponding perfectly to the ideal type.

Where traditional authority is decentralized through the appropriation of governing powers by privileged social groups, this may become a formal case of the separation of powers when organized groups of the members of such a privileged class participate in political or administrative decisions by a process of compromise with their chief.

The subjects of such compromises may be rules or concrete administrative decisions or measures regulating the administrative process. The members of such groups may possibly exercise imperative control on their own authority and by means of their own administrative staff.

1. Under certain circumstances groups, such as peasants, which do not enjoy a privileged social position, may be included. This does not, however, alter the concept. For the decisive point is the fact that the members of the privileged group exercise independent rights. If all kinds of socially privileged groups were absent, the case would obviously belong under another type.

2. This type has been fully developed only in the Western World. Both its peculiar organization in more detail and the reasons for its development in that case will be discussed separately below.

3. The possession of his own administrative staff by a member of such a privileged group has been unusual. The exercise of independent governing authority on his part is still more exceptional.

The Relations of Traditional Authority and the Economic Order

The primary effect of traditional authority on modes of economic activity is usually in a very general way to strengthen traditional attitudes. This is most conspicuous in gerontocratic and purely patriarchal situations since those exercising authority are not in possession of any distinct administrative machinery which is not available to the other members of the group. Thus they are, in upholding their own legitimacy, most strongly dependent on the safeguarding of tradition in every respect.

1. Beyond this, the consequences for the economic order are in the first instance a function of the mode in which the group exercising imperative authority is financed. In this respect, patrimonialism is open to a wide variety of different possibilities. The following, however, are particularly important.

(a) An *oikos* maintained by the chief where needs are met on a liturgical basis wholly or primarily in kind in the form of contributions of goods and compulsory services. In this case, economic relationships tend to be strictly bound to tradition. The development of markets is obstructed, the use of money is primarily oriented to consumption, and the development of capitalism is impossible.

(b) Provision by the services of socially privileged groups has very similar effects. Though not necessarily to the same extent, the development of markets is also limited in this case by the fact that ownership exists in kind, is pre-empted on a non-monetary basis, and purchasing power correspondingly reduced. Furthermore, the productive capacity of individual economic units is to a large extent pre-empted for the needs of the gov-

erning group.

(c) Finally, it is possible for patrimonialism to be organized on a monopolistic basis of meeting its needs, partly by profit-making enterprise, partly by fees, and partly by taxes. In this case, the development of markets is, according to the type of monopolies involved, more or less seriously limited by irrational factors. The important openings for profit are in the hands of the chief and the members of his administrative staff. In so far as productive enterprises are directly administered by the governing group itself, the development of capitalism is thereby directly obstructed. If, on the other hand, there is tax farming, leasing or sale of offices, and provision for armies and administration on a capitalistic basis for fiscal reasons, there is an opening for capitalistic development; but it is diverted in the direction of political orientation.

Even where it is carried out in money terms, the financing of patrimonialism and even more of Sultanism tends to have irrational consequences for the following reasons:

1. The obligations placed on sources of direct taxation tend both in amount and in kind to remain bound to tradition. At the same time there is complete freedom—and hence arbitrariness—in the determination of fees and of newly imposed obligations, and in the organization of monopolies. This element of arbitrariness is at least claimed as a right. It is, however, historically effective to a widely varying extent.

2. Two fundamental bases of the rationalization of economic activity are entirely lacking; namely, a basis for the calculability of obligations and of the extent of freedom which will be allowed to private acquisitive activity.

3. It is, however, possible that in individual cases patrimonial fiscal policy can, by systematic attention to the prosperity of its sources of taxation

and by the rational organization of monopolies, have a rationalizing effect. This, however, is structurally fortuitous and is dependent on specific historical circumstances, some of which have, however, existed in the Western World.

Where the groups appropriating governing powers are formally organized, fiscal policy typically tends to be a result of compromise. This results in making the burdens relatively predictable and in eliminating or at least sharply limiting the arbitrary powers of the chief to impose new burdens and, above all, to create monopolies. Whether the resulting concrete fiscal policy tends to promote or to limit rational economic activity depends largely on the type of group occupying the predominant position of power, above all, whether it is a feudal or a patrician[2] class.

The dominance of a feudal class tends, because the structure of feudalized powers of government is normally predominantly patrimonial, to set rigid limits to the freedom of acquisitive activity and the development of markets. It may even involve deliberate attempts to suppress them to protect the power of the feudal group. The predominance of a patrician class may have the opposite effect.

1. What has been said above must suffice for the present. It will be necessary to return to these questions repeatedly in different connexions.

2. The *oikos* has been found in ancient Egypt and in India. Provision by socially privileged groups is found in large parts of the Hellenistic world, in the late Roman Empire, in China, in India, and to some extent in Russia

---

2 "Patrician" is here used not in the Roman sense, but in that of the privileged commercial classes of the Free Cities of the German Empire, such as the Hanseatic cities.—ED.

and the Mohammedan states. The monopolistic type under direct control of the regime is illustrated by the Egypt of the Ptolemies, to some extent by the Byzantine Empire, and in a different way by the regime of the Stuarts in England. The other type of monopolistic organization, which has been favorable to politically oriented capitalism, has been most highly developed in the patrimonial states of the Western World in the period of "enlightened despotism." The system organized by Colbert is the best-known example.

3. It is not only the financial policy of most patrimonial regimes which tends to restrict the development of rational economic activity, but above all the general character of its administrative practices. This is true in the following respects:

(a) Traditionalism places serious obstacles in the way of formally rational regulations, which can be depended upon to remain stable and hence are calculable in their economic implications and exploitability.

(b) A staff of officials with formal technical training is typically absent. The fact that such a class developed in the patrimonial states of the Western World is, as will be shown, accounted for by a set of very peculiar conditions. These were present only in this particular case and developed for the most part out of sources wholly different from the general structure of patrimonialism.

(c) There is a wide scope for actual arbitrariness and the expression of purely personal whims on the part of the chief and the members of his administrative staff. The opening for bribery and corruption, which is simply a matter of the disorganization of an unregulated system of fees, would be the least serious effect of this if it remained a constant quantity, because then it would become calculable in

practice. But it tends to be a matter which is settled from case to case with every individual official and is thus highly variable. If offices are leased, the incumbent is put in a position where it is to his immediate interest to get back the capital he has invested by any available means of extortion, however irrational.

(d) Running through patriarchalism and patrimonialism generally, there is an inherent tendency to substantive regulation of economic activity. This is derived from the character of the claim to legitimacy and the corresponding interest in the contentment of the subjects. Its effect is to break down the type of formal rationality which is oriented to a formally technical legal order. This type of influence is conspicuous, indeed decisive, in the case of the type of patrimonialism organized on a hierocratic basis. In the case of pure Sultanism, on the other hand, it is fiscal arbitrariness which is likely to be most important.

For all these reasons, under the dominance of a patrimonial regime only certain types of capitalism are able to develop. It leaves room for a certain amount of capitalistic mercantile trade, for capitalistic organization of tax farming, and the sale and lease of offices, for the provision of supplies for the state, the financing of wars and, under certain circumstances, capitalistic plantations and other colonial enterprises. All these forms are indigenous to patrimonial regimes and often reach a very high level of development. This is not, however, true of the type of profit-making enterprise with heavy investments in fixed capital and a rational organization of free labour which is oriented to the market purchases of private consumers. This is altogether too sensitive to all sorts of irrationalities in the administration of justice, in other forms of administrative practice, and in taxation. For these upset the basis of calculability.

The situation is fundamentally different only in cases where a patrimonial ruler, in the interest of his own power and financial provision, develops a rational system of administration with technically specialized officials. For this to happen, it is necessary in the first place that technical training should be available. Secondly, there must be a sufficiently powerful incentive to embark on such a policy. This is notably supplied by sharp competition between a plurality of patrimonial powers within the same cultural area. Finally, a very special factor is necessary, namely, the participation of urban communes as a financial support in the competition of the patrimonial units.

the egyptian pharoah

nine

The Memphite Theology

HENRI FRANKFORT

The Memphite Theology presents the religious teaching for Menes' new capital. It combines views which we can recognize as new, since they concern the new foundation; others which we suspect to be new because they run counter to common Egyptian beliefs and could hardly have gained acceptance if they had not been part of the great movement at the dawn of history. Other doctrines again seem to be rooted in Egyptian, or even African, traditions of the greatest antiquity.

The text is a cosmology: it describes the order of creation and makes the land of Egypt, as organized by Menes, an indissoluble part of that order. Ptah, the *genius loci,* to whom a temple south of the wall of Memphis had been dedicated, is proclaimed the Creator of All; and in an argument of astonishing boldness and profundity the intellectual advantages of monotheism are combined with the variety of recognized Egyptian gods. But these remarkable speculations (for which the text is famous) form only its middle part, our Section V, set in a treatise upon the place of

Reprinted from *Kingship and the Gods,* pp. 24–35, by permission of The University of Chicago Press. Copyright 1948 by The University of Chicago Press. [Footnotes and hieroglyphs omitted]

society in nature. It is characteristic of the Egyptian view of kingship that it should be clarified within such a context.

The document, in its present damaged state, suggests a division into six parts; there may have been more, or sections which now seem separate may originally have been joined together. It is exceptionally difficult to judge in this matter, since the text is not formally subdivided. The transition from our Section V to Section VI, for instance, shows that the literary construction is of the flimsiest; the text consists simply of a succession of statements (or, in the case of the related Mystery Play of the Succession, of scenes) which, from a formal point of view, are all equivalent and in no way subordinated to one another. As literary forms, these early texts are most primitive.

Section I is badly damaged, but the main themes are recognizable. On the one hand, the land of Egypt is proclaimed to have its being in the creator-god Ptah-Ta-Tjenen, Ptah "the Risen Land." On the other hand, reference is made to the appearance of a united country under one king. What is left of this section reads:

...Ptah, that is, this [land] named with the Great Name of Ta Tjenen....
He who unified this [land] has appeared as King of Upper Egypt and as King of Lower Egypt.

The succeeding sentence states that Atum, the sun-god-creator of common Egyptian beliefs, acknowledged that Ptah had created him and all the other gods. The significance of this phrase will become clear as we proceed.

The various references to "the land" have to be understood with some appreciation of that polyphony of meaning which the Egyptians loved. It means the country, Egypt, with all that it contains. But it also means the fertile soil, and as such it is one with the creator Ptah-Ta-Tjenen. The "Risen Land" possesses, again, a multiple significance. It alludes to the universal Egyptian belief that creation started with the emergence of a mound, the Primeval Hill, above the waters of chaos. Ptah, the fruitful earth, is one with this hill—the starting-point of all that is, even of life itself. But the epithet alludes, at the same time, to the land which Menes had reclaimed from the marsh waters to build Memphis and the temple of Ptah; and it furthermore alludes to the "Great Land," the name of the province of This, which, as we shall see, possessed some significance for the new theology.

Section II deals with the end of conflict which precedes the establishment of order both in the universe and in the state. The gods Horus and Seth, contending for the rulership of Egypt, are separated; and Geb, the earth-god, acts as arbiter. He first divides the country between the two, but he regrets this decision and rescinds it, giving the whole land to Horus. The two crowns of Upper and of Lower Egypt are now said to "grow" from the head of Horus; and Horus appears in the role of Menes (a role assumed by each king at his coronation) "uniting the lands" in his single rule. The Ennead, or nine gods, who assist, represent...a formula which expresses the relation between king and gods. The text is damaged at the beginning of this section:

...the Ennead gathered to him (Geb) and he separated Horus and Seth.... He prevented them from quarreling and installed Seth as Upper Egyptian king, in Upper Egypt, at the place where he was born, in *Su* (near Herakleopolis). And Geb put Horus as Lower Egyptian king in Lower Egypt, at the place where his father was drowned, at the "Half of the Two Lands" (probably near Memphis). And so Horus was in his place, and Seth was in his place; and they agreed with each other as regards the Two Lands in Ajan (opposite Cairo), which is the frontier (or separation) of the Two Lands....

It suited Geb's heart ill that the portion of Horus was like that of Seth, and so Geb gave his heritage (entirely) to Horus, that is, the son of his son, his eldest (literally, "his opener-of-the-body").

Geb calls Horus an "opener-of-the-body" with a reference to the fact that he was a firstborn son. Horus is then identified with the wolf-god, Upwaut, whose name means "Opener-of-the-Ways," and whose ensign is closely associated with Pharaoh at all great ceremonies, as we shall see....

The treatment of Horus in this text is remarkable. At the first division of the land, Seth goes to the place where he was born, but Horus to the place where his father was drowned. Horus, in contrast to Seth, seems to appear not as king in his own right but as the legitimate successor to his father Osiris. And, again, when Geb changes his mind and assigns the whole country to Horus, he justifies his act by acclaiming Horus as the eldest son of his predecessor. Horus assumes kingship over the Two Lands, not as conqueror, but as rightful heir. If we remember that this text was probably composed in the reign of Menes, a Horus king who had just conquered Egypt, we can gauge the relative importance, to the Egyptian mind, of historical and theological facts.

It is interesting that Geb acts as arbiter. He was doubly entitled to do so, as father of Osiris and as earth-god. In the first function he could act as head of the family with primitive, but universally acknowledged, authority. As god of the earth he was obviously concerned in a division of the land of Egypt. His successive decisions clearly represent the mythological form in which the whole complex of ideas involved in Menes' dual monarchy could be expressed: the fundamental view of a world in static equilibrium between conflicting forces (Horus and Seth); the kingship of Upper and Lower Egypt as the corresponding political form; and withal a rulership vested in the person of a single king.

The text, continuing, reasserts the relation between the land and Ptah—a relationship which was the subject of Section I also.

Horus stood (as king) over the land. And so became united this country named with its Great Name, Ta-Tjenen-who-is-to-the-south-of-his-wall, the Lord of Eternity.
The two "Great in Magic" (the crowns) grew out of his head. Thus it was that Horus appeared as King of Upper Egypt and as King of Lower Egypt who united the Two Lands in the province of The (White) Wall, at the place where the Two Lands are united.

Now follows a ritual act signifying the acquiescence of the two parts of Egypt in the union. The heraldic plants—sedge for Upper, papyrus for Lower, Egypt—are placed at the entrance of the temple of Ptah:

It happened that sedge and papyrus were put at the two outer gates of the temple of Ptah. That means: Horus and Seth, who bore with each other and united in fraternizing so that their quarrel is ended wherever they may be. They are united in the temple of Ptah, the "Balance of the Two Lands in which Upper Egypt and Lower Egypt have been weighed."

Section III is very much damaged. It seems that the text, after having established the succession of Horus as rightful heir, now turns to his predecessor, Osiris, and explains the relation of this god to Ptah and to the new capital. Too much is lost for us to judge this relationship. Memphis is said to derive its significance as the "granary" of Egypt from the fact that Osiris was buried there. This statement is repeated in Section VI, where it is better preserved.

Section IV deals with the construction of the royal castle at Memphis, mentioned just before as the place where Osiris was buried and important also as the seat of authority over the whole of Egypt established by Menes. But the text is too damaged to allow further comment.

Section V is the famous exposé of the sole creatorship of Ptah, a closely reasoned theological argument which reduces the gods of Egypt to aspects or manifestations of Ptah. We shall be better able to appreciate its meaning when our study has progressed further, but we may summarize it here. It is argued that everything that exists found its origin in the conceptions of Ptah's mind ("heart"), which were objectified by being pronounced by his "tongue." In this process of creation, one god after the other came into being; and through them Ptah evolved the visible and invisible universe and all living creatures, as well as justice, the arts, etc. This account imparts, at the same time, the character of an established order, valid for all time, to the phenomenal world. The cities and sanctuaries of Egypt are part of this order.

And the final phrase of the section closes the circle: while it had started by stating that the gods came forth from Ptah, objectified conceptions of his mind, it ends by making those gods "enter into their bodies" (statues) of all kinds of material—stone, metal, or wood—which had grown out of the earth, that is, out of Ptah.

The text starts with a series of eight equations in which the polytheism of Egypt is taken into account, but superimposed upon it is the novel thought of the ultimate oneness of the divine. The gods are declared to be manifestations of Ptah. The number eight is chosen in deference to a widely held view of creation which acknowledged the sun-god as creator but maintained at the same time that the sun had been brought forth from the waters of chaos by eight strange gods, who were no more than a conceptualizing of chaos, as their names (Darkness, Primeval Ocean, etc.) testify. Here, then, was a point where the Memphite Theology could build up a claim for Ptah as Creator; here were divinities older than the sun. Our text maintains that even these—in other words, chaos—were of the substance of Ptah, uncreated manifestations of his being. Thus the second of the eight equations runs: "Ptah—Nun the father who begat Atum." Nun is the primeval ocean from which Atum, the creator-sun, came forth. But Ptah is manifest in every god, hence in Atum: "Ptah—the Great One who is heart and tongue of the Ennead." The Great One stands for Atum, who created the Ennead of Heliopolis and who is called its heart and tongue because these are the organs of creation, according to the Memphite Theology. The epithet is no doubt given here because it throws the unique power of Ptah in bold relief: even Atum, generally worshiped as the creator of gods and cosmos, is but an emanation of Ptah.

The eight equations appear under a heading which reads: "The gods who came forth from Ptah"; they present the whole theology of the text as a formula. But the theory is then stated once more in the form of a narrative of creation. And there we can watch how the ancient Egyptian language—which, as an instrument of expression for a mentality tending toward the concrete, is ill equipped to frame abstract thoughts—is made the vehicle of some truly astonishing abstractions. The author expresses no less than the conviction that the basis of existence is spiritual: ideas conceived by the Creator and objectified by his utterances. The text expresses this by describing the "heart" and the "tongue" as the organs of creation. These terms are concrete enough. But we should misread our document completely if we took them at their face value. We know from numerous other texts that "heart" stands for "intellect," "mind," and even "spirit." The "tongue" is realizing thought; it translates concepts into actuality by means of "Hu"—authoritative utterance. We must, then, read these passages as the true Egyptian equivalent of John's "In the beginning was the Word, and the Word was with God, and the Word was God." The Egyptian mode of expression strikes us as clumsy because we assume involuntarily that a more abstract mode was available; but, of course, it was not.

(There) originated in the heart and on the tongue (of Ptah) (something) in the image of Atum.

Great and exalted is Ptah who bequeathed his power to all the gods and their Ka's through his heart and on his tongue. . . .

It happened that heart and tongue prevailed over (all other) members, considering that he (Ptah) is (as heart) in every body, (as tongue) in every mouth, of all gods, people, beasts, crawling creatures, and whatever else lives, while he thinks (as heart) and commands (as tongue) everything that he wishes. . . .

Every divine word came into being through that which was thought by the heart and commanded by the tongue.

And thus the Ka's were made and the Hemsut were created—they that make all sustenance and all food—by this speech (that was thought by the heart and was spoken by the tongue).

(And so justice is done to him) who does what is liked, (and evil is done to him) who does what is hated.

And so life is given to the peaceful, death to the criminal.

And so are done all labor and all arts, the action of the arms, the going of legs, the movement of all members according to this command which was thought by the heart and issued from the tongue and which constitutes the significance of all things.

Here we find, then, expressed in a most refractory medium, a statement proclaiming the unity of the divine, its spiritual character, and its immanence in living nature.

We have omitted a theological argument which once again establishes that the thought and utterance of Ptah underlies Atum's work of creation, and a similar assertion follows the lines we have quoted. After that we read: "And so Ptah rested (or was satisfied) after he had made all things and all divine words." It has been argued that these "divine words" really stood for a "divine order" in which "all things" found their appropriate places. The expression would rather seem once more to emphasize Ptah's peculiar process of creation through utterance of thought. For such "creative speech" turns each divine word into the *causa materialis, causa formalis,* and *causa movens* of an element of creation—all in one.

It is true, however, that the text describes how Ptah established a cer-

tain order. Our quotation explained that gods and other living beings, nay, their very life and the mechanics of their life, derived from Ptah's action as a demiurge. And the text continues by ascribing to him the establishment of the religious order of the land, namely, the local cults and all their peculiarities down to the very shapes in which the gods were worshiped; for their statues were made by Ptah and that from material "grown" upon him as earth-god.

He created the (local) gods, he made the cities, he founded the provincial divisions; he put the gods in their places of worship, he fixed their offerings, he founded their chapels. He made their bodies resemble that which pleased their hearts (i.e., the forms in which they wished to be manifest). And so the gods entered into their bodies of every kind of wood, of every kind of stone, of every kind of clay, of every kind of thing which grows upon him, in which they have taken form. Thus all the gods and their Ka's are at one with him, content and united with the Lord of the Two Lands.

The diversified cults of all Egypt appear here as sanctioned by, or even due to, the initiative of the god of the united country. Our text thus imparts unity of a sort even to them.

Section VI continues to elaborate the close connection between the god and the land of Egypt by speaking about Memphis, the site of the temple of Ptah and the new capital of the country. Memphis is said to have a special significance for the "sustenance" of Egypt, and this fact is explained by the presence on its soil of the interred body of Osiris. The text acknowledges that Osiris had not always been connected with Memphis. He reached the city in the water of the Nile. Like the later myth, it speaks of Osiris' drowning, after which his body was drawn ashore by Isis and Nephthys. But the word "drowning" has connotations in connection with this god to which the straightforward translation cannot do justice. The paradox of Osiris consists precisely in this—that in death the god becomes a center of vitalizing force. Hence the Nile, and especially the Nile in flood, counts as a manifestation of him. Osiris' connection with the river is not, therefore, rendered adequately by the statement that he was destroyed by the water—that he was drowned. The god was in the waters, and we have translated the verb here "to float." The notion that the god is the active force in, the beneficial influence of, the inundation can be expressed with the concreteness requisite in myth only by describing the anthropomorphic figure of Osiris as floating or submerged, "drowned," in the river; the "finding" of Osiris, which our text describes as the recovery of his body by Isis and Nephthys, is represented in the ritual by the lifting-up of a jar of fresh Nile water. The statement that Osiris was buried at the new capital proclaimed it the center from which the vitalizing forces radiated. Hence Memphis could be said to be the "granary... where the sustenance of the Two Lands is taken care of."

Since the text acknowledges explicitly that Osiris was not at home at Memphis, one may ask whence he "reached" that city. We are inclined to think of Abydos, contrary to current opinion. We shall consider the claims of Abydos in detail below, but we may ask here why the god should be related to the capital founded by Menes at the apex of the Delta. It would seem, as we shall see, that Osiris was the dead ancestor of the kings of Menes' line, and the significance of dead kings—in ancient Egypt as in modern Africa—was so great that no blessing could rest upon the transference of the royal residence from the Thinite nome, in which Abydos is situated, unless the ancestral figure of Osiris was brought into a definite relationship with the new site. The Nile, in which Osiris was manifest and which streamed past Memphis as past Abydos, offered a means of creating a relationship that was expressed mythologically in the story of the rescue of Osiris' body from the waters.

The Memphite Theology, like the myth, ascribes the actual rescue to Isis and Nephthys; but the Theology, in contrast with the myth, insists that the goddesses acted on the orders of Horus. It agrees in this with the pyramid texts where Horus, the living king, appears as the instigator of all acts benefiting Osiris, his late predecessor.

The text continues by describing the fate of Osiris after burial. His is a twofold destiny: he joins the sun-god in his daily circuit, but he also joins "the Court of Ptah-Ta-Tjenen," who must dwell where Ptah is god, within the earth. In fact, he "becomes earth." This is the crucial phrase in this section, since it explains (as it did also in Sec. III) the extraordinary fertility of the region of Memphis where Osiris is buried. Immediately after the interment of Osiris comes the statement that Horus ascended the throne; and with this the text ends. This section reads:

Granary of the god (Ptah-Ta-Tjenen) was the Great Throne (Memphis) which rejoices the hearts of the gods who are in the temple of Ptah, Mistress of Life (epithet of temple), where the sustenance of the Two Lands is taken care of, because Osiris floated in his water. Isis and Nephthys perceived it. They saw him and were aghast. But Horus ordered Isis and Nephthys to grasp Osiris without delay and to prevent him from floating away. They turned their heads in time, and thus they let him reach land.

He entered the Secret Gates (of the Netherworld?), the glory of the Lords of Eternity (the dead), in step with Him who shines in the Horizon (the sun), on the path of Re, in the Great Throne (Memphis).

He joined the court and fraternized with the gods of Ta-Tjenen, Ptah, Lord of Years.

Thus Osiris became earth in the Royal Castle on the north side of this land which he had reached. His son Horus appeared as king of Upper Egypt and as king of Lower Egypt in the arms of his father Osiris in the presence of the gods that were before him and that were behind him.

If we now consider the Memphite Theology as a whole, the most remarkable feature, besides its spiritual view of creation, is the manner in which reality and mythology are intermingled. It is true that all the personages are gods; but we have already seen in our Introduction that Egyptian art presents Pharaoh consistently as a deity, and we shall presently deal with similar inscriptional evidence. In Section II the gods Horus and Seth are contending, but the subject of their quarrel is dominion over Egypt; and we have seen that Pharaoh is occasionally called "Horus-and-Seth" to indicate that his rule marks the end of discord. Section V, the account of creation, ends by assigning to the Creator the kingly title "Lord of the Two Lands," while the concluding Section VI is explicitly concerned with the capital, Memphis, and with the myth of Osiris. The locale of the action is, in fact, not mythological but real. It is Memphis, and, more precisely, the royal castle, the newly established seat of authority for the united country, which is the place where Osiris is interred; and the figure of Osiris is not exclusively at home in mythology either. Each king, at death, becomes Osiris, just as each king, in life, appears "on the throne of Horus"; each king *is* Horus. It is then possible that the Horus who appears at the end of the text as king of Egypt in the arms of his father Osiris (though the latter is dead and buried) is not only the god but also the king; rather, it is the royal succession as it appears upon the superhuman plane which is here referred to, and the question whether Horus and Osiris are here gods or kings is, for the Egyptian, meaningless. These gods are the late king and his successor; these kings are those gods.

There is unequivocal evidence that this is so. The embrace of Horus and the dead Osiris, with which our text ends, is realized by a ritual in the Mystery Play of the Succession; here the new king acts in person, and the burial of his father is performed in effigy. The embrace is a true communion of spirits, involving the actual ruler and his deceased predecessor in a rite performed at the accession of each new king; in the same way it appears, timeless, in the Memphite Theology involving the gods Horus and Osiris. Better than any other feature of Egyptian kingship, it shows that the monarchy was conceived as a reality in the world of the gods no less than in the world of men.

It is for this reason that we find a theory of kingship implied in a cosmological text. Nature itself could not be conceived without the king of Egypt. The Memphite Theology shows this specifically; it demonstrates that the dual monarchy, centered in Memphis, realized a divine plan. The order of society as established by Menes is presented as part of the cosmic order.

Let us, then, consider of what the Egyptian theory of kingship consists. One proposition, that the king is divine, we have mentioned already. The other proposition is even more remarkable. It is clearly indicated that kingship is conceived in its profoundest aspect, on the plane of the gods, as involving two generations.

We have seen, in commenting upon the second section of the Theology, that Horus is acknowledged by the assembled gods, through Geb, not because he possesses greater power than Seth, but solely because he is the eldest son of Osiris and the legitimate heir. And in the final phrases of the text we found again that Horus and Osiris are inseparable, even at the moment when Horus appears as the ruler of Egypt, after the burial of his father. It seems that the actual occupancy of the throne creates a fusion of the powers of the late king and his successor.

This view is peculiarly Egyptian, though it is not unconnected with the more widely held belief that the king is divine. It is, therefore, important to determine the relation of the two propositions which make up the Egyptian theory of kingship.

The basic view, namely that rulership implies characteristics denied to the common man, is a conventional one. In primitive societies, and among them many in East Africa, the chieftain is also the medicine man or magician; in other words, he is believed to entertain closer relationship with the powers in nature than other men. The African "rain-maker-king" is a well-known example of this type of ruler. Of the Dinka tribe it is said: "A rainmaker is buried in a cattle byre, which continues to be used (as was the royal castle of Memphis where Osiris was buried)....He is said to take the food of the community into the grave, so when the next season arrives a hole is dug at the side of the byre so that the food may come out again." And of the Komde: "The health of the...[Chungu] (chieftain) and the welfare of the whole community were inseparably bound up together. A Chungu in health and vigour meant a land yielding its fruits, rain coming in its season, evil averted." Much farther to the west the king of Jukun is addressed as "*Azaiwo* (our guinea corn), *Afyewo* (our ground nuts), *Asoiwo* (our beans)....The king of Jukun is therefore able to control the rain and winds. A succession of droughts or bad harvests is ascribed to his negligence or to the waning of his strength, and he is accordingly secretly strangled." We insist on this widespread aspect of kingship in Africa to indicate the premises upon which Menes' position rested. We know that King Scorpion, who probably preceded Menes, was considered an incarnation of the god Horus; we may then assume for the predynastic period the belief that the chieftains were charged with the power of divinity. The unification increased the significance of kingship; it did not destroy any of its aspects. The superhuman associations remained valid. The uncertain services which the medicine man had given to the community became institutionalized. Kingship in Egypt remained the channel through which the powers of nature flowed into the body politic to bring human endeavor to fruition.

Now this view of kingship entailed, furthermore, two generations. If the living ruler is the intermediary between men and nature, his potency continues to profit the community even after his death. This belief is, again, widespread. The dead rulers of Uganda continue to give audiences and to advise their people through oracles. Other tribes, too, seek advice at the tombs of their dead rulers in times of perplexity and do not bury them before the succession is regulated. The Kizibu know of a supreme god but actually worship the spirit of an ancient king who now rules the dead. Nyakang, the dead ruler of the Shilluk, plays a much greater part in their religious life than the supreme deity Juok and sends them rain and crops. We have just seen that the rainmaker of the Dinka is supposed to take the food of the people with him in death. In Egypt the power of the buried king was seen to break forth from the earth in which he rested: plants sprouting, Nile waters flooding the banks, the moon and Orion rising from the horizon—all were manifestations of his vital power. But it is at this point that we leave the sphere of universal primitive thought for that of peculiarly Egyptian conceptions. In Egypt the dead kings were represented by a single divine figure; each one, at death, became the chthonic god Osiris, manifest in the various phenomena which come forth from the earth after apparent death. Hence the succession of earthy rulers assumed an unchanging mythological form, Horus succeeding Osiris, at each new succession, forever.

The tendency to interpret changes in unchanging mythological terms is strong in Egypt. We have found it necessary to point this out when describing Egyptian art. We have also met it in the motif of the contending gods, Horus and Seth, who stand for all conflict and strife in nature and the state, with Horus victorious in a stable equilibrium of opposing powers. The Egyptians viewed the world as essentially static. The incidents of history, therefore, lacked ultimate reality. It is true that kings died and that one ruler succeeded another, but this merely proved to the Egyptian that the essential quality of kingship could not be the *praesens,* "this king rules"; it had to be the *perfectum,* "this king has ascended the throne," or, in mythological terms, "Horus has succeeded Osiris." Throughout Egyptian history the texts reflect a curious mood of recent achievement: "the land *has been* united; discord *has been* terminated; the king *has ascended* the throne; he *has placed* truth in the place of falsehood."

It is on this very note that the Memphite Theology ends. The concluding phrases which show Horus in the embrace of his father, though the latter is buried and has become earth, show that death does not destroy the kings. There is a mystic communion between father and son at the moment of succession, a unity and continuity of divine power which suggests a stream in which the individual rulers come and go like waves.

The King's Person: Horus

HENRI FRANKFORT

Horus, The Great God, Lord of Heaven

Pharaoh is Horus, and of this god little enough is known. His symbol is the falcon, but we do not know whether the bird was thought in some way to be merely the god's manifestation; whether the god was embodied, temporarily or permanently, in a single bird or in the species as a whole; or whether the falcon was used as a sign referring to a much more intangible divinity. The latter possibility does not exclude the others, and modern parallels suggest, as we shall see, that we must not expect a rigid doctrine on matters of this type but rather a fluid belief of interrelationship which may assume almost any specific form.

Horus is generally called "the Great God, the Lord of Heaven"; and texts call up a strangely compelling image. The bird has acquired gigantic proportions, as in a vision. His outstretched wings are the sky, his fierce eyes sun and moon. The speckled breast of the falcon is seen when, toward evening, the clear Egyptian sky becomes spotted with feathery clouds. And since these share the glories of sunrise and sunset, Horus is called "feathered in many hues." He is also called "wide breasted"; and the winds, especially the north wind, are his breath. This image is obviously of great antiquity, but it casts its spell throughout Egyptian history. The New Kingdom still uses it: "Thou art

Reprinted from *Kingship and the Gods,* pp. 37–44.

the god who came first into being when no (other) god had yet come into existence, when no name of any thing had yet been proclaimed. When thou openest thine eyes so as to see, it becomes light for everyone." In Ptolemaic times the god is still addressed as "the venerable bird in whose shadow is the wide earth; Lord of the Two Lands under whose wings is the circuit of heaven; the falcon radiating light from his eyes."

This visionary conception of Horus is not found in pictorial art. For art requires definiteness. It cannot well render the allusions and associations of language, poetry, and the poetical intuitions of the popular mind. Once, however, in the formative phase of Egyptian culture when experiments were common, the sky was rendered as the outspread wings of the great god. The design is instructive. In the first place, we find already here, on a simple ivory comb belonging to a courtier of the First Dynasty, a completely symbolical design including standard motifs of classical Egyptian art. The great wings which render the sky span the distance between, and seem supported by, two verticals which have the shape of the *was* scepter, denoting "welfare." In the Old Kingdom a similar combination sometimes frames the name of the king. The sky symbol above is then the hieroglyph *pet;* and below we find the double-headed hieroglyph of the earth-god Akeru, a feature absent on the older comb.

The Old Kingdom design is relevant to our subject. It proclaims that the ruler acts within a harmony between heaven and earth, which means welfare. The design alludes at the same time to a well-known epithet of the king, "Lord of that which the sun encircles." The wings of heaven and the *was* scepters on the comb form so curious a combination that we must assume them to express the same thought as the more complete Old Kingdom framework, and that the more so since the comb, too, shows the king's name inclosed by the design. It is written with a snake and set in a panel crowned by the falcon. . . . On the comb the god Horus is thus represented a second time, first as the Lord of Heaven whose outspread wings are the sky, and second as incarnate in the king named in the panel. He appears a third time, in the boat above the wings, as the sun sailing across the sky. As such he is known from the First Dynasty to Greek times as "Harakhte," Horus of the "Horizon" or of the "Land of Sunrise." In the clumsy parlance of modern science we say that Horus was a sun-god as well as a sky-god; and we often forget that the spurious precision of such terms may effectively preclude an understanding of their true significance and suggest inconsistencies which are of our own making. Since Horus was a god of heaven, the most powerful object in the sky, the sun, was naturally considered a manifestation of his power.

Later art used a more compact formula to express the association of Horus with both sky and sun. It is the winged sun disk, in which the wings stand for the expanse of the sky, as on the First Dynasty comb. When the god Harakhte is depicted, he appears as a falcon or a falcon-headed man crowned by the sun disk.

The association of Horus with the sun is subsidiary to the notion of the sky-god. That follows from the prevalence and persistence of the imagery which we have discussed. The god's name seems suitable for a sky-god. "Horus" does not mean "the falcon"; the bird is called *bik,* and there are various other names for the falcon standards and symbols. Horus (*Hrw*) seems to mean "the distant one."

The king is an embodiment of this god. The epithet of Horus, "the Great God," appears also with the names of the kings in the Fourth and Fifth Dynasties—Snefru, Khufu (Cheops), and Sahure. Even Pepi I is called, on his coffin, "The Great God, Lord of the Horizon," and also "Horus of the Horizon, Lord of Heaven." In the tombs the dead call themselves "honored before the Great God," meaning the dead king. They also write in their tombs texts like the following: "Any noble, any official, or any man who may destroy any stone or any brick in this my tomb, I will be judged with him by the Great God." It has been shown that this judgment took place in the Hereafter; yet the Great God is here, too, the king, who remained the leader upon whom the subjects continued to depend when they had joined him in death. With the decline of the prestige of royalty in the troubles which actually destroyed the Old Kingdom, the epithet "Great God" was replaced by "Good God" when texts referred to the living ruler. And in the funerary texts the "Great God" envisaged was no longer the individual but the mythological aspect of each dead king—Osiris, who became "The Great God, Lord of the West."

It remains to explain why it should have been Horus who was thought to be incarnate in the king. It is assumed by most authors (with total disregard of the religious nature of the problem) that the explanation is political, namely, that the House of Menes derived from a region worshiping the falcon-god. It is true that the city of Nekhen-Hierakonpolis, within the state of the pre-Menite chieftains, was a center of Horus worship. It is also true that in different localities differing manifestations of divine power received the main share of the people's devotion. But these so-called "local gods" were not necessarily unknown outside their chief centers of worship, nor were they all equals in the estimation of the Egyptians. If Horus, in preference to a dozen or more Upper Egyptian gods, came to be looked upon as the animating spirit of the ruler of Egypt, it was because Horus was widely recognized as a supreme god. We should expect as much on the strength of the impressive image in which he was conceived. But there is more tangible evidence, too. The symbol of Horus, the falcon on its perch, may serve in the pyramid texts for the notion "god" in general, or follow, as a determinative, the name of any deity. Horus, apparently, was the god par excellence. It has even been maintained that the epithet *netjer aa*, "the Great God," which pertains to Horus preeminently, really means "the greatest god." Finally, falcon-gods were worshiped throughout Egypt; and, though it is usual to treat these as "local gods" of independent origin and nature, it is at least as probable that they were predynastic differentiations of one and the same deity who had been worshiped as supreme by the ancestral Egyptians.

Horus, Son of Osiris

Pharaoh, then, is an incarnation of Horus the Great(est) God, Lord of Heaven. But the Memphite Theology describes how Horus, son of Osiris, ascends the throne. The question arises, therefore, whether these two gods with the same name may or may not be one.

It seems difficult, at first sight, to bring the elusive and somewhat uncanny "Horus feathered in many hues" within the family group of the Osiris cycle. The figures of Osiris, Isis, and Horus and their adventures, as told in the myth, would fit any folk tale. But this very fact should make us suspicious. Gods so strikingly human are without parallel in Egypt, and we are probably misled by the tradition that preserved their story. The fullest account derives from Plutarch, and the purely human characteristics of the main figures may be due to the enlightened age in which he wrote. The older Egyptian sources suggest, indeed, that this is so. It is true that they nowhere add up to a complete version of the myth. But the reliefs and the texts agree in giving to the members of the cycle that admixture of animal features which characterizes most Egyptian gods. Seth, the murderer, is almost always rendered by his enigmatical animal or as an animal-headed god. Horus appears with equal regularity as a falcon-headed man. A relief in Seti I's temple at Abydos shows Isis as a falcon-like bird hovering over the prostrate body of Osiris, which, as the myth records, she succeeded in reviving for the posthumous conception of his son Horus. This pictorial tradition survived in Ptolemaic times; it was also put into words, and that already in the Eighteenth Dynasty. In a hymn to Osiris it is said that Isis "made shadow with her feathers and made an air current with her wings." She "erected the tiredness of the powerless one" and conceived. In the tomb of Queen Nefertari of the Nineteenth Dynasty, Isis and Nephthys are shown on either side of the bier as falcons or kites wearing the hieroglyphs of their names upon their heads. But the birdlike characteristics of the personages of the Osiris myth are not a late development and would, in fact, be inexplicable as such. Already in the pyramid texts, and also in later tombs, Isis and Nephthys bewailing Osiris are often called "The Two Kites"; the comparison was no doubt furthered by the shrill plaintive cries which the kite, *Falco milvus,* utters when circling aloft; but this poetic fantasy cannot account for the other instances just quoted. We shall see presently that Isis has originially nothing to do with the falcon. Horus, even when adoring Osiris, appears as a falcon-headed man. It seems, then, that the falcon Horus, god of the sky, is the same as Horus, son of Osiris, and that Isis, and occasionally Nephthys, received their birdlike characteristics through their relation to Horus.

Another feature of the Egyptian (as contrasted with the Greek) texts supports this view. In the conflict with Seth, Horus temporarily loses his eye, or is said to be wounded in the eye. This episode is always referred to Horus, son of Osiris; and the conflict, though it has a most general significance, is indeed most often referred to in connection with the succession to Osiris' kingship. Yet the story is relevant to Horus the heavenly falcon whose eyes were the sun and moon. We find, in fact, that the waning moon counts as Horus' ailing eye and that the sun is attacked by clouds and thunderstorms which are a manifestation of Seth. It is therefore a mistake to separate "Horus, the Great God, Lord of Heaven," from "Horus, son of Osiris," or to explain their identity as due to syncretism in comparatively late times. The two gods "Horus" whose titles we have set side by side are, in reality, one and the same. Their identity is also confirmed by an important pyramid text which addresses the king as follows: "Thou art Horus, son of Osiris, the eldest god, son of Hathor." The mother of Horus, son of Osiris, is Isis. The name of Hathor means "House of Horus" and refers, with obvious imagery, to her motherhood. But *her* son is Horus, Lord of Heaven. And Osiris is never the husband of Hathor.

Seeing inconsistencies in texts like the one we have just quoted means ignoring a very fundamental fact. Religious teachings are attempts to put into the conceptual form of language notions which cannot be entirely rationalized—"truths" which are sensed rather than known. The function of the king as the intermediary between humanity and the powers in nature is one of these notions which can be adumbrated but not adequately formulated in words.

Our own language disposes of many means of expression which are either totally lacking in ancient Egyptian or very poorly represented. Abstract nouns, adverbs, and conjunctions which enable us to modulate meaning were relatively little used by the Egyptian. His mind tended toward the concrete; his language depended upon concrete images and therefore expressed the irrational, not by qualifying modifications of a principal notion, but by admitting the validity of several avenues of approach at one and the same time. The king is the "sky-god" Horus; he is also Horus the son of his predecessor who had become Osiris at the moment of his death. The latter identification—Horus, son of Osiris—is appropriate when the king is considered in connection with his father, as heir in the legitimate line, as the incumbent of a royalty which involved...two generations. But, when the avenue of approach is not the king's place in the succession, or his relationship with the ancestral spirits, or the continuity of kingship;

when, on the contrary, the king is considered in the fulness of his power—then he is Horus, the Great God.

The two viewpoints corresponding to "Horus, son of Osiris," and "Horus, the Great God," do not exhaust the possible avenues of approach to kingship. In polytheism the interrelations require definition. The king, even as the god Horus, must be brought in relation to other deities. Here, again, the scheme of father and son is applied; and, wherever there is a local cult, the king appears as the son of the deity. It has been thought that this relationship represents a generalization of the scheme Horus-Osiris. This view is erroneous. The king is the son of Osiris, because Osiris is the deceased ruler who was normally the father of his successor. The relationship Horus-Osiris has its foundation in the physical fact of fatherhood viewed in the mythological context which we have discussed. In connection with the other gods the sonship of the king expresses a relationship of intimacy, dependence, and piety; but it is not exclusive. In other words, it is possible to find that two male gods, Atum and Monthu, address King Seti I as "our beloved son"; and Ramses II returns from the Battle of Kadesh to be greeted by the assembled gods with the words: "Welcome beloved son of ours!" Similarly, Tuthmosis III appears as son of Atum at Medinet Habu, as son of Re at Amada, as son of Dedun at Semneh, as son of Amon, Ptah, and Hathor at Karnak. All such phrases, but especially the common "Son of Re," are subject to considerable elaboration on occasion. King Piankhi is made to say in reference to Re: "I am he who was fashioned in the womb and created in the divine egg, the seed of the god being in me. By

his Ka there is nothing which I shall do without him; it is he who commands me to do it."

Such texts accentuate, again, the difference between the designations "Son of Re" and "Son of Osiris." The term "Son of Re" establishes a relationship with the sun-god which is equivalent to the designation Horus in that it stresses the divine nature of the king, although it does not claim identity with the god; it emphasizes that Pharaoh, "on the throne of Atum," is a distant successor of the Creator and the champion of the created order. It is significant that the epithet "Son of Re" in the titulary precedes the *nomen,* the name given at birth. The combination indicated that the prince who had been known by this name up to the coronation had been recognized as the son of the Creator and therefore possessed the essential nature of a ruler.

As the king could be proclaimed the son of various gods to express a relation of dependence and intimacy, so all goddesses could be addressed as his mother. But this consideration does not dispose of the problem presented by the pyramid text quoted above: "Thou art Horus, son of Osiris, the eldest god, son of Hathor." As we have said already, Osiris is never the husband of Hathor; and Hathor is not the mother of Horus, son of Osiris.

In the myth Osiris begets Horus on Isis, his sister and wife. Since the king's father and predecessor becomes Osiris at his death, we should expect the queen-mother to be Isis. This, however, is not the case, or rather, when in late texts it does occur, it is either part of a series of identifications of goddesses with the queen or a mere literary figure. It plays no part in any of the ceremonials of kingship and is thereby shown not to be a religious reality at all—this is in striking contrast to the transfiguration of the dead king Osiris.

If, then, the queen-mother does not count as Isis, we must ask what Isis stands for. Her name gives us a clue. It suggests that Isis was originally the deified throne. This at first startling solution has a considerable amount of evidence to support it. Ceremonial objects are very likely to become personified in Egypt. We know, for instance, that sacrifices of food and drink were offered to a standard of the god Amon. We also have hymns addressed to the king's crowns. The throne is shown by various expressions which have become established to have been an object of veneration in Egypt in early times. We have seen that Memphis was called "The Great Throne" in the Memphite Theology. The capital of a western Delta state, which the Greeks called Buto, was "Pe" in Egyptian—a word meaning seat, stool, or throne. Amon-Re was called "Lord of the Thrones of the Two Lands who commands in Karnak." Dominion over the earth is expressed by the phrase "the thrones of Geb." Among the Shilluk of the upper Nile, who retain many traits recalling Egyptian usages and beliefs, the king becomes charged with the supernatural power of royalty by being enthroned on the sacred stool which normally supports the fetish Nyakang, who, like Osiris, is both a god and the ancestor of the new monarch. In Egypt, too, the central ceremony of the accession took place when the ruler was enthroned and received the diadems and scepters. Thus the Egyptian might well refer to the throne, which had received a prince who arose king, as the ruler's "mother." In the same way a pyramid text states that the dead king goes to heaven to sit upon the "great throne which made the gods."

The myth of Osiris and Seth, Isis and Horus, which presents religious conceptions in the guise of a narrative, described Isis as the embodiment of marital devotion and motherly love, thus laying the foundation for the widespread veneration she found throughout the Roman Empire. But she lacks distinctive attributes when she is depicted, perhaps as a result of her origin. Like all personifications, she appears in human shape; but she wears on her head cow's horns borrowed from Hathor. In later times the two goddesses are often treated as one because both found their principal function in motherhood. But in relation to the king, Isis and Hathor remained distinct. When the emphasis was laid on his divinity per se, the king was Horus, son of Hathor, suckled by the divine cow called Sekhat-Hor, "She who remembers Horus." But, viewed as the heir and successor in the royal line, the king was the son of Osiris, borne by the throne, Isis, who is therefore called his mother in this context. This significance of the title "son of Isis," which occurs already in the First Dynasty, is very clearly defined in a text of Ramses IV: "I am a legitimate ruler, not an usurper, for I occupy the place of my sire, as the son of Isis, since I have appeared as king on the throne of Horus."

Pharaoh's human mother does not seem to have played any part in the theology of kingship. She was no more than the vehicle of the incarnation. The succession of one of her sons proved that particular son—generally the eldest—to have been divine, "powerful in the egg" or "ruling in the egg," or, in other words, qualified to rule, since a god had begotten him. For, in contrast with physical motherhood, physical fatherhood was a subject of theological speculation. It was normally viewed as an element in the perennial truth that Horus succeeded Osiris. But we know of rulers of the New Kingdom who stressed their affiliation with the god Amon-Re, possibly because their claim to the throne was irregular. We have seen that the king counted as the son of Re. Hence we find reliefs in New Kingdom temples in which it is shown that Amon-Re embodied himself in the king and thus visited the queen to beget a successor.

two aspects of the feudal period in ancient egypt

ten

The Question of Feudal Institutions in Ancient Egypt

WILLIAM F. EDGERTON

The Old Kingdom and the First Intermediate Period

In theory, at all times, the Egyptian king was a god, ordained by the greater gods to rule over mankind. His expressed will not merely had the force of law; it *was* the law. No other human source of legislation was acknowledged in Pharaonic Egypt.

In the Fourth Dynasty reality corresponded rather closely to this theory, or so it seems. The government was an autocratic bureaucracy headed by the king. A single official, the vizier, probably exercised supreme administrative and judicial authority under the king throughout the kingdom. Territorially the kingdom was divided into a number of administrative districts called nomes (perhaps twenty-two in Upper Egypt and twenty in Lower Egypt; complete lists are not available before the Ptolemaic period). Many nomes were derived from independent states of great antiquity. They were governed by

Reprinted from Rushton Coulborn, ed., *Feudalism in History* (Princeton, N.J., 1956), pp. 121–26, by permission of the Princeton University Press; copyright 1956 by the Princeton University Press. [Footnotes omitted]

nomarchs, royal appointees whose highest ambitions in this period were concerned with the central administration and the royal court rather than with their particular nomes. Administratively the central government was organized in a number of departments each of which doubtless functioned throughout the country; to what extent the nome administrations may have been similarly organized is not known. There is evidence tending to show that officials whose work pleased the king were freely moved from job to job. Princes of the royal house often held the highest offices; with this exception, some Egyptologists believe that birth was of little importance, though I personally am skeptical of this proposition. (The view of Junker, that descendants of kings filled the majority of public offices, depends in part on the precise interpretation of an obscure title, *rh-nyśwt*, which may mean perhaps "descendant of a king" or perhaps merely "acquaintance of the king.")

By making and maintaining canals and dikes throughout the country, the government regulated the intake and discharge of the Nile flood. Such regulation has always been, and is today, the indispensable prerequisite for decent living conditions in Egypt.

Irrigation and drainage consume a very large part of the total labor force which is or can be usefully employed in Egyptian agriculture. The task cannot be effectively performed on a purely local basis. Hence, the difference in terms of human well-being between a strongly unified kingdom and a congeries of mutually hostile localities is immensely greater in Egypt than in most parts of the world. Hence also, the government must exercise effective control over a large labor force. The compulsory labor of his subjects constituted an important part of the king's income, in the Old Kingdom as in most later periods. Another important part of his income was the right of his officials to requisition accommodations and materials of various kinds when traveling on the king's business. Perhaps the most important part of his revenue may have been derived from the royal domains: it is believed that these were partly managed directly by the king's salaried officials and partly farmed out on lease. I personally do not doubt that he also collected taxes on lands held by the temple and tomb endowments and by private individuals, but almost nothing can be stated with absolute certainty regarding land taxes in Egypt before Alexander.

The supreme task of government in the Fourth Dynasty was the erection of the king's pyramid, and in general the provision of those material benefits which would insure eternal blessedness for the king and for those about him. By the king's favor, the high officials of the kingdom built their tombs close around his pyramid so that they would be closely associated with him in the hereafter as they had been on earth. Expensive tombs remote from the capital are extremely rare before the Fifth Dynasty.

Kings and officials endeavored to endow their tombs in perpetuity. Such an endowment might include lands, cattle, and "people" (serfs or slaves?). It might also include income consisting of future offerings which were first to be presented but not consumed at the temple of some god or at the tomb of some exalted personage of an earlier generation. The endowment was to be administered by a "soul-servant" or a group of such; a man's soul-servants might or might not be his own descendants. Such endowments were sometimes gifts of the king, and sometimes erected by the tomb-owner out of his private property. The "god-servants" (priests) who maintained the divine service in temples were supported by similar endowments.

In these two cases, therefore (soul-servants and god-servants), there was a direct connection between the tenure of lands and other property and the rendering of stated services. In neither of the two cases was the ostensible recipient of the services a living human being. Probably the recipient (the god, or the deceased tomb-owner) was the owner of the endowment in Egyptian legal theory, but it is also probable that the individual god-servant or soul-servant could effectively dispose of his individual rights and duties, at least by testament. In the Middle Kingdom and later, priestly offices were bought and sold like any other kind of property, but we do not know whether this was true in the Old Kingdom.

The reigning king paid his officials partly by stipends of food, drink, clothing, etc., and partly by donations of lands. We have no evidence to suggest that continuing ownership of land so donated depended in any way on continuing service; on the contrary, it is the current belief of Egyptologists that the holder and his heirs could keep such lands indefinitely, and I am one of those who suppose that such lands could also be freely sold. The progressive impoverishment of the royal government through the cumulative effect of donations of land to officials, to temples, and to mortuary endowments, is believed to have been one of the principal causes of the collapse of the Old Kingdom. Even at the beginning of the Fourth Dynasty (the earliest period for which relevant information is available) some lands could be bought, sold, and bequeathed.

The Fifth and Sixth Dynasties are characterized by progressive governmental decentralization. Nomarchs, instead of being freely shifted from one nome to another, became permanently attached to their individual nomes and made their tombs there. A new office, "governor of Upper Egypt," came between the Upper Egyptian nomarchs and the vizier: this office may have been created to keep the nomarchs from becoming independent, but the nomarchs continued to grow increasingly independent. At some times several different nomarchs were simultaneously "governors of Upper Egypt," each functioning in a limited number of nomes. Offices tended to become hereditary (a condition always desired by the officials themselves). By the end of the Sixth Dynasty the nomarch was usually chief priest in the principal temple of the nome. A nomarch who inherited the highest civil (administrative and judicial) and the highest priestly offices in his nome together with important landed estates was obviously in a position to take advantage of any weakness which might appear in the central government.

A practice which surely contributed to the collapse of the Old Kingdom was the granting of "immunities" from forced labor and from other exactions which might be imposed by royal officials or by other powerful or influential persons. A number of such grants have come down to us, issued by kings of the Fifth, Sixth, and Eighth Dynasties in favor of various temples and mortuary endowments. Some such grants actually forbid agents of the government to enter lands of the privileged temple. By the time of Pepi II (late Sixth Dynasty) the granting of immunities had attained such proportions that the king had to authorize certain officials on certain occasions to requisition what they needed from towns, temples, etc., "without allowing any immunity." The next step was to issue new grants of immunity, taking cognizance of the commissions "without allowing any immunity," and specifying that even such commissions should be void against the new immunities now granted. We are dependent on our imaginations for the consequences of this double contradiction. . . .

The Sixth Dynasty was followed by a period of disorganization known to Egyptologists as the First Intermediate Period. A horde of Asiatics overran at least the entire Delta and occupied it for a considerable period. Ipuwer's description suggests that they may also have wrought much havoc in Upper Egypt; many of them may have established themselves there, perhaps in positions of authority. The invasion was doubtless facilitated by the greatly diminished efficacy of the royal government and the increasing disunity of the country. Whatever the causes, it is certain that public authority was not consistently maintained. The splendid tombs of the kings and grandees of the Old Kingdom were generally looted and wrecked in this period: in ancient Egypt, nothing could more clearly register a state of anarchy. The new tombs and other works produced during the period are unambitious in scale and poor in execution.

The Eighth Dynasty succeeded the Sixth at Memphis with little or no interval. The Eighth Dynasty was formally recognized at least as far south as Coptos, and probably to the First Cataract: I share the view... that Sethe's "Coptite" Dynasty is really the Memphite Eighth. But it is unlikely that these last Memphite rulers exercised much real power. Rival families in the chief provincial centers were more concerned with their own aggrandizement than with serving king or country. The nomarchs of Heracleopolis (XXth nome of Upper Egypt) took the kingly title, forming the Ninth and Tenth Dynasties. They reconquered the Delta and most if not all of Upper Egypt, but succumbed to the nomarchs of Thebes (IVth nome) who formed the Eleventh Dynasty. In the middle of the twenty-first century B.C. Mentuhotep II or III of the Eleventh Dynasty conquered Heracleopolis and reunited all Egypt. The period of union thus begun, the Middle Kingdom, lasted nearly three centuries.

During the First Intermediate Period many nomarchs became practically petty kings (not counting, of course, those of Heracleopolis and Thebes who actually assumed the full royal titles). The reunification of the kingdom under the Eleventh and Twelfth Dynasties did not proceed without conflict. Some of the great nomarchic families opposed the new Theban power, and disappeared. Others were on the winning side, and prospered. A major task of the early Twelfth Dynasty kings was the complete establishment of royal power over the traditional independence of those nomarchic families which had supported them. This task is believed to have been completed by the time of Sesostris III (second quarter of the nineteenth century B.C.).

Our knowledge of the institutions of the First Intermediate Period is scant and unsatisfactory. A nomarch might date by the years of his own tenure of power (as only kings had done before) and append the pious wish "may he live, be prosperous, and be healthy!" to his name (another royal prerogative). These superficial phenomena undoubtedly epitomize the basic realities: even though a nomarch might acknowledge the superior authority of a distant king and perhaps even pay regular tribute to the royal court, he himself was really an autocrat within his nome. The nomarch collected taxes, administered justice, suppressed robbers, protected widows and orphans, raised and commanded troops in war, and did everything which a wise, vigorous, and benevolent king might be expected to do; such, at least, is the ideal which emerges from the mortuary "autobiographies" of the period.

The Values of Life in Ancient Egypt

JOHN A. WILSON

It was easy to worship success as long as success conferred its benefits on all men, as long as well-tended pyramids and tombs were the visible symbols of the lasting power of worldly success. But that happy state did not last. The Old Kingdom of Egypt collapsed into turmoil heels over head. The old values in position and property were swept away in an anarchy of force and seizure. The Egyptians ascribed their woes in part to a dissolution of their own character, but also to the violent presence of Asiatics in the Egyptian Delta. However, it is doubtful whether the Asiatics came in as an invading and suppressing horde; it is much more likely that an inner breakdown of rule in Egypt permitted small groups of Asiatics to come in and settle but that these insignificant penetrations were result rather than cause of the breakdown.

The real source of the collapse was a progressive decentralization. Rulers other than the dynastic pharaohs felt their individual capacity for independence and set up competitive government until the strain fractured Egypt into a lot of warring factions. This was part of the individualistic, self-seeking trend which had been gaining momentum throughout the Old Kingdom. Now, with the single, cen-

Reprinted from "Egypt" in H. Frankfort, H. A. Frankfort, J. A. Wilson, and T. Jacobsen, *The Intellectual Adventure of Ancient Man* (Chicago: The University of Chicago Press, 1948), reprinted as *Before Philosophy* (Baltimore, Md.: Penguin Books Ltd., 1951), pp. 110–15, by permission of Penguin Books.

tral control dissipated, there was anarchy in the competing grabs for power, which went right down to the lowest strata of society. Egypt had been moving away from autarchy in the direction of separatism based on individual capacity to act, but the nation was unprepared to take advantage of the breakdown of autarchy by the immediate institution of a system of rule on a broader basis. In the confusion there was no rule.

We have many expressions of the bewilderment of the Egyptian at the overturn of his old world. Instead of the prized stability and security, the land whirled around dizzily like a potter's wheel. The former rich and powerful were now in rags and hunger, whereas the former poor had property and power. We of the present day read with a wry amusement the protests that there was a thoroughgoing cheapening of the high court of justice and a disregard for the statutes of the law, that poor men were now able to wear fine linen, that servant girls were insolent to their mistresses, and the laundryman arbitrarily refused to carry his bundle. The visible continuity of life through the care and preservation of the tombs of the great was abruptly fractured; tombs were plundered, including the pyramids of the pharaohs, and the treasured dead lay exposed upon the desert plateau. The crisp frontier lines which had given geometric order to Egypt were erased; the red desert pushed its way into the fertile black soil, the provincial states were "hacked to pieces," and foreigners from abroad had entered Egypt. When the provinces refused to pay taxes, the central control of agriculture broke down, and no one would plough even when the Nile was in beneficial flood. The old profitable commerce with Phoenicia and Nubia had disappeared, so that the appearance of a few miserable traders from the desert offering herbs and birds was now a remarkable phenomenon.

Egypt may have been moving steadily toward individualism and decentralized power, but it had still had the single keystone of the kingship. When this had been removed, the whole arch had fallen. "Behold, it has come to a point where the land is robbed of the kingship by a few irresponsible men. . . . Behold, the secret of the land, unknowable in its extent, has been exposed, and the (royal) residence has been overthrown within an hour." . . . In the earlier wisdom literature . . . the norm for the good life had been the successful official. Now the officials were in hunger and want. "Behold, no office at all is in its (proper) place, like a stampeded herd without its herdsman" "Changes have taken place, so that it is no (longer) like last year, but one year is more burdensome than another." The old values of a successful individual career, which showed to the world property, administrative position, and a tomb provisioned unto eternity had been swept away. What values could be found to replace them?

In the upset, some found only the negative answers of despair or scepticism. Some turned to suicide, and we read that the crocodiles of the river were sated because men went to them of their own accord. One of the finest documents of Egyptian literature records the debate of a would-be suicide with his own *ka,* or soul. Life was too much for him, and he proposed to seek his death by fire. It was symptomatic of the times that the soul, which should have exhibited the consistent and directing attitude toward death, was the wavering member to the debate and could find no satisfactory answer to the man's melancholy. It first was inclined to accompany him no matter what his end might be; then it shifted and tried to hold him back from violence. Still it had no constructive arguments for realizing a good life on this earth and could only urge the man to forget his cares and seek sensual enjoyment. Finally, after the man had contrasted the miseries of this life with the sober pleasures of the next world, the soul agreed to make a home with him no matter what his fate might be. There was no answer except that this world was so bad that the next must be a release.

This document carries a philosophy of pessimism worth our study. The man presented his argument to his soul in four poems of uniform tristichs contrasting life with the release of death. The first poem urged that the man's name would be in bad odour if he followed the advice of his soul to give himself up to pleasure. He had his own standards still, and he would not permit his good name to be damaged.

> Behold, my name will reek through thee
> More than the stench of fishermen,
> More than the stagnant swamps where they have fished.

> Behold, my name will reek through thee
> More than the stench of bird-droppings,
> On summer days when the sky is hot.

In six more stanzas the man presented the evil odour of his reputation if he followed the cowardly advice of his soul. Then in a second poem he turned to a lament over the breakdown of standards in the society of his day. Three of the stanzas in this poem run as follows:

> To whom can I speak today,
>   (One's) fellows are evil;
>   The friends of today do not love.

> (To whom can I speak today?)
>   The gentle man has perished,
>   But the violent man has access to
>   everybody.

> To whom can I speak today?
>   No one remembers (the lessons of)
>   the past;
>   No one at this time does (good in
>   return) for doing (good).

From these evils of life the man turned to contemplate death as a blessed release.

> Death (stands) before me today
>   (Like) the recovery of a sick man,
>   Like going out-doors (again) after
>   being confined.

> Death (stands) before me today
>   Like the fragrance of myrrh,
>   Like sitting under a shade on a
>   breezy day.

> Death (stands) before me today
>   As a man longs to see his house,
>   After he has spent many years held
>   in captivity.

Finally, the man urged the high privileges of the dead, who had the power to oppose evil and who had free access to the gods.

> Nay, but he who is yonder
>   Shall be a living god,
>   Inflicting punishment upon the doer
>   of evil.

> Nay, but he who is yonder
>   Shall be a man of wisdom,
>   Not stopped from appealing to Rē
>   when he speaks.

This man was ahead of his day in rejecting the active values of this life in favour of the passive values of future blessedness. As we shall see, such submissiveness characterized a period a thousand years later. This was a tentative move in the pessimism of the period—that one should seek death as a release instead of emphasizing the continuance of the life as known here.

In this debate the man's soul at one point urged upon him the futility of taking life seriously and cried out: "Pursue a holiday (mood) and forget care!" This theme of non-moral hedonism occurs again in another text of the period, where the argument is: The old standards of property and position have broken down; we have no certainty about future happiness, so let us grasp what happiness we can in this world. The past shows only that this life is brief and transitory—but transitory to an unknowable future.

Generations pass away and others go on since the time of the ancestors. . . . They that build buildings, their places are no more. What has been done with them? I have heard the words of (the past sages) Imhotep and Hardedef, with whose sayings men speak so much—(but) what are their places (now)? Their walls are crumbled, their places are nonexistent, as if they had never been. No one returns from (over) there, so that he might tell us their disposition, that he might tell us how they are, that he might still our hearts until we (too) shall go to the place where they have gone.

Since that wisdom which was so highly prized in the earlier age had not guaranteed for the wise a visible survival in well-kept tombs, and since it was impossible to tell how the dead fared in the other world, what was left for us here? Nothing, except to snatch at the sensual pleasures of the day.

Make holiday and weary not therein!

Behold, it is not given to a man to take his property with him. Behold, no one who goes (over there) can come back again!

the theological aspect of
mesopotamian kingship

eleven

HENRI FRANKFORT

In historical times the Mesopotamian, no more than the Egyptian, could conceive of an ordered society without a king. Yet he did not regard kingship as an essential part of the order of creation. According to Egyptian views, the universe was the outcome of one single creative process, and the activity of the creator had found its natural sequel in the absolute rule which he exercised over the world he had brought forth. Human society under Pharaoh formed part of the cosmic order and repeated its pattern. In fact, Re, the creator, headed the lists of the kings of Egypt as the first ruler of the land who had been succeeded by other gods until Horus, perpetually reincarnated in successive Pharaohs, had assumed the legacy of Osiris.

In Mesopotamia the theological aspect of kingship was less impressive; the monarchy was not regarded as the natural system within which cosmic

Reprinted from *Kingship and the Gods,* pp. 231–48, by permission of The University of Chicago Press. Copyright 1948 by The University of Chicago Press. [Footnotes omitted; further materials on the myths analyzed here can be found in Alexander Heidel, *The Babylonian Genesis* (Chicago: University of Chicago Press, 1942).]

and social forces were effective. Kingship had gained universal acceptance as a social institution, but nature did not appear to conform to a simple scheme of forces co-ordinated by the will of a ruler.

It is true that Anu and Enlil were habitually styled "King of the Gods" and that words derived from their names (*anutu, enlilutu*) denoted kingship. Yet it is peculiar that there should have been two kings: Anu, the aloof heaven, personifying the majesty of kingship, and Enlil, the violent storm-wind, its executive power. The matter becomes clearer when we observe that the texts usually describe the gods, not under the absolute authority of these kings, but rather following their guidance. The gods made decisions after general discussion, and Anu and Enlil derived their exceptional positions from the fact that they were the leaders of the assembly.

The title "king" has a less strict meaning in Mesopotamia than it has in Egypt. We have seen that a "governor" of Lagash might be called "king" by his subjects. In the same way, city-gods like Ningirsu of Lagash, who never appear as "kings" among the gods, are constantly called so by their liegemen upon earth. Neither among the gods nor among men did the title "king" denote the summit of a rigid hierarchical pyramid which was acknowledged as the only possible structure of society—for the memory of a kingless period in the past was never lost.

The Origin of Kingship Among the Gods

The Mesopotamian myth of beginnings knew neither single origin nor single authority. The primeval chaos contained two elements, sweet water and salt water—the male Apsu and the female Tiamat. This couple brought forth a multitude of gods whose liveliness disturbed the inertia congenial to Chaos. So Chaos rose to destroy its progeny. In this conflict the older gods proved inadequate, and a young deity was chosen king. After his victory he created the world as we know it.

The violence and confusion depicted in this story are poles apart from the serene splendor of the Egyptian creator rising from the primeval ocean on the first morning to shape the world he was to rule. In the Mesopotamian epic the actual creation forms, not the beginning, but the end of the narrative. On the other hand, the Egyptian, who viewed the universe as an immutable order, could not conceive anything preceding the establishment of his static world. For him the act of creation stood truly at the beginning. It was said to have occurred amid a stagnancy of water, an immeasurable potential of fertility, Nun. At Hermopolis chaos had been conceptualized in an Ogdoad of which Nun was one. But hardly anything could be said about these eight gods, since neither action nor order was possible before creation. When the Ogdoad is called "the waters that made the light," we must remember that mythopoeic thought habitually expresses itself in narrative form and

that, consequently, such phrases mean no more than the sun emerged from the waters of chaos. The Egyptians, positing an Ogdoad of deities named "Darkness," "the Boundless," and so forth, merely rendered with the concreteness to which mythopoeic thought is prone a chaos such as Milton conceived:

> ...a dark
> Illimitable Ocean without bound,
> Without dimension, where length,
>   breadth and height
> And time and place are lost.

Nothing could occur in this chaos until the miraculous appearance of the creator heralded the first act of all— creation—and the beginning of his reign.

The Egyptian and Mesopotamian views of creation were, then, diametrically opposed. The contrast between them is thrown into relief by certain resemblances which are, perforce, of a secondary nature. Common to both is the description of the starting point in negative terms. The first lines of the Babylonian Epic read:

> When on high the heavens had not
>   (yet) been named,
> And below the name of firm ground
>   had not (yet) been thought of....

And we read in the pyramid texts:

> When heaven had not yet come into
>   existence,
> When men had not yet come into
>   existence,
> When gods had not yet been born,
> When death had not yet come into
>   existence....

This negative description of creation is by no means confined to the ancient Near East. In fact, the most obvious way of introducing an account of creation is to emphasize the absence of all familiar phenomena.

In the Sumerian myths we find this purpose served by phrases like "the wolf did not snatch away lambs," or "eye disease did not say, 'I, Eye-disease.'" Both sentences mean: this familiar phenomenon did not yet exist. Elsewhere this piling-up of negatives shows a more ambitious purpose. In the Rigveda, for instance, it constitutes an attempt to escape from the tendency toward the concrete which characterizes mythopoeic thought and to conceive the act of creation without a material substratum. Egyptian and Mesopotamian thought were never aware of bondage to the concrete, and the second similarity between the creation myths of the two countries consists precisely in an agreement about the nature of the material substratum. It was held to be water. Now the belief that the world emerged from a primeval ocean has been one of those most widely held throughout the world, among all kinds of peoples and at all periods. The reason is a simple one: the universe is viewed as endowed with life; and the emergence of life, whether of plants or of animals, is preceded by water—be it rain, the floods of rivers inundating fields, or the outflow of the amniotic liquid.

A third resemblance between the Egyptian and Mesopotamian creation stories consists in the fact that they reflect certain natural features of their respective countries. But it is a mistake to see in the contrast of physiographical conditions the basis of the difference between the myths. The Mesopotamians could have built from their material—had they been so inclined—a story as serene as that of Atum's appearance in Egypt. In fact, the first section of the Epic of Creation, which reflects the Mesopotamian scene, lacks precisely the destructive nihilism, the anxiety, and the violence which dominate the central and major portion of the poem. It depicts in mythical terms the curious conditions which prevail even to-day in the southern part of the country where civilization arose. There, in the lagoons at the head of the Persian Gulf, the waters of Euphrates and Tigris mingle with those of the sea and deposit their silt. The contrast of land and water is blurred; men, moving in boats, pitch their tents on the reeds which grow from the marsh bottom, beating them down to form a shallow mattress upon the slime. Hence Ea, the god of water, was originally called Enki, the Lord of Land. And so we read in the Epic of Creation that Apsu, sweet water, and Tiamat, salt water, were inter-mingled in the primeval chaos. Next

> Lahmu and Lahamu appeared, and they were named;
> Increasing through the ages, they grew tall.

The names of this, the second couple in chaos, have been interpreted as meaning "silt." At the edges of the watery waste, all round the horizon, a deposit of mud slowly mounted, form-ing a great double circle—the begin-ning of earth and sky: the earthy horizon *kishar* and the heavenly hori-zon *anshar*.

> Anshar and Kishar (then) were formed, surpassing them;
> They lived for many days, adding year unto year.
> Their son was Anu, equal to his fathers.

With Anu we have reached the head of the Mesopotamian pantheon, but not yet creation. Before the extant universe could be said to exist, it was necessary that the solid disks formed by a continuing process of deposition out of the silt circles, Kishar and Anshar, should be separated. This separation was the act of creation, and it was originally ascribed to Enlil, the storm-wind. Again we observe a parallel with Egypt, where Shu, the god of air, was said to have lifted the sky from the earth. But we do not know the details of this myth in Mesopotamia; in the extant version Marduk has displaced Enlil. And Marduk made the sky and the earth from the two halves of Tiamat's body. It is unlikely that the older story gave a more peaceful account of creation, for Enlil was the god of the storm, and the Mesopotamian myths impart to the gods characters which, for all their plausibility, express the nature of the peculiar element in which the god is manifest. Enlil, consequently, appears as moody, impulsive, and passionate. We must, however, discount this version of the epic and consider the one which is preserved and in which Marduk is the creator. This last term has, of course, to be taken in a somewhat restricted sense. For we have seen that all the gods and much else existed and that many events had taken place before Marduk created heaven and earth. The Mesopotamians saw the world in perpetual flux, and even the creation of the existing universe was not an absolute beginning. Creation was but an episode in a larger story which was known as far back as the joint existence of Apsu and Tiamat.

The battles of the gods against Chaos moved from a promising start to a crisis which forced them to subordinate themselves to a king. The first threat of Tiamat and Apsu was countered by the destruction of the latter when Ea "cast a spell upon the waters." (Note that the victor was not a king but a magician.) The reaction of Chaos was terrifying. Its powers gathered (using the forms of Primitive Democracy), and prolific

Tiamat spawned a numerous brood of monsters to strengthen their ranks:

> Angry, scheming, restless day and night,
> they are bent on fighting, rage and prowl like lions.
> Gathered in council, they plan the attack.
> Mother Hubur—creator of all forms—
> adds irresistible weapons, has borne monster serpents,
> sharp toothed, with fang unsparing;
> has filled their bodies with poison for blood.
> Fierce dragons she has draped with terror,
> crowned with flame and made like gods,
> so that whoever looks upon them shall perish with fear,
> and they, with bodies raised, will not turn back their breast.

The gods stood aghast. Even Anu, the embodiment of authority, was helpless

> ...when Anu approached and saw the mood of Tiamat
> He could not stand before her and turned back.
> He went in terror....

We have now reached the crisis of the conflict. Note that the story has so far proceeded without assigning any significance whatsoever to the concept of kingship. Only at this point in the emergency was Marduk asked to take charge.... Consequently, the gods imparted their collective power to their elected king, and after due preparations the battle was joined:

> The Lord raised up the floodstorm, his mighty weapon.
> He mounted the chariot, the irresistible, terrifying cyclone....
> For his clothing he wore armor that inspires fright;

His head was covered with frightening
    radiance.
The Lord set out and pressed toward
    her,
Toward the place of raging Tiamat he
    set his face
He held between his lips a talisman(?)
    of red clay;
An herb to destroy the poison he
    grasped in his hand.
Then they crowded around him, the
    gods crowded around him;
The gods, his fathers, crowded around
    him, the gods crowded around him.

These excited phrases introduce the description of Marduk's victory. His election was justified, and his kingship was made permanent while the gods intoned a magnificat proclaiming his fifty names.

Since our copy of the Epic of Creation was written in Late Assyrian times, it shows that throughout Mesopotamian history the kingship of the gods was believed to have originated, not as a natural concomitant of an orderly society, but as the product of confusion and anxiety. This genesis of kingship among the gods followed the pattern of its inception among men. The same rule holds good in Egypt, where the origin of kingship was made to coincide with that of the universe because personal rule had existed in Africa since time immemorial.

However, the ruler of the Mesopotamian gods differed from the human ruler in one respect: in the ideal world of the gods the limitations of kingship were maintained. It is true that the Epic of Creation ends in a glorification of Marduk, but this is understandable, since the text was recited annually in the Marduk temple in Babylon. Other gods, too, were hymned as mighty rulers in their own shrines by their devotees. Yet it is significant that the very phrases in which the gods proclaim their submission to Marduk (words which might

mutatis mutandis have been spoken in many an early assembly of the city-states) exalt the power of his "word" or judgment in their deliberations:

Thou, O Marduk, art our champion;
We gave thee kingship, power over all
    things.
Take thy seat in the council; may thy
    word prevail.
May thy weapon not yield, may it
    smite thy foes.
Grant breath of life to lord(s) who
    put (their) trust in thee.
But if a god embraces evil, shed his
    life.

In the Mesopotamian view the assembly of the gods remained the *fons et origo* of divine decrees. In a text dealing with the destruction of Ur, it is said to have decided the ruin of the leading city of the land; in the "Song of Ishtar and Saltu," it is credited with having curbed Ishtar's warlike propensities; at every New Year's festival, at the critical turn of the seasons, it was thought to decide what would be the destiny of mankind. Two thousand years after it had been superseded by monarchy in human society, Primitive Democracy was believed to survive among the gods.

The Origin of Kingship upon Earth

The origin of kingship among men was also bound to be a subject of speculation in Mesopotamia, and it is evident that the secular and historical explanations which we have given in the preceding chapter would have been meaningless to people who regarded human destiny as the outcome of divine decrees. The Mesopotamians asserted that in the earliest times, and again after the Flood, "kingship had descended from heaven." This remarkable formula combines the awareness that kingship had not always existed with the fact that it represented the only known form of government in historical times. Moreover, the phrase indicated that the office, and not the office-holder, was of superhuman origin. The majesty of kingship, the awe and sanctity of him who symbolized the community and represented it before the gods, was acknowledged as it was in Egypt. But while the Egyptians saw Pharaoh as a god, the Mesopotamians viewed their king as a mortal endowed with a divine burden. "Kingship descended from heaven," as if it were something tangible. In fact, another text, placing kingship in exact parallelism with the insignia of royalty, suggests that it was somehow inherent in crown, tiara, and staff:

> They (the gods) had not yet set up a king for the beclouded people
> No headband and crown had (yet) been fastened. . . .
> No scepter had (yet) been studded with lapis lazuli. . . .
> Scepter, crown, headband and staff
> Were (still) placed before Anu in heaven
> So that there was no counseling of its (i.e., kingship's) people.
> (Then) kingship descended from heaven.

The first line of the quotation intimates that the people were lost, lacking all direction, moving, as it were, in a fog, because there was no king. But the specific power of kingship existed from the first; it was immanent in the royal insignia, and these were in heaven, before Anu, the god who personified authority and from whom, therefore, all order ultimately emanated. When kingship had been brought down to earth, Enlil and Inanna sought "a shepherd of the people," but there "was no king in the land. Kingship (descended from heaven) and Enlil bethought himself (to institute a king.)" In these early texts the basic conception of kingship in Mesopotamia is clearly expressed: Royalty was something not of human origin but added to society by the gods; the king was a mortal made to carry a superhuman charge which the gods could remove at any time, to bestow it upon another.

The Choice of the Gods

We do not know by what means the gods conveyed whom they had chosen for the throne. Omens, dreams, and the pragmatic proof of success were accepted at different times as indications of their choice. The texts use many different phrases instead of describing a formal ritual of divine election as is often thought. They name gods with whom the new ruler stood in a particularly close relationship, and these are described as concurring explicitly with the choice of the assembly by some gracious act. For instance, Eannatum, an Early Dynastic ruler of Lagash, called himself one "whose name was called to mind by Enlil; endowed with strength by Ningirsu; envisaged by Nanshe in (her) heart; truly and rightly suckled by Ninhursaga; named by Inanna." But on another brick of the same Eannatum these actions are divided somewhat differently among the various deities. He is a ruler "endowed with strength by Enlil; truly and rightly suckled by Ninhursaga; whose name was called to mind by Ningirsu; envisaged by Nanshe in (her) heart." Gudea calls himself:

Shepherd envisaged by Ningirsu in (his) heart; steadfastly regarded by Nanshe; endowed with strength by Nindar; the man described(?) by Baba; child borne by Gatumdug; endowed with dignity and the sublime scepter by Ig-alima; well provided with the breath of life by Dunshagar; he whom Ningiszida his god has made to appear in the assembly with (proudly) raised head.

The later texts continue to use similar expressions, but they also introduce others. The king was, as before, said to have been singled out by a god's glance: "When Shamash...with radiant face had joyfully looked upon me—me, his favorite shepherd, Hammurabi." Or in a text of Shalmaneser III of Assyria: "When the great lord Assur, in the steadfastness of his heart, had singled me out by his dazzling gaze." Or in Esarhaddon's phrase: "In the gladness of their hearts the gods, lifting their eyes to me, had chosen me to be truly and rightly king."

Sometimes the king is said to have been predestined to rule, and one meets phrases which recall the Egyptian view of kingship but which sound almost like mockery when applied to rulers so harassed by fear of the gods' changing favor. Assurbanipal stated of himself: "Assur and Sin have pronounced (my) name for rulership since time immemorial." And Nabonidus said that "Sin and Ningal determined that he should rule when he was still in his mother's womb." Other rulers emphasize the discrepancy between their status in youth and the position which they ultimately occupied and which could, therefore, be explained only as a result of divine election. This was no doubt the purpose of the "birth legend of Sargon of Akkad," who is described as the son of a priestess, set out in a reed basket and found and brought up by a gardener. A similar tendency underlies the following verses which Assurnasirpal II addressed to Ishtar:

I was born amid mountains which no
  one knew
I did not recognize thy might and did
  not pray to thee.
The Assyrians did not know of thy
  godhead and did not pray to thee.
But thou, O Ishtar, fearsome mistress
  of the gods,

Thou didst single me out with the
  glance of thine eyes; thou didst
  desire to see me rule.
Thou didst take me from among the
  mountains.
Thou didst call me to be a shepherd
  of men.
Thou didst grant me the scepter of
  justice.

Sargon was not of royal descent, but Assurnasirpal II was the son of King Shamsi-Adad IV. We could desire no clearer proof that even in Late Assyrian times divine election and not descent was regarded as the source of the king's authority.

The reasons which prompted the god's choice are sometimes indicated, and they are quite surprising; they betray a concern with the welfare of the people for which the theological tenets we are considering do not provide a basis. For man was specifically created as the servant of the god and did not, therefore, have a claim to their sympathy. But the gods mercifully desired that their people should enjoy just rule; in other words, if the living faith of the Mesopotamians comprised a feeling of utter dependence upon the gods, it also sustained the conviction that the gods had decreed justice as the foundation of society. In the text of Assurnasirpal II, Ishtar equips the king with the "scepter of justice." Hammurabi is more explicit. He declares to be called by Anu and Marduk "to make justice appear in the land, to destroy the evil and the sinful, to prevent the strong from oppressing the weak." The same motivation appears in late texts, last of all in an inscription of the very ruler who ended the independence of Mesopotamia while modeling his kingship on Mesopotamian prototypes. Cyrus, the Persian, said: "(Marduk) reviewed the totality of the lands, and having seen them, he searched for a just king, a king after his own heart, whom he could guide by the hand. He pronounced his name "Cyrus of Anshan" and he signified his name for kingship over all."

Kingship of the City and Kingship of the Land

The gods might call a man to rule over a city or to rule over the land. Early rulers, as we have seen, were not concerned with "kingship over all" nor yet with kingship over the land, but with rulership over a city. An early text reflects the original division of the country among many city-states by describing how kingship, when it had been created, was assigned to several cities at once. But in historical times a much more complex situation prevailed. Rulership over the country had become an ideal which men attempted to realize even though the central government had for the time being succumbed to the centrifugal force of particularism. Often it would be impossible to know to what type of dominion the gods had called the man of their choice, for rulership over the land was always an extension of rulership over a city. Every local ruler might aspire to hegemony, and his relation with the world of the gods did not differ from that of an overlord of the whole of Mesopotamia. Let us consider these two relationships.

As one would expect, the call to rulership over a city issued from the city-god. He acted, however, in agreement with the divine assembly. A text of Gudea gives us a clear impression of the hierarchical relationship of city-ruler, city-god, and the pantheon at large. Enlil, the leader of the divine assembly, initiated the execution of his decree by instructing Ningirsu to withhold the annual rise of the Tigris at Lagash as a sign to the inhabitants that something was required of them. Ningirsu did this,

and he furthermore ordered his temple Eninnu to "manifest its powers" in a manner we cannot reconstruct—perhaps by omens:

> On a day when destinies were being
> determined in heaven and upon
> earth,
> Lagash held her head high in pride
> of her great powers.
> Enlil looked deliberately upon Lord
> Ningirsu:
> "Let the proper occurrences fail to
> take place in our city!
> Let the 'heart' fail to overflow!
> Let the 'heart of Enlil' fail to overflow!
> Let the 'heart' fail to overflow!
> Let the high flood, filled with brilliance and awesomeness,
> Let the good waters not be brought
> down in the "heart of Enlil,' that is
> (to say) in the Tigris!"

> To the house (temple) its owner
> (Ningirsu) called out,
> And (the temple) Eninnu began manifesting its powers in heaven and on
> earth.

> The governor being a man of understanding—took notice.

A similar hierarchical order was acknowledged in an older inscription of Lagash in which Entemena gives the history of a boundary dispute between Lagash and the neighboring city of Umma. Enlil was said to have determined the boundary between the estates of the respective city-gods, Ningirsu and Shara. On the human plane this decision was given effect by Mesilim, the king of Kish, probably the most powerful ruler in the land at that time.

> Enlil, the king of all countries, the father of the gods, established the boundary for both Ningirsu and Shara by his unalterable command. And Mesilim, King of Kish, measured the fields and set up a stela in that place at the command of his god Sataran.

Ush, Governor of Umma, repeatedly transgressed the agreement. He tore out that stela and moved it into the plain of Lagash.

The warrior of Enlil, Ningirsu, at his (Enlil's) just command, did battle with Umma. At Enlil's command he clapped (his) *shushkallu* net down on its (people) and lined up their burial mounds in the plain at that place.

Note that Enlil did not address himself to Mesilim directly but that the king's personal god transmitted the order. Our text goes on to relate that a later ruler of Umma had not respected the boundary; Entemena had defeated him and now represented his victory as an achievement of the god of Lagash. This obviously leaves unsolved the thorny problem of the god of Umma's part in the course of events; another text frankly admits that the ruler of Umma acted "by command of his god."

Thus the conflicts between city-states were viewed as conflicts between their divine owners. The human victor could speak with a certain complacency of the justice of his cause, as Entemena did. The loser faced an insolvable moral problem if he was convinced of being without guilt. Such was the case with Urukagina of Lagash when he was conquered by Lugalzaggesi of Umma and Erech:

The man of Umma, after he destroyed Lagash, committing a crime against Ningirsu—the hand which he laid upon it (Lagash) shall wither! There was no crime on the part of Urukagina, King of Girsu (in Lagash).

Let that crime be on the head of Nidaba, the (personal) goddess of Lugalzaggesi, the Governor of Umma.

The men of Lagash felt that the causes of the calamity which had overtaken them transcended human relationships. The conviction that rulers, as well as ordinary men, were tools in the hands of the gods allowed them, if not to explain, then at least to express their helplessness and perplexity.

When rulership over the land as a whole had become well established, a new theological concept was introduced. For now an explanation was needed, not merely of the occasional success of individual rulers, but of the centuries of predominance which cities such as Akkad, Ur, or Babylon enjoyed. The assembly of the gods was credited with assigning temporary rule of the land to one city after another. The earliest embodiment of this view is probably the Sumarian king list, which was drawn up when the Dynasty of Akkad had definitely established rulership over the whole land. The list combined the older historical traditions of the separate city-states and expressed its new concept in an old form when it opened with the statement: "When kingship was lowered from heaven, the kingship was in Eridu," or when it summarized the First Dynasty of Ur: "four kings reigned its 177 years," or when it continued: "Ur was smitten with weapons; its kingship was carried to Awan."

But if one city profited as a result of the divine decree which gave it the leadership of the land, another city suffered eclipse; and its inhabitants were no more able to account for their misfortune than the subjects of Urukagina of Lagash had been. There was no reason why they should explain it as a result of their own shortcomings rather than of decisions which altogether transcended the sphere of man in their motivation. Yet they felt the need to account for the ineffectualness of their city-god on whom they had relied for help and whose estate was now ravaged. Conflicts between gods could be postulated to explain wars between city-states, even though man could not presume to explain how the gods could transgress a decree of Enlil. But changes in the rulership of the land could not be due to conflicts between individual gods, since these changes were approved by unanimous decision at the highest level in the divine assembly. Man imagined, however, that the deliberations of the assembly sometimes reached a dramatic tension which induced individual gods to concur with actions to which they objected at heart. A text dealing with the destruction of Ur describes how Nanna (Sin), the city-god, joined in the unanimous pronouncement of the gods: "Let it be!" When the city was in ruins, he bitterly regretted that action. But the decree could not be annulled:

> Enlil answered his son Sin concerning it:
> The deserted city, with throbbing heart, weeps bitterly;
> Sobbing thou passest the day in it.
> (But), Nanna, through thy own submission thou didst accept the "Let it be!"
> By the verdict, by the word (of) the assembly of the gods,
> By command of Anu and Enlil...
> Was the kingship of Ur...carried away.
> Since olden days when the country was founded
> Have the terms of kingship been constantly changed;
> As for its (Ur's) kingship, its term has now been changed for a different term.

The Accession

The Mesopotamian king derived his authority from divine election, but we do not know how the choice of the gods was recognized. We do know that in Assyrian times the death of a king more often than not called

forth several pretenders to the throne who did not even require the qualification of royal descent. The most that could be said for it was this: the gods in assigning hegemony to a particular city—to start under a king whom they chose and to last through several generations—might be credited with the intention of appointing that king's descendants to succeed him. The argument was not conclusive, and its weakness is proved by the disturbances that occurred at the beginning of almost every new reign. Once more the contrast with Egypt is illuminating; there the inflexible rule of an established order became operative at the death of Pharaoh and supplied the country with its next king. In Mesopotamia each succession was essentially an *ad hoc* solution.

The Late Assyrian kings attempted to smooth the transition from their reigns to those of their successors by an equivalent of the Egyptian institution of coregency. In Assyria the king inquired of the gods whether they desired one of his sons to succeed him; and if they answered favorably, the heir apparent was installed. The crown prince was not always the eldest son, and the solemn oath of allegiance sworn at his investiture did not prevent his brothers from contesting the succession at their father's death. But officially the problem of the succession was solved once a prince had been inducted in the "House of Succession" or "Palace of the Crown Prince," hence Assurbanipal adored the Ishtars, saying: "From the House of Succession (they) have magnified my kingship." Esarhaddon's account of his installation as crown prince is characteristic:

I was the younger brother of my adult brothers. (Yet) my father who begat me exalted me in the assembly of my brothers at the command of Assur, Shamash, Marduk, Nebo, Ishtar of

Nineveh, and Ishtar of Arbela, saying: "This one is my successor." He questioned Shamash and Adad through oracles. They replied to him in the affirmative: "It is he who should be thy successor." Honoring this important pronouncement, he called together the people of Assyria, great and small, as well as my brothers born in the paternal house. Before the gods Assur, Sin, Shamash, Nebo, Marduk, the gods of Assyria, the gods who inhabit Heaven and Earth, he made them swear to respect my primacy. In the month of Nisan, on a propitious day, according to the august will of the gods, I entered gladly in the House of Succession, the awesome place of royal destinies.

In the House of Succession the crown prince was initiated in the craft of kingship. He took an active part in the government, representing the king in official celebrations, carrying out special missions, and supervising religious festivals. He was therefore in the best possible position to take over when the king died.

It should be emphasized that in Mesopotamia the funeral rites of a king were in no way connected with his successor's accession. The reason is that the relationship between the two had little theological significance. In Egypt kingship involved two generations, and the burial and transfiguration of Osiris were part of the celebrations at the succession of Horus. In Mesopotamia the king arranged for the funeral of his predecessor as a simple act of piety. A Late Assyrian account of a royal funeral—the only account that has come down to us—describes how the body was lying in state, decked out with the regalia and surrounded with the various objects which were to be interred with it:

> (In the) tomb, place of mystery,
> on the Royal Esplanade,
> I made him goodly rest.

> The sarcophagus, the groove for its
>   cover,
> I sealed its opening with solid bronze.
> I established its spell (against robbers
>   and demons)

> Equipment of gold and silver
> fitting for a tomb
> (and) the royal insignia which he
>   (my father) loves
> I exhibited in the light of the sun.

> I put all this in the tomb,
> with my father who begot me.

> I offered sacrifice
> to the divine rulers, the Anunnaki,
> and to the gods who inhabit the earth.

> The channels complain
> and the watercourses respond.
> Of trees and fruit
> the face is darkened.
> The orchards weep
> and what was green. . . .

The last lines suggest that nature, too, mourned; and we know from other texts that the people gathered to bewail their late ruler. But nowhere is there any suggestion that these rites were related to the ceremonies of the accession.

The accession of the new king was formally sealed by the ritual of coronation. To view such solemnities as purely symbolical distorts the significance which they had for the ancients. For them the first contact between the new ruler and the royal insignia was but the outward sign of a union in which the unchanging powers of kingship took possession of his person and made him fit to rule. Because the insignia of kingship were charged with these powers, they were divine. The primitive awareness of a confrontation with power brings with it an imputing of personality. Consequently, the inanimate object in or through which power becomes manifest is perceived as a god. We remember that in Egypt at the coronation the throne which made a prince king became the mother-goddess Isis. The crowns of Upper and Lower Egypt were also goddesses and the "mothers" of the king. A Sumerian text similarly treats the royal insignia as goddesses, "Lady of the Crown" and "Lady of the Scepter."

The king received the insignia in the temple of the city-god who disposed of kingship during the period for which the assembly had decreed the ascendancy of the city in the land. While in the mythical time before "kingship descended from heaven, scepter, crown, tiara, and staff *were placed before Anu* in heaven," the proper place for the insignia after the introduction of kingship was the temple of the city-god. The Sumerian text which describes a coronation in Erech states that the "Lady of the Scepter" and the "Lady of the Crown" stood on a "throne dais." An Assyrian text which we shall quote presently describes their supports as "seats." Such seats are commonly depicted supporting symbols of the gods, and notably the crowns of Anu and Enlil. In shape the "seats" resemble altars.

We shall now quote first the description of the coronation ritual in Erech. The ceremony took place in Eanna, the temple of Ishtar (Inanna), the mistress of Erech:

He (the ruler) entered into Eanna.
He drew near the resplendent throne dais.
He placed the bright scepter in his hand.

He drew near the throne dais of Nin-men-na ("Lady of the Crown")
He fastened the golden crown upon his head.
He drew near to the throne dais of Nin-PA ("Lady of the Scepter")
Nin-PA, fit for heaven and earth. . . .

After she had discarded his "name (of) smallness,"
She did not call his *bur-gi* name
But called his "name (of) rulership."

Though the expression "*bur-gi* name" remains unexplained, the translator suggests that the last phrases describe a change of the ruler's name during the coronation. This supposition has much in its favor. One of the phrases in which divine election is described claims that a god has "pronounced the name" of the chosen ruler. That formula may well mean, pregnantly, that the god proclaimed the throne name by which his favorite was henceforth to be known.

In Egypt, where the king was born to the purple, the throne name, together with the rest of the titulary, could be made known throughout the country immediately upon his accession. In Mesopotamia the new name was given at the coronation when the choice of the gods became effective in the world of men. The "name of smallness" is presumably the name which the new ruler bore before his accession, and this interpretation finds support in the fact that the Sumerian word for "king," *lugal*, means "*great man*."

The Assyrian description of a coronation does not mention change of name; otherwise the ritual resembles those of earlier times. The king went to the temple of the god Assur, where the royal insignia rested upon "seats." (It is interesting that the Assyrian kings were crowned, not in Calah or Nineveh, the capitals of the empire, but in the ancient city of Assur from which the empire took its rise.) The king on his portable throne was carried to the temple on the shoulders of men, while a priest going in front beat a drum and called out: "Assur is king! Assur is king!" This phrase emphasized that the new ruler—as yet uncrowned, and hence not "king" in the fullest sense of the word—was on his way to the god who was the depositary of kingship in Assyria. The king entered the temple, kissed the ground, burned incense, and mounted the high platform at the end of the sanctuary where the statue of the god stood. There he touched the ground with his forehead and deposited his gifts: a gold bowl with costly oil, a *mina* of silver, and an embroidered robe. He then arranged Assur's offering-table while priests set those of the other gods. Next followed the last preparations for the coronation. The text is damaged here, but it seems likely that the king was anointed with the oil brought in the gold bowl. The account then continues: "The crown of Assur and the weapons of Ninlil (Assur's spouse) are brought," and they were put on "seats" at the foot of the platform before the god. However, the central ceremony of the coronation is preserved in one text. The priest carried crown and scepter, still on the felt cushions which supported them when lying on their "seats," and brought them to the king. Then, while crowning the king, he said:

> The diadem of thy head—may Assur and Ninlil, the lords of thy diadem, put it upon thee for a hundred years.
> Thy foot in Ekur (the Assur temple) and thy hands stretched towards Assur, thy god—may they be favored.
> Before Assur, thy god, may thy priesthood and the priesthood of thy sons find favor.
> With thy straight scepter make thy land wide.
> May Assur grant thee quick satisfaction, justice, and peace.

After the priest had spoken, the great dignitaries present at the ceremony pronounced prayers; and, upon the return of the procession to the palace, they gathered before the throne to do homage to the king. They presented gifts, deposited their badges and other insignia of office before him, and placed themselves in an irregular fashion, avoiding the order of precedence of the ranks they had just relinquished. It is clear that this usage was intended to allow the new ruler to choose his advisers to his own liking; but in Assyrian practice changes in the administration must have been made in an earlier or a later phase of the new reign, for the ritual of the coronation states simply: "The king then says: 'Everyone resumes his office.' The dignitaries take up their badges and their order of precedence."

We cannot but be struck by the simplicity and sobriety of this Assyrian ritual, especially if we remember the tone of its Egyptian counterpart. The very odor which characterized the gods emanated from Pharaoh when the feathers were bound upon his forehead, and the goddesses of the crowns were reborn in the union with his divine person. It may be an accident that we have no Mesopotamian equivalents of the song which celebrated Pharaoh's accession, for in Mesopotamia, too, the opening of the new reign must have been an occasion of rejoicing, if only because man greets every new beginning with new hope. But for the ruler and those near him sobriety was the appropriate mood. The gods, in choosing the king, had given him signal proof of their favor; but the task which he now faced was hazardous in the extreme. The coronation, though it made him capable of ruling, did not diminish the gulf which separated him from the gods. Great as his power was relative to that of his people, he remained subject to the inadequacies of man in relation to nature. Nature was the realm of the gods, and the Assyrian king stood outside it, a servant of its masters, while Pharaoh was himself one of these. In Egypt, Hatshepsut could say—referring to *maat,* the "truth" or ruling principle of cosmic order—

> I have made bright Truth which the god loves. . . .
> I eat of its brightness. I am a likeness from his limbs, one with him.

But the Mesopotamian king was not conscious of such superhuman resources within him. When confronted with one of those disquieting portents which were never absent for long and which were so hard to interpret, he could only pray:

> In the evil eclipse of the moon which took place in the month of Kislimu, on the tenth day;
> in the evil of the powers, of the signs, evil and not good,
> which are in my palace and my country,
> I fear, I tremble, and I am cast down in fear!
> . . .At thy exalted command
> let me live, let me be perfect and let me behold thy divinity!
> Whenever I plan, let me succeed!
> Cause truth to dwell in my mouth!

Pharaoh's acts were divine revelations, acclaimed by the people and inspired, admired, and supported by the other gods. But the Mesopotamian king was obliged to grope his way through omens and oracles. It was with full knowledge of the burden which royalty imposed upon the new king that the priest prayed at the height of the coronation ceremony: "May Assur grant thee quick satisfaction, justice, and peace!"

three aspects of mesopotamian law

twelve

Legal and Social Institutions of the Babylonians and Assyrians

SABATINO MOSCATI

Legal and Social Institutions

A constant and typical feature of the habits of thought of the Mesopotamian peoples, and one which left its mark on all forms of their social life, was their juridical outlook. A natural tendency to distinguish and codify lies behind the vast system of jurisprudence which was developed by Babylonian and Assyrian civilization and which served in its turn as one of the chief vehicles for the extension of that civilization to the surrounding world.

The fusion of Sumerian and Semitic elements which is so typical of Mesopotamian culture as a whole is here especially noteworthy; once more it is difficult to separate the elements inherited from the Sumerians from those of Semitic origin, though some traces of nomadic inspiration may be distinguished in certain legal provisions and customs.

The great discovery in the field of Mesopotamian law was that of the Code of Hammurapi, which came to

light at the beginning of the present century in the ruins of Susa, whither it had been carried off by an Elamite king after an invasion of Babylon. It is in the form of a large stele bearing on its upper portion a relief of the king standing before his god. Under the relief the inscription begins with an introductory passage in which the king exalts the task which the gods have set him of bringing justice on the earth, defending the poor against the rich, and the righteous against wrongdoers. Next follows the body of laws, and then finally a conclusion in which the king once more exalts his work, and trusts that the oppressed may find in it words of comfort and of justice.

Hammurapi's legislation was for long regarded as a highly original creation, but this judgement has since been modified thanks to the discovery of more ancient bodies of law, namely the Code of Bilalama, sovereign of Eshnunna about two centuries before the time of Hammurapi, contained in two tablets found between 1945 and 1947; the equally ancient code, in Sumerian, of Lipit-Ishtar of the dynasty of Isin, found, in four fragments, in Nippur at the end of the last century, but only recently identified and interpreted; and finally, most ancient of all, also in Sumerian, the laws of Ur-Nammu, founder of the third dynasty of Ur, around 2050 B.C., found in 1952. These new discoveries show that the importance of Hammurapi's legislation lies rather in its having collected and codified what was already traditional, than in the originality of its content. This however does not alter the fact that Hammurapi's Code enjoyed a most widespread diffusion and renown, and influenced all subsequent legislation.

We have also a collection of laws from Assyria, belonging to the time of the Middle Empire; as compared with the laws of Hammurapi the Assyrian ones are marked by a much greater severity and a much lower cultural level. Finally, we have neo-Babylonian laws. There is a notable difference in emphasis between Babylonian and Assyrian law, and between the law of one period and that of another.

In addition to the laws, we have a number of contracts, judicial decisions, reports of trials, accounts and receipts, and fiscal and other documents, which complete our acquaintance with Mesopotamian jurisprudence, and show the complexity and high level of development of the legal system.

Babylonian society is represented in the Code of Hammurapi as consisting of three classes. The members of the highest of these, who were called *awīlum*, were the "patricians," enjoying full liberty and all the rights and privileges of citizenship. The second class is composed of citizens called *mushkēnum*, who may be termed "plebeians"; though free men, they were subject to certain legal restrictions, notably in connection with the transfer of immovable property. The third class is that of the *wardum*, that is, the slaves. Among the Assyrians too there was a division into three classes; the two extremes of this divi-

sion correspond to those of the Babylonian one, but the exact status of the middle class is not certain.

The three classes differ from one another in legal status. For example, offences against plebeians are punished much less severely than offences against patricians; or rather, they are punished according to a different principle:

If a patrician has destroyed the eye of another, they shall destroy his eye.
If he has broken the bone of another, they shall break his bone.
If he has destroyed the eye of a plebeian or broken the bone of a plebeian, he shall pay one mina of silver.

Here we see an application, restricted to the patricians, of the law of retaliation, of which more will be said in the section on penal law.

Slaves were naturally rated much lower than free men:

If a patrician has given the marriage-gift for the daughter of a patrician, but another takes her by force, without asking the leave of her father and her mother, and takes away her virginity, this is a capital offence, and he shall die. . . .
If a patrician takes away the virginity of the slave-girl of another patrician, he shall pay two thirds of a mina of silver; the slave-girl shall remain her master's property.

Slaves were regarded simply as the chattels of their masters, and the only advantage of their state was the protection given them by their masters for that very reason.

Within the family the father had supreme though not unlimited authority. Marriages were concluded by written contract, without which the union was not valid in law. The Code of Hammurapi is explicit on this point:

If any man has taken a wife, but has

not made with her a written contract, that woman is not his wife.

The marriage was preceded by a gift made by the bridegroom to the parents of the bride, a relic of the ancient custom of buying the bride. This gift served as a guarantee against the breach of the contract by either party.

A second wife was commonly taken if the first was childless. Such second wives were often slaves; though they had not the same rights as free spouses, their condition was fairly satisfactory.

Divorce was permitted, and in certain cases, such as the husband's prolonged absence or refusal to support his wife, came into effect automatically. According to the Code of Hammurapi, childlessness was grounds for divorce, but in that case the woman kept her dowry and the marriage-gift. A woman might also divorce her husband, if he neglected her or left her; in such a case she had the right to remarry.

Adultery and rape were punished with the utmost severity, as also were assaults on close relations.

From the Assyrian laws we learn that in that region, from even before the first millennium, it was the custom for ladies of rank and married women to wear veils, whereas this was forbidden under heavy penalties to slaves and harlots.

The status of women in Mesopotamian society was, in conclusion, relatively satisfactory; at least, along with the increase in the force of law in the new social conditions, great progress had been made from the state of affairs that had obtained in desert life.

Right of inheritance in Babylonia was founded on legal succession. The inheritance was divided among the legitimate or legitimated sons without distinction, whether born of the first wife or of another, whether natural or adoptive. Daughters were excluded from inheriting except in the absence of male heirs, but they retained a certain right of usufruct, which was however for life only; in addition they had the right to a gift on the occasion of their marriage. An heir might be disinherited only for grave reasons, certified by the judge.

Written wills were not in use, but their purpose was to some extent served by contracts of adoption, since adopted sons were thereby legal heirs, while the adoptive father might make the validity of the contract of adoption dependent on the execution of certain conditions.

The notion of property underwent a notable evolution in Mesopotamia, when the few movable goods of the desert-dwellers were succeeded by the possessions of a settled community, comprising both movable property, such as grain, gold and silver, boats and the like, and immovable, such as houses, gardens and fields. Immovable property was registered in the administrative archives; a special status was accorded to such property granted in fee by the state to certain categories of its subjects; these concessions carried with them the obligation to military service, and, according to circumstances, a contribution levied on the fruits of the earth.

A great part of the documents that have so far come down to us from Babylonian civilization is made up of contracts, which bear witness to the great development of commercial life which had accompanied that of property-owning, and to the elaborate legal system by which commercial dealings were regulated. We have deeds relating to deposits, to transport, to buying and selling and transfer of property, to loans at interest, to leases, to partnership. The Code of Hammurapi lays down certain prescriptions for contracts, for example in the interesting case of land-leases.

The multitude of contracts gives us an insight into the economic life of Mesopotamia. The principal occupation of the people was agriculture. The land was very fertile so long as it was irrigated by an efficient canal-system, hence the work of controlling and distributing the waters to which the valley owed its prosperity and its very life was the first care of king and people alike. The seemingly sterile sand-waste transformed itself as soon as it was watered into a green plain, on which in a very short time there arose the date-palms which were the country's great source of wealth. The principal cereal of Mesopotamia was barley, but wheat and rye were also grown. Wine had been known from Sumerian times. Other plants cultivated were sesame, for its oil, the pomegranate, and the mulberry.

Assyria lent itself less well than Babylonia to the cultivation of cereals. A large amount of its territory, however, was mountainland, where there grew forests, which were a source of timber for building and for tool-making. Even stone, extremely rare in Babylonia, was less so in Assyria, where many temples and even private houses were built of stone. Babylonia on the other hand had to use brick, and brick-making was its principal manufacture, as is to be seen from the many commercial deeds relating to it.

Though stock-raising was no longer for the Semitic peoples of Mesopotamia what it had been for their ancestors in the desert, it retained its own importance, and reached a considerable development, and its exercise was regulated by law. Dairy-farming ensured the supply of milk, butter and cheese.

The canals were not only the foundation of agricultural prosperity, but also the highways of commerce. Great barges laden with oil and grain and all manner of other wares passed continually along them. The waterways were likewise the bearers of much of the passenger-traffic, and of many of the processions of the gods. The Mesopotamians made great use of "collapsible boats" in the form of large bladders of hide. On the banks of the waterways arose great warehouses and provisioning-centres, and the prosperity even of the cities came from their nearness to the water.

Trade with regions inaccessible by sea or river was carried on by caravaneers. From the mouth of the Persian Gulf they set out across the Arabian peninsula, or followed its coastline, making mainly for Arabia Felix. To the north, in addition to the sources of Tigris and Euphrates, there were other routes into Asia Minor, where there was a large Assyrian commercial colony. Babylonian manufactured goods penetrated to the cities of India, whither traders brought them by sea or through Persia.

This vast and active organization of the economic life of the Mesopotamian valley is all the more impressive when we reflect that it was built up at a time when over a large part of the Mediterranean world there had as yet arisen no comparable form of society.

Law and Statecraft in Babylon

H. W. F. SAGGS

One of the most marked features of ancient Mesopotamian civilization was its respect for the rule of law. A very large proportion of the cuneiform documents so far recovered—put as high as 95 per cent in the case of those in the Sumerian language, and probably not far short of that in the case of Akkadian—consist of the type of records sometimes referred to loosely as "contracts," though actually mainly receipts, accounts and records of transactions of various other kinds concerning property. It was generally recognized that a property transaction without written record was not valid, and to alter such a document was a heinous offence.

. . . .

Justice—for which the word used meant literally "the straight thing"—was an accepted concern of the king. Hammurabi, for example, made the establishment of justice one of his first concerns at his accession; and the formula by which his second regnal year was known was "the year in which he set forth justice in the land," a formula also employed by certain other rulers. This does not refer to the publication of the famous so-called "Code," which can be shown to have been published much later in Hammurabi's reign, but rather to cer-

tain measures taken for the amelioration of the lot of the citizens. The "justice" referred to meant, primarily, economic justice, and there is clear evidence that for the king to "set forth justice in the land" involved some kind of moratorium or general remission of debts. Once the old Sumerian system of state-socialism had begun to break down, . . . a situation arrived where it was the individual peasant, holding land as private property or rented land rather than as a fief from the temple, who took the first shock of catastrophes such as flood, drought, blight or sickness. Whereas in the original system the temple, as lord and owner of everything, both land and people, took steps by the issue of rations from the temple granaries to tide the community over such difficulties, the independent land-owning peasant now had to borrow from the temple, and borrow at interest. Over the years this would result in the greater part of the peasantry becoming the victims to a crippling load of debt, and the situation could only be cleared by drastic measures, namely by a general remission and a fresh start. There are traces of the same situation in the Old Testament, and the twenty-fifth chapter of *Leviticus*, which deals with the Year of Jubile, lays down that in the fiftieth year the poor man who had to pledge property or mortgage land or sell himself into bondage should have restored to him all his former rights.

Although in the case of Hammurabi's year-formula, "to set forth justice in the land" does not refer specifically to the promulgation of the laws, it may well have been from economic measures of the kind referred to that the issue of specific collections of laws ultimately arose. One of the concerns of the king, to prevent exploitation of the population by the temples and holders of large estates, with consequent economic distress and political instability, involved the issue of decrees fixing prices and wages. It seems likely that a monument such as the stele of Hammurabi, set up in Babylon or elsewhere to give the text of the royal laws, goes back in origin ultimately to similar but simpler monuments bearing a list of authorized prices. Hammurabi's "Code" contains sections dealing with rates of hire and wages at the end of the laws immediately before the epilogue, whilst the laws of the state of Eshnunna, ante-dating Hammurabi by at least a century, begin with a list of controlled prices of most of the commodities (barley, oil of various kinds, lard, wool, salt, spices and copper) basic to the economy, followed by clauses fixing the rate of hire of wagons and boats and the wages of various agricultural workers.

Hammurabi and his successors are known to have issued "royal ordinances" to their officials as guidance in certain matters, such as procedure in lawsuits, breach of contract, and so on, and that these royal ordinances were definite written instructions and do not denote merely Law in the abstract is clear from a passage in a royal letter; in this letter the king, writing to an official, directs him to try a case "according to the ordinances which are in your presence." Such royal ordinances, modifying customary law, deciding between variant practices as between two cities, or recapitulating laws falling into desuetude, may lie behind such an imposing document as the "Code" of Hammurabi: some scholars go so far as to regard the "Code" as containing not so much decrees as collections of decisions in particular cases.

The earliest collection of laws now known—which the accidents of archaeological discovery may at any day rob of priority—are those of Ur-Nammu, founder and first king of the Third Dynasty of Ur: these have only been published since 1952. The text (in Sumerian) begins with a brief review of the history of the world and the rise to supremacy of Ur, with its king Ur-Nammu as representative of the city's god, Nanna. After establishing the political and military security of his city, Ur-Nammu turned to economic measures, and rectified a number of abuses: he

established justice in the land.... He did away with the duties, the Big Sailors [whatever that may mean], those who by force seized the oxen, sheep or donkeys,

and ensured that

the orphan was not given over to the rich, the widow was not given over to the powerful, the man of one shekel was not given over to the man of one mina....

The remainder of the introduction is broken away, and when the text again becomes legible the laws themselves have begun. Unfortunately they are very badly damaged, but enough remains to enable five laws to be restored with some confidence. These concern respectively, trial by water ordeal, return of a runaway(?) slave to his master, and compensation for injury (which takes up three of the five sections). One of the laws concerning personal injury may be translated approximately

If a man has broken another man's bones with a weapon, he shall pay one mina of silver, and the other two are on similar lines. The great interest of these is that they show that already in Sumer the *lex talionis,* or principle of "an eye for an eye," had—if it ever existed there —been superseded. The same is true in the laws of Eshnunna, possibly under Sumerian influence. The more barbaric principle, found in the laws of Hammurabi, of Assyria and of the Hebrews, reflects the unmodified practice of the less civilized Semites.

There are other laws known which are written in Sumerian. Foremost amongst these are the laws of Lipit-Ishtar king of Isin, who reigned half-way between Ur-Nammu and Hammurabi. These are now known in a text made up from seven fragments of tablets, which bear a partial prologue and epilogue and thirty-seven sections of laws, the whole amounting to about a third of what can be computed as the extent of the original text. Four of the fragments, which show chaotic arrangement and many mistakes, are in fact excerpts of laws from Lipit-Ishtar's 'code' used as exercises for the training of scribes. The other three are pieces of a large tablet which a passage in the epilogue—

When I had established the well-being of Sumer and Akkad I set up this stele—

shows to have been a copy of an original inscribed on a public monument.

.   .   .

It should be clear from the summary and from the specimens of laws translated that the "Code" of Hammurabi does not constitute a complete system of law. Hammurabi in his prologue and epilogue makes no claim to having codified the whole of the existing law, and many matters which must at times have needed legal decisions are not included. For instance, there is no reference to parricide, cattle-lifting, or kidnapping a person other than a freeman's son. It therefore has to be concluded that Hammurabi was simply dealing with matters which needed amendment, adoption of one of a number of alternatives found in different cities, or simply recapitulation of regulations liable to fall into desuetude. It has been pointed out that "there is not a single case in the thousands of legal documents and reports which have been preserved in which reference is made to the wording of the text of the Laws," and this is clear evidence that whatever the Laws were, they were not statute law to be given a verbal interpretation but rather incorporated principles to be observed, or which actually had been observed, in particular cases.

That the principles in question were observed in Babylonia, even more than a millennium after the time of Hammurabi, is clear from a number of records of court cases. One, dating from as late as 527 B.C., may be quoted. Four workmen were arraigned before the Assembly of Erech on a charge of having stolen two ducks belonging to the temple, and the case was heard in the presence of the two principal temple administrators and representatives from the capital. Reference to the laws of Hammurabi sheds light on why the theft of two ducks should set in motion such ponderous legal machinery. Section 6 of the laws decrees that "if a man has stolen property of a god or the palace, that man shall be put to death," whilst section 8 says "If a man has stolen either ox, sheep, ass, pig or a boat, if it belongs to a god or the palace, he shall pay thirty-fold." The distinction between the two cases is that in the more serious case the theft was from within the temple or palace precincts and therefore sacrilegious, whilst in the lighter case the theft was from outside the temple precincts. Clearly the question at issue in the case adduced was whether the offence was a capital one. This is borne out by the nature of the evidence given by the accused, who testified "On the eleventh of the month Tebet...we...were digging behind the wall by the river; the two ducks...that we killed we buried in the mud." Clearly the men claimed to be on the river side of the boundary wall of the temple, and thus outside the precincts, at the time of the offence. Their evidence was accepted and the penalty was the lighter one—thirty-fold restitution.

Courts and Punishments in Babylon

G. R. DRIVER   J. C. MILES

The king was the *fons justitiae* in the realm, as Ḫammu-rabi's letters make abundantly clear. He might deal with offenders administratively and punish them himself but apparently preferred generally to remit questions for trial to his local governors or to a court of law; and his decision or that of his delegate would without doubt be final. The parties might make petition to him if justice was refused to them or in the case of bribery or of the abuse of an official position; and there are instances of his intervening in two cases which have dragged on for a number of years and of his referring another to a local court. This, however, does not mean that there was any system of appeal from a lower to a higher court; for no definite evidence of this has as yet been found. The only direct reference to the judicial activity of the king in the Laws is in § 129, which provides that, if a husband spares the life of his wife taken in adultery, the king may or shall see that her paramour receives the same treatment.

The "judge" appears to have been a member of a profession, since he is so described even when acting in a private capacity. The judges, since they are almost always mentioned in the plural number, seem normally to have sat as a college or bench; when, therefore, a single judge is mentioned, the probability is that he is acting not alone but as president of the court. The judges are generally mentioned *co nomine* without other qualification, but there are known to have been various classes of them. Thus there are "the judges of the temple of Samaš" and "the judge of the cloister". . . , other judges are royal or local, the former being called "the king's judges" and the latter being named after the chief towns in the country (Babylon, Sippar, Larsa, Dilbat, Barsippa). These titles have suggested that there were two types of judges, the ecclesiastical and the secular. The view that the judges were originally members of the priesthood is in itself not improbable, since priests were once the best if not the only educated class, and statistics show that there was a gradual transition from the priestly to lay judges in the course of the first Babylonian dynasty, with the turning-point in the reign of Ḫammu-rabi. There is, however, no trace of an ecclesiastical as distinct from a secular law; and, as nothing is known of the manner in which a man acquired the title of judge and, as no records of criminal cases have survived, only the slightest inferences can be drawn in respect to the nature of and the distinction between the various classes of judges. Indeed, the *daiyānum* of the temple may merely have been a judge sitting there; for the temple was one of the most convenient places in which courts could be held, especially as a frequent method of trial was by ordeal.

Reprinted from *The Babylonian Laws,* vol. I, *Legal Commentary* (1952), pp. 490–94, by permission of The Clarendon Press, Oxford. [Footnotes omitted]

There appear to have been several types of courts, which cannot be clearly distinguished. Twice the "palace" is mentioned in the Laws: in § 18 a fugitive slave, when taken, is brought there for identification and in § 109 an innkeeper is required to bring there malefactors plotting a crime in her house. Similarly, in the Middle-Assyrian Laws a harlot or slave-girl found improperly wearing a veil in the street is ordered to be brought to it for punishment. The *ekallum,* however, was at the same time both the royal palace in the capital city and the official residence of the governor in the main centres of administration, and there was probably one, if not in every town, at any rate in every district or province; in it the king or the governor heard the cases brought before him, and it served in some respects as a police-court.

Where the judges held their courts is not always clear. In § 5 they seem to have sat "in the assembly," but the documents usually show them sitting in the temple since there are numerous references to judicial proceedings "in the temple of Samas." Otherwise the place of the court is mentioned only very rarely, but one passage definitely refers to "the house of judgement," while another very obscure text speaks of this place and of "the house of the judgement of the land." There is no direct evidence to show that they sat anywhere else, for example "in the gate," where Oriental justice was so often administered; but the mention of "the gate of the judges" in an apparently Old-Babylonian document suggests that this may occasionally have served as a court.

There were other courts besides those of the king or his representative and the regular judges. Sometimes the judges and "the elders of the city" ... sat together, at other times the elders sat alone to try cases, or the "mayor" alone or with the elders acted as a court. This last officer is mentioned once in [sections] 23–4, where he and the city are made responsible for any robbery committed within their jurisdiction. Sometimes the "assembly" of a town, for example of Nippur and Dilbat and elsewhere, or a "merchant-guild" alone or with the judges is found acting as a court of law, though not in the Laws.

Again, the "gate" or "district," which seems to have been an assembly of the free men of a district or of the neighbours acting as a court to deal with local affairs, is mentioned both in contemporary documents and in the Laws. So in § 126 it takes part in a complaint that goods belonging to a man have been stolen within its jurisdiction, in § 142 it determines a question as to the character of a wife, and in § 251 it notifies a man that his ox is dangerous. Lastly, the "free men" alone occasionally constituted a court; these presumably were the chief men of the district or the neighbours of the parties to the case.

A considerable number of officers were connected with the courts, of whom there is here no need to say anything as their functions are for the most part quite unknown and few of them are found in the Laws. Three or four, however, who are directly or indirectly involved may be mentioned: they are "the runner of the district," and the *rīdûm* of the judges, the "herald," the judges' "surgeon-barber," to whom the "clerk" and the "archivist" of the judge may be added. Their titles explain their functions, which require no detailed examination.

How far, if at all, the decisions of a court were enforced by public authority is not known; there was no police, no public prosecutor, and no public executioner. The duty of the judge was to find the facts of the case before him and to declare what was the law applicable, but he seems to have had no power to execute his judgement. The *rēdûm* presumably acted only under orders from the appropriate authority; but there is nothing, apart from his title which suggests a sheriff's officer, to indicate that his duties were other than those of an usher, to keep order and to take messages and to summon persons to court. If the king or the local governor inflicted a penalty, it would be carried out *manu militari*; but, if indeed the actual execution in any case was left to the aggrieved party, his relations or his neighbours, it was perhaps carried out, as in § 127, in the presence of the judges, who thus saw that the sentence pronounced by them was not exceeded. Possibly, in the last resort, the successful party in a civil case would be entitled to distrain the loser's property or in some cases to seize his body as that of a judgement-debtor and hold him as a bondslave until he had worked off the amount awarded by the court.

Part 4

historic
civilizations

The historic civilizations, which attained the highest levels of socio-cultural evolution before the rise of modern societies, emerged out of archaic backgrounds under the impacts of philosophic breakthroughs and their attendant religious and cultural movements. The transcendent orders envisioned by the breakthrough movements entailed highly generalized conceptions of the nature of desirable conditions for human life and society. As elaborated and interpreted by cultural specialists, these charismatic social ideals, which Weber termed religious ethics, provided ultimate grounds for the reconstruction of the traditional normative orders. Religious commitment to the new transcendent ideals required that institutional traditions be subjected to thorough examination, with illegitimate elements being rejected and the valuable elements being generalized into firm principle, adapted to new conditions, and reorganized in terms of their logical interrelations. In each of the historic civilizations, the normative framework that evolved from these processes was fundamentally more highly rationalized than that of any archaic society. What all historic civilizations contained in common, most basically, was normative culture systematically rationalized in terms of the evaluative implications of a transcendent religious ideal.

By considering the very general and diffuse effects upon systems of social organization generated by the emergence of rationalized normative frameworks, we can outline some key components of the historic type of social structure. In the pattern maintenance sphere, historic societies were characterized by a need for institutionalization of salvation religion through which individuals could gain meaningful contact with the transcendent sacred, and major institutional patterns could receive transcendent legitimation. This functional need was met by the emergence, though to different degrees of autonomy, importance, and scope of control, of privileged groups of cultural specialists who served not only as ritual leaders but also as guardians, developers, and interpreters of the classic traditions of the sacred learning. In all historic societies, learned cultural specialists gained important monopolies over the capacity to provide normative guidance that was authoritative in terms of the standards of the sophisticated classical culture.

The rationalization of constitutive symbolism accomplished by the cultural specialists had a massive impact upon integrative functioning in historic societies. Societal community and loyalty came to be defined less in particularistic fashion, such as by ethnicity, and more in terms of adherence to and common implementation of sets of transcendent ideals. Legal regulation of the statuses and interests of societal units underwent systematic rationalization in terms of transcendent social values, but also adaptation to the expanded and more differentiated structuring of societal community. As compared with archaic systems, all historic stratification was more differentiated and flexible in its articulation with the evaluation of various types of responsibility for the classical learning, with ethnic membership and kinship relations, with levels of political authority, and with economic participation and ecological location in the society (e.g., such differences as rural-urban, artisan-merchant-bureaucrat, peasant-landlord). Yet, we will see that historic systems varied greatly in terms of the numbers of classes, the solidarity of classes, the ethnic and economic heterogeneity of classes, the scope of ascriptive privileges, and the importance of power in relations among classes.

Not all historic polities have been larger and more powerful than all archaic polities, but historic civilization did bring more effective means of rule. The rationalization of the normative order freed political leadership from the more particularistic of traditional controls on the development of policy and the setting of goals. The differentiation of the societal community into larger numbers of more independent solidary groups enabled political leaders to become less dependent on particular supporting groups and heightened the competition among groups for privileged influence with the central authorities. In particular, the emergence of administrations manned by groups having a special status-honor and ethic somewhat differentiated from those of other privileged groups made the implementation of policy both more effective and more secure from obstruction by established aristocracies.

The principal effect of normative rationalization upon economic organization seems to have been further development of market mechanisms. Although specialized productive roles continued to be institutionalized in highly ascriptive ways, e.g., with lineages, castes, or localities devoting themselves to given specialties by tradition, the number and range of specialized roles often expanded very markedly. The scale and internal complexity of the agricultural, hand manufactural, and mercantile enterprises managed by upper-class households generally increased. The management of economic enterprise tended to become more autonomous from central political control and more strongly oriented to the operations of economic markets. The market system came to mediate relations among units having stronger and larger needs for multiple types of exchange, and became increasingly differentiated by types of resource (e.g., life necessities vs. luxuries) and scale of exchange (local peasant markets vs. major mercantile exchanges). Political authority came to rely more heavily on market mechanisms for mobilizing resources for its operations and especially for support of its administrative personnel. The main type of economic concern of government became not direct control of the production of economic resources usable for its particular purposes but the protection of the general economic mechanisms of the society through the prevention of both inflation and the withdrawal of resources from the market.

Our readings on historic civilization begin with two comparative, generalizing essays. The first is concerned with comparison of the orientations to the transcendent that provided the different evaluative frameworks in terms of which the normative structures of the various historic civilizations were rationalized. The second is concerned with the role of administrative bureaucracies in the functioning of historic polities, but especially with surveying the great variation among societies in the ways in which different bureaucratic groups related, on the one hand, to the policies of the rulers and on the other, to other privileged groups in the societal communities. The readings which follow discuss major aspects of the societal structuring of China, India, Islam, and the Roman Empire in their classic historic phases of evolution. Each reading has been selected less as a general treatment of a particular historic civilization than as an analysis of institutional complexes that assumed special dynamic importance within the distinctive structural configuration evolved by the civilization. It is hoped that comparison of these key institutions and of the ways in which they articulated into the broader social structures will lead to an understanding of the radical nature of the variation among societies that normative rationalization imparted to the historic stage of socio-cultural evolution.

Talcott Parsons' essay presents a concise review of the systematic typology of religious orientations Max Weber developed in the course of his comparative studies of religion and social structure. Weber emphasized the role of charismatic movements in generating philosophic breaks with traditional orders and setting up religious problems about the meaning of human existence which could not be answered in traditionalistic fashion. As crystallization points for religious speculation, charismatically posed questions of ultimate meaning could be adequately "answered" only in terms of thought oriented to a transcendent order set off against the experiential "world." In his treatment of prophecy, Weber argued that the nature of a charismatic movement was a major factor in determining what type of attitude or stance toward the transcendent sacred would become rationalized and systematized. He distinguished two polar types of prophets or leaders who bear transcendently ordained missions into the world.

The ethical prophet brings man a new ethical system that has been commanded by God. In attempting to generate commitments to the new ethics, he leads men to see themselves as the instruments of God who should perfect their abilities to transform the sinful world so as to bring its evils under control and establish God's way on earth. The emphasis on mastery of the world comprises an ascetic stance toward the sacred. Always hostile toward tradition, it provides the strongest religious grounding for processes of rationalization of social structure. By contrast, the exemplary prophet stands as a charismatic model of how men should live in harmony with all existence. He establishes a mystical religious stance that emphasizes abnegation of all spiritual attachment to the world and contemplation of the transcendent sacred as the charismatic source of universal harmony. Tension with the world and with tradition is to be maximally reduced, hence there is little impetus to systematic reorganization of society except insofar as philosophic and normative rationalization is necessary for or follows from the contemplative spiritual life of the religious and cultural elite. Parsons indicates that very fundamental differences of institutional pattern among historic and modern civilization—concerning especially their openness to thorough-going change—may be attributed to variation among the religious stances in terms of which their normative structures gained rationalization. When used to analyze differences among elements providing the highest levels of cybernetic control in socio-cultural systems, therefore, the asceticism-mysticism dimension, and secondarily the cross-cutting dimension of inner-worldliness–other-worldliness, may be taken as demarking basically different "paths" along which societies have evolved after undergoing philosophic breakthrough.

S. N. Eisenstadt discusses the processes of the emergence, stabilization, alteration, and breakdown of the positions of bureaucratic administrative groups in centralized empires, most but not all of which are "historic" in the sense of our evolutionary typology. The creation of the bureaucracies generally originated in the attempts of kings further to centralize their rules and to enhance their autonomy from aristocracies in the setting of policy. However, the degree to which bureaucracies came to be institutionalized as differentiated structures in the society depended upon three sets of basic conditions: the extent of the development of the economic market through which resources could be mobilized for support of bureaucratic activities and personnel; the degree of differentiatedness and flexibility of structures of stratification within which bureaucratic groups would enter the competition for prestige and privilege; the extent to which the culture had gained universalistic formulation through normative rationalization. As bureaucracies emerged to positions of importance in societal power structures, they became engaged in continual political struggles between the central rulers and various peripheral groups that expected services from and control over them.

With varying degrees of success, the bureaucracies escaped from the status of creatures of the political struggle by formulating new ethics and standards of service for their activities. Such service ethics emphasized the contributions the bureaucracies made to the state rather than to the rulers personally, drawing upon elements of cultural universalism to break with the personalistic cast of authority legitimated in purely traditional fashion. Eisenstadt emphasizes that a broad range of strains often operated to distort the service ethics, for example, leading them to emphasize mainly the aggrandizement of the bureaucratic groups. Depending on the position of the bureaucratic groups in the stratification hierarchies and in relation to the controlling powers of the rulers, the bureaucracies became more or less accountable to other authorities and groups for the performance of their services and more or less aligned with other powerful elements in the goals that they pursued. In these respects, the bureaucracies sometimes carved out great autonomy for themselves, but often they became largely absorbed into other aristocratic groups or the ruling interests. Depending on the nature of the societal value system, bureaucratic services might encompass a broad or a narrow range of operations and might emphasize the regulation of the activities of other social units or direct attainment of collective goals. Eisenstadt argues that the most stable type of bureaucracy emerged where a strong service ethic emphasizing regulative operations was maintained in response to effective pressures from differentiated sets of flexibly interrelated status-groups.

Max Weber essays the complex, diffuse role of the literati in shaping, integrating, and stabilizing the Confucianist institutional core of classic, premodern Chinese civilization. An extensive elite located throughout the countryside, the literati carried the charisma of the Confucian classics, occupied a status of diffuse honor and influence central to the stratification and integration of the societal community, and comprised the qualified group from which the state recruited its administrative officials. The literati gained their status of special qualification by passing state administered examinations which tested their knowledge and command of Confucian thought with a universalism that was perhaps unparalleled in the pre-modern world. That only scholars profoundly learned and committed to the Confucian culture could gain the positions of diffuse honor and leadership held by the literati ensured the evolution of the society along the path ordained by the orthodox classical philosophy.

Weber emphasizes how vastly the Confucian learning differed from the Western classics. It was not founded on a conception of logic; it was not speculative or systematic; and it had no rhetorical organization. It consisted of parables that conveyed ceremonial and ethical understandings which were to be contemplated as considerations guiding proper conduct. The literatus was not educated as a priest or a technical specialist, but as a genteel layman. Representing the charisma of the classical learning, the literatus as gentleman was to exhibit social beneficence and ethical excellence, ceremonial refinement, favorable spiritual-magical abilities, and a cultivated style of thought. Especially when serving in office as a mandarin, the literatus was to live and take action as a public model of refined propriety. The Confucian ceremonialethical emphasis may be contrasted with the Western emphasis on instrumental effectiveness as a measure of the difference between China and the West regarding the standards that normatively orient the development of structures of collective action.

The Confucian literati claimed to monopolize the competence to conduct the administrative affairs of the state with propriety. The charismatic underpinning of the state and the position of the Emperor were said to depend upon adherence to the conceptions of official duty and public weal contained in the service ethic of the Confucian mandarinate. Administration by officials not qualified in the Confucian classics would lead to loss of the "mandate of Heaven" by which the Emperor's rule was legitimated. Thus, the Confucianists were able to restrict the access to power of rival claimants such as the patrimonial relatives and dependents of the Emperor, merchants attempting to purchase offices and privileges, technical experts, especially the military leaders, and the court eunuchs and favorites. More basically, they were able to restrict the status-honor obtainable through alternative lines or careers of activity and to maintain the preeminence of a style of life which could be led only by those having a Confucian education. Consequently, potential social developments such as the political absolutism advocated by the court favorites or the capitalism of the merchant groups were contained within strong institutional boundaries. Weber concluded his *Religion of China* with the argument that, given the very general institutionalization of Confucianism, its evaluative emphases blocked the types of rationalization of social structure that could have generated movement towards modern levels of adaptive capacity.

In Weber's comparative studies, Indian civilization was treated as approaching the pure type of a large-scale society in which the major institutional frameworks have been rationalized in terms of an orientational pattern of other-worldly mysticism. Social arrangements were so structured as to maximize the opportunities for individuals, especially members of the religious and cultural elites, to merge themselves through contemplation in the transcendent sources of being. The caste system, both in its general organization and in its many component regulations ordering different ways of life, comprised the structural core of the institutional implementation and preservation of the predominant value orientations. Our two readings on India analyze the caste system from quite different but complementary perspectives. Heinrich Zimmer's essay discusses the cultural grounding in religious and moral philosophy of the caste system and of the formal ideals by which the elites were to order their individual life cycles. A. L. Basham's essay provides a general overview of the institutional functioning of the caste system during the classic "historic" phase of Indian civilization.

Zimmer's analysis focuses on the Indian belief in *Dharma* or sacred moral order as an entity bringing together or interrelating the transcendent sacred, the established social order, and individual life courses. *Dharma* so legitimated the social order, including the various different statuses within the caste system, that the individual could act morally only by living within and through his established caste position. By assimilating himself to the impersonal qualities of his caste status and by realizing all the particularities of his caste role, especially through following the regulations of the appropriate caste laws, the individual could efface his own selfhood and gain absorption in the timeless, boundless, universal transcendent. To break the caste law would be to presume to live in the ways which *Dharma* had set for others and to personalize one's self as an entity set off against the universal. Only by accepting and acquiescing in all the givens of one's life could one attain the thorough depersonalization that was requisite for total service to the divine.

The ideals of the four life stages profoundly embodied the principle of systematic depersonalization. The pupil was to make himself a vessel to receive the sacred knowledge provided by his guru. The householder was to take on a productive role, a wife, and a family, but to delimit his worldly involvements so as always to maintain the primacy of his ritual obligations. The purpose of having and supporting a family was to continue the fulfillment of ritual duties. In the third stage of life, one ideally turned away from one's worldly attachments and concerns in order to seek the essence of one's self as merged in the transcendent being. The devotion to such contemplative activity was to culminate in the final stage of life in which the individual was to attain complete indifference to all of the world, wandering as a beggar without a home or fixed social ties.

Basham's treatment of the caste system is built about the crucial distinction between *varna* and *jati*. The *jati* is the local or regional group into which the individual is bound by particular institutions of endogamy, commensality, craft specialization, ritual service, and loyalty. The *varna* is the divinely ordained class with which particular *jati* may be identified and to which normative theory of the classic texts applies. The four *varna* of the classical learning correspond to the principal categories of distinct moral status which were believed to be established by the *Dharma*. While in theory a clear moral and prestige hierarchy obtained among the four *varna*, Basham shows that other social forces often complicated the actual relationships among the *jati* of particular localities. One must be sensitive to the fact that caste theory was constructed by the Brahmans and in certain respects represented their special views.

The Brahmans, as the spiritual and ritual leaders who mediated the charisma of the transcendent into the society and as the specialists in cultural learning and religious philosophy, comprised the *varna* with the highest moral standing. In actuality, the Brahmans were divided into many *jati* grouped more or less into subcastes. Some groups were devoted strictly to the religious life and held the full status-honor of Brahmans, while others entered government service, certain special trades, or farming in order to support themselves, and then often had difficulty in claiming the full privileges of their *varna*. Some Brahmans were highly learned in the religious philosophy, while other groups were deeply penetrated by magical rites and beliefs of relatively low rationality. The groups of the Ksatriya *varna* were dedicated to political rule and war-making. Where kings and royal castes were powerful and wealthy, they tended to rival the Brahmans in prestige and to check Brahman predominance in the stratification hierarchy. In many times and places, Ksatriya prestige tended to support an emphasis on inner-worldly interests and concerns that varied importantly from the values of the Brahman philosophy. The Vaisyas, who were generally merchants, often very wealthy ones, but sometimes clerks, lawyers, and government advisors or bureaucrats, constituted the third privileged *varna*, usually well below the first two in prestige. Their distinctly upper-class status, however, gave important autonomy, authority, and resource control to their performance of worldly functions. The fourth *varna*, the Sudra, was distinctly second-class in status. While Sudras were given a definite role in religious life, they were not privileged to hear the Vedas and could hope to lead the fully religious life only in a higher reincarnation. Various Sudra *jati* differed considerably in ritual status: some were servants to the privileged castes, while others were practically untouchable. Some Sudras were free peasants who might gain wealth as landowners and adopt certain of the customs of the higher castes, but most were confined to mean occupations and styles of life.

Below the Sudras were the untouchable *jati* and tribes who lived in segregation from the rest of the community and were sharply excluded from its ritual life. Their occupations and ways of life were regarded as profoundly defiling for practically all of the caste community; hence they were not in general recognized as having significant rights within the community. Nevertheless, the pattern of ranking all groups took hold within the untouchable realm, and untouchables formed their own rules of hierarchy and of exclusion of inferior groups.

Basham strongly emphasizes the looseness and flexibility, especially over time, of the articulation of *jati* into the framework of the *varna*. Caste rules bound the individual tightly into his own *jati,* with breaches of the rules that were not absolved by ritual penance making him an outcaste. Thus, there could be no mobility of individuals among *jati*. However, particular *jati* were often able to improve their standing within the entire caste system by changing their type of work, adapting their styles of life to higher standards, gaining power, or becoming more wealthy. Indeed, the *jati* were objects of strong corporate sentiments and ambitions, so that much competition, dispute over rank, and jealousy often emerged among them as each group strove to better its own caste position.

Our selections from the collaborative work of Hamilton Gibb and Harold Bowen present a broad, developmental treatment of Islamic civilization, with special reference to the religious and political dimensions of its organization. Gibb and Bowen show that the intensely charismatic origins of Islam stamped it with some very enduring and fundamental characteristics. The Arab originators of Islam zealously spread their religion with great rapidity over a vast area and very diverse set of peoples largely by means of military conquest. Yet, close contact and diffuse identification with the sources of charisma remained the only bases of accession to any form of authority, leadership, and prestige in the emergent empire. The highest levels of control remained closely associated with Arab ethnicity and culture, and the integrity of Islam came to depend upon the success of Arabization of the very heterogenous, often highly civilized, subject populations. Moreover, the charismatic grounding of the centers of authority allowed little room for movements toward differentiation of political and religious functioning, so that no distinction emerged at the highest levels between secular and religious offices. These basic conditions severely limited the capacity of Islam, as the community of believers, to develop integrative institutions that could provide firm solidarity in support of a cohesive empire. Not only did the early Caliphate fall subject to forces of fragmentation, but the various successor states also tended to be loosely structured in terms of institutions of societal community.

As the religious situation crystallized somewhat with the waning of the early, intensely charismatic phase, it came to reflect the general structuring of ethnic and cultural groups in Islam. By the end of the early phase, with its Arab predominance and rapid spread of the religion, the preponderance of the privileged and governing groups adhered to the Sunni "orthodoxy." Though quite traditionalistic, the Sunni position proved rather flexible in its tolerance of variant cultural elements and of their penetration into the religious tradition, e.g., in the syncretism of some non-Arab converts. The Sunni "orthodoxy" was not developed and promulgated by an organizational structure devoted to the establishment of an authoritative dogma—Islam created no "church" in that sense. It was comprised merely of the loosely-defined operating consensus of the learned that emerged from open and competitive discussion of religious issues. Thus, there was ample opportunity for the emergence of variant, sometimes oppositional, forms of Islam. The first to arise were the Siite sects among the lower classes and in the countryside, especially in enclaves of continued attachment to pre-Islamic, non-Arabic cultural patterns. Later came the Sufi movement, a stronger challenge to Sunni orientations, which presented a concern for social justice, appeals to the individual conscience, opposition to the worldliness of the orthodox, and elements of mysticism. In places, as in the Ottoman Empire, Sufism and its brotherhoods challenged the official *ulema* or religious leaders so strongly that the latter had to strengthen their seminaries and make accommodations with Sufi ideas in order to protect their positions of predominance.

Despite the theory of fusion of religious and political authority, operative religious organizations were in general quite autonomous from the state. Political authorities tended to cultivate and provide general support for religious institutions, but to focus assertion of authoritative control upon the administration of the *seria* or holy law and upon supervision of public morality. Thus, the *kadis* or religiously qualified judges who administered justice according to the *seria* stood as mediators between government and the religious organizations, having important roles in both. Aside from teaching that allegiance to the rulers under the *seria* was a religious duty, religious institutions tended to be apolitical and even aloof from the civil powers. Local religious organizations sought their grounding in their respective communities and in providing a focus for ties of solidarity among people of all ranks and roles in society. Linkages among the religious organizations of different localities tended not to be highly developed.

The effectiveness of Islamic political organization was importantly limited by the remove of the ruling class of soldiers and officials from the governed class of merchants, artisans, and peasants. No rigid caste system separated the classes, and there was much social mobility between them. However as Gibb and Bowen emphasize, the masses of the commoner class were divided into large numbers of local groups which were autonomous in their dealings with the government bureaucracy. Not only were such groups comparatively weak in capacity to pressure government officials effectively, but also their fragmentation prevented government from developing policy that could further the expressed interests of extensive sectors of the society. Each group tended to be represented in all of its dealings with the bureaucracy by a single leader whose position rested on thoroughly traditionalistic bases, for example, in the village. The bureaucracy generally submitted to the limitations of custom and tradition in exercizing its powers both because of the generalized reverence in Islam for tradition and because the institutionalization of more highly rationalized arrangements would have required more effective oversight of bureaucratic policy and activities and would thereby have undermined the autonomy of the bureaucratic officials. Thus, Gibb and Bowen demonstrate that the apparent absolutism of the rulers was strongly checked by the entrenched power position of the bureaucracy and by the traditionalism with which all power was used.

Our reading on the Roman Empire differs from our readings on the other historic civilizations in that it deals with a more specific set of structures in the society. Rudolf Sohm's venerable essay is concerned with the adaptation of the Roman legal system to Rome's rise from a small city-state republic to an immense empire embracing an extremely heterogenous set of peoples and cultures. While Sohm does not treat the actual functioning of a major sector or subsystem of Roman society in sociological fashion, he does trace the evolution of structures essential to the establishment and maintenance of societal community over the far-flung territories and diverse segments of the empire. Within the institutional framework provided by its law, the Roman Empire contained the most differentiated and dynamic economic and political forces and the most flexibly integrated societal community that emerged anywhere on a comparable scale before the onset of the modern era. The Roman legal system constituted the most highly rationalized normative structure of a large-scale society that evolved in the entire course of man's pre-modern history. Thus, Roman law occupies a very distinctive and important position in socio-cultural evolution, deserving of our special attention. Sohm's analysis is particularly suitable to our interests in that it gives more direct and detailed attention to an actual instance of the process of normative rationalization than our readings on other historic societies.

The active relations of the early Roman Republic with other peoples of the ancient Mediterranean world gave rise to a portion of the Roman civil law known as the *jus gentium* or law among nations, which regulated trade between Romans and citizens of other states. Although fully a part of Roman law—and enforceable by Roman law alone—the *jus gentium* was conceived on universal grounds as consisting of the elements of law which were in accord with the legal systems of all civilized nations. Although the universalism of the conception of "natural law" in Greek Stoicism came to be a major influence upon the development of the *jus gentium*, Sohm emphasizes that it was constructed far less through philosophical elaboration of universalistic principles than by the efforts of legal officials to provide equity in extremely various cases by attending carefully to the details of the matters in question. The Roman devotion to following legal form, i.e., to formal rationalization, combined with the steady rise in importance of cases falling under the *jus gentium,* led inexorably to an expansion of the legal parameters of the *jus gentium* that undermined the traditional *jus civile.* By the time the Empire achieved maturity, the former *jus gentium* had been transformed into the principal foundation of the law of the Empire.

Sohm discusses the transformation of the *jus gentium* in terms of the contributions made by three interacting but distinct agencies within the evolving legal system, namely the praetorian edicts, the schools of jurisprudence, and imperial legislation. Each of these agencies predominated at a different phase in the evolution of the law.

The praetorian edict was the formal statement by which the praetor or Roman official charged with administering justice promulgated the principles from which he would take guidance in deciding cases. Since the praetor could permit or grant an action but not legislate, the edict was not a law in the sense of an act of the people. However, it was formally binding over the limited range of legal activities over which the particular praetor held jurisdiction. Moreover, it was both a highly formalized statement and an extremely flexible one, since each praetor customarily announced his own revised edict upon taking office.

The importance of the praetorian edict declined with the concentration of power about the office of the emperor. The early emperors carefully instructed the praetors on the principles that should govern the provision of justice. With Hadrian, the emperors began to establish the edicts for the praetors and to monopolize the right to revise edicts. The edicts then became comparatively set in form and much less a dynamic factor in the evolution of the law.

The origins of Roman jurisprudence lay in the knowledge of the *pontifices* or religious authorities on the letter of the traditional law as it pertained to the taking of legal actions. The *pontifices* traditionally controlled the right to bind the courts with regard to determination of the laws under which particular cases were to be decided. The judges questioned the *pontifices* about disputed or uncertain points of law and were bound to render their decisions in terms of the pontifical statements of the law. In the early Republic, the legal authority of the *pontifices* was deeply embedded in the secrets and mysteries of their sacred religious leadership. When the legal formulae of which they had originally monopolized authoritative knowledge were later made public, their powers were greatly altered. It was no longer possible to restrict the scope of legal questions under consideration to particular cases. Law had then to be formulated more universalistically so that it would apply to general classes and categories of cases and legal considerations. Commentaries on the law began to appear, and the law gradually became more systematized and rationalized. Sohm emphasizes that the publicizing and formalizing of the processes of determining the law for specific cases operated importantly to suppress certain particularistic privileges which had formerly advantaged the patrician class in legal action.

After Augustus, who combined the office of *pontifex maximus* with the role of "first citizen," the authority to bind the courts on points of law passed to the emperors. With Tiberius, it became the practice for the emperor to delegate this authority to particular prominent jurists. The legal role of the pontifical college was thereby thoroughly undermined, and the courts became bound by opinions obtained from the official jurists by the parties to particular cases. Gradually, the jurists' opinions came to be binding not only in particular cases, but as precedents in all cases involving similar legal problems.

In response to the rise in importance of legal learning of a universalistic and systematic type, the first schools of jurisprudence emerged in Rome. Influenced both by Greek Stoic philosophy and its emphasis upon abtract principle and by the Roman concern with details of specific cases, the schools stressed the use of casuistry to systematize the law. Despite the emergence of two competing schools, one of which emphasized principles of legal progress while the other was more traditional in its orientation, Roman jurisprudence as a whole sustained the effort to restructure the law in terms of, in Sohm's phrase, "legal principles of universal validity." Over the long run, the jurists managed to fuse the *jus civile,* the edicts, and imperial legislative law into one harmonious whole. Especially in the complicated areas of contract and implicit contract, the jurists developed a calculable, rational law for the guiding and regulating of the very flexible interplay of the economic interests of diverse social units.

The concentration of formal authority about the office of the emperor, a vast process which commenced with Augustus' assumption of the position of "first citizen" and continued through centuries of, first, political expansion and, then, adjustment to declining resources, social integration, and effective power, enabled the emperors to make law in a number of ways. In either rendering decisions or offering opinions in particular cases, the emperors could affect the lasting body of legal precedents. In issuing instructions or mandates to subordinate officials or in promulgating edicts or public ordinances, each emperor could set binding arrangements for the duration of his own rule. The later emperors also monopolized the right to enter motions for decrees in the Senate, and thus came to control the process of legislation. In addition, they gained increasing control over the work of the jurists until imperial opinions supplanted the opinions of an autonomous "scientific" jurisprudence almost entirely. From the reign of Diocletian, the emperors practically monopolized the development of the law.

The emperors of this period were engaged in continual contests with forces of political entropy, such as ethnic and territorial fragmentation and scarcity of resources necessary for central rule, which constantly ate away at their powers. In order to shore up the integrity of the Empire, they introduced a long series of reforms intended to homogenize or unify the laws applying to the various territories under their rule. They attempted at the same time to broaden the scope of the laws which were binding throughout the Empire. Thus, with the very Greek ideal of a universal law of the Empire, they extended the *jus gentium* over the *jus civile* throughout practically the whole range of codified legal subject matter.

The culmination of the emperors' efforts to unify the law was the *Corpus juris* of Justinian, completed practically on the eve of the dissolution of the Western Empire. This work consisted of three parts, the Institutes, the Digest, and the Code. The institutes provided a systematic introduction to the law. The Digest was a set of selections from the classical jurists, altered and arranged so as to provide a systematic statement of the *jus,* the traditional and jurist-made law. Justinian gave statutory bindingness to the Digest and attempted to forbid all other references to the classical jurists in the hope of fixing the *jus* to a permanent form. Justinian's Code was similar to the codes of a number of previous emperors. It arranged the body of imperial legislation by subject and chronologically, introducing changes in particular *leges* or legislated laws in order to make the system of laws internally consistent. Justinian nullified the bindingness of all *leges* not included in the Code, banned the writing of new commentaries, and decreed that all subsequent legal difficulties were to be resolved personally by the Emperor. Although the *Corpus juris* succeeded neither in permanently fixing the law nor in containing the forces of dissolution acting upon the Empire, it provided ideals of universal law that survived the ensuing "Dark Ages." The history of modern law begins with the late Medieval renaissance of study of the *Corpus juris* and Roman legal universalism.

max weber's systematic typology of religion

thirteen

TALCOTT PARSONS

Weber's comparative sociology of religion did not consist only of a series of separate studies of "cases" which serve to bring out religious elements inhibiting the development of capitalism elsewhere than in the modern West. It is mainly preoccupied with the problem of capitalism and its main theoretical framework focuses upon it. But out of it emerges a general system or religious typology which gives the final breadth to the perspective of the religious aspect of the problem of capitalism. It is possible to give here to complete the preceding presentation only a bare sketch of some of the major concepts.

Even a sketchy presentation of this systematic typology is not possible without some reference to Weber's general conception of historical development.... It was his view that in what is relevant to his analysis there is something like a point of common

origin for processes of religious development, a general "primitive religion." The various possible types of "developed" religious system are then to be thought of as arising by a process of differentiation from the common starting point. They represent possibilities which are to a large extent mutually exclusive. The present concern is not, however, with the historical applications, but with the logical relations of the different type elements.

For the "primitive" type it is not, Weber thinks, possible to differentiate religious and nonreligious elements on the basis of rationality as such or of the character of "ends." The ends are in general worldly and a certain relative rationality applies to religious and magical actions as well as to secular techniques. The distinction in such terms is rather one brought in from the point of view of modern views of nature and not to be found in the primitive material itself. The fruitful starting point is rather the observation that religious as distinct from secular actions involve qualities, forces, etc. which are exceptional, removed from the ordinary (*ausseralltäglich*), to which a special attitude is taken and a special virtue attributed. This exceptional quality Weber calls *charisma*. It is exemplified in such conceptions as mana.

From this conception of things "set apart" can easily arise that of a "world" of entities different from that involved in the ordinary affairs of everyday life—in this sense and only this, a "supernatural" world. The ways in which these entities may be conceived and the character of their relations to the "natural" world are most various. They may, for example, be distinguished as "personal" and "impersonal," but Weber does not for present purposes lay great stress on these distinctions; the important thing is the difference of attitude toward these entities, however conceived, from that toward everyday things. They tend to issue in two types of entity; in so far as this supernatural world is involved in the individual personality itself, it becomes the "soul," or if outside the individual, "gods" or "demons." Whether or not the conceptions are anthropomorphic is of secondary importance. The ordering of the relations of these entities to men is what Weber designates as the realm of religious action.

One further element of this complex is important. This quality of special apartness, charisma, is often attributed to objects, acts, human beings, which in other respects belong to the everyday world or are closely related to it. This quality is in some sense a manifestation of these supernatural forces or entities. Some distinction between the natural and the supernatural elements in these concrete things is imperative. Among the possible interpretations of the relation of the two elements is that the former symbolizes the latter. As Weber says, "Now not only do things play a part in life which are merely there and happen, but also which have a 'meaning' and are there because of this meaning. With this, magic, from the direct action of forces, becomes symbolism." However different the "na-

tive" interpretation of this may be from our own self-conscious symbolism, here is an element of fundamental importance.

From this basal idea Weber draws one of his fundamental theses, that the first effect of "religious ideas" on action including economic action—an effect everywhere present—is to sanction the stereotyping of tradition. "Every magical procedure which has been 'proved' efficacious is naturally repeated strictly in the successful form. That is extended to the whole realm of symbolically meaningful actions. The slightest departure from the approved norm may vitiate the action. All branches of human activity get drawn into this circle of symbolic magic." While there are specific acts and complexes of action which are in Durkheim's term typically "profane," that is not true of any of the great spheres of conduct, economic or political activity, love or war. In so far as these are brought into relation with charismatic forces they become traditionalized. As Weber says, "The sacred is that which is specifically unalterable."

The above characterization is that of only a very broad basis of "primitive" religion. In a large number of different respects there can, on this general basis, be variations of different types and developments in different directions. Weber treats them at considerable length and with at least the beginnings of a systematic classification. There is no space here to follow through these complexities. There may be, however, great variations in the character of the supernatural entities involved, their relations to each other, to men of different classes and to the nonhuman world. There may be variations in the ways in which these sacred traditions are maintained and transmitted, by word of mouth or in written form, in the degree of specialization as between those who do and do not have especially intimate relations with sacred things and the relations of specialists such as the magician and the priest to other classes in the community.

However important these differences may be in other connections, they do not touch what is for Weber the central question of the way out of traditionalism. Religion remains on this level an aspect of the general social community and on the whole sanctions the general structure of this community and its practices, including ritual. What is lacking is a rationally systematized attitude toward the religiously significant aspects of life.

Once the level of symbolism is reached the question arises of the "meaning" of things and events of this world. Rationalization of these discrete meanings into a coherent system, an inclusive interpretation of the world as a whole and man's place in it, is an "immanent" need of the intellect once the question of meaning is raised. It is as one of the points where this question is most acutely raised that Weber lays such great stress on the problem of suffering, more broadly that of evil. This leads up, by the process of rationalization, to the great theodicy conceptions. But this rationalization is deeply inhibited by traditionalism. For the traditionalistic situation will inevitably have assimilated and given its traditional sanction to very diverse elements which cannot all be accepted in *any* single rational system.

Hence a carrying of the rationalization process beyond a certain point involves a break with traditionalism and, conversely, every sharp break with traditionalism involves rationalization—for the breaker of tradition is by his very act forced to define his attitudes toward that with which he has broken. When such breaks with tradition involve religious elements, that is, when the breaker claims charismatic authority, Weber calls the process "prophecy" and the personal agent of it a "prophet." It is with prophecy and its implications and effects that the main body of his sociology of religion is concerned. The prophet is significant as the initiator of a great process of rationalization in the interpretation of the "meaning" of the world and the attitudes men should take toward it. The possible attitudes they can take Weber holds to be conditioned by the structure of ideas which results from this process.

As has been pointed out, Weber is interested in systems of religious ideas as *differentiating* elements in social development. Underlying this interest is his basic thesis that the process of religious rationalization is not predetermined by its immanent nature in *one* particular direction, but that it can proceed in a limited number of possible directions according to various circumstances. Though the subtypes are numerous, the major directions can be reduced to two—a dualism, which runs through all of Weber's work on this subject.

Weber defines the prophet as "a purely personal[1] bearer of *charisma* who by virtue of his 'mission' preaches a religious doctrine or a divine command." He is always one who has a mission, who feels himself in particularly close connection with a "supernatural" entity or order. And he undertakes his mission without authorization by any human agency, in fact in conscious opposition to all such agencies. Jesus' words, "It is written..., but *I* say unto you...,"

---

[1] He is not "legitimized" by any human authority, especially neither by tradition nor an "office."

the opposite, are typical. Of the two forms of mission, a command, if it is to make sense, implies a doctrine but a doctrine need not imply any commands.

It is on this basis that Weber distinguishes his two fundamental types of prophecy. Either the prophet feels himself to be the instrument of a divine will, bringing in the latter's name a concrete command or a norm with which people should comply as an ethical duty. This is ethical prophecy (Mohammed, Jesus). Or he is one who by his personal example shows others the way to religious salvation (Buddha), what Weber calls exemplary prophecy. But whichever type is involved, prophecy always implies "first for the prophet, then for his followers a unified attitude toward life gained by a deliberate meaningful stand taken toward it." Human action must, to realize religious interests, be in conformity with the coherent meaning of the world implied in such a stand.

The ethical prophet feels himself to be the instrument of a divine will. As such a part of his mission is to give men ethical norms with which they are expected to conform. And by definition these norms are different from the existing traditional state of affairs. The rationalization of this situation leads in a particular direction. The will of which the prophet is an instrument, the source of the new norms, cannot be merely a manifestation of the immanent order of the world as it is. Only the conception of a transcendental personal God, concerned with, but not in his essence involved in, the existing cosmic and human order, can be adequate to ethical prophecy. This is not to say that such a conception of God arose only as a "rationalization" of ethical prophets, or vice versa, but that they are phenomena mutually interdependent.

Thus Weber holds that the pantheistic conceptions of India and China, once firmly established, were enough to prevent the development of ethical prophecy.

On the other hand, such a pantheistic conception of the divine as an immanent principle of order is related to the emergence of the exemplary prophet. A norm or command to change the world is out of the question, but not an attempt to live in harmony with it. And there is no inherent reason why traditional modes of achieving this "harmony" should be beyond criticism; indeed they certainly are not. In the sense of a path to salvation, an exemplary prophet may well have a new doctrine that is not traditional, and others may follow his example and his teaching of the doctrine.

There is one immediate social implication of the appearance of a prophet. If his prophecying is efficacious he gathers about him a community of disciples. The fact that prophecy itself involves a break with traditionalism means that the relation of both the prophet and his followers to the society in which they appear is highly problematical, especially to the bearers of its religious tradition, but also to other elements. Moreover, in the course of its own development, this community or *Gemeinde* inevitably undergoes changes within itself, particularly the change of leadership from the founder to his successors. In all these matters a large number of different possibilities are open according to the character of the prophet and his doctrine and to the circumstances. But the main fact is that prophetic religion is a source of social organization independent of the immanent development of the traditional order. It may also itself become retraditionalized, but not necessarily so. Religion thus becomes not merely an aspect of a social community, but the basis of one.

The social implications of a prophetic movement, both within its *Gemeinde* and without, depend, in relation to the character of the prophecy and the system of ideas it involves, on the means it takes to the realization of its religious interests. These again fall into a dichotomy of two main types which Weber calls asceticism and mysticism. Their significance, however, only becomes understandable on the basis of Weber's view, already noted, that *no* traditional order can be made to conform completely to the requirements of *any* fully rationalized conception of the meaning of the world. Hence it is inevitable that certain elements at least of the worldly order will come into conflict with religious values. It is this conflict that indeed forms the basis of the need for "salvation."

In this conflict there are in principle two generally possible attitudes compatible with a consistent rational view. It is obvious that the world cannot be simply "accepted." Then worldly things can, so far as possible, be controlled, mastered in the interest of the religious idea. Or, on the other hand, they may be radically devalued and become indifferent. In Weber's terminology the former course is the ascetic, the latter the mystical. Each may, in turn, be subdivided into worldly[2] and otherworldly types.

Both are carried through in a radical form only by a minority of religious virtuosos. The unequal religious qualification of men is a fact on which Weber lays great stress. The

ascetic type of salvation is associated with ethical prophecy. The individual feels himself to be an instrument of God's will. He must hence, in terms of the latter, subject the traditional ethical code to a radical criticism, and set for himself ideals far above those of the mass even of "good" men. The "world" becomes sinful, in the extreme case radically evil, something to be combated and, if possible, controlled.

According to circumstances this may take one of two directions. The "world" to be fought and mastered may be only within oneself—for such a person there are no positive duties beyond that. Then the ascetic will flee the world, as hermit or monk. Or, where this retirement from the world is excluded as it was in Protestantism, the only recourse is to control, not only oneself, but also the rest of the world, which still, however, remains sinful. Otherworldly asceticism is also compatible with the pantheistic background as a means of mastering the interfering desires and interests of the flesh, thus rendering them harmless.

On the other hand, the end of salvation may be the attainment of an exceptional higher "state," through "mystical experience." This is attained only by a minority, using a systematic technique, that of "contemplation." The interests of the world can appear only as disturbances. To one with such an experience there can be no positive relation to such interests; they can only be avoided. The result is indifference to the world, attained either by avoiding it as far as possible—"otherworldly mysticism" —or living in it but not of it, allowing no inner attachment to it— "worldly mysticism." The connection of this attitude with the immanent, impersonal conception of the divine is evident.

---

2 "Worldly" here means remaining within the order of society, not an inner attachment to "worldly" goods. "Otherworldly" involves, on the other hand, a break with the everyday social order.

The relations of these different roads to salvation to the different elements of social life are by no means simple and cannot be analyzed here. But in general it can be said that the farther over on the mystical side the position is, the more difficult it is for a stable social organization to grow up on a religious basis, even a *Gemeinde,* without a reversion to traditionalism, and the less influence the system of religious ideas will have on the life of the society except indirectly in stereotyping tradition. Buddhism represents the extreme in this direction.[3]

On the other hand, the farther over the position is in the ascetic direction, the more the opposite is true under certain conditions. Otherworldly asceticism may become radically antisocial, but the worldly asceticism of Protestantism represents the extreme of possible religious interest in shaping the organization of life in this world in the image of a rationalized religious ideal.

Weber sharply rejects the view that these rationalized systems of religious ideas can be understood as the creation of any "material" conditions. They are, no the contrary, the outcome of the immanent *Eigengesetzlichkeit* of solving the problem of the meaning of the world from different starting points. He does, however, allow a very considerable role for nonreligious factors in the concrete processes by which they develop and in the particular directions the development takes. A few of the main relations may be noted.

In the first place, the emergence of prophecy itself, and hence the start of the whole process, is to be attributed in a larger degree to social situations. Above all, where the tradiional values have been shaken and overt conflicts arisen, a strong stimulus is given to "taking a stand." In fact prophets have often been related to social conflicts. Secondly, when a society is differentiated, the problems of the meaning of the world will not be entirely the same for all classes of society. Just as the social significance of a system of religious ideas lies in its canalization of interests, so the kinds of ideas one will turn to will depend on the kind of problems one is faced with. Not in the sense that class interests determine religious ideas, but that some types of class situation make its members more receptive to a given line of religious thought than to another—or to the idea of salvation at all. Third, the chances for a given religious doctrine to gain a predominant position in a culture are bound up with the position in the social "balance of power" of the class who are its principal bearers. This has been illustrated above in the case of the Brahmans.

On the other side it must again be made clear what is Weber's conception of the mode of influence of systems of religious ideas on practical life and through that on social structure. Society is not in any sense merely an "emanation" product of the religious idea. The process is, on the contrary, highly complex. The central theoretical concept is that of religious "interest." Ideas are effective in action because they determine the directions of practical activity in which the interests can be pursued.

But the very conception of interest implies another factor. Human action is subject not only to "ideal" but to real conditions. Moreover the rationalization that is the characteristic of these religious systems involves sacrifice of many potential values which are more or less embodied in

---

[3] That is, in its asocial character. It did not provide so strong a sanction of "lay" traditionalism as did Brahmanic Hinduism.

social institutions. The process is, then, one of highly complex interaction between these various elements. In the process a selective influence at least may be exercised on the course of the development of the religious system itself. Finally, the elements of potential conflict, especially between religious interests and the "world," which are absolutely fundamental to Weber, ensure that the process shall be highly dynamic. Nothing is more unjust than to accuse Weber, because he insisted on the social importance of religious ideas, of a naïve monistic "emanation" theory of the mode of their influence.

The Protestant ethic can now be set in the broad perspective of Weber's comparative treatment of religion. Certain fundamental features were common to the religious developments of both China and India, however much these two may differ from each other. Rationalization of religious thought in both cases went in the immanent, impersonal, pantheistic direction, starting from the conception of an impersonal order of ritual forces, tao and rita. Connected with this is the fact that in neither development did there appear a movement of *ethical* prophecy, setting up ethical standards in opposition to the traditional order.

Another circumstance on which Weber lays great stress was that the rationalized religious ideas in both areas were the creation of cultivated intellectual classes. In both the status of the class and its highest religious good were bound up with "knowledge," not the empirical knowledge of modern Western science but knowledge of a totally different order. It was either the knowledge of a literary tradition, as in China predominantly, or a mystic gnosis. In either case faith, in the Christian sense, was excluded. And since this knowledge was accessible only to the cultivated few there was a great chasm between the sophisticated religion of the elite and the religion of the masses. The latter was not shaken out of its state of magical traditionalism; it remained "primitive."

In China, in keeping with the character of the mandarin class who were the bearers of the Confucian tradition, the rationalization process took an entirely worldly direction. All metaphysical speculation was rigidly avoided. But precisely on this account a radical rationalization of the meaning of the world did not arise at all. Rationalization remained confined to adaptation to a given order of things. This order itself, including its ritual and magical elements, was left unquestioned. There was hence no motive for salvation by escape from it, and equally no Archimedean point from which to undertake its radical reconstruction. Confucian rationality is that of prudent conservatism, adaptation to a given order. In so far as sophisticated minds departed from this worldliness it was not in the direction of worldly asceticism but of Taoist mysticism, the counterpart of the Indian movements.

In India, on the other hand, the radical rationalization did take place in the hands of the cultivated intellectuals. This process yielded the doctrines of karma and transmigration. For the masses, linked with the caste hierarchy, there resulted only the sanction of an extreme of traditionalized immobility; as Weber says, "the one completely logically consistent form of an 'organic' theory of society which has ever arisen." For the elite, on the other hand, salvation could lie only in turning away from the things of this world in mystical contemplation and otherworldly asceticism. The traditional order was either left untouched as in Buddhism or radically sanctioned as in Hinduism. In both religions, to use Weber's words,

...the layman [in China the man without literary schooling] to whom the gnosis and hence the highest religious goal is denied, or who repudiates it for himself, acts ritualistically and traditionally in the pursuit of his everyday interests. Everywhere the unlimited acquisitiveness of the Asiatic is famous as unequalled, and on the whole rightly. But it is an "acquisitive impulse" which is served with all possible means of deception and with the help of the ubiquitous recourse to magic. There was lacking precisely what was decisive for the economic life of the West—the rational disciplining of this impulsive character of acquisition and its incorporation into a system of rational ethical conduct in the world. This was brought about by the "worldly asceticism" of Protestantism carrying the beginnings of a few related predecessors to completion. For such a development the necessary elements were lacking in the Asiatic religions.[4]

The differences of the ethic of ascetic Protestantism from the religious ethics of both China and India should now be clear. In Weber's typology it is the extreme logical antithesis of the Buddhistic, more generally that of Indian mysticism. China lies between. In its radical Calvinistic form the Protestant rationalization of the world combines the following elements: (1) the transcendental God, (2) predestination, involving the complete cutting off of the individual from salvation by his own efforts including the gnosis of mystical contemplation, (3) the sinfulness of the flesh leading to the most radical possible tension between ideal and real, (4) the conception of man as the instrument of God's will in building the Kingdom of God on Earth with its tendency to guide religious interests in the direction of active ascetic mastery over the world in the interest of an ideal, finally (5) the complete corruption of the world which implied the absolute devaluation of traditionalism, especially magical, ritual or symbolic. If *any* system of religious ideas could constitute an active social force, surely it was this.[5]

---

4 *Gesammelte Aufsätze zur Religionssoziologie* (Tübingen: J. C. B. Mohr, P. Siebeck, 1920–21), vol. ii, p. 372.

5 Calvinism and Buddhism represent the antithetical polar extremes of Weber's classification so far as his empirical material goes. Whether they are maxima in any more general theoretical sense need not be discussed.

political orientations
of bureaucracies in
centralized empires

fourteen

S. N. EISENSTADT

I

The purpose of this essay is to analyze the main types of social and political orientations of bureaucratic administrations (especially of their upper echelons) and their participation in the political struggle in historical centralized empires. . . .

The analysis here . . . is rooted in a number of pre-modern historical examples: the Ancient Egyptian Empires, the Sassanid Empire of Persia, the Chinese Empires from the period of Han onward, the Byzantine Empire, the Abbasid and Ottoman Empires, certain European countries in the 11-18th centuries, and the Spanish-American Empire. For reasons of space we shall not be able to present in full analysis a case study of any single society, and most of the materials presented here will be mainly descriptive, although we shall attempt, as far as possible, to present these illustrations in a systematic way, related to the major problem of the analysis.

Reprinted from *Essays on Comparative Institutions,* pp. 216–42, by permission of the publisher. Copyright 1965 by John Wiley and Sons. [Notes omitted]

. . . In most of these societies the bureaucratic administrations were either created or reorganized by the rulers—the Emperors or Kings—as one of the most important instruments in their attempts to create a relatively centralized, unified polity and to develop ways for the implementation of autonomous political goals.

The success of the rulers in the establishment of these polities and in the development and maintenance of the bureaucratic administrations was usually dependent either on the existence or development of specific conditions in the structure of their societies. The most important of these conditions were a relatively differentiated social structure, emergence to some extent of a market economy, a relatively flexible status system, and the growth of some universalistic cultural orientations. All these were connected with the development of various free-floating resources and with relative predominance of various nonascriptive rural and urban groups in the social structure of these societies.

The rise of bureaucratic organizations and their very activities have played an important part in the establishment and continuation of the basic conditions and premises of these polities. Their rise has also helped in the development of those relatively differentiated and non-traditional strata that provided the backbone of these polities and of the "free" resources needed by the rulers, and in the maintenance of continuous interrelations between the rulers and these strata.

But these conditions were not always given or assured for an indefinite period of time. Various social groups, such as the aristocracies, some more traditional ascriptive urban groups, and religious elites, often waged a struggle against the rulers and the institutional structure of these polities and attempted to undermine those conditions which enabled the maintenance of these premises. The rulers attempted with varying degrees of success to counteract these tendencies through the implementation of policies which could ensure the continuous maintenance of basic conditions, especially the existence of some free-floating resources, on the one hand, and the ruler's control over these resources, on the other.

In the implementation of these aims the bureaucratic administrations have played, as indicated above, a very important part. But in this way the bureaucratic administrations were necessarily caught in the political struggle that developed in these societies between different social groups and between the administrations and the rulers.

Thus the bureaucratic administrations in these societies were posed between the rulers, who very often wanted to use them almost exclusively for their own needs and purposes, and some of the major groups and strata, from whom the rulers and the administrations wanted to mobilize various resources and who usually developed on their part some expectations of services from the bureaucracy.

In conjunction with these different pressures the bureaucratic administrations (and especially their higher echelons) developed several rather diversified types of activities and some specific organizational characteristics of their own. The most important of these was the tendency to emphasize, to some extent, their internal organizational and professional autonomy and self-perpetuation.

This tendency was manifest in two major aspects of their activities. First, the bureaucratic administrations tended, insofar as they did take into account the demands and interests of both the rulers (the monarch) and the various strata, to develop some autonomy vis-à-vis both of them. They usually developed and maintained certain general usages or rules and standards of service, executed them with regard to the strata and groups to which they applied, took into consideration some general interests of the population, and withstood the pressure of those interested in changing these usages continuously or intermittently for their own benefit. Second, most of these bureaucracies developed some conception of themselves as servants of the "state" or of the community (even if the state was symbolized mainly by a dynasty) and not only as *personal* servants of the rulers. Even though in none of these cases were all these manifestations of the autonomy of the bureaucracy as developed as in modern "civil service," they did exist in an embryonic form.

Such autonomy of the bureaucracy was, however, very often suspected by the rulers, who therefore tried to restrict it, to maintain some measure of political control over it, so as to minimize the possibility of its developing relatively independent political goals and activities. Thus, throughout the implementation of their different tasks, the bureaucratic administrations were faced with the problem of striking some equilibrium between these different pressures and tendencies, namely between organizational and social autonomy, and controls and pressures from the rulers and some of the major strata.

But the attainment of balance between all these tendencies and pressures was not always easy, as there could easily develop a strong preponderance of one of the tendencies, undermining or weakening the others, and influencing accordingly the scope and direction of the activities of the bureaucracy. This development occurred for several reasons, all of them connected with the basic conditions of development of the bureaucratic administrations in these polities and with the fact that the bureaucracy was caught in the political struggle that developed therein.

First, the very power position which these bureaucracies acquired, in societies in which there usually existed but few "constitutional" limits on power and in which the access to power was relatively limited, placed the members of the bureaucracy in an especially privileged position. Second, the great emphasis, in these societies, on some sort of ascriptive symbols of status necessarily "tempted" the members of the bureaucracy to use their position for acquisition of symbols or to make these positions into bases of such symbols. Third, the relatively low level of economic development and social differentiation enabled only a little development of special professional roles and of adequate remuneration for such roles. The fact that in most of these societies the sale of offices was very common attests to this.

As a result of all these conditions, the different echelons of bureaucra-cies may have often distorted many of their customary or explicit rules and diverted many of their services for the benefit of some social group with whom they might become identified and/or for their own benefit, in order to become both alienated from other strata and groups in the society and oppressive toward such groups. In other words, the bureaucratic echelons may have displaced their service goals to the rulers and/or to the various social strata and emphasized goals of self-interest and aggrandizement instead.

On the other hand, the relative weakness of many political groups and the great dependence of the bureaucracy on the kings could often cause the undermining of the relative autonomy of the bureaucracy. This could happen through the bureaucracies' total subjugation to the rulers by the ruler diverting all the activities of the bureaucracy for his own exclusive use without allowing it to perform any continuous services to different strata in the society and to uphold any general rules of provision of services.

For all these reasons the bureaucratic administration in these societies could develop political orientations which were to some extent opposed to the basic premises of their polities, undermine the polities' foundations, and generate processes of change which could not be contained within the framework of these polities.

It is the main purpose of this paper to analyze the major types of such political orientations of the main echelons of the bureaucratic administrations in the historical-bureaucratic empires, and to investigate the conditions under which each of these orientations and patterns of activities tends to develop.

II

The preceding discussion indicates that the major types of political orientations developed by the bureaucracies in the historical-bureaucratic societies were the following: (a) maintenance of service orientations to both the rulers and the major strata (with, in the societies studied here, usually greater emphasis on services to the rulers); (b) development into a merely passive tool of the ruler with but little internal autonomy or performance of services to the different strata of the population; (c) displacement of bureaucracies' service goals to various strata and to the rulers in favor of goals of self-aggrandizement and usurpation of power exclusively in its own favor and/or in favor of a group with which it becomes closely identified; (d) displacement of bureaucracies' service goals to the major strata in favor of goals of self-aggrandizement and attainment of political power—but together with maintenance of service goals to the rulers.

Needless to say all the bureaucratic administrations in the historical-bureaucratic polities usually evinced some mixture or overlapping of all these four tendencies or orientations, although a particular tendency was usually predominant, for at least part, if not the whole, of the history of a particular bureaucratic-historic polity. It is with this relative predominance and its influence on the continuity of the political systems of these societies that we are mainly concerned here.

The discussion of the political orientations of the bureaucracies would be incomplete without considering how these were related to the scope of their activities. Various studies...

have shown that in general the scope of the activities of a bureaucracy, as measured by the institutional spheres in which it was active and by the extent of specialization of departments, was closely related to the extent of development of the basic conditions of these societies—i.e., the extent of differentiation of the institutional structure of these societies and the scope of the autonomy of political spheres within them.

However, in all these discussions we have not differentiated between several types of activities in which the bureaucracy may be engaged and especially between technical or regulatory activities, i.e., between activities oriented mainly to the performance of technical services and between activities oriented to social and political regulation of different groups. While it is obvious that every bureaucratic administration in any of the historical-bureaucratic societies is engaged in both types of activities, the predominant activity may vary greatly from one case to another.

Moreover, there necessarily existed also great variations as to the criteria of such regulation and especially for whose benefit the regulation was done. All these variables were, as we shall see in greater detail, influenced by the political orientations and activities of the bureaucracy.

III

We shall begin with a description of the major types of political orientations and activities of the bureaucracies that can be found in the historical-bureaucratic societies.

We start with analysis of those cases in which the bureaucracy maintained its service orientation to both the rulers and some of the major strata, even if, in the societies with which we are concerned, there was always a greater emphasis on service to the ruler. Such political orientations and tendencies of the bureaucracy were developed and maintained in the Sassanid Empire, especially during the first period of its history and during the reign of Khawad, in the Byzantine Empire through most of the period between the 7th and 10th centuries, in the Spanish-American Empire in the first century and a half of its existence, in France, especially in the period from the Fronde to the last decades of Louis XIV*e* reign, in England in the 17th and 18th centuries, in the Chinese Empire throughout the first and middle periods of most of its dynasties, and in the Abbasid Empire until the 11th century.

In most of these cases, the bureaucracy maintained some of its internal organizational autonomy while at the same time the ultimate control of the rulers was not weakened—even if there always developed many tensions and quarrels within the bureaucracy and between it and the rulers. In most of these cases continuous and general usages or even explicit rules of service, appointment, and promotion were maintained with the bureaucracy. There also developed some relatively strong professional and even departmental *esprit de corps,* some extent of internal collegiality and responsibility, and various internal supervisory and disciplinary bodies which attempted to maintain the standards of discipline and service.

At the same time rulers successfully held their control over the bureaucracy through special officials (private officials of the inner courts, special *intendants* or visitors), through a relatively strong control over allocation of budget and over private traffic in offices, and through the monarch's direct participation in the process of decision making within the upper echelons of the bureaucracy.

IV

The second main type of political orientation of bureaucracy that can be found in the historical-bureaucratic societies is characterized by the bureaucracy's total subservience to the king, to the exclusion of almost any subservience, except for some minimal technical services, to the major strata of the population. The best examples of this development can be found in Prussia in the 17th and 18th centuries, and in the Ottoman Empire, especially during the first century and a half of its existence, while more embryonic developments can be discerned also in other conquest empires like the Spanish-American Empire in the first stages of its development, in periods of rapid change and of reorganization of royal power in Sassanid Persia under Khusro, and in Byzantium, in periods of great external dangers, especially under Heraclius.

In all these cases the strong hand of the rulers over the bureaucracy could be discerned first in the internal organization of the bureaucracy. The bureaucracy's most crucial characteristic, in such cases, was the very small extent of internal autonomy. This was manifested in the continuous shifting of officials from place to place and office to office without any fixed general rules, in the destruction by the rulers of any distinct career patterns, in the maintenance by them of strong and often arbitrary discipline not based on any general rules or criteria, in their destruction of any departmental or professional *esprit de corps* and cooperation, and in their insistence on the bureaucrats being "personal" servants of the ruler and of the "State" as personified by the ruler. This strong and often ruthless direction of the bureaucracy by the rulers made it for sometime—especially during the first stages of the establishment of new polities—a relatively efficient instrument for the implementation of the rulers' main goals, such as mobilization of resources, unification of the country, and suppression of opposition. From a long-term point of view, however, this "strong hand" of the rulers often diminished the efficiency of the bureaucracy, quashed the initiative of officials, and gave rise to overformalistic attitudes and activities and to many subterfuges and tricks through which officials tried to avoid the rulers' control. Moreover this often led, as we shall see, to the growing rapacity and self-assertion of the bureaucracy.

V

The third main type of political orientation of a bureaucracy was that which stressed the bureaucracy's own autonomy and self-interest to an extent that may have involved evasion of all political supervision from above and/or the displacement of its service goals to different strata. In these cases the upper echelons of the bureaucracy attempted to act almost exclusively in their own self-interest or in the interest of groups or strata with which they became allied or identified and, insofar as possible, they attempted to minimize their service orientation and professional and political responsibility.

The most extreme manifestations of this tendency, in our case studies, can be found during the various periods of aristocratic predominance in Sassanid Persia, the decadent stages of the Chinese dynasties when the bureaucracy became rapacious and almost fully identified with some specific gentry groups, the final period of the Byzantine empire, the period of aristocratic reaction in France in the 18th century, and, to some extent, at the close of the Hapsburg era, during the decline of the Spanish-American Empire, and in the later stages of the Abbasid Empire.

This type of socio-political orientation of the bureaucracy was usually connected also with several developments in its internal structure. All these developments were rooted in the partial or total transformation of the administration into a relatively inefficient, self-seeking group, concerned mostly with the maximization of its own benefits with but minimal regard to public duties or efficiency.

The most important manifestations of these developments were: (a) recruitment of bureaucratic personnel, mainly through various nepotistic channels within the bureaucracy itself; (b) conception of bureaucratic posts by their holders, as mainly sinecures, private, even hereditary property, and the consequent development of an intensive unrestricted and unregulated traffic in office; (c) a consequent proliferation of bureaucratic personnel beyond the necessities of bureaucratic tasks, and a tendency toward the implementation of "Parkinson's Law"; (d) a growing proliferation of departments with consequent difficulties in coordination; (e) a weakening of the effectiveness of the bureaucracy; (f) a growing "formalization" and "ritualism" in bureaucratic practice, both in the internal relations within the bureaucracy and in the bureaucracy's relations with its clients.

VI

The fourth type of political orientation of bureaucracy which tended to develop in the historical-bureaucratic societies was characterized by the combination of strong self-orientation of the bureaucracy (i.e., orientation of self-aggrandizement in the social, economic, and political spheres), together with service orientation to the poli[t]y and the rulers with an almost total lack of any service orientation to other strata or social groups. Two main types of such semiusurpatory bureaucracies which maintained some political responsibility and service can be found in our material.

First, we find such a type in the less developed, more "traditional" societies, such as Ancient Egypt and Sassanid Persia (in its patrimonial stages, e.g., in the first two periods of its history where a relatively autonomous bureaucracy was often closely allied with a traditional, semipatrimonial ruler). Second are the cases, best exemplified by Prussia and Austria in the late 18th and early 19th centuries, when the bureaucracy, together with some of the aristocratic groups, developed some *modus vivendi* with the kings within the framework of a relatively differentiated bureaucratic polity.

In both these cases the organizational pattern and the patterns of activities of the bureaucracy differed in some important respects from both a totally subservient and a totally aristocratized bureaucracy. Although, in most of these cases, the bureaucracy evinced many of the characteristics of a relatively "closed" group, with membership restricted mainly to members of upper social groups, at the same time it maintained a relatively efficient administrative structure and some type of departmental division of labor and internal system of supervision which enabled it to implement, in a relatively efficient way, various policies and political goals. Moreover, in most of these cases

the various echelons of the bureaucracy tended to maintain some professional or "service" ideology and status image, in which service to the polity was to some extent at least emphasized.

VII

What were the conditions under which each of these major types of political orientation in the bureaucracy developed? Our preceding analysis indicates that the development of different political orientations of the bureaucratic administrations was very closely related to its standing within the society and especially to its relations to the rulers and to various strata in the society. Therefore, in order to understand the variations of the bureaucracy's political orientation, it is necessary first to examine its position in the social structure.

This position may be analyzed according to the following criteria: (a) the position of the main echelons of the bureaucracy in the hierarchy of status and power; (b) the extent to which the bureaucracy, or its upper and middle echelons, constituted an independent status group, or, conversely, the extent to which its different echelons were considered parts of other social strata; (c) the criteria according to which the bureaucracy (or its different echelons) was differentiated from other strata or substrata, and especially the extent to which the proximity to the ruler and exercise of power served as such criteria; (d) the extent to which the bureaucracy was alienated from other social groups.

VIII

The analysis of material bearing on the societies referred to above indicates that there existed a very close relation between the social position of the bureaucracy (and especially of its upper echelons) and its major political orientations, and that one of the main mechanisms through which these two were connected was the patterns and avenues of recruitment into the bureaucracy.

Thus the material shows, first, that the maintenance of service orientation to both the rulers and the major strata by the bureaucracy was very closely related to either its partial incorporation in various flexible and "free" strata or at least nonalienation from such strata, and, second, that the greater the extent of the bureaucracy's incorporation within such strata, the greater was the emphasis, by the bureaucracy, of service orientation to both the rulers and the main strata.

The greatest extent of such incorporation of the bureaucracy within "flexible," nontraditional, upper and middle, urban and peasant (or gentry) groups developed in England and China. In these cases the bureaucracy was largely viewed as a part of these strata, using the same major symbols of status and participating largely in similar styles of life, although it developed and emphasized its distinctive occupational roles and career patterns. These specific bureaucratic careers usually ranked, in such cases, as one possibility within the range of occupational and status roles open to members of these (respective) strata.

Thus in England we find that the administrative careers were, to a very large extent, one of the possibilities within the accepted way of life of the upper rural classes and to a smaller extent of the upper urban classes. In China the bureaucracy, although greatly subordinated in every instance to the ruler and deriving part of its prestige from him, emphasized, through the system of examination, classical (Confucian) education as the main criterion of status. This bureaucracy was generally considered to be a part of the wider literati group and was greatly, although not entirely, rooted in the gentry. Its official prestige was derived from the examination degrees and from its devotion to the Confucian ideals which it shared with the literati. Although the extent to which the Chinese bureaucracy constituted an entirely autonomous group, differentiated from the gentry is yet subject to debate, there can be little doubt that there existed very strong interrelations between these two terms of a common cultural tradition.

Less fully developed incorporation of the bureaucracy in various middle and social strata can also be found in France during the reign of Henri IV and immediately afterward. There such incorporation could be seen especially with respect to the middle echelons of the bureaucracy, in the very strong relation between the developing *noblesse de robe* and the rising urban groups.

In these cases the members of the higher and middle echelons of the bureaucracy were recruited from various higher and middle flexible strata, i.e., mostly from upper and middle urban groups, from professional circles, and from the gentry and upper peasant groups, and these members continued, to a very great extent, to maintain close relations with their groups of origin. They often constituted an important channel of linkage with the more traditional groups and the provinces, and with the differentiated types of political activity that had developed at the centers of these polities.

A somewhat different social pattern among a service-oriented bureaucracy (with special emphasis on service to the rulers) could be found in Sassanid Persia under the reigns of Khawad and Khusro, during early and middle Byzantium, in the Spanish-American Empire, and in the Abbasid Caliphate. Here the upper echelons of the bureaucracy developed into relatively autonomous status groups emphasizing either their services and political position and/or power as the main criterion of their distinct status. However, in these cases, the bureaucracy, even while constituting a nearly separate group emphasizing its own criteria of status, continued to maintain some relation with different upper and middle urban, professional gentry and upper peasant groups, from whom many of its members were recruited. In most of these societies the members of the bureaucracy were not alienated from these strata and constituted an important link between these groups and the central political institutions—even if the bureaucracy and these strata were not entirely identical, and even when there existed between them great differences of style of life and of social and political participation.

Thus, in early and middle Byzantium we find that the bureaucracy constituted a comparatively independent status group, oriented mostly to the implementation of the Emperor's goals and policies, given to his supervision, and tending to emphasize service both to the Emperor and to the polity. In conjunction with all these characteristics, its members usually stressed the occupation of a bureaucratic office as basic status criteria. In the social sphere the bureaucracy was relatively autonomous and distinct from other groups but closely associated with some major social strata, especially with the upper peasant merchant and urban profes-sional and cultural groups. This applies to most periods of the 7th through 10th century Byzantium (with the partial exception, perhaps, of the reign of Heraclius) which was then at its prime. It was only during its decline, when the State was weakened and the aristocracy became powerful, that the bureaucracy became very closely associated with the aristocracy and to some extent (although never entirely) incorporated into it, becoming alienated from the more differentiated middle groups and oppressive toward them and toward lower groups.

A similar situation can be found in the Spanish-American Empire. Here the bureaucracy initially constituted a separate group, differentiated from both the Spanish settlers and the natives and emphasizing (with the full approval of the Crown) its autonomous status. But it was also closely associated with the upper classes of the local settlers and the groups of local aristocracy. As in Byzantium, the bureaucracy tended toward aristocratization and assimilation into the upper strata when the power of the rulers and their ability to implement their goals weakened. Similarly, such tendencies toward social autonomy, based on the bureaucracy's service to the rulers and its power positions but linked with a relatively close and positive relation to various (especially middle urban and rural) groups, can be found in the Abbasid Empire up to the end of the 9th and middle of the 10th centuries.

In these societies the upper and middle echelons of the bureaucracy were usually also recruited from various middle urban and rural groups, but the process of recruitment was a rather selective one, tending to emphasize the distinctiveness of the bureaucratic career pattern, to remove the recruits from their groups of origin, and to weaken their relations with groups—even if no special attitudes or alienation were developed or stressed.

IX

The bureaucracy's subservience to the rulers was usually closely connected with its being a separate status group, with strong emphasis on power and service to the rulers as the main distinctive social characteristic. Although socially autonomous, with a status based on its special position, such bureaucracies were subject politically to the rulers' supervision. In the first stages of the Ottoman Empire, both the political subservience and social autonomy of the bureaucracy were assured by the "slave" system wherein most of the bureaucracy's members were the Sultan's personal slaves, recruited from alien elements. In Prussia in the 17th century the Hohenzollerns established a widespread bureaucratic organization entirely subordinate to the ruler, deriving its status and power from its relation to the ruler, and markedly hostile, in the first stages of its development, to the aristocracy, older town autonomies and the various "Stande" organizations.

In these cases the upper and middle echelons of the bureaucracy were usually recruited from the lower or from the very weak, middle strata and sometimes from alien groups. They were removed from their groups of origin, and the process of recruitment stressed their alienation and total distinctiveness from any established social status.

The bureaucracy was usually, at least for the period during which the rulers were able to control it, alienated from the strata from which many of its members were recruited,

and its members developed a marked "punishment" orientation toward [these] strata. It tended very often to develop monolithic status aspirations and often, with the encouragement of the rulers, it strove to establish itself as the sole apex of a status hierarchy based largely on the criterion of power.

However, the bureaucracy's great dependence on the king made difficult the full realization of its aspirations to autonomous power and status. As long as the rulers maintained their strong control, the bureaucracy could not usually develop into a separate and cohesive status group; its members and their families were very often subject to the vicissitudes and arbitrariness of the monarch's will. Therefore it often happened that, as the bureaucracy developed and became more stabilized and diversified, it tried to find various ways to assert its own status and sought allies among some especially aristocratic groups which could provide it with symbols of status and social standing against the rulers.

X

The development by the bureaucracy, or rather by its upper echelons, of tendencies toward displacement of service goals to the various strata and/or the rulers was closely connected with the development of the bureaucracy into some sort of strongly ascriptive stratum, either an independent semiaristocratic or "gentry" stratum (emphasizing power as a status criterion) or a part of an existing aristocratic stratum. These bureaucracies were alienated, to some extent at least, from the rulers. Such development took place in the periods of decline (from the 13th century onward) in Byzantium and in the Abbasid Empire, during the aristocratic reaction in 18th century France, and to a smaller extent in the period of decline of several Chinese dynasties.

In such cases the bureaucracy tended usually to weaken and de-emphasize the distinctiveness of its occupational and career patterns and its professional ideology and self-image as servants of the country. It tried to lend the basic attributes of aristocratic status to its position, to make the offices into some sort of private hereditary possessions or fiefs, to limit recruitment into the bureaucracy to members of bureaucratic families, and to minimize its accountability to various strata and, in extreme cases, to the rulers as well.

It was only insofar as an aristocratized bureaucracy was not alienated from the rulers and was not strongly opposed to one of the other strata, as was the case in Ancient Egypt and to some extent in Prussia and Russia in the 17th and 18th centuries, that it maintained some orientation toward the maintenance of public service.

XI

Thus we see that each of the main political orientations of the bureaucracy was connected with the occupation by its members of specific types of positions in the social structure. What were the specific conditions that influenced the nature of the social standing of the bureaucracy and, through this standing, its political orientations and patterns of activities?

The main variables influencing the political orientations and activities of the bureaucracy were, first, the extent of differentiation and the goals of the rulers. Second, however, because of the special position of the bureaucracy in the political and social structure of these societies, the very constellation of the political forces and process in the society and especially the extent of compatibility between the goals of the rulers and the political orientations of the major groups were of crucial importance in influencing the development of the social status and political orientations of the bureaucracy.

We may start with a brief analysis of the influence of the major goals of the rulers on the social standing and political orientation of the bureaucracy. In cases where the rulers emphasized political, collective goals (i.e., military and expansionist goals, or goals of internal political consolidation), the bureaucracy emphasized its own autonomous status position. Such goals stressed the autonomy and the special position of the rulers who were in a way the main bearers of these goals and therefore of the bureaucracy. In cases where the rulers emphasized mainly cultural or economic goals (as in China, Abbasid Empire, or England), the bureaucracy usually became incorporated into some wider, relatively flexible groups and strata.

However, the predominant goals of the rulers provided only the framework within which the social and political orientations of the bureaucracy (and its patterns of activities) could develop. The concrete developments of these orientations depend to a large extent on the other conditions specified above, namely the extent of compatibility between the goals of the rulers and those of the major groups and the extent of differentiation of the social structure.

When the goals and interests of the major strata were basically incompatible with those of the rulers, the bureaucracy, aided by the rulers, developed power as its main autonomous criterion of status. It either became entirely autonomous and alienated from other strata and greatly dependent on and subservient to the rulers, or it tried to find some *modus vivendi* with some of these strata—the choice depending on the relative strength of the rulers and these "opposing" strata. Where these strata were not very powerful or politically active or where the rulers had sufficient power to repress them and make them politically passive, the bureaucracy (and especially its higher echelons) established power as a main criterion of status and attained autonomous status on the basis of this criterion. The two best examples of such development, from our cases, are Prussia and the Ottoman Empire. In both these countries the bureaucracy originally constituted an independent group or stratum, differentiated from all other strata and oriented against the aristocracy, the town, and estates. This bureaucracy was initially considered the monarch's means of implementing his goals, and it derived its status entirely from him and from its service to him.

In these two cases, however, both the social autonomy and political subservience of the bureaucracy diminished with time—as a result of the financial and social stability attained by its members and in close connection with a realignment of the relations between the rulers and some of the aristocratic groups and forces.

When the opposing strata were stronger, and when the rulers were weak and unable to control them, as was the case in many periods of decline of the historical polities, then the bureaucracy tended to ally itself with these (mostly aristocratic) groups at the expense of both the rulers and other strata and to develop a tendency to displacement of its service goals.

On the other hand, the greater the compatibility between the major goals of the rulers and the political orientations of the major strata, the more the bureaucracy tended to become incorporated into some free stratum or at least to be nonalienated from the rulers and major strata and to maintain its service orientation to the rulers and these strata. In such cases the bureaucracy's potential aspirations for social and political autonomy were curbed by the strength of both the rulers and the various flexible strata. At the same time, however, the very interaction between different strata and between the rulers exerted pressures on the bureaucracy and enabled it to develop some organization, occupational autonomy, and some autonomous professional image. Yet, the bureaucratic occupational patterns were easily incorporated into the general style of life of these strata. Such maintenance of service orientation was most developed in those cases in which the flexible "middle" strata were strong and relatively predominant in the social structure—i.e., when the extent of the differentiation of the social structure was relatively great, as in Byzantium between the 7th and 12th centuries, in China throughout most of its history, or in Western Europe in the 17th century.

Some such orientations could also develop when the scope of differentiation of the social structure was small and when the aristocracy or an aristocratized bureaucracy constituted the predominant social strata and when there existed a basic compatibility between the political goals of the rulers and those of the politically active aristocracy and the more passively oriented weak middle strata. In such cases the aristocracy, although relatively predominant in the social and economic hierarchy, was to some extent "domesticated" within the framework of the bureaucratic polity. Its own power and economic positions were to a great extent dependent on the existence of these frameworks and hence tended to develop some *modus vivendi* with the rulers.

Two such main types of aristocratized service bureaucracy can be found. One developed in the traditional, relatively nondifferentiated societies, such as Ancient Egypt or Sassanid Persia. In these cases the bureaucracy developed in two major directions. When the autonomous aristocratic-patrimonial hierarchy was relatively strong (as was the case through the greater part of Sassanid Persia's history), the upper echelons of the bureaucracy were usually incorporated into and absorbed by these elements. If the aristocracy was weak, however, as in Ancient Egypt, or oppressed by the rulers, as during several periods in Sassanid history (to some extent in the beginning of its history and especially in the reign of Khawad and Khusro), the upper echelons of the bureaucracy usually developed into a more autonomous stratum with some emphasis of the power criterion as an autonomous designate of status. But even in such cases the tendency to adopt an aristocratic style of life prevailed, although the new aristocracy was mainly one of service (*Amteraristokratie*).

The lower and middle echelons of the bureaucracy were, in such cases, usually recruited from the society's marginal groups or from outside, and, whatever their personal prestige and power, they rarely developed into an independent stratum. These echelons were either, to the extent that they aimed at economic position and security, in the same category as the lower strata (e.g., the peasantry) or outside the main status hierarchy of the society.

The second type of aristocratized service bureaucracy can be found especially in Prussia, from the time of Frederick the Great, and to a lesser extent in Austria and Russia in the 18th and 19th centuries. After an initial period when the bureaucracy constituted an avenue for social advancement for the middle classes and was anti-aristocratic in its orientation, there was in Prussia, under Frederick the Great, an aristocratic reaction on the part of the rulers and a growing infusion of the bureaucracy with aristocratic elements. Similar developments can also be seen in Austria and Russia. In these cases the ruler's control over the bureaucracy and the bureaucracy's service orientation were not entirely weakened as a result of the bureaucracy's partial aristocratization. They were greatly increased by the ruler's dependence on the bureaucracy and the political power of both the bureaucracy and the aristocratic group.

This development followed a period during which various aristocratic groups and, to a smaller degree, the (traditional) towns became adjusted to the demands of the rulers. They benefited economically from the political framework, and, when the rulers themselves, after some "flirting" with various middle groups, tended to emphasize their conservative orientations and distrust of some of the more flexible groups, these groups continued to be of some importance in the social structure.

A total displacement of service goals by an aristocratized bureaucracy developed mainly in those cases when the policies of the ruler depleted or alienated the various origins of free-floating resources and political support. This displacement also occurred when the ruler became less able to uphold his distinct political orientations and goals and more dependent on various conservative-aristocratic forces. These forces attempted to monopolize the most important economic and political positions in the society, thus furthering the dwindling of the "flexible" strata or their alienation from the framework and symbols of the existing political institutions. Usually in such cases the bureaucracy attempted either to incorporate some of these strata with its own status hierarchy, based on the criterion of power, or to develop as an independent aristocratic stratum and acquire for itself many of the symbols of aristocratic status.

Such conditions could develop both in societies, like the Ottoman Empire and (to a smaller extent) the Spanish-American Empire, in which the bureaucracy was initially subservient to the rulers, and in those societies, like Byzantium, the Abbasid Empire, and France, in which for relatively long periods of time there existed a service-oriented bureaucracy.

XII

The various conditions connected with the development of the different types of political orientations of the bureaucracy were not fixed. In any society these conditions could change throughout its history, and these changes would bring about alterations in the social standing and political orientation of the bureaucracy.

Thus in many of the societies studied here an initially strong subservice of the developing bureaucracy to the ruler very often gave way to a more differentiated service orientation of the bureaucracy to both the ruler and the major strata. This was the case, for instance, in Byzantium after the 7th and 8th centuries and in the Spanish-American Empire in the first two centuries of its development. In some circumstances, especially in periods of external danger, such service orientation again became weakened, and subordination to the rulers developed or was re-established.

In many other cases the ruler attempted to check the tendencies of the aristocracy to self-aggrandizement. The various periodic attempts by the ruler (or his active ministers) to effect reforms of the bureaucracy are very instructive from this point of view. Many reforms, such as those of Frederick Wilhelm in Prussia, Wang An-shih in China, and Heraclius and Leo in Byzantium, aimed at the re-establishment of the control of the ruler over the bureaucracy and aimed against the growing usurpation of power and displacement of service goals by the upper echelons of the bureaucracy. They were very often directed against those structural characteristics of the bureaucracy which were seen as the most important manifestations of its total independence, and especially against: (a) the narrowing of the base of recruitment to the bureaucracy; (b) the conception of the bureaucratic position as a sort of sinecure; (c) overformalization and ritualization; (d) proliferation of uncoordinated activities and departments and lack of control.

In all of these cases, and especially where reforms were successful, the rulers were aided by different social groups in their attempts at reforms of the bureaucracy, especially by the rising middle classes (or in some instances, like that of Byzantium, by the rural middle classes).

The most frequent and prevalent change to be found in the political orientations of the bureaucracy, in periods of decline of the political systems studied here, was the development of a ruler-centered or a service-oriented bureaucracy into a self-centered aristocratic or semi-aristocratic body.

XIII

The preceding analysis has illustrated and substantiated the thesis that the political orientations of the bureaucracy in centralized, bureaucratic, political systems can be fully understood only in connection with the bureaucracies' status position in the social structure and its relation to the constellation of political forces within this social structure. We have seen that the nature of the political orientation and the patterns of activities of the bureaucracy were greatly influenced by the bureaucracy's social position within the society, and that this position was influenced by, first, the extent of differentiation of the social structure, second, the major goals of the rulers, and, third and most important, by the relative strength of the major social strata vis-à-vis the ruler and vis-à-vis one another and by the extent of compatibility between the goals of the ruler and the political orientation of these strata.

We have seen also that these social and political conditions which influenced the development of the political orientations of the bureaucracy were not fixed in any society, but tended to change according to the relative strength of social forces and the outcome of the political struggle.

Because of the crucial position of the bureaucracy in the political struggle, these different political orientations and activities may have had many repercussions on the changes in the constellation of political forces in the bureaucratic societies. In order to fully understand such repercussions it is worthwhile to analyze the patterns of activities developed by the different types of bureaucracies in the historical-bureaucratic societies.

As indicated above, the scope of the activities of the bureaucracy was mainly influenced by the extent of structural differentiation and by the major goals of the rulers of these societies. However, as also indicated, the political orientations of the bureaucracy greatly influenced several aspects of its activities, especially the relative importance of technical or regulative activities.

The emphasis on technical and regulative activities was mainly developed by those bureaucracies that maintained service orientations to both the rulers and the major strata. The extent to which these bureaucracies emphasized more technical or regulative activities and the criteria according to which such regulation was effected depended on the relative predominance of the rulers or the major strata in the political field and on the scope of the autonomous regulative mechanisms developed by the different strata.

Thus, in Byzantium or in the Spanish-American Empire, where the rulers were predominant, the bureaucracies provided many technical services to the population. At the same time, they also implemented many regulative policies in the major institutional spheres—economic, political, and cultural—policies that were mainly guided by the interests of the rulers. On the other hand, as in England and to a more limited extent in China, where several of the social groups and strata were very strong, the bureaucracies emphasized the provision of technical services more, and only the indirect control of major social strata and institutional spheres and their regulative activities were greatly influenced by the interests of the politically strong strata.

In most cases in which there existed

a dominant emphasis on the regulative activities of the bureaucracy, the extent of the political participation of the major groups in the organs of political struggle was small. We find the same situation where there was an emphasis on regulative and technical activities, and where the extension of the scope of the bureaucratic activities was usually evident in the growing participation of the major strata in the organs of political struggle.

The second factor which influenced the relative importance of regulative or technical activities of the bureaucracy was the scope of the autonomous mechanisms developed by the major social strata in the main institutional fields. The greater the scope of the activities of these autonomous mechanisms, the smaller the extent of regulative activities of the bureaucracy.

XIV

The predominance of regulative activities, with small emphasis on technical service, developed usually in those types of bureaucracies that minimized the service orientations to various groups and strata and strongly emphasized service to the rulers and/or self-aggrandizement.

Where the bureaucracy was entirely subservient to the ruler (as in Prussia and the Ottoman Empire), it tended to develop, under his direction, various regulative activities which aimed to assure the power position of the ruler and the bureaucracy—and the resources needed by them—in opposition to the potentially active social strata.

The most important among these activities were: (a) attempts to regulate *in toto* most of the social spheres, aiming not only at providing different groups and strata with technical services but also at establishing the general principles governing the regulation of social, economic, political, and cultural activities and/or at creating many new types of such organizations and activities; (b) attempts to penetrate into many social spheres and groups, even if they did not seem to be in need of these specific services of the bureaucracy; (c) attempts to develop various legal activities aiming at regimentation and prescription of many aspects of social life; and (d) attempts to develop various party-political and propagandist activities, the main purpose of which was to control and even monopolize the free-floating political potential in the society and to minimize the possibility of development of independent centers of power.

A similar pattern of activities was developed by bureaucracies that displaced goals of service in favor of goals of self-interest and self-aggrandizement. In those cases the bureaucracy usually developed various usurpatory regulative-prescriptive activities, serving mostly the interests of the upper echelons of the bureaucracy and allied groups instead of the rulers and other groups and strata.

Activities of these bureaucracies were not, in these cases, geared to the implementation of any predominant political goals or of any consistent set of policies. They served the diverse and often inconsistent interests of different bureaucratic and aristocratic groups. Hence such bureaucracies usually evinced a much smaller degree of efficiency and unity of policy than were found in the initial stages of "oppressive" bureaucracies, totally subservient to the rulers.

Those bureaucracies which combined a tendency to *partial* usurpation of power and strong autonomy together with orientations to performance of public services emphasized strong regulation of most aspects of social life in the society. However, they were usually not as oppressive and self-oriented as those of the totally aristocratized bureaucracies. The various echelons of the bureaucracies tended to maintain some professional ideology and image, in which service to the polity was strongly emphasized; hence their regulative activities were often guided by some consistent policies and goals.

XV

The preceding analysis demonstrates the ways in which activities of the bureaucracy influenced the basic social conditions of the political systems of the historical-bureaucratic societies, the constellations of political power, and the political process.

Insofar as the bureaucracy maintained its basic service orientations to both rulers and major strata, it usually contributed to the continuity and stability of the regime, and especially to the maintenance of the basic conditions of the centralized bureaucratic regimes. In those societies or periods in which such service orientations were maintained by bureaucracies, the rulers were able, with the help of the bureaucracies, to maintain their own positions and the positions of those strata supporting them, and to keep in check those strata opposed to the basic prerequisites of the centralized political systems. Insofar as the bureaucracy was able to monopolize the highest social, political, and economic positions and to minimize its political responsibility and responsiveness to the ruler and/or the major flexible strata, it tended very often to contribute to the weakening of the institutional frameworks of these Empires.

Because of the strong (actual or potential) involvement of the bu-reaucracy in the political struggle in these societies, the development of different political orientations of the bureaucracy has necessarily many repercussions on this political struggle.

Thus the total subservience of the bureaucracy to the ruler, as in Prussia and the Ottoman Empire, was usually connected with the utilization of a very high degree of force in the implementation of the ruler's goals, against strong opposition, and with relatively little direct support from those groups (such as urban classes, free peasantry) which could provide the requisite resources needed for the implementation of the ruler's goals and the development of centralized, bureaucratic polities. Such political orientation of the bureaucracy was usually connected with the establishment of rigid political systems. Because of the paucity of requisite free resources and the strongly prescriptive orientations of the rulers, these systems ultimately had to turn to the more traditional and ascriptive (aristocratic) groups, to use their social prestige, and ultimately to reach some sort of *modus vivendi*. These systems very often contributed to the weakening or alienation of the more flexible groups and strata.

The displacement of the bureaucracy's service goals by goals of illegitimate, self-aggrandizement, usually connected with at least partial aristocratization and with development of usurpatory policies, tended to contribute to the grave weakening of those flexible, nontraditional strata, which were the mainstay of usurpatory policies, as well as to the dwindling of both economic resources and political support requisite for the continuous functioning of these policies. This in turn . . . was a contributory cause in the gradual disintegration of these political systems, either by the strengthening of the aristocratic, ascriptive elements and the development of a prebureaucratic (patrimonial or feudal) system, by outright disintegration and dismemberment of the polity under external pressure, or by the development, usually through some revolutionary movement, of a more differentiated, "modern" type of political structure.

XVI

The preceding analysis indicates the rather paradoxical relationship of the bureaucracy to the basic prerequisites of the functioning of the political systems of historical-bureaucratic societies.

The bureaucracy, by virtue of its central regulative functions in the society, performed very important tasks in the internal regulation of free-floating power in the historical-bureaucratic societies, and in the ensurance of a continuous and regulated flow of such power and resources. Insofar as the bureaucracy became a semi-independent stratum, or was not effectively controlled in the political field, it may become itself an omnivorous consumer of such free resources, and it may greatly impede the functioning of the basic institutional frameworks of these societies, constituting a stumbling block on the continuous flow of regulated, generalized power. This relation of the bureaucracy to these prerequisites of the functioning of political systems in historical-bureaucratic societies can be seen in the differences in the conditions which make for growth of the scope of bureaucratic activities, as compared with those which increase the possibilities of bureaucracy's usurpation of political power and social position.

The general scope of activities (especially technical) of the bureaucracy was closely related to increased differentiation, growing development of free resources, and the rise of various mobile strata. But the scope of *regulative* activities of the bureaucracy was inversely related to the social and political strength of these strata. Although the range of technical activities of the bureaucracy usually increased wtih growing social differentiation, the extent to which the bureaucracy was able to become a socially and politically independent group was severely limited insofar as this differentiation was connected with growing social, economic, and political self-regulation of the major social groups and with the existence of politically powerful ruler[s] and groups.

This incompatibility, between the conditions which gave rise to the extension of the technical and service activities of the bureaucracy and between those which enabled its usurpation of political control and displacement of service goals, was inherent in the structural position of the bureaucracy and in the bases for its growth. It was inherent in the fact that the bureaucracy was, on the one hand, a functional group performing relatively specific tasks and, on the other, a group so closely related to the bases of power as to be able to monopolize power positions and develop into an independent social stratum, which could impede the continuity of the political systems.

It is this potential contradiction in the structure and orientation of the bureaucracy that accounts for the fact which has been, in a way, the focus of our analysis here; although bureaucracy's political orientations always and necessarily presuppose the basic premises of the bureaucratic polity, some of them may undermine the bases of these premises. In other words, the bureaucracy's tendency toward displacing its goals and activities, a tendency which may develop under certain conditions inherent in bureaucracy's growth, might nullify the possibility of its performing its basic tasks in the social structure, thus contributing to the weakening of the fundamental premises of centralized polities.

the chinese literati

fifteen

MAX WEBER

For twelve centuries social rank in China has been determined more by qualification for office than by wealth. This qualification, in turn, has been determined by education, and especially by examinations. China has made literary education the yardstick of social prestige in the most exclusive fashion, far more exclusively than did Europe during the period of the humanists, or as Germany has done. Even during the period of the Warring States, the stratum of aspirants for office who were educated in literature—and originally this only meant that they had a scriptural knowledge—extended through all the individual states. Literati have been the bearers of progress toward a rational administration and of all "intelligence."

As with Brahmanism in India, in China the literati have been the decisive exponents of the unity of culture. Territories (as well as enclaves) not administered by officials educated in literature, according to the model of

Reprinted from *From Max Weber: Essays in Sociology,* edited and translated by H. H. Gerth and C. Wright Mills, pp. 416–44. Copyright 1946 by Oxford University Press, Inc. Reprinted by permission. This material also appeared as Chapter V in *The Religion of China* by Max Weber (New York: The Free Press of Glencoe, 1951). [Footnotes omitted]

the orthodox state idea, were considered heterodox and barbarian, in the same way as were the tribal territories that were within the territory of Hinduism but not regulated by the Brahmans, as well as landscapes not organized as *polis* by the Greeks. The increasingly bureaucratic structure of Chinese polities and of their carriers has given to the whole literary tradition of China its characteristic stamp. For more than two thousand years the literati have definitely been the ruling stratum in China and they still are. Their dominance has been interrupted; often it has been hotly contested; but always it has been renewed and expanded. According to the Annals, the Emperor addressed the literati, and them alone, as "My lords" for the first time in 1496.

It has been of immeasurable importance for the way in which Chinese culture has developed that this leading stratum of intellectuals has never had the character of the clerics of Christianity or of Islam, or of Jewish Rabbis, or Indian Brahmans, or Ancient Egyptian priests, or Egyptian or Indian scribes. It is significant that the stratum of literati in China, although developed from ritual training, grew out of an education for genteel *laymen.* The "literati" of the feudal period, then officially called *po-shih,* that is, "living libraries," were first of all proficient in ritualism. They did not, however, stem from the sibs of a priestly nobility, as did the *Rishi* sibs of the *Rig-Veda,* or from a guild of sorcerers, as did in all likelihood the Brahmans of the *Atharva-Veda.*

In China, the literati go back, at least in the main, to the descendants, probably the younger sons, of feudal families who had acquired a literary education, especially the knowledge of writing, and whose social position rested upon this knowledge of writing and of literature. A plebeian could also acquire a knowledge of writing, although, considering the Chinese system of writing, it was difficult. But if the plebeian succeeded, he shared the prestige of any other scholar. Even in the feudal period, the stratum of literati was not hereditary or exclusive—another contrast with the Brahmans.

Until late historical times, Vedic education rested upon oral transmissions; it abhorred the fixing of tradition in writing, an abhorrence which all guilds of organized professional magicians are apt to share. In contrast to this, in China the writing of the ritual books, of the calendar, and of the *Annals* go back to prehistoric times. Even in the oldest tradition the ancient scriptures were considered magical objects, and the men conversant with them were considered holders of a magical charisma. As we shall see, these have been persistent facts in China. The prestige of the literati has not consisted in a charisma of magical powers of sorcery, but rather in a knowledge of writing and of literature as such; perhaps their prestige originally rested in addition upon a knowledge of astrology. But it has not been their task to aid private persons through sorcery, to heal the sick, for instance, as the magician does. For such purposes there were special professions. . . . Certainly the significance of magic in China, as everywhere, was a self-understood presupposition. Yet, so far as the interests of the community were concerned, it was up to its representatives to influence the spirits.

The emperor as the supreme pontifex, as well as the princes, functioned for the political community. And for the family, the head of the sib and the housefather influenced the spirits. The fate of the community, above all of the harvest, has been influenced since olden times by rational means, that is, by water regulation; and therefore the correct "order" of administration has always been the basic means of influencing the world of the spirits.

Apart from knowledge of scriptures as a means of discerning tradition, a knowledge of the calendar and of the stars was required for discerning the heavenly will and, above all, for knowing the *dies fasti* and *nefasti,* and it seems that the position of the literati has also evolved from the dignified role of the court astrologer. The scribes, and they alone, could recognize this important order ritually (and originally probably also by means of horoscopes) and accordingly advise the appropriate political authorities. An anecdote of the Annals shows the results in a striking manner.

In the feudal state of the Wei, a proved general—Wu Ch'i, the alleged author of the textbook in ritually correct strategy which was authoritative until our time—and a literary man competed for the position of first minister. A violent dispute arose between the two after the literary man had been appointed to the post. He readily admitted that he could neither conduct wars nor master similar political tasks in the manner of the general. But when the general thereupon declared himself to be the better man, the literary man remarked that a revolution threatened the dynasty, whereupon the general admitted without any hesitation that the literary man was the better man to prevent it.

Only the adept of scriptures and of tradition has been considered competent for correctly ordering the internal administration and the charismatically correct life conduct of the prince, ritually and politically. In sharpest contrast to the Jewish prophets, who were essentially interested in foreign policy, the Chinese literati-politicians, trained in ritual, were primarily oriented toward problems of internal administration, even if these problems involved absolute power politics, and even though while in charge of the prince's correspondence and of the chancellery they might personally be deeply involved in the guidance of diplomacy.

This constant orientation toward problems of the "correct" administration of the state determined a far-reaching, practical, and political rationalism among the intellectual stratum of the feudal period. In contrast to the strict traditionalism of the later period, the Annals occasionally reveal the literati to be audacious political innovators. Their pride in education knew no limit, and the princes—at least according to the layout of the Annals—paid them great deference. Their intimate relations to the service of patrimonial princes existed from ancient times and has been decisive for the peculiar character of the literati.

The origin of the literati is veiled from us in darkness. Apparently they were the Chinese *augurs*. The pontifical cesaro-papist character of the imperial power has been decisive for their position, and the character of Chinese literature has also been determined by it. There were official Annals, magically proved hymns of war and sacrifice, calendars, as well as books of ritual and ceremony. With their knowledge the literati supported the character of the state, which was in the nature of an ecclesiastic and compulsory institution; they took the state for granted as an axiomatic presupposition.

In their literature, the literati created the concept of "office," above all, the ethos of "official duty" and of the "public weal." If one may trust the Annals, the literati, being adherents of the bureaucratic organization of the state as a compulsory institution, were opponents of feudalism from the very beginning. This is quite understandable because, from the standpoint of their interests, the administrators should be only men who were personally qualified by a literary education. On the other hand, they claimed *for themselves* to have shown the princes the way toward autonomous administration, toward government manufacture of arms and construction of fortifications, ways and means by which the princes became "masters of their lands."

This close relation of the literati to princely service came about during the struggle of the prince with the feudal powers. It distinguishes the Chinese literati from the educated laymen of Hellas, as well as from those of Ancient India *(Kshatriya)*. It makes them similar to the Brahmans, from whom, however, they differ greatly in their ritualist subordination under a cesaro-papist pontifex. In addition, no caste order has existed in China, a fact intimately connected with the literary education and the subordination under a pontifex.

The relation of the literati to the *office* has changed its nature [in the course of time]. During the period of the feudal states, the various courts competed for the services of the literati, who were seeking opportunities for power and, we must not forget, for the best chances for income. A whole stratum of vagrant "sophists" *(che-she)* emerged, comparable to the wayfaring knights and scholars of the occidental Middle Ages. As we shall later see, there were also Chinese literati who, in principle, remained unattached to any office. This free and mobile stratum of literati were carriers of philosophical schools and antagonisms, a situation comparable to those of India, of Hellenic Antiquity, and of the Middle Ages with its monks and scholars. Yet, the literati as such felt themselves to be a unitary status group. They claimed common status honors and were united in the feeling of being the sole bearers of the homogeneous culture of China.

The relation of the Chinese literati to princely service as the normal source of income differentiated them as a status group from the philosophers of Antiquity and from at least the educated laymen of India, who, in the main, were socially anchored in fields remote from any office. As a rule, the Chinese literati strove for princely service both as a source of income and as a normal field of activity. Confucius, like Lao-tzu, was an official before he lived as a teacher and writer without attachment to office. We shall see that this relation to state-office (or office in a "church state") was of fundamental importance for the nature of the mentality of this stratum. For this orientation became increasingly important and exclusive. The opportunities of the princes to compete for the literati ceased to exist in the unified empire. The literati and their disciples then came to compete for the existing offices, and this development could not fail to result in a unified orthodox doctrine adjusted to the situation. This doctrine was to be *Confucianism*.

As Chinese prebendalism grew, the originally free mental mobility of the literati came to a halt. This development was fully underway even at the time when the Annals and most of the systematic writings of the literati originated and when the sacred books, which Shih Huang Ti had destroyed, were "rediscovered." They were "rediscovered" in order that they might be revised, retouched, and interpreted by the literati and therewith gain canonical value.

It is evident from the Annals that this whole development came about with the pacification of the empire, or rather that it was pushed to its conclusions during this period. Everywhere war has been the business of youth, and the sentence *sexagenarios de ponte* has been a slogan of warriors directed against the "senate." The Chinese literati, however, were the "old men," or they represented the old men. The Annals, as a paradigmatic public confession of the prince Mu Kung (of Ch'in), transmitted the idea that the prince had sinned by having listened to "youth" (the warriors) and not to the "elders," who, although having no strength, did have experience. In fact, *this* was the decisive point in the turn toward pacifism and therewith toward traditionalism. Tradition displaced charisma.

1. Confucius

Even the oldest sections of the classic writings connected with the name of K'ung-tzu, that is, with Confucius as editor, permit us to recognize the conditions of charismatic warrior kings. (Confucius died in the year 478 B.C.) The heroic songs of the hymnbook *(Shih Ching)* tell of kings fighting from war chariots, as do the Hellenic and Indian epics. But considering their character as a whole, even these songs are no longer heralds of individual, and in general, purely human heroism, as are the Homeric and Germanic epics. Even when the *Shih Ching* was edited, the king's army had nothing of the romance of the warrior followings or the Homeric adventures. The army already had the character of a disciplined bureaucracy, and above all it had "officers." The kings, even in the *Shih Ching*, no longer win simply because they are the greater heroes. And that is decisive for the spirit of the army. They win because before the Spirit of Heaven they are morally right and because their charismatic virtues are superior, whereas their enemies are godless criminals who, by oppression and trespass upon the ancient customs, have wronged their subjects' weal and thus have foregone their charisma. Victory is the occasion for moralizing reflections rather than heroic joy. In contrast to the sacred scriptures of almost all other ethics, one is struck at once by the lack of any "shocking" expression, of any even conceivably "indecent" image. Obviously, a very systematic expurgation has taken place here, and this may well have been the specific contribution of Confucius.

The pragmatic transformation of the ancient tradition in the Annals, produced by official historiography and by the literati, obviously went beyond the priestly paradigms performed in the Old Testament, for example, in the Book of Judges. The chronicle expressly ascribed to Concius' authorship contains the driest and most sober enumeration of military campaigns and punitive expeditions against rebels; in this respect it is comparable to the hieroglyphic protocols of Assyria. If Confucius really expressed the opinion that his character could be recognized with special clarity from this work—as tradition maintains—then one would have to endorse the view of those (Chinese and European) scholars who interpret this to mean that his characteristic achievement was this systematic and pragmatic correction of facts from the point of view of "propriety." His work must have appeared in this light to his contemporaries, but for us its pragmatic meaning, in the main, has become opaque.

The princes and ministers of the classics act and speak like paradigms of rulers whose ethical conduct is rewarded by Heaven. Officialdom and the promotion of officials according to merit are topics for glorification. The princely realms are still ruled hereditarily; some of the local offices are hereditary fiefs; but the classics view this system skeptically, at least the hereditary offices. Ultimately they consider this system to be merely provisional. In theory, this pertains even to the hereditary nature of the dignity of the emperor. The ideal and legendary Emperors (Yao and Shun) designate their successors (Shun and Yü) without regard to birth, from the circle of their ministers and over the heads of their own sons, solely according to their personal charisma as certified by the highest court officials. The emperors designate their ministers in the same way, and only the third Emperor, Yü, does not name his first minister (Yi) but his son (Ch'i) to become his successor.

In contrast with the old and genuine documents and monuments, one looks in vain for genuinely heroic minds in most of the classic writings. The traditional view held by Confucius is that caution is the better part of valor and that it ill behooves the wise man to risk his own life inappropriately. The profound pacification of the country, especially after the rule of the Mongols, greatly enhanced this mood. The empire became an empire of peace. According to Mencius, there were no "just" wars within the frontiers of the empire, as it was considered as one unit. Compared to the size of the empire, the army had finally become very tiny. After having separated the training of the literati from that of the knights, the emperors retained sport and literary contests and gave military certificates in addition to the state examinations of the literati. Yet for a long time the attainment of such military certificates had hardly any connection with an actual career in the army. And the fact remained that the military were just as despised in China as they were in England for two hundred years, and that a cultivated literary man would not engage in social intercourse on an equal footing with army officers.

2. The Development of the Examination System

During the period of the central monarchy, the mandarins became a status group of certified claimants to office prebends. All categories of Chinese civil servants were recruited from their midst, and their qualification for office and rank depended upon the number of examinations they had successfully passed.

These examinations consisted of three major degrees, which were considerably augmented by intermediary, repetitive, and preliminary examinations as well as by numerous special conditions. For the first degree alone there were ten types of examinations.

The question usually put to a stranger of unknown rank was how many examinations he had passed. Thus, in spite of the ancestor cult, how many ancestors one had was not decisive for social rank. The very reverse held: it depended upon one's official rank whether one was allowed to have an ancestral temple (or a mere table of ancestors, which was the case with illiterates). How many ancestors one was permitted to mention was determined by official rank. Even the rank of a city god in the Pantheon depended upon the rank of the city's mandarin.

In the Confucian period (sixth to fifth century B.C.), the possibility of ascent into official positions as well as the system of examinations was still unknown. It appears that as a rule, at least in the feudal states, the "great families" were in the possession of power. It was not until the Han dynasty—which was established by a parvenu—that the bestowal of offices according to merit was raised to the level of a principle. And not until the T'ang dynasty, in 690 A.D., were regulations set up for the highest degree. As we have already mentioned, it is highly probable that literary education, perhaps with a few exceptions, was at first actually, and perhaps also legally, monopolized by the "great families," just as the Vedic education in India was monopolized. Vestiges of this continued to the end. Members of the imperial sib, although not freed from all examinations, were freed from the examination for the first degree. And the trustees, whom every candidate for examinations, until recently, had to name, had to testify to the candidate's "good family background." During modern times this testimony has only meant the exclusion of descendants of barbers, bailiffs, musicians, janitors, carriers, and others. Yet alongside this exclusion there was the institution of "candidates for the mandarinate," that is, the descendants of mandarins enjoyed a special and preferred position in fixing the maximum quota of examination candidates from each province. The promotion lists used the official formula "from a mandarin family and from the people." The sons of well-deserved officials held the lowest degree as a title of honor. All of which represent residues of ancient conditions.

The examination system has been fully carried through since the end of the seventh century. This system was one of the means the patrimonial ruler used in preventing the formation of a closed estate, which, in the manner of feudal vassals and office nobles, would have monopolized the rights to the office prebends. The first traces of the examination system *seem* to emerge about the time of Confucius (and Huang K'an) in the sub-state of Ch'in, a locality which later became autocratic. The selection of candidates was determined essentially by military merit. Yet, even the *Li Chi* and the *Chou Li* demand, in a quite rationalist way, that the district chiefs examine their lower officials periodically with regard to their morals, and then propose to the emperor which of them should be promoted. In the unified state of the Han Emperors, pacifism began to direct the selection of officials. The power of the literati was tremendously consolidated after they had succeeded in elevating the correct Kuang Wu to the throne in 21 A.D. and in maintaining him against the popular "usurper" Wang Mang. During the struggle for prebends, which raged during the following period, ... the literati developed into a unified *status group*.

Even today the T'ang dynasty irradiates the glory of having been the actual creator of China's greatness and culture. The T'ang dynasty, for the first time, regulated the literati's position and established colleges for their education (in the seventh century). It also created the *Hanlin Yüan,* the so-called "academy," which first edited the Annals in order to gain precedents, and then controlled the emperor's correct deportment. Finally, after the Mongol storms, the national Ming dynasty in the fourteenth century decreed statutes which, in essence, were definitive. Schools were to be set up in every village, one for every twenty-five families. As the schools were not subsidized, the decree remained a dead letter—or rather we have already seen which powers gained control over the schools. Officials selected the best pupils and enrolled a certain number in the colleges. In the main, these colleges have decayed, although in part they have been newly founded. In 1382, prebends in the form of rice rents were set aside for the "students." In 1393, the number of students was fixed. After 1370, only examined men had claims to offices.

At once a fight set in between the various regions, especially between the North and the South. The South even then supplied candidates for examinations who were more cultured, having experienced a more comprehensive environment. But the North was the military foundation stone of the empire. Hence, the emperor intervened and *punished* (!) the examiners who had given the "first place" to a Southerner. Separate lists for the North and the South were set up, and moreover, a struggle for the patronage of offices began immediately. Even in 1387 special examinations were given to officers' sons. The officers and officials, however, went further, and demanded the right to designate their successors, which meant a demand for re-feudalization. In 1393 this was conceded, but in the end only in a modified form. The candidates presented were preferentially enrolled in the colleges, and prebends were to be reserved for them: in 1465 for three sons, in 1482 for one son. In 1453 we meet with the purchase of college places, and in 1454 with the purchase of offices. During the fifteenth century, as is always the case, these developments arose from the need for military funds. In 1492 these measures were abolished, but in 1529 they were re-introduced.

The *departments* also fought against one another. The Board of Rites was in charge of the examinations after 736, but the Board of Civil Office appointed the officials. The examined candidates were not infrequently boycotted by the latter department, the former answering by going on strike during the examinations. Formally, the minister of rites, actually, the minister of offices (the major-domo) were in the end the most powerful men in China. Then merchants, who were expected to be less "stingy," came into office. Of course, this hope was quite unjustified. The Manchus favored the old traditions and thus the literati and, as far as possible, "purity" in the distribution of offices. But now, as before, three routes to office existed side by side: (1) imperial favors for the sons of the "princely" families (examination privileges); (2) easy examinations (officially every three to six years) for the lower officials by the higher officials who controlled patronage; this inevitably led each time to advancement also to higher positions; (3) the only legal way: to qualify effectively and purely by examination.

In the main, the system of examinations has actually fulfilled the functions as conceived by the emperor. Occasionally (in 1372), it was suggested to the emperor—one can imagine by whom—that he draw the conclusion from the orthodox charisma of virtues by abolishing the examinations, since virtue *alone* legitimizes and qualifies. This conclusion was soon dropped, which is quite understandable. For after all, both parties, emperor and graduates, had a stake in the examination system, or at least they thought they had. From the emperor's standpoint, the examination system corresponded entirely to the role which the *mjestnitshestvo*, a technically heterogeneous means, of Russian despotism played for the Russian nobility. The system facilitated a competitive struggle for prebends and offices among the candidates, which stopped them from joining together into a feudal office nobility. Admittance to the ranks of aspirants was open to everybody who was proved to be educationally qualified. The examination system thus fulfilled its purpose.

3. The Typological Position of Confucian Education

We shall now discuss the position of this educational system among the great types of education. To be sure, we cannot here, in passing, give a sociological typology of pedagogical ends and means, but perhaps some comments may be in place.

Historically, the two polar opposites in the field of educational ends are: to awaken charisma, that is, heroic qualities or magical gifts; and, to impart specialized expert training. The first type corresponds to the charismatic structure of domination; the latter type corresponds to the *rational* and bureaucratic (modern) structure of domination. The two types do not stand opposed, with no connections or transitions between them. The warrior hero or the magician also needs special training, and the expert official is generally not trained exclusively for knowledge. However, they are polar opposites of types of education and they form the most radical contrasts. Between them are found all those types which aim at cultivating the pupil for a *conduct of life*, whether it is of a mundane or of a religious character. In either case, the life conduct is the conduct of a status group.

The charismatic procedure of ancient magical asceticism and the hero trials, which sorcerers and warrior heroes have applied to boys, tried to aid the novice to acquire a "new soul," in the animist sense, and hence, to be reborn. Expressed in our language, this means that they merely wished to *awaken* and to test a capacity which was considered a purely personal gift of grace. For one can neither teach nor train for charisma. Either it exists *in nuce*, or it is infiltrated through a miracle of magical rebirth—otherwise it cannot be attained.

Specialized and expert schooling attempts to *train* the pupil for practical usefulness for administrative purposes—in the organization of public authorities, business offices, workshops, scientific or industrial laboratories, disciplined armies. In principle, this can be accomplished with anybody, though to varying extent.

The pedagogy of cultivation, finally, attempts to *educate* a cultivated type of man, whose nature depends on the decisive stratum's respective ideal of cultivation. And this means to educate a man for a certain internal and external deportment in life. In principle this can be done with everybody, only the goal differs. If a separate stratum of warriors form the decisive status group—as in Japan—education will aim at making the pupil a stylized knight and courtier, who despises the pen-pushers as the Japanese Samurai have despised them. In particular cases, the stratum may display great variations of type. If a priestly stratum is decisive, it will aim at making the disciple a scribe, or at least an intellectual, likewise of greatly varying character. In reality, none of these types ever occurs in pure form. The numerous combinations and intermediary links cannot be discussed in this context. What is important here is to define the position of Chinese education in terms of these forms.

The holdovers of the primeval charismatic training for regeneration, the milk name, the previously discussed initiation rites of youth, the bridegroom's change of name, and so on, have for a long time in China been a formula (in the manner of the Protestant confirmation) standing beside the testing of educational qualifications. Such tests have been monopolized by the political authorities. The educational qualification, however, in view of the educational means employed, has been a "cultural" qualification, in the sense of a general education. It was of a similar, yet of a more specific nature than, for instance, the *humanist* educational qualification of the Occident.

In Germany, such an education, until recently and almost exclusively, was a prerequisite for the official career leading to positions of command in civil and military administration. At the same time this *humanist* education has stamped the pupils who were to be prepared for such careers as belonging socially to the *cultured* status group. In Germany, however—and this is a very important difference between China and the Occident—rational and specialized *expert* training has been added to, and in part has displaced, this educational status qualification.

The Chinese examinations did not test any special skills, as do our modern national and bureaucratic examination regulations for jurists, medical doctors, or technicians. Nor did the Chinese examinations test the possession of charisma, as do the typical "trials" of magicians and bachelor leagues. To be sure, we shall presently see the qualifications which this statement requires. Yet it holds at least for the technique of the examinations.

The examinations of China tested whether or not the candidate's mind was thoroughly steeped in literature and whether or not he possessed the *ways of thought* suitable to a cultured man and resulting from cultivation in literature. These qualifications held far more specifically with China than with the German humanist gymnasium. Today one is used to justifying the gymnasium by pointing to the practical value of formal education through the study of Antiquity. As far as one may judge from the assignments given to the pupils of the lower grades in China, they were rather similar to the essay topics assigned to the top grades of a German gymnasium, or perhaps better still, to the select class of a German girls' college. All the grades were intended as tests in penmanship, style, mastery of classic writings, and finally—similar to our lessons in religion, history, and German—in conformity with the prescribed mental outlook. In our context it is decisive that this education was on the one hand purely secular in nature, but, on the other,

was bound to the fixed norm of the orthodox interpretation of the classic authors. It was a highly exclusive and bookish literary education.

The literary character of education in India, Judaism, Christianity, and Islam resulted from the fact that it was completely in the hands of Brahmans and Rabbis trained in literature, or of clerics and monks of book religions who were professionally trained in literature. As long as education was Hellenic and not "Hellenist," the Hellenic man of culture was and remained primarily ephebe and hoplite. The effect of this was nowhere thrown into relief more clearly than in the conversation of the Symposium, where it is said of Plato's Socrates that he had never "flinched" in the field, to use a student term. For Plato to state this is obviously at least of equal importance with everything else he makes Alcibiades say.

During the Middle Ages, the military education of the knight, and later the genteel education of the Renaissance salon, provided a corresponding though socially different supplement to the education transmitted by books, priests, and monks. In Judaism and in China, such a counterbalance was, in part altogether, and in part as good as altogether, absent. In India, as in China, the literary means of education consisted substantially of hymns, epic tales, and casuistry in ritual and ceremony. In India, however, this was underpinned by cosmogonic as well as religious and philosophical speculations. Such speculations were not entirely absent from the classics and from the transmitted commentaries in China, but obviously they have always played only a very minor role there. The Chinese authors developed rational systems of social ethics. The educated stratum of China simply has never been an autonomous status group of scholars, as were the Brahmans, but rather a stratum of officials and aspirants to office.

Higher education in China has not always had the character it has today. The public educational institutions *(Pan kung)* of the feudal princes taught the arts of the dance and of arms in addition to the knowledge of rites and literature. Only the pacification of the empire into a patrimonial and unified state, and finally, the pure system of examinations for office, transformed this older education, which was far closer to early Hellenic education, into what has existed into the twentieth century. Medieval education, as represented in the authoritative and orthodox *Hsiao Hsüeh,* that is "schoolbook," still placed considerable weight upon dance and music. To be sure, the old war dance seems to have existed only in rudimentary form, but for the rest, the children, according to age groups, learned certain dances. The purpose of this was stated to be the taming of evil passions. If a child did not do well during his instruction, one should let him dance and sing. Music improves man, and rites and music form the basis of self-control. The magical significance of music was a primary aspect of all this. "Correct music"—that is, music used according to the old rules and strictly following the old measures— "keeps the spirits in their fetters." As late as the Middle Ages, archery and charioteering were still considered general educational subjects for genteel children. But this was essentially mere theory. Going through the schoolbook one finds that from the seventh year of life, domestic education was strictly separated according to sex; it consisted essentially of instilling a ceremonial, which went far beyond all occidental ideas, a ceremonial especially of piety and awe toward parents and all superiors and older persons in general. For the rest, the schoolbook consisted almost exclusively of rules for self-control.

This domestic education was supplemented by school instruction. There was supposed to be a grade school in every *hsien*. Higher education presupposed the passing of the first entrance examination. Thus two things were peculiar to Chinese higher education. First, it was entirely nonmilitary and purely literary, as all education established by priesthoods has been. Second, its literary character, that is, its *written* character, was pushed to extremes. In part, this appears to have been a result of the peculiarity of the Chinese script and of the literary art which grew out of it.

As the script retained its pictorial character and was not rationalized into an alphabetical form, such as the trading peoples of the Mediterranean created, the literary product was addressed at once to both the eyes and the ears, and essentially more to the former. Any "reading aloud" of the classic books was in itself a translation from the pictorial script into the (unwritten) word. The visual character, especially of the old script, was by its very nature remote from the spoken word. The monosyllabic language requires sound perception as well as the perception of pitched tone. With its sober brevity and its compulsion of syntactical logic, it stands in extreme contrast to the purely visual character of script. But in spite of this, or rather—as Grube has shown in an ingenious way—in part because of the very rational qualities of its structure, the Chinese tongue has been unable to offer its services to poetry or to systematic thinking. Nor could it serve the development of the oratorical arts as have the structures of the Hellenic, Latin, French, German, and Russian languages, each in its own way. The stock of written symbols remained far richer than the stock of monosyllabic words, which was inevitably quite delimited. Hence, all phantasy and ardor fled from the poor and formalistic intellectualism of the spoken word and into the quiet beauty of the written symbols. The usual poetic speech was held fundamentally subordinate to the script. Not speaking but writing and reading were valued artistically and considered as worthy of a gentleman, for they were receptive of the artful products of script. Speech remained truly an affair of the plebs. This contrasts sharply with Hellenism, to which conversation meant everything and a translation into the style of the dialogue was the adequate form of all experience and contemplation. In China the very finest blossoms of literary culture lingered, so to speak, deaf and mute in their silken splendor. They were valued far higher than was the art of drama, which, characteristically, flowered during the period of the Mongols.

Among the renowned social philosophers, Meng Tzu (Mencius) made systematic use of the dialogue form. That is precisely why he readily appears to us as the one representative of Confucianism who matured to full "lucidity." The very strong impact upon us of the "Confucian Analects" (as Legge called them) also rests upon the fact that in China (as occasionally elsewhere) the doctrine is clothed in the form of (in part, probably authentic) sententious responses of the master to questions from the disciples. Hence, to us, it is transposed into the form of speech. For the rest, the epic literature contains the addresses of the early warrior kings to the army; in their lapidar forcefulness, they are highly impressive. Part of the didactic *Analects* consists of speeches, the character of which rather corresponds to pontifical "allocutions." Otherwise speech plays no part in the official literature. Its lack of development, as we shall see presently, has been determined by both social and political reasons.

In spite of the logical qualities of the language, Chinese thought has remained rather stuck in the pictorial and the descriptive. The power of *logos,* of defining and reasoning, has not been accessible to the Chinese. Yet, on the other hand, this purely scriptural education detached thought from gesture and expressive movement still more than is usual with the literary nature of any education. For two years before he was introduced to their meaning, the pupil learned merely to paint about 2,000 characters. Furthermore, the examiners focused attention upon style, the art of versification, a firm grounding in the classics, and finally, upon the expressed mentality of the candidate.

The lack of all training in calculation, even in grade schools, is a very striking feature of Chinese education. The *idea* of positional numbers, however, was developed during the sixth century before Christ, that is, during the period of Warring States. A calculative attitude in commercial intercourse had permeated all strata of the population, and the final calculations of the administrative offices were as detailed as they were difficult to survey, for reasons mentioned above. The medieval schoolbook enumerates calculation among the six "arts." And at the time of the Warring States, there existed a mathematics which allegedly included trigonometrics as well as the rule of three and commercial calculation. Presumably this literature, apart from fragments, was lost during Shih Huang Ti's burning of the books. In any case, calculation is not even mentioned in later pedagogy. And in the course of history, calculation receded more and more into the background of the education of the genteel mandarins, finally to disappear altogether. The educated merchants learned calculation in their business offices. Since the empire had been unified and the tendency toward a rational administration of the state had weakened, the mandarin became a genteel literary man, who was not one to occupy himself with the "$\sigma\chi o\lambda\acute{\eta}$" of calculation.

The mundane character of this education contrasts with other educational systems, which are nevertheless related to it by their literary stamp. The literary examinations in China were purely political affairs. Instruction was given partly by individual and private tutors and partly by the teaching staffs of college foundations. But no priest took part in them.

The Christian universities of the Middle Ages originated from the practical and ideal need for a rational, mundane, and ecclesiastic legal doctrine and a rational (dialectical) theology. The universities of Islam, following the model of the late Roman law schools and of Christian theology, practiced sacred case law and the doctrine of faith; the Rabbis practiced interpretation of the law; the philosophers' schools of the Brahmans engaged in speculative philosophy, in ritual, as well as in sacred law. Always ecclesiastic dignitaries or theologians have formed either the sole teaching staff or at least its basic corps. To this corps were attached mundane teachers, in whose hands the other branches of study rested. In Christianity, Islam, and Hinduism, prebends were the goals, and for the sake of them educational certificates were striven after. In addition, of course, the aspirant wished to qualify for ritual activity and the curing of souls. With the ancient Jewish teachers (precursors of the Rabbis), who worked "gratis," the goal was solely to qualify for instructing the laymen in the law, for this instruction was religiously indispensable. But in all this, education was always bound by sacred or cultic scriptures. Only the Hellenic philosophers' schools engaged in an education solely of laymen and freed from all ties to scriptures, freed from all direct interests in prebends, and solely devoted to the education of Hellenic "gentlemen."

Chinese education served the interest in prebends and was tied to a script, but at the same time it was purely lay education, partly of a ritualist and ceremonial character and partly of a traditionalist and ethical character. The schools were concerned with neither mathematics nor natural sciences, with neither geography nor grammar. Chinese philosophy itself did not have a speculative, systematic character, as Hellenic philosophy had and as, in part and in a different sense, Indian and occidental theological schooling had. Chinese philosophy did not have a rational-formalist character, as occidental jurisprudence has. And it was not of an empirical casuist character, as Rabbinic, Islamite, and, partly, Indian philosophy. Chinese philosophy did not give birth to scholasticism because it was not professionally engaged in logic, as were the philosophies of the Occident and the Middle East, both of them being based on Hellenist thought. The very concept of logic remained absolutely alien to

Chinese philosophy, which was bound to script, was not dialectical, and remained oriented to purely practical problems as well as to the status interests of the patrimonial bureaucracy.

This means that the problems that have been basic to all occidental philosophy have remained unknown to Chinese philosophy, a fact which comes to the fore in the Chinese philosophers' manner of categorical thought, and above all in Confucius. With the greatest practical matter-of-factness, the intellectual tools remained in the form of parables, reminding us of the means of expression of Indian chieftains rather than of rational argumentation. This holds precisely for some of the truly ingenious statements ascribed to Confucius. The absence of speech is palpable, that is, speech as a rational means for attaining political and forensic effects, speech as it was first cultivated in the Hellenic *polis*. Such speech could not be developed in a bureaucratic patrimonial state which had no formalized justice. Chinese justice remained, in part, a summary Star Chamber procedure (of the high officials), and, in part, it relied solely on documents. No oral pleading of cases existed, only the written petitions and oral hearings of the parties concerned. The Chinese bureaucracy was interested in conventional propriety, and these bonds prevailed and worked in the same direction of obstructing forensic speech. The bureaucracy rejected the argument of "ultimate" speculative problems as practically sterile. The bureaucracy considered such arguments improper and rejected them as too delicate for one's own position because of the danger of innovations.

If the technique and the substance of the examinations were purely mundane in nature and represented a sort of "cultural examination for the literati," the popular view of them was very different: it gave them a magical-charismatic meaning. In the eyes of the Chinese masses, a successfully examined candidate and official was by no means a mere applicant for office qualified by knowledge. He was a proved holder of magical qualities, which, as we shall see, were attached to the certified mandarin just as much as to an examined and ordained priest of an ecclesiastic institution of grace, or to a magician tried and proved by his guild.

The position of the successfully examined candidate and official corresponded in important points, for example, to that of a Catholic chaplain. For the pupil to complete his period of instruction and his examinations did not mean the end of his immaturity. Having passed the "baccalaureate," the candidate came under the discipline of the school director and the examiners. In case of bad conduct his name was dropped from the lists. Under certain conditions his hands were caned. In the localities' secluded cells for examinations, candidates not infrequently fell seriously ill and suicides occurred. According to the charismatic interpretation of the examination as a magical "trial," such happenings were considered proof of the wicked conduct of the person in question. After the applicant for office had luckily passed the examinations for the higher degrees with their strict seclusion, and after, at long last, he had moved into an office corresponding to the number and rank of examinations passed and depending on his patronage, he still remained throughout his life under the control of the school. And in addition to being under the authority of his superiors, he was under the constant surveillance and criticism of the censors. Their criticism extended even to the ritualist correctness of the very Son of Heaven. The impeachment of the officials was prescribed from olden times and was valued as meritorious in the way of the Catholic confession of sins. Periodically, as a rule every three years, his record of conduct, that is, a list of his merits and faults as determined by official investigations of the censors and his superiors, was to be published in the *Imperial Gazette.* According to his published grades, he was allowed to retain his post, was promoted, or was demoted. As a rule, not only objective factors determined the outcome of these records of conduct. What mattered was the "spirit," and this spirit was that of a life-long pennalism by office authority.

4. The Status-Honor of the Literati

As a status group, the literati were privileged, even those who had only been examined but were not employed. Soon after their position had been strengthened, the literati enjoyed *status privileges.* The most important of these were: first, freedom from the *sordida munera,* the *corvée;* second, freedom from corporal punishment; third, prebends (stipends). For a long time this third privilege has been rather severely reduced in its bearing, through the financial position of the state. The *Sheng* (baccalaureate) still got stipends of $10.00 yearly, with the condition that they had to submit every three to six years to the *Chü jen* or Master's examination. But this, of course, did not mean anything decisive. The burden of the education *and* of the periods of nominal pay actually fell upon the sib, as we have seen. The sib hoped to recover their expenses by seeing their member finally enter the harbor of an office. The first two privileges were of importance to the very end; for the *corvée* still existed, although to a decreasing extent. The rod, however, remained the national means of punishment. Caning stemmed from the terrible pedagogy of corporal punishment in the elementary schools of China. Its unique character is said to have consisted in the following traits, which remind one of our Middle Ages but were obviously developed to even greater extremes. The fathers of the sibs or of the villages compiled the "red cards," that is, the list of pupils *(Kuan-tan).* Then for a certain period they engaged a schoolmaster from among the over-supply of literati without office, which always existed. The ancestral temple (or other unused rooms) was the preferred schoolroom. From early until late the howling in unison of the written "lines" was to be heard. All day long the pupil was in a condition of mental daze, which is denoted by a Chinese character, the component parts of which signify a pig in the weeds *(meng).* The student and graduate received slaps on the palm of his hand, no longer on what, in the terminology of German mothers of the old hue, was called "the God-ordained spot."

The graduates of high rank were entirely free from such punishment so long as they were not demoted. And in the Middle Ages freedom from the *corvée* was firmly established. Nevertheless, in spite and also because of these privileges, the development of feudal ideas of honor was impossible on their basis. Moreover, as has been observed, these privileges were precarious because they were immediately voided in the case of demotion, which frequently occurred. Feudal honor could not be developed on the bases of examination certificates as a qualification for status, possible degradation, corporal punishment during youth, and the not quite infrequent case of degradation even in old age. But *once,* in the past, such feudal notions of honor had dominated Chinese life with great intensity.

The old Annals praise "frankness" and "loyalty" as cardinal virtues. "To die with honor" was the old watchword. "To be unfortunate and not to know how to die is cowardly." This applied particularly to an officer who did not fight "unto the death." Suicide was a death which a general, having lost a battle, valued as a *privilege.* To permit him to commit suicide meant to forego the right to punish him and therefore was considered with hesitation. The meaning of feudal concepts was changed by the patriarchal idea of *hsiao. Hsiao* meant that one should suffer calumny and even meet death as its consequence if it served the honor of the master. One could, and in general should, compensate for *all* the mistakes of the lord by loyal service. The *kotow* before the father, the older brother, the creditor, the official, and the emperor was certainly not a symptom of *feudal* honor. For the correct Chinese to kneel before his love, on the other hand, would have been entirely taboo. All this was the reverse of what held for the knights and the *cortegiani* of the Occident.

To a great extent, the official's honor retained an element of student honor regulated by examination achievements and public censures by superiors. This was the case even if he had passed the highest examinations. In a certain sense, it is true of every bureaucracy (at least on its lower levels; and in Württemberg, with its famous "Grade A, Fischer," even in the highest positions of office); but it held to quite a different extent in China.

5. The Gentleman Ideal

The peculiar spirit of the scholars, bred by the system of examinations, was intimately connected with the basic presuppositions from which the orthodox and also, by the way, nearly all heterodox, Chinese theories proceeded. The dualism of the *shen* and *kuei,* of good and evil spirits, of heavenly *Yang* substance as over against earthly *Yin* substance, also within the soul of the individual, necessarily made the sole task of education, including self-education, to appear to be the unfolding of the *Yang* substance in the soul of man. For the man in whom the *Yang* substance has completely gained the upper hand over the demonic *kuei* powers resting within him also has power over the spirits; that is, according to the ancient notion, he has magical power. The good spirits, however, are those who protect order and beauty and harmony in the world. To perfect oneself and thus to mirror this harmony is the supreme and the only means by which one may attain such power. During the time of the literati, the *chün tze,* the "princely man," and once the "hero," was the man who had attained all-around self-perfection, who had become a "work of art" in the sense of a classical, eternally valid, canon of psychical beauty, which literary tradition implemented in the souls of disciples. On the other hand, since the Han period at the latest, it was a firmly established belief among the literati that the spirits reward "beneficence," in the sense of social and ethical excellence. Benevolence tempered by classical (canonical) beauty was therefore the goal of self-perfection.

Canonically perfect and beautiful achievements were the highest aspiration of every scholar as well as the ultimate yardstick of the highest qualification certified by examination. Li Hung-chang's youthful ambition was to become a perfect literary man, that is, a "crowned poet," by attainment of the highest degrees. He was, and he remained, proud of being a calligrapher of great craftsmanship and of being able to recite the classics by heart, especially Confucius' "Spring and Autumn." This ability occasioned his uncle, after having tested it, to pardon the imperfections of his youth and to procure him an office. To Li Hung-chang all other branches of knowledge (algebra, astronomy) were only the indispensable means of "becoming a great poet." The classical perfection of the poem he conceived in the name of the Empress-Dowager, as a prayer in the temple of the tutelary goddess of silk-culture, brought him the Empress' favor.

Puns, euphemisms, allusions to classical quotations, and a refined and purely literary intellectuality were considered the conversational ideal of the genteel man. All politics of the day were excluded from such conversation. It may appear strange to us that this sublimated "salon" cultivation, tied to the classics, should enable man to administer large territories. And in fact, one did not manage the administration with mere poetry even in China. But the Chinese prebendary official proved his status quality, that is, his charisma, through the canonical correctness of his literary forms. Therefore, considerable weight was placed on these forms in official communications. Numerous important declarations of the emperors, the high priests of literary art, were in the form of didactic poems. On the other hand, the official had to prove his charisma by the "harmonious" course of his administration; that is, there must be no disturbances caused by the restless spirits of nature or of men. The actual administrative "work" could rest on the shoulders of subordinate officials. We have noticed that above the official stood the imperial pontifex, his academy of literati, and his collegiate body of censors. They publicly rewarded, punished, scolded, exhorted, encouraged, or lauded the officials.

Because of the publication of the "personal files" and all the reports, petitions, and memorials, the whole administration and the fateful careers of the officials, with their (alleged) causes, took place before the broadest public, far more so than is the case with any of our administrations under parliamentary control, an administration which puts the greatest weight upon the keeping of "official secrets." At least according to the official fiction, the official *Gazette* in China was a sort of running account of the emperor before Heaven and before his subjects. This *Gazette* was the classic expression for the kind of responsibility which followed from the emperor's charismatic qualification. However dubious in reality the official argumentation and the completeness of publication may have been—that, after all, also holds for the communications of our bureaucracy to our parliaments—the Chinese procedure at least tended to open a rather strong and often a quite effective safety-valve for the pressure of public opinion with regard to the official's administrative activities.

6. The Prestige of Officialdom

The hatred and the distrust of the subjects, which is common to all patrimonialism, in China as everywhere turned above all against the lower levels of the hierarchy, who came into the closest practical contact with the population. The subjects' apolitical avoidance of all contact with "the state" which was not absolutely necessary was typical for China as for all other patrimonial systems. But this apolitical attitude did not detract from the significance of the official education for the character formation of the Chinese people.

The strong demands of the training period were due partly to the peculiarity of Chinese script and partly to the peculiarity of the subject matter. These demands, as well as the waiting periods which were often quite long, forced those who were unable to live on a fortune of their own, on loans, or on family savings of the sort discussed above, to take up practical occupations of all sorts, from merchant to miracle doctor, before completing their educational careers. Then they did not reach the classics themselves, but only the study of the last (the sixth) textbook, the "schoolbook" *(Hsiao Hsüeh)*, which was hallowed by age and contained mainly excerpts from the classic authors. Only this difference in the *level* of education and not differences in the *kind* of education set these circles off from the bureaucracy. For only classic education existed.

The percentage of candidates who failed the examinations was extraordinarily high. In consequence of the fixed quotas, the fraction of graduates of the higher examinations was proportionately small, yet they always outnumbered many times the available office prebends. They competed for the prebends by personal patronage, by purchase money of their own, or by loans. The sale of prebends functioned here as in Europe; it was a means of raising capital for the purposes of state, and very frequently it replaced merit ratings. The protests of the reformers against the sale of offices persisted until the last days of the old system, as is shown by the numerous petitions of this sort in the *Peking Gazette.*

The officials' short terms of office (three years), corresponding to similar Islamic institutions, allowed for intensive and rational influencing of the economy through the administration as such only in an intermittent and jerky way. This was the case in spite of the administration's theoretical omnipotence. It is astonishing how few permanent officials the administration believed to be sufficient. The figures alone make it perfectly obvious that as a rule things must have been permitted to take their own course, as long as the interests of the state power and of the treasury remained untouched and as long as the forces of tradition, the sibs, villages, guilds, and other occupational associations remained the normal carriers of order.

Yet in spite of the apolitical attitude of the masses, which we have just mentioned, the views of the stratum of applicants for office exerted a very considerable influence upon the way of life of the middle classes. This resulted, first and above all, from the popular magical-charismatic conception of the qualification for office as tested by examination. By passing the examination, the graduate proved that he was to an eminent degree a holder of *shen.* High mandarins were considered magically qualified. They could always become objects of a cult, after their death as well as during their lifetime, provided that their charisma was "proved." The primeval magical significance of written work and of documents lent apotropaic and therapeutic significance to their seals and to their handwriting, and this could extend to the examination paraphernalia of the candidate. A province considered it an honor and an advantage to have one of its own sons selected by the emperor as the best graduate of the highest degree, and all whose names were publicly posted after having passed their examinations had "a name in the village." All guilds and other clubs of any significance had to have a literary man as a secretary, and these and similar positions were open to those graduates for whom office prebends were not available. The officeholders and the examined candidates for office, by virtue of their magical charisma and of their patronage relations—especially when they stemmed from petty bourgeois circles—were the natural "father confessors" and advisers in all important affairs of their sibs. In this they corresponded to the Brahmans *(Gurus)* who performed the same function in India.

Alongside the purveyor to the state and the great trader, the officeholder, as we have seen, was the personage with the most opportunities for accumulating possessions. Economically and personally, therefore, the influence on the population of this stratum, outside as well as inside their own sibs, was approximately as great as was the combined influence of the scribes and priests in Egypt. Within the sib, however, the authority of old age was a strong counterweight, as we have already emphasized. Quite independent of the "worthiness" of the individual officials, who were often ridiculed in popular dramas, the prestige of this literary education as such was firmly grounded in the population until it came to be undermined by modern Western-trained members of the mandarin strata.

7. Views on Economic Policy

The social character of the educated stratum determined its stand toward economic policy. According to its own legend, for millennia, the polity had the character of a religious and utilitarian welfare-state, a character which is in line with so many other typical traits of patrimonial bureaucratic structures bearing theocratic stamps.

Since olden times, to be sure, actual state policy, for reasons discussed above, had again and again let economic life alone, at least so far as production and the profit economy were concerned. This happened in China just as in the ancient Orient— unless new settlements, melioration through irrigation, and fiscal or military interests entered the picture. But military interests and interests in military finance had always called forth liturgical interventions in economic life. These interventions were monopolistically or financially determined, and often they were quite incisive. They were partly mercantilist regulations and partly in the nature of regulations of status stratification. Toward the end of national militarism, such planned "economic policy" eventually fell into abeyance. The government, conscious of the weakness of its administrative apparatus, confined itself to the care of the tide and the maintenance of the water routes, which were indispensable for provisioning the leading provinces with rice; for the rest, to the typically patrimonial policy of dearth and consumption. It had no "commercial policy" in the modern sense. The tolls the mandarins had established along the waterways were, so far as is known, merely fiscal in nature and never served any economic policy. The government on the whole pursued only fiscal and mercantilist interests, if one disregards emergency situations which, considering the charismatic nature of authority, were always politically dangerous. So far as is known, the most grandiose attempts to establish a unified economic organization were planned by Wang An-shih, who during the eleventh century tried to establish a state trading monopoly for the entire harvest. In addition to fiscal gains, the plan was intended to serve the equalization of prices and was connected with a reform in land taxes. The attempt failed.

As the economy was left to itself to a large extent, the aversion against "state intervention" in economic matters became a lasting and basic sentiment. It was directed particularly against monopolistic privileges, which, as fiscal measures, are habitual to patrimonialism everywhere. This sentiment, however, was only one among the quite different attitudes which resulted from the conviction that the welfare of the subjects was dependent upon the charisma of the ruler. These ideas often stood in unmediated fashion beside the basic aversion to state intervention, and continually, or at least occasionally, made for bureaucratic meddling in everything, which again is typical of patrimonialism. Moreover, the administration of course reserved the right to regulate consumption in times of dearth—a policy which is also part of the theory of Confucianism [as reflected] in numerous special norms concerning all sorts of expenditures. Above all, there was the typical aversion against too sharp a social differentiation as determined in a purely economic manner by free exchange in markets. This aversion, of course, goes without saying in every bureaucracy. The in-creasing stability of the economic situation under conditions of the economically self-sufficient and the socially homogeneously composed world-empire did not allow for the emergence of such economic problems as were discussed in the English literature of the seventeenth century. There was no self-conscious bourgeois stratum which could not be politically ignored by the government and to whose interests the "pamphleteers" of the time in England primarily addressed themselves. As always under patrimonial bureaucratic conditions, the administration had to take serious notice of the attitude of the merchants' guilds only in a "static" way and when the maintenance of tradition and of the guilds' special privileges were at stake. Dynamically, however, the merchant guilds did not enter into the balance, because there were no expansive capitalist interests *(no longer!)* of sufficient strength, as in England, to be capable of forcing the state administration into their service.

8. Sultanism and the Eunuchs as Political Opponents of the Literati

The total *political* situation of the literati can be understood only when one realizes the forces against which they had to fight. We may disregard the heterodoxies here.

In early times the main adversaries of the literati were the "great families" of the feudal period who did not want to be pushed out of their office monopolies. Having to accommodate themselves to the needs of patrimonialism and to the superiority of the knowledge of script, they found ways and means of paving the way for their sons by imperial favor.

Then there were the capitalist purchasers of office: a natural result of the leveling of status groups and of the fiscal money economy. Here the struggle could not lead to constant and absolute success, but only to relative success, because every demand of war pushed the impecunious central administration toward the jobbery of *office-prebends* as the *sole* means of war finance. This held until recent times.

The literati also had to fight the administration's rationalist interests in an expert officialdom. Specialist, expert officials came to the fore as early as 601 under Wen Ti. During the distress of the defensive wars in 1068 under Wang An-shih, they enjoyed a short-lived and full triumph. But again tradition won out and this time for good.

There remained only one major and permanent enemy of the literati: sultanism and the eunuch-system which supported it. The influence of the harem was therefore viewed with profound suspicion by the Confucians. Without insight into this struggle, Chinese history is most difficult to understand.

The constant struggle of the literati and sultanism, which lasted for two millennia, began under Shih Huang Ti. It continued under all the dynasties, for of course energetic rulers continually sought to shake off their bonds to the cultured status group of the literati with the aid of eunuchs and plebeian parvenus. Numerous literati who took a stand against this form of absolutism had to give their lives in order to maintain their status group in power. But in the long run and again and again the literati won out. Every drought, inundation, eclipse of the sun, defeat in arms, and every generally threatening event at once placed power in the hands of the literati. For such events were considered the result of a breach of tradition and a desertion of the classic way of life, which the literati

guarded and which was represented by the censors and the "Hanlin Academy." In all such cases "free discussion" was granted, the advice of the throne was asked, and the result was always the cessation of the unclassical form of government, execution or banishment of the eunuchs, a retraction of conduct to the classical schemata, in short, adjustments to the demands of the literati.

The harem system was of considerable danger because of the way in which successorship to the throne was ordered. The emperors who were not of age were under the tutelage of women; at times, this petticoat-government had come to be the very rule. The last Empress-Dowager, Tz'u Hsi, tried to rule with the aid of eunuchs. We will not discuss at this point the roles which Taoists and Buddhists have played in these struggles, which run through all of Chinese history— why and how far they have been natural coalitionists, specifically of the eunuchs, and how far they have been coalitionists by constellation.

Let us mention in passing that, at least by modern Confucianism, astrology has been considered an unclassical superstition. It has been thought to compete with the exclusive significance of the emperor's *Tao* charisma for the course of government. Originally this had not been the case. The departmental competition of the Hanlin Academy against the board of astrologers may have played a decisive part; perhaps also the Jesuit origin of the astronomic measures had a hand in it.

In the conviction of the Confucians, the trust in magic which the eunuchs cultivated brought about all misfortune. Tao Mo in his Memorial of the year 1901 reproached the Empress that in the year 1875 the true heir to the throne had been eliminated through her fault and in spite of the censors' protest, for the censor Wu Ko-tu had acknowledged this by his suicide. Tao Mo's posthumous memorial to the Empress and his letter to his son were distinguished by their manly beauty. There cannot be the slightest doubt of his sincere and profound conviction. Also the belief of the Empress and of numerous princes in the magical charisma of the Boxers, a belief which alone explains her whole policy, was certainly to be ascribed to the influence of eunuchs. On her death bed this impressive woman left as her counsel: (1) never again to let a woman rule in China, and (2) to abolish the eunuch system forever. This counsel was fulfilled in a different way than she had undoubtedly intended—if the report is accurate. But one may not doubt that for the genuine Confucian everything that has happened since, above all the "revolution" and the downfall of the dynasty, only confirms the correctness of the belief in the significance of the charisma of the dynasty's classic virtue. In the improbable but possible event of a Confucian restoration, the belief would be exploited in this sense. The Confucianists, who are ultimately pacifist literati oriented to inner political welfare, naturally faced military powers with aversion or with lack of understanding. We have already spoken of their relationship to the officers, and we have seen that the whole *Annals* are paradigmatically filled with it. There are protests to be found in the *Annals* against making "praetorians" into censors (and officials). As the eunuchs were especially popular as favorites and generals in the way of Narses, the enmity against the purely sultanist patrimonial army suggested itself. The literati took pride in having overthrown the popular military usurper Wang Mang. The danger of ruling with plebeians has simply always been great with dictators, yet only this one attempt is known in China. The literati, however, have submitted to *de facto* established power even when it was created purely by usurpation, as was the power of the Han, or by conquest, as was the power of the Mongol Manchus. They submitted even though they had to make sacrifices—the Manchus took over 50 per cent of the offices without having the educational qualifications. The literati have submitted to the ruler *if* the ruler in turn submitted to their ritualist and ceremonial demands; only *then,* in modern language, have they accommodated themselves and taken a "realistic" stand.

"Constitutionally"—and this was the theory of the Confucians—the emperor could rule *only* by using certified literati as officials; "classically" he could rule only by using orthodox Confucian officials. Every deviation from this rule was thought capable of bringing disaster and, in case of obstinacy, the downfall of the emperor and the ruin of the dynasty.

caste and the four life-stages
in traditional india

sixteen

HEINRICH ZIMMER

In India everybody wears the tokens of the department of life to which he belongs. He is recognizable at first glance by his dress and ornaments and the marks of his caste and trade class. Every man has the symbol of his tutelary deity painted on his forehead, by which sign he is placed and kept under the god's protection. Maiden, married woman, widow: each wears a distinctive costume. And to each pertains a clear-cut set of standards and taboos, meticulously defined, scrupulously followed. What to eat and what not to eat, what to approach and what to shun, with whom to converse, share meals, and intermarry: such personal affairs are minutely regulated, with severe and exacting penalties for accidental as well as for intentional infringement. The idea is to preserve without pollution-by-contact the specific spiritual force on which one's efficacy as a member of a particular social species depends.

Reprinted from *Philosophies of India* by Heinrich Zimmer. "Caste and the Four Life-Stages." Bollingen Series XXVI. Pantheon Books. Pages 151–59. Reprinted with the permission of the Bollingen Foundation, Princeton University Press, and Routledge and Kegan Paul, Ltd. [Some footnotes omitted]

For insofar as the individual is a functioning component of the complex social organism, his concern must be to become identified with the tasks and interests of his social role, and even to shape to this his public and private character. The whole group takes precedence over any of its components. All self-expression, as we know and care for it, is therefore ruled out, the precondition to participation in the group consisting not in cultivating, but in dissolving, personal tendencies and idiosyncrasies. The supreme virtue is to become assimilated—wholeheartedly and without residue — to the timeless, immemorial, absolutely impersonal mask of the classic role into which one has been brought by birth (*jāti*). The individual is thus compelled to become anonymous. And this is regarded, furthermore, as a process not of self-dissolution but of self-discovery; for the key to the realization of one's present incarnation lies in the virtues of one's present caste.

Caste is regarded as forming an innate part of character. The divine moral order (*dharma*) by which the social structure is knit together and sustained is the same as that which gives continuity to the lives of the individual; and just as the present is to be understood as a natural consequence of the past, so in accordance with the manner in which the present role is played will the caste of the future be determined. Not only one's caste and trade, furthermore, but also all the things that happen to one (even though apparently through the slightest chance) are determined by, and exactly appropriate to, one's nature and profoundest requirement. The vital, malleable episode at hand points back to former lives; it is their result—the natural effect of bygone causal factors operating on the plane of ethical values, human virtues, and personal qualities, in accordance with universal natural laws of elective attraction and spontaneous repulsion. What a person is and what he experiences are regarded as strictly commensurate, like the inside and the outside of a vase.

The correct manner of dealing with every life problem that arises, therefore, is indicated by the laws *(dharma)* of the caste *(varṇa)* to which one belongs, and of the particular stage-of-life *(āśrama)* that is proper to one's age. One is not free to choose: one belongs to a species— a family, guild and craft, a group, a denomination. And since this circumstance not only determines to the last detail the regulations for one's public and private conduct, but also represents (according to this all-inclusive and pervasive, unyielding pattern of integration) the real ideal of one's present natural character, one's concern as a judging and acting entity must be only to meet every life problem in a manner befitting the role one plays. Whereupon the two aspects of the temporal event—the subjective and the objective—will be joined exactly, and the individual eliminated as a third, intrusive factor. He will then bring into manifestation not the temporal accident of his own personality, but the vast, impersonal, cosmic law, and so will be, not a faulty, but a perfect glass: anonymous and self-effacing. For by the rigorous practice of prescribed virtues one actually can efface oneself, dissolving eventually the last quirk of impulse and personal resistance—thus gaining release from the little boundary of the personality and absorption in the boundlessness of universal being. Dharma is therefore fraught with power. It is the burning point of the whole present, past, and future, as well as the way through which to pass into the transcendental consciousness and bliss of the purest spiritual Self-existence.

Everybody is born to his own place *(sva-dharma)* in the phantasmagoric display of creative power that is the world, and his first duty is to show it, to live up to it, to make known by both his appearance and his actions just what part of the spectacle he is. Every feminine being is a manifestation on earth of the universal Mother, a personification of the productive, alluring aspect of the holy mystery that supports and continually creates the world. The married woman is to be all decency; the harlot is to pride herself on her ability to keep her allurements effective and sell her charms. The mother and housewife is to breed sons without cease, and to worship her husband as the human embodiment of all the gods. Husband and wife are to approach each other as two divinities; for he, through her, is reborn in his sons, just as the Creator is made manifest in the forms and creatures of the world through the magical operation of his own power, his śakti, personified in his goddess. And as the male member of the community is co-ordinated to the whole through the particular religious devotions and services proper to his social position, so the wife is co-ordinated to society as the śakti of her spouse. Her service to him is her religion, just as his religion is the service to his "Fathers" and the deities of his vocation. Thus the whole of life is lived as, and understood to be, a service to the Divine, all things being known as images of the one and universal Lord.

Every profession has its special tutelary divinity, who embodies and personifies the very skill of the trade, and wields or exhibits its tools as his distinguishing attributes. The tutelary divinity of writers, poets, intellectuals, and priests, for example, is the goddess Sarasvatī Vāc: the goddess of riverlike, streaming speech. And the patroness of magic priestcraft, Brāhmanhood, is Sāvitrī: not the human princess, daughter of King Aśvapati, who, according to the legend, rescued her husband, Prince Satyavān, from the dominion of King Death, but the female counterpart and divine energy, śakti, of Savitar-Brahmā, the Creator of the world; she is the all-moving, all-inspiring, divine principle of creation. Kāma, the Hindu Cupid, is the tutelary divinity of courtesans, and of those who stand in need of the lessons of the kāmaśāstra, the authorized code of traditional revealed wisdom in the lore of love and sex. While Viśvakarman, the divine "Expert of All Crafts," the carpenter, architect, and master craftsman of the gods, is the patron deity of workmen, artisans, and artists.

Each of these, representing the principle and sum total of a certain highly specialized department of knowledge and skill, is a jealous and exclusive god and master. The human creature called by birth to the deity's service is to dedicate all of his powers and devotion to worship; the slightest failure can entail disaster. Like a mistress, charming and generous if faithfully and exclusively served, but baleful, wrathful, terrific, if not duly paid her whole requirement, the god blossoms like a flower, yielding sweetness, fragrance, and fruit abundantly for the devotee of perfect concentration, but otherwise is touchy and revengeful. India's static, departmentalized, and mutually cooperative hierarchy of the crafts and professions, that is to say, demands and inculcates the most extreme one-sidedness. There is to be no choice, no floundering around, no sowing of wild oats. From the very first breath of life, the individual's energies are mastered, trained into channels, and co-ordinated to the general work of the superindividual who is the holy society itself.

This depersonalizing principle of specialization is pressed even further by the subdivision of the ideal lifecourse of the individual into four stages (āśrama). The first stage, that of the pupil (antevāsin), is ruled exclusively by obedience and submission. The pupil, eager to receive, under the magic spell of the spiritual teacher, the whole charge, the total transference, of the divine knowledge and magic craft of his vocation, seeks to be nothing but the sacred vessel into which that precious essence flows. Symbolically, by the spiritual umbilical cord of the "sacred thread" with which he is solemnly invested, he is linked to his guru as to the one and only, all-sufficient human embodiment and source (for him) of superhuman spiritual nourishment. Strict chastity (brahmacarya) is enjoined; and if through any experience with the other sex he violates this interdict, thereby breaking the continuity of the life-generating, lifebegetting intimacy and identification with the guru, the most severe and complex punishments descend upon him. This is the period for śraddhā (blind faith in the master-technician who knows the path), and śuśrūṣā (the will and desire to "hear" [śru] and to learn by heart; to hear, to obey, and to conform). This is the period when the mere natural man, the human animal, is to be absolutely sacrificed, and the life of man in the spirit, the supranormal wisdom-power of the "twice-born," to be made effective in the flesh.

Then, abruptly, when the stage of pupilship is finished, and without any transitional period, the youth, now a man, is transferred—one might say, hurled—into married life, the stage of householdership (*gṛhastha*). Taking over the paternal craft, business, or profession, he receives a wife (chosen for him by his parents), begets sons, supports the family, and does his best to identify himself with all the tasks and ideal roles of the traditional *pater familias,* member of the guild, etc. The young father identifies himself with the delights and worries of married life (*kāma*), as well as with the classic interests and problems of property and wealth (*artha*), so that he may have the means at his disposal, not only to support his growing family according to the standards proper to his birth or human species (*jāti*), but also to meet the more or less costly demands of the orthodox sacramental cycle of rituals. For the house-priest, the Brāhman guru, whom he now must employ and heed—even as Indra must employ and heed the divine Bṛhaspati— blesses and assists the family on every possible occasion, as a combination spiritual adviser and confessor, family doctor, consulting practical psychologist, exorcist, conjuror, and wizard. And these professional men charge their fees: that is part of the cause of the real effectiveness of their cryptic, holy, psychotherapeutic dealings. The gurus, linking themselves with full surrender (like everyone else in the community) to the privileges and duties of their own immemorial role,

serve as conduits of supernatural wisdom and holy power (*brahman*), like nerves of consciousness throughout the social body.

The guru tends to become petrified into an idol—just as everyone tends to become petrified, dehumanized, stabilized, and purged of spontaneous individuality—in proportion to the degree of perfection he achieves in the intensely stylized enactment of his timeless role. In the second half of the individual's life cycle, therefore, these brittle roles are to be put aside. Having identified himself wholly with the functions of his social personality (his social actor's mask, or *persona*), he must now as radically step away from that—throw off possessions and all the concerns of wealth (*artha*), break from the desires and anxieties of his now flowered and variously fruitful life-in-marriage (*kāma*), turn even from the duties of society (*dharma*) which have linked him to the universal manifestation of Imperishable Being through the stable archetypes of the human tragicomedy. His sons are now bearing the joys and burdens of the world; himself, in late middle life, may step away. And so he enters upon the third āśrama, that of the "departure to the forest" (*vanaprastha*). For we are not only social, professional masks, representing ageless roles in the shadow-world of time, but also something substantial; namely, a Self. We belong, cannot but belong, to the world, yet are not adequately described by our caste marks and costume, not fathomed to our essence by secular and moral functions. Our essence transcends this manifested nature and everything that belongs to it, our property, delights, our rights and duties, and our relationship to the ancestors and the gods. To seek to reach that unnamed essence is to enter upon the path of the quest for the Self; and this is the aim and end of the third of the four life-stages.

The man and wife in the period of the retreat to the forest cut off the cares, duties, joys, and interests that linked them to the world and begin the difficult inward quest. And yet, not even this idyl of the life of holiness in the forest can mark the end of their adventure; for, like the first period—that of studenthood—this is only a preparation. In the fourth and last āśrama—that of the wandering holy beggar (*bhikṣu*)—no longer linked to any exercise, no longer linked to any place, but "taking no thought of the future and looking with indifference upon the present," the homeless wanderer "lives identified with the eternal Self and beholds nothing else." "He no more cares whether his body, spun of the threads of karma, falls or remains, than does a cow what becomes of the garland that someone has hung around her neck; for the faculties of his mind are now at rest in the Holy Power (*brahman*), the essence of bliss."

Originally, Jaina saints went about "clothed in space" (*digambara*), i.e., stark naked, as a sign that they did not belong to any recognized group, sect, trade, or community. They had discarded all determining marks; for determination is negation by specialization.[1] In the same spirit, the wandering Buddhist monks were instructed to go clad in rags, or else in an ochre-colored garment—the latter being traditionally the garb of the criminal ejected from society and condemned to death. The monks donned this disgraceful raiment as a sign that they too were dead to the social

hierarchy. They had been handed over to death and were beyond the boundaries of life. They had stepped away from the world's limitations, out of all the bond ages of belonging to something. They were renegades. Likewise the Brāhman pilgrim-mendicant has always been likened to the wild goose or swan (*haṁsa*), which has no fixed home but wanders, migrating with the rain-clouds north to the Himalayas and back south again, at home on every lake or sheet of water, as also in the infinite, unbounded reaches of the sky.

Religion is supposed finally to release us from the desires and fears, ambitions and commitments of secular life—the delusions of our social, professional, and family interests; for religion claims the soul. But then religion is necessarily a community affair, and so itself is an instrument of bondage, tying us more subtly, by less gross and therewith more insinuative delusions. Anyone seeking to transcend the tight complacencies of his community must break away from the religious congregation. One of the classic ways of doing this is by becoming a monk—joining, that is to say, still another institution, this time dedicated to isolation from, and insurance against, the ordinary human bondages. Or people take the step into the forest, becoming hermit-solitaries—tied now to the gentle idyl of the hermitage and the innocent details of its primitive life-ritual. Where in all the world can one be totally free?

What is a man really, behind and beyond all the marks, costumes, implements, and activities that denote his civil and religious status? What being is it that underlies, supports, and animates all the states and changes of his life's shadowlike becoming? The anonymities of the forces of nature that operate within

---

[1] Later on, as a concession, the Jaina holy men donned the white garment and became *śvetāmbara,* "clothed in white." This was the most non-committal dress that they could find.

him; the curious performances, successful or unsuccessful, upon which his social character depends; the landscape and life incidental to his time and place of birth; the materials that pass through and constitute for a time his body, charm his fancy, and animate his imagination: none of these can be said to be the Self.

The craving for complete release from limitations, which is identical with the craving for absolute anonymity, one may seek to fulfill by turning homeless beggar-mendicant, with no fixed place to lay one's head, no regular road, no goal, no belongings. But then—one is still carrying oneself around. All those stratifications of the body and psyche that correspond to the demands and offerings of the environment and link one to the world wherever one may be are present, active still. To reach the Absolute Man (*puruṣa*) that is sought, one must somehow discard those garbs and obscuring sheaths. From the skin, down through the intellect and emotions, the memory of things past and the deep-rooted habits of reaction—those acquired spontaneities, the cherished automatisms of one's profoundly rooted likes and dislikes—all must be cast aside; for these are not the Self but "super-impositions," "colorings," "besmearings" (*añjana*), of its intrinsic radiance and purity. That is why before entering upon the fourth āśrama, that of the wandering nonentity, the Hindu practices the psychological exercises of the third, that of the idyl of the forest. He must put off himself to come to the adamantine Self. And that is the work of yoga. Yoga, Self-discovery, and then the absolutely unconditional identification of oneself with the anonymous, ubiquitous, and imperishable ground of all existence, constitute the proper end of the second half of the cycle of the orthodox biography. This is the time for wiping off the actor's paint that one wore on the universal stage, the time for the recollection and release of the unaffected and uninvolved, yet all-sustaining and enacting, living Person who was always there.

laws of class and stage of life in india

seventeen

A. L. BASHAM

Often and in many contexts we read of "the *Dharma* of class and stage of life" (*varṇāśrama-dharma*), which, in the golden age of the remote past, was self-evident and uninfringed, but which is now vague, misunderstood and partly forgotten, and which the brāhmans interpret and the king preserves and enforces. The implication of this phrase is that Dharma is not the same for all. There is indeed a common Dharma, a general norm of conduct which all must follow equally, but there is also a dharma appropriate to each class and to each stage in the life of the individual. The dharma of men of high birth is not that of humbler folk, and the dharma of the student is not that of the old man.

This thoroughgoing recognition that men are not the same, and that there is a hierarchy of classes, each with its separate duties and distinctive way of life, is one of the most striking features of ancient Indian sociology. Criticisms of the pretensions of the

Reprinted from *The Wonder that was India* (London: Sidgwick & Jackson, 1954; New York: Evergreen, 1959), pp. 137–51, by permission. Copyright 1954 by Sidgwick & Jackson Ltd.

higher classes were heard from time to time, and equalitarian propositions were occasionally put forward, but in general this concept has held its ground from the end of the Ṛg Vedic period [about 1500 to 1000 B.C.] to the present day.

The Four Great Classes

...By the end of the Ṛg Vedic period the fourfold division of society was regarded as fundamental, primeval, and divinely ordained. The four varnas of India developed out of very early Aryan class divisions, for some class stratification existed in many Indo-European communities, and ancient Irān had four *piśtras* or classes, comparable in some respects to those of India. In India class stratification grew more rigid when, in the Vedic period, a situation arose rather like that prevailing in South Africa today, with a dominant fair minority striving to maintain its purity and its supremacy over a darker majority. Tribal class-divisions hardened, and the dark-skinned aboriginal found a place only in the basement of the Aryan social structure, as a serf with few rights and many disabilities. Soon the idea of varna had become so deeply embedded in the Indian mind that its terminology was even used for the classification of precious commodities such as pearls, and useful materials like timber. Theoretically all Aryans belonged to one of the four classes, with the exception of children, ascetics and widows, who were outside the system.

Varṇa came to the Dravidian South comparatively late, for the earliest Tamil literature shows a society divided into tribal groups with little sense of the precedence of one over the other. Succeeding centuries saw the gradual hardening of class, until South Indian brāhmaṇs became even stricter in their ritual observances and the untouchables even more debased than in the North.

A sharp distinction was made between the three higher classes and the śūdra. The former were twice-born (*dvija*), once at their natural birth and again at their initiation, when they were invested with the sacred thread and received into Aryan society.[1] The śūdra had no initiation, and was often not looked on as Aryan at all. The fourfold division was in theory functional. Manu lays down that the duty of the brāhmaṇ is to study and teach, to sacrifice, and to give and receive gifts; the kṣatriya must protect the people, sacrifice, and study; the vaiśya also sacrifices and studies, but his chief function is to breed cattle, to till the earth, to pursue trade and to lend money; the śūdra's duty is only to serve the three higher classes—and "it is better," Manu adds elsewhere, "to do one's own duty badly than another's well." This epigram, elaborated so beautifully in the *Bhagavad Gītā,* was the leading theme of most Indian social

thought; for each man there was a place in society and a function to fulfil, with its own duties and rights.

This was the ideal, but though in the Middle Ages it was perhaps approached, it has never been wholly reached. The precepts of the texts which lay down the laws for the conduct of the four classes were rarely fully carried out in practice, and were often blatantly infringed. The texts ...were written by brāhmaṇs and from the brāhmaṇic point of view, and represent conditions as the brāhmaṇs would have liked them to be. Thus it is not surprising that they claim the utmost honour for the priestly class and exalt it above measure.

The brāhmaṇ was a great divinity in human form. His spiritual power was such that he could instantly destroy the king and his army, if they attempted to infringe his rights. In law he claimed great privileges, and in every respect he demanded precedence, honour and worship. Even the Buddhist scriptures, though they do not admit the more extravagant brāhmaṇical claims and regularly exalt the kṣatriya over the brāhmaṇ, recognize his greatness, if he is pious and sincere.

These Buddhist sources show us two types of brāhmaṇ. There were learned brāhmaṇs, performing all the rites of the Aryan and receiving great respect; but there were also village brāhmaṇs, who made much of their living by fortune-telling and sorcery, and who were less honoured. For all the rigidity of the class system the brāhmaṇs soon lost their racial purity, and it has even been suggested that, as Aryan culture expanded, schools of aboriginal sorcerers and medicine men managed to obtain a footing in the brāhmaṇic order, just as aboriginal chiefs were certainly assimilated to

---

[1] In later texts the term "twice-born" was often reserved for brāhmaṇs, but strictly it applies to kṣatriyas and vaiśyas also if they have been initiated.

the warrior class. Thus, it may well be, the proto-Hinduism of the Harappā culture was ultimately assimilated to the Aryan faith.

Of professional priests there were various types and classes—in the earliest times we read of the semi-legendary *ṛṣis*, or seers, who composed the Vedic hymns, while the sacrificial ritual demanded a number of priests (*ṛtvij*) with specialized duties—invokers (*hotṛ*), cantors (*udgātṛ*), and priests to perform the manual operations of the ceremony (*adhvaryu*). The term *brāhmaṇa* meant originally "one possessed of *brahman*," a mysterious magical force of the type widely known to modern anthropologists by the Polynesian word *mana*. It was first applied to the specially trained priest who superintended the whole sacrifice, and was ready to counteract with his magic spells any evil influence caused by minor errors of ritual. By the end of the Ṛg Vedic period the term was used for all members of the priestly class.

There were other divisions within the order. The brāhmaṇs of the later Vedic period were divided into exogamous septs (*gotra*), a system which was copied in part by other classes and has survived to the present day. Later the brāhmaṇ class formed many castes, linked together by endogamy and common practices. A further division was the *śākhā* or branch, based on the recension of the Vedic texts accepted as authoritative by the family in question.

Often the brāhmaṇ lived under the patronage of a king or chief, and was provided for by grants of tax-free land, farmed by peasants, who would pay their taxes to the brāhmaṇ instead of to the king; but there were also land-owning brāhmaṇs, who cultivated large estates by hired labour or serfs. The religious brāhmaṇ might have a high post at court, and the purohita's[2] importance in the state has already been noted. Other brāhmaṇs might earn a competence as teachers of the Veda, and of other branches of learning.

At all times many brāhmaṇs led truly religious lives. Kālidāsa's *Sakuntalā* gives a charming picture of a settlement of such pious brāhmaṇs, living simply but not too austerely in huts in the forest, where even the wild deer were unafraid of the gentle hermits, and the woodland was forever perfumed with the fragrance of their sacred fires. Such brāhmaṇ colonies were supported by the gifts of kings and chiefs and of the peasants of the neighbourhood. Other brāhmaṇs became solitary ascetics, while in the Middle Ages brāhmaṇ monastic orders were founded, rather on the Buddhist model.

But the varied religious activity of ancient India did not provide a livelihood for more than a few of the brāhmaṇs. The Smṛti literature contains special sections on "duty when in distress" (*āpad-dharma*), which carefully define what a man may legitimately do when he cannot earn a living by the profession normally followed by his class, and professions. Many were employed in important government posts, and several royal families were of brāhmaṇ origin. Generally the lawbooks disapprove of brāhmaṇs engaging in agriculture, because it inflicts injury on animals and insects, but this rule was often ignored. A brāhmaṇ is forbidden to trade in certain commodities—among them cattle and other animals, slaves,

---

2 This term was extended to mean a family priest, who performed the many rites and ceremonies of Hinduism for a family or group of families, and has survived in this sense to the present day.

weapons, and spirituous liquor—and his lending money at interest is also disapproved of, though Manu allows him to lend at low interest to "wicked people," by whom he probably means those who do not maintain Aryan rites. But though he kept these rules rigidly, a brāhman would find many trades and professions open to him.

Opinions differed as to whether a brāhman engaged in a secular profession was worthy of the respect accorded to the practising member of his class, and no clear ruling is laid down. Manu, the most authoritative of the Smṛtis, is uncertain on this point, and in different parts of the text diametrically opposed views are given. As far as can be gathered from general literature the special rights of the brāhman were usually only granted to those who lived by sacrifice and teaching. Cārudatta, the poor brāhman hero of the play "The Little Clay Cart," receives scurvy treatment at the hands of the court, probably because he is a brāhman by birth only, and not by profession.

For all his prestige, the brāhman was often the butt of satire. Even in the *Rg Veda* the croaking of frogs at the beginning of the rainy season is compared to the monotonous reciting of the priests, though here no sarcasm may be intended. But there can be no other explanation of a remarkable passage in the early *Chāndogya Upaniṣad*, which describes a vision of the sage Vaka Dālbhya, wherein dogs move round in a circle, each holding the tail of the preceding dog in its mouth, "just as the priests do when about to sing praises"; and then, repeating the very sacred syllable *Om*, they sing: "*Om!* let us eat! *Om!* let us drink! *Om!* may the gods Varuṇa, Prajāpati and Savitr bring us food!" Another early reference to the gluttony of brāhmaṇs occurs in the *Aitareya Brāhmaṇa,* in an interesting passage which describes the other three classes from the point of view of the warrior; here the brāhman is "a receiver of gifts, a drinker of soma, an eater of food, to be expelled at will." The *vidūṣaka,* the fool of Sanskrit drama, an amiable but gluttonous figure of fun, is invariably a brāhman.

There are, however, few frontal attacks on brāhmaṇical pretensions, even in the literature of the Buddhists, who came nearest to an anti-brāhmaṇical point of view; but one brief Buddhist tract, the "Diamond Needle," ascribed to Aśvaghoṣa, of the 1st or 2nd century A.D., attacks the claims of the priesthood, and indirectly the whole class system, with vigorous dialectical skill. The claims of the brāhman were, in fact, often ignored, and not wholly unchallenged.

The second was the ruling one, the members of which were in the Vedic period called *rājanya,* and later *kṣatriya.* The theoretical duty of the kṣatriya was "protection," which included fighting in war and governing in peace. In early times he often claimed precedence over the brāhman; this claim is implicit in the *Aitareya Brāhmaṇa* passage which we have quoted, the inclusion of which in a brāhmaṇical scripture is hard to account for. According to Buddhist tradition, in times when the brāhmaṇs are the highest class Buddhas are born in that class, while when kṣatriyas are the highest they are born as kṣatriyas. The historical Buddha was a kṣatriya, and his followers evidently had few doubts about class priorities. Where the names of the four classes are mentioned together in the Pāli scriptures that of the kṣatriya usually comes first.

A strong king was always a check on brāhmanic pretensions, just as the brāhmaṇs were a check on the pretensions of the king. Tradition speaks of many anti-brāhmaṇical kings who came to evil ends, and the legend of Paraśurāma, who destroyed the whole kṣatriya class for its impiety, must contain a recollection of fierce strife between the two classes in pre-Buddhist times. After the Mauryan period the brāhman's theoretical position was established throughout most of India, but the kṣatriya was in fact still often his equal or superior.

The martial class of ancient India, from great emperors to petty chiefs, was recruited from all races and ranks, and all the invaders of India down to the coming of the Muslims were given a place in the social order in this way. Manu describes the warlike peoples on the fringes of Aryan civilization, including the Greeks, the Scyths, and the Parthians, as kṣatriyas who had fallen from grace through their neglect of the Sacred Law, but who could be received once more into the Aryan fold by adopting the orthodox way of life and performing appropriate penitential sacrifices. This provision might be applied to almost any conquering people, and the Rājputs, in later times the kṣatriyas *par excellence,* were no doubt largely descended from such invaders.

The kṣatriyas claimed and received certain privileges. They continued old customs not in keeping with orthodoxy, with such persistence that the brāhmaṇic lawgivers were forced to give them legal status. Thus marriage by capture was permitted to the kṣatriya, as were the clandestine liaison and the *svayaṃvara,* at which a girl chose her husband from among the assembled suitors. Like the brāhmans, they did not always live by fulfilling their ideal function. The rules of *āpad-dharma* applied to them also, and there are many records of men of warrior stock becoming merchants and craftsmen.

In Vedic times the *vaiśya,* or mercantile class, though entitled to the services of the priesthood and to the sacred thread of initiation, was but a poor third to the brāhmans and kṣatriyas. In the *Aitareya Brāhmaṇa* passage to which we have referred the vaiśya is described as "paying tribute to another, to be lived on by another, to be oppressed at will." Other passages in early brāhmaṇic literature show him as a wretched and downtrodden cultivator or petty merchant, who is of no interest to his betters except as a source of profit.

According to Manu the special duty of the vaiśya was keeping cattle, which were made over to his charge at the creation of the world. The class evidently originated in the ordinary peasant tribesman of the *Ṛg Veda,* but long before the lawbook ascribed to Manu was composed it had many other activities. The śūdras, the humblest of the four classes, had by now taken to agriculture, and Manu admits many other legitimate vaiśya occupations besides cattle rearing and farming. The ideal vaiśya has expert knowledge of jewels, metals, cloth, threads, spices, perfumes, and all manner of merchandise—he is, in fact, the ancient Indian business-man.

Though the Brāhmaṇa literature gives the vaiśya few rights and humble status, the Buddhist and Jaina scriptures, a few centuries later in date and of more easterly provenance, show that he was not always oppressed in practice. They mention many wealthy merchants living in great luxury, and powerfully organized in guilds. Here the ideal vaiśya is not the humble taxpaying cattle-breeder, but the *asītikoṭivibhava,* the man possessing eight million *paṇas.* Wealthy vaiśyas were respected by kings and enjoyed their favour and confidence. It was they, rather than the kṣatriyas, who chiefly favoured the rising unorthodox religions of Buddhism and Jainism. They formed by this time, at least in the regions of Magadha and Kosala, a true bourgeoisie, no doubt small in number, but very important. Numerous inscriptions from Sunga times onward record the great donations of vaiśya merchants and skilled craftsmen to religious causes, especially to Buddhism, and show that they were prosperous and influential.

If the vaiśya, according to the *Aitareya Brāhmaṇa,* was to be oppressed at will, the lot of the *śūdra* was even more unfortunate. He was "the servant of another, to be expelled at will, to be slain at will"—but the latter phrase may be interpreted "to be beaten at will," and the import of the whole passage seems to be satirical.

Sūdras were not "twice-born." For them there was no initiation into full Aryan status, and they were not regularly considered Aryans, though the *Arthaśāstra* in its chapters on slavery specifically mentions them as such. The śūdra was in fact a second-class citizen, on the fringes of Aryan society. The word śūdra is of doubtful etymology, and occurs only once in the *Ṛg Veda;* it was perhaps originally the name of a non-Aryan tribe, which became subordinate to the conquerors, and the origin of the śūdra class may be accounted for in this way, though it certainly included other elements. As the rigidity of brāhmaṇic observances increased, groups which refused to accept orthodox custom, or clung to old practices which were no longer respectable, fell to the rank of śūdras. There are today castes which themselves claim to be kṣatriyas, but which are branded by the brāhmaṇs as śūdras because they adhere to customs which have long become objectionable, such

as meat eating or the remarriage of widows. Persons born illegitimately, even when of pure high-class blood, were officially counted as śūdras.

Sūdras were of two kinds, "pure" or "not-excluded" (*aniravasita*) and "excluded" (*niravasita*). The latter were quite outside the pale of Hindu society, and were virtually indistinguishable from the great body of people later known as untouchables. The distinction was made on the basis of the customs of the śūdra group in question, and the profession followed by its members. According to the brāhmaṇical textbooks the chief duty of the pure śūdra was to wait on the other three classes. He was to eat the remnants of his master's food, wear his cast-off clothing, and use his old furniture. Even when he had the opportunity of becoming wealthy he might not do so, "for a śūdra who makes money is distressing to the brāhmaṇs." He had few rights, and little value was set on his life in law. A brāhmaṇ killing a *śūdra* performed the same penance as for killing a cat or dog. The śūdra was not allowed to hear or repeat the Vedas. A land where śūdras were numerous would suffer great misery.

Thus the textbooks give small hope of happiness to the wretched śūdra, who could do little but serve his betters in unpleasant and servile tasks, and whose only hope was rebirth in a higher social class; but there is good evidence that śūdras did not always live the humble and wretched life laid down for them in the Sacred Law. There is mention of śūdras engaged in manufacture and commerce, and by Mauryan times many śūdras were free peasants. The śūdra had a place of sorts in the Hindu fold, and was encouraged to imitate the customs of the higher classes. Though he might not hear the Vedas, the Epics and Purāṇas were open to him, and he had a part in the devotional religion which became more and more popular from post-Mauryan times onwards, and ultimately eclipsed the older cults; in the *Bhagavad Gītā* the lord Kṛṣṇa himself promises full salvation to those śudras who turn to him. From the point of view of most medieval sects, class and caste were affairs of the body rather than of the spirit, and verses expressing the fundamental equality of all men are to be found in Dravidian devotional literature and in vernacular religious literature of later times. Theoretically Buddhism and Jainism made no class distinctions in religious affairs. As we have seen, śudra kings were not unknown, and many śudras, despite the injunctions of the lawbooks, must have been prosperous.

Untouchables

Below the śudras were the early representatives of the people who were later called untouchables, outcastes, depressed classes, or scheduled castes. Buddhist literature and the early Dharma Sūtras show that several centuries before Christ there already existed groups of people who, though serving the Aryans in very menial and dirty tasks, were looked on as quite outside the pale. Sometimes they were called the "fifth class" (*pañcama*), but most authorities rejected this term, as if to insist that they were excluded from the Aryan social order altogether.

Numerous groups of these people are mentioned, by names which are non-Aryan in origin, and were probably those of aboriginal tribes which came under the sway of the advancing Aryans. Chief of these groups was the *caṇḍāla,* a term which came to be used loosely for many types of untouchable. The caṇḍāla was not allowed to live in an Aryan town or village, but had to dwell in special quarters outside the boundaries. Though some caṇḍālas had other means of livelihood, in theory their main task was the carrying and cremation of corpses, and they also served as executioners of criminals.

According to the lawbooks the caṇḍāla should be dressed in the garments of the corpses he cremated, should eat his food from broken vessels, and should wear only iron ornaments. No man of higher class might have any but the most distant relations with a caṇḍāla, on pain of losing his religious purity and falling to the caṇḍāla's level. By Gupta times caṇḍālas had become so strictly untouchable that, like lepers in medieval Europe, they were forced to strike a wooden clapper on entering a town, to warn the Aryans of their polluting approach.

Certain classes of outcastes or untouchables seem to have gained their unenviable position through the growth of the sentiment of non-violence—for instance the *niṣāda,* who was a hunter, the fishing caste called *kaivarta,* and the leather worker. The *pukkusa,* who appears as a sweeper in Buddhist literature, may have fallen in status because members of his class made and sold alcoholic liquor. More difficult to account for are such base classes as basket-maker and the chariot-maker. In early Vedic times the latter was a most respected craftsmen, but soon fell to the status of an impure śudra or outcaste.

By the beginning of the Christian era the outcastes themselves had developed a caste hierarchy, and had their own outcastes. Manu mentions the *antyāvasāyin,* a cross between a caṇḍāla and a niṣāda, who was despised even by the caṇḍālas themselves. In later India every untouchable group imagined that some other group was lower than itself, and this stratification evidently began quite early.

Even the lot of the untouchable was not altogether without hope. Though he was denied access to the temples and the comforts of orthodox religion, Buddhist monks preached to him, and the more enlightened wandering ascetics would give him instruction. The untouchable dying in defence of brāhmaṇs, cows, women, and children secured a place in heaven. Orthodox texts contain frequent warnings on the evils which arise when śūdras and outcastes grow too powerful, and this would seem to show that a caṇḍāla might occasionally become influential.

Another class of untouchable was the *mleccha,* the word commonly used for outer barbarians of whatever race or colour. As an invader he was loathed, but once he had come into contact with Indian ways and was less strange and forbidding his status might improve. In fact it was not blood which made a group untouchable, but conduct. Generally there was no chance of an individual rising in the social scale, but for a group this was possible, over a number of generations, by adopting more orthodox practices and following the rules of the Smṛtis. Thus the Indian class system was always somewhat fluid.

"Confusion of Class"

An early legend tells of Viśvāmitra, a kṣatriya who, by penance and piety, became a brāhmaṇ and a seer (*ṛṣi*) to boot; but as time went on such raising of one's status became more and more difficult, and finally virtually impossible, though convenient fictions sometimes permitted kings and chiefs of low status to find legen-

dary kṣatriya ancestors and advance in the class hierarchy. While it became very difficult for the individual to rise, it grew progressively more easy for him to fall. Every breach of the manifold regulations of one's class entailed impurity and outcasting, either permanent or temporary. The lawbooks give long lists of penances for the restoration of the unfortunate offender, ranging from trivial ones, such as bathing, or touching Ganges' water, to others so rigorous that they must usually have resulted in the death of the penitent. Secular literature, however, tells many stories of high-class people infringing the rules of purity without doing penance, and no doubt the more sophisticated townsman often took his class responsibilities lightly.

The continual injunctions to the king to ensure that "confusion of class" (*varṇa-saṃkara*) did not take place indicate that such confusion was an ever-present danger in the mind of the orthodox brāhmaṇ. The class system was indeed a very fragile thing. In the golden age the classes were stable, but the legendary king Vena, among his many other crimes, had encouraged miscegenation, and from this beginning confusion of class had increased, and was a special feature of the *Kali-yuga,* the last degenerate age of this æon, which was fast nearing its close. The good king, therefore, should spare no effort to maintain the purity of the classes, and many dynasties took special pride in their efforts in this direction.

Before the tightening of the social system in the Middle Ages confusion of class was comparatively frequent, and some forms of interclass marriage were expressly permitted. The type of marriage known to anthropologists as hypergamous, when the husband is of higher class than the wife, was by no means disapproved of; on the other hand hypogamous marriage, when the wife's status was higher than that of the husband, was always frowned on. The former was "in accordance with the direction of the hair," smooth and natural, while the latter was "against the hair," or "brushing the wrong way." This distinction is to be found in other societies; for instance in Victorian England the peer who married an actress rarely incurred the same scorn and ostracism as the lady who married her groom.

The earlier legal literature permitted *anuloma* or hypergamous marriage, provided that a man's first wife was of his own class. Generally brāhmaṇs were forbidden to take śūdra wives, but one lawbook allowed even this, and Bāṇa, the 7th-century poet, who was a brāhmaṇ, had a step-brother by a śūdra mother. Various mixed classes, many of them the forerunners of later castes, were said to be the products of marriages of this type, and their members were not looked on as in any way unclean, but enjoyed a position intermediate between that of the two parents. Of the groups thought to have descended from hypergamous marriage only the niṣāda, in theory a cross between a brāhmaṇ and a śūdra woman, was thought to be impure.

Hypogamous or *pratiloma* marriage, on the other hand, produced offspring whose status was lower than that of either parent. Thus the caṇḍālas were believed to have descended from marriages between śūdras and brāhmaṇ women. The only exceptions were the class of charioteers, or *sūtas,* thought to have sprung from the hypogamy of kṣatriyas and brāhmaṇs, and the bards or *māgadhas,* descended from vaiśya fathers and kṣatriya mothers, both of whom were well respected. The complex system of sub-classes low in the social scale, out of which the Indian caste system developed, was believed to be wholly the result of "confusion of class." This tradition was accepted by early Indologists, but, as we shall see, is completely unfounded.

Caste

Relations between classes and social groups in later Hinduism were governed by rules of endogamy (marriage was only legitimate within the group), commensality (food was only to be received from and eaten in the presence of members of the same or a higher group), and craft-exclusiveness (each man was to live by the trade or profession of his own group, and not take up that of another). Megasthenes noted seven endogamous and craft-exclusive classes in India—philosophers, peasants, herdsmen, craftsmen and traders, soldiers, government officials and councillors. His sevenfold division is certainly false, but he gives evidence to show that in Mauryan times class divisions were already hardening. Even in the Gupta period, however, the regulations were by no means rigid. Hypergamous intermarriage was recognized, the rule of craft-exclusiveness was often ignored, or circumvented by the convenient escape clauses of *āpaddharma,* and in the earlier lawbooks the brāhmaṇ was permitted to accept food from any Aryan. It was only in late medieval times that it was finally recognized that exogamy and sharing meals with members of other classes were quite impossible for respectable people. These customs, and many others such as widow-remarriage, were classed as *kalivarjya*—customs once permissible, but to be avoided in this dark *Kali* age, when men are no longer naturally righteous.

In the whole of this chapter we have hardly used the word which in most minds is most strongly connected with the Hindu social order. When the Portuguese came to India in the 16th century they found the Hindu community divided into many separate groups, which they called *castas,* meaning tribes, clans or families. The name stuck, and became the usual word for the Hindu social group. In attempting to account for the remarkable proliferation of castes in 18th- and 19th-century India, authorities credulously accepted the traditional view that by a process of intermarriage and subdivision the 3,000 or more castes of modern India had evolved from the four primitive classes, and the term "caste" was applied indiscriminately to both *varna* or class, and *jāti* or caste proper. This is a false terminology; castes rise and fall in the social scale, and old castes die out and new ones are formed, but the four great classes are stable. They are never more or less than four, and for over 2,000 years their order of precedence has not altered. All ancient Indian sources make a sharp distinction between the two terms; *varna* is much referred to, but *jāti* very little, and when it does appear in literature it does not always imply the comparatively rigid and exclusive social groups of later times. If caste is defined as a system of groups within the class, which are normally endogamous, commensal and craft-exclusive, we have no real evidence of its existence until comparatively late times.

Caste is the development of thousands of years, from the association of many different racial and other groups in a single cultural system. It is impossible to show its origin conclusively, and we can do little more than faintly trace its development, since early literature paid scant attention to it; but it is practically certain that caste did not originate from the four classes. Admittedly it developed later than they, but this proves nothing. There were subdivisions in the four classes at a very early date, but the brāhman gotras, which go back to Vedic times, are not castes, since the gotras are exogamous, and members of the same gotra are to be found in many castes.

Perhaps the first faint trace of caste is to be found in the careful cataloguing of trades and professions in later Vedic literature, as if their members were looked on almost as distinct species. In the Pāli scriptures many trades and professions are described as living apart; thus we read of villages of brāhmans, potters, hunters and robbers, and of separate quarters in the towns for different trades and professions. Many trades were organized in guilds, in which some authorities have seen the origin of the trade castes; but these trade groups cannot be counted as fully developed castes. A 5th-century inscription from Mandasor shows us a guild of silk-weavers emigrating in a body from Lāta (the region of the lower Narmadā) to Mandasor, and taking up many other crafts and professions, from soldiering to astrology, but still maintaining its guild-consciousness. We have no evidence that this group was endogamous or commensal, and it was certainly not craft-exclusive; but its strong corporate sense is that of a caste in the making. Hsüan Tsang, in the 7th century, was well aware of the four classes, and also mentioned many mixed classes, no doubt accepting the orthodox view of the time that these sprang from the intermarriage of the four, but he shows no clear knowledge of the existence of caste in its modern form.

To the present day the life of the lower orders is much more affected by caste than by varna—it is not being a vaiśya or a sūdra, but being an *ahīr,* a *kāyasth,* or a *sonār* which matters, and corporate feeling is centred around this caste group, whether based on region, race, profession or religion. The same strong corporate sense existed among the Mandasor silk weavers, and evidence of its existence at an even earlier date can be gathered from many sources. Indian society developed a very complex social structure, arising partly from tribal affiliations and partly from professional associations, which was continuously being elaborated by the introduction of new racial groups into the community, and by the development of new crafts. In the Middle Ages the system became more or less rigid, and the social group was now a caste in the modern sense. Professor J. H. Hutton has interpreted the caste system as an adaptation of one of the most primitive of social relationships, whereby a small clan, living in a comparatively isolated village, would hold itself aloof from its neighbours by a complex system of taboos, and he has found embryonic caste features in the social structure of some of the wild tribes of present-day India. The caste system may well be the natural response of the many small and primitive peoples who were forced to come to terms with a more complex economic and social system. It did not develop out of the four Aryan varṇas, and the two systems have never been thoroughly harmonized.

By the end of our period many of the present-day caste groups were already in existence. Even the brāhmaṇ class was much subdivided into endogamous groups, often based on locality and race, with many different practices. The Rājputs were divided into clans which, if not regularly endogamous, were castes of a sort, and the vaiśyas, śūdras, and untouchables had evolved hundreds of castes. They were governed by local committees of elders, usually hereditary, which had the power to expel members and regulate caste rules, and whose decisions, from the time of the *Arthaśāstra* onwards, had the force of law.

After the large joint family, the caste provided social security, helping destitute members and providing for widows and orphans. A man expelled from his caste was also automatically expelled from his family, unless the whole family accompanied him in his social ostracism. He was lost to society, and could only consort with the lowest of the low. Though he might sometimes retain some of his former wealth he was isolated, a tree torn up by the roots. Permanent loss of caste was the greatest catastrophe, short of death and the major chronic diseases, which could happen to a man.

Early Tamil literature gives no evidence of caste, but the growth of Aryan influence and the development of a more complex political and economic structure produced a system in some ways more rigid than that of the North. By the Cōla period an important feature of South Indian caste structure had appeared, which has survived to the present day. In the Dravidian country families claiming to be kṣatriyas were few, other than the ruling families, and vaiśyas were equally rare. Nearly the whole of the population were brāhmaṇs, śūdras or untouchables, and the śūdra castes, which formed the mass of the people, were divided into two great caste groups, known as the right and left hands. The great animosity and rivalry which still exists between these groups is at least a thousand years old. On the right are the trading castes, some weaving castes, musicians, potters, washermen, barbers, and most of the cultivating and labouring castes; on the left are various castes of craftsmen, such as weavers and leather workers, cowherds, and some cultivating castes. We have no evidence of how this strange bisection of society arose.

Hypergamy never wholly disappeared. In Malabār, where matrilinear succession has continued almost to modern times, men of the great brāhman caste of Nambūdiris have regularly married the women of the dominant secular caste, the Nayyars. In Bengal the Rādhī caste of brāhmans and the important and respectable castes of scribes (*kāyastha*) and doctors (*vaidya*) are divided into subcastes, which are hypergamous. The system is known as "kulīnism," from the name of the highest subcaste of the brāhmans (*kulīna*); it was by tradition imposed by the Bengal king Vallāla Sena (12th century), but is no doubt a survival from much earlier times.

The organization of the castes, independent of the government, and with social ostracism as its most severe sanction, was a powerful factor in the survival of Hinduism. The Hindu, living under an alien political order imposed from above, retained his cultural individuality largely through his caste, which received most of the loyalty elsewhere felt towards king, nation and city. Caste was so strong that all attempts at breaking it down, until recent years, have ended in failure. Equalitarian religious reformers of the late Middle Ages, such as Basava, Rāmānand, and Kabīr, tried to abolish caste among their followers; but their sects soon took on the characteristics of new castes, and in some cases divided into castes within themselves. The Sikhs, despite the outspoken sentiments of their *gurus* and the adoption of rites deliberately intended to break down caste prejudice, such as the ritual meal eaten in common, did not overcome caste feeling. Even the Muslims, for all their equalitarian faith, formed caste groups. The Syrian Christians of Malabār early divided into sections which took on a caste character, and when in the 16th century Roman Catholic missionaries began to make converts in South India their flocks brought their caste prejudices with them, and high-caste converts held themselves aloof from those of the lower orders.

Only in the last fifty years has the caste system shown real signs of breaking down, thanks to the many inventions of the West not designed for use in a society divided into watertight compartments, the spread of Western education, growing national sentiment, and the intensive propaganda of enlightened leaders. The process is not yet complete, and it will be many years before all trace of caste feeling is eradicated; but when Mahātmā Gāndhī, in many ways socially conservative, persuaded his followers to sweep their own floors and clean their own latrines he sounded the death knell of the old Hindu social order, which, for all its faults, has preserved the identity of Indian society over centuries of foreign domination.

government, social structure, and the religious institution in islamic society

eighteen

The Religious Institution

HAMILTON GIBB   HAROLD BOWEN

...From the very first, Islam stood in the minds of its adherents not for a body of religious beliefs only, but for a community which was animated by those beliefs and had the duty laid upon it of actively promoting them. The earliest political pronouncement of the Prophet Muhammad was "Ye are one Community over against Mankind." Henceforth the Religion and the Community were inseparable in theory. No distinction was made at first between the secular and the religious offices of government; the Imâm was omnicompetent, and even in later times sovereignty carried with it an authority which was more than purely secular. But in practice the religion had to create the larger community. The task, already difficult in the limited area of Arabia, became infinitely more so when, as a result of the conquests of the first century, the religion was spread from Central Asia to the

Atlantic. Wide variations in language, in culture, in prior religious tenets, and in customs and institutions precluded any prospect of early unification. The imposing Empire of the early Caliphs, so far from forming a unity of any kind, consisted of an ill-assorted group of provinces held together by the military forces and moral prestige of the central government. The Community was represented by a relatively small body, chiefly of Arabs, who formed a governing caste in the midst of vast populations which had submitted to their rule. This was destined to have two consequences of the utmost importance. It associated Islâm, in the minds of Arabs and subjects alike, with Arabdom, and it gave to the form of Islâm patronized by the governing classes (for already sectarian differences had begun to appear amongst the Arabs) the character of a state Church or "established" religion. The result of the first of these consequences was to place Arabicization before Islamization in the process of moulding the constituent elements

Reprinted from *Islamic Society and the West,* Part II (London: Oxford University Press, 1957), pp. 70–80, by permission of the publisher. [Some footnotes omitted]

of the Empire into a unity. The result of the second was to cause those who accepted Islâm but who were hostile to the governing classes to lean towards the sectarian rather than the "established" interpretation of the religious creed. This is most clearly seen among the Persian converts; the nobles and the official class generally adopted the *Sunnî* creed of the Arab aristocracy, while the population of the great cities and some parts of the country-side showed a preference for the extremer forms of Şî'ism, or even, in some provinces, for the *Hârici* or literalist doctrine.[1]

The gradual spread of Islâm among the subject peoples did not, therefore, imply that a corresponding degree of religious unity had been attained. On the contrary, whereas the disputes amongst the Arabs themselves had been political rather than doctrinal in essence, the infiltrations from without widened and deepened the cleavage. Thus, by an apparent paradox, the stronger Islâm grew in numbers, the weaker became its power to promote a genuine religious unification and the more persistently was the established church (already rent internally by disputing parties) challenged by the *Şî'î*—and more pacifically by the *Sûfî*—sectaries. Yet such divisions were almost inevitable in a church which was itself rapidly expanding in an age of expanding material culture. They were, indeed, a sign of vigour and religious zeal—however much the latter, from the orthodox point of view, might appear to be misplaced.

By the end of the ninth century A.D. the contrast between the *Sunnî* or established church, and the *Şî'î* or opposition sects, appears in its most intense form in the open revolutionary movement led by the *Karmatîs* or "Carmathians." To the former belong the Court, aristocracy, and army, the bureaucracy, the *'Ulemâ* or representatives of the orthodox religious institution, and all who were associated with these groups. To the latter belong large sections of the lower classes in the towns and country-side and of the nomadic Arabs on their frontiers. With such a distribution of forces the consequences of open revolt might be foreseen, but forcible suppression of the rebels could not in itself furnish a solution of the underlying problem.

The real strength of the orthodox party lay, however, as we can now see, not in its stronger military force but in its more practical idealism. Whereas Şî'ism never ceased to be conscious of its character as a sectarian and opposition movement, the orthodox *'Ulemâ* held unswervingly to the conviction that they represented the Universal Church,[2] and that the task before them was to realize in fact the theory of the Religious Community. We have already seen the consequences in political theory of this steady effort to maintain the doctrine of the "Community in being," and the same spirit of tolerance and realism with which they patiently laboured to accommodate unwelcome actualities in this field was shown in the wider field also. Their attitude and conduct may be labelled as unheroic, but it saved them from falling into the irreparable error of persecuting their opponents, save in a few isolated and untypical instances, and it is impossible not to admire the con-

---

1 The inheritance of pre-Islamic religious beliefs also played a part in this, which may, however, be neglected here.

2 This is implied in the word *Sunni,* which, though interpreted as "adhering to the *Sunna* or Tradition of Muhammad and the Elders," means in fact "adhering to the *Sunna* of the Community." On the other hand, the *Şî'î* writers speak of those who deserted Şî'ism for Sunnism as "joining the majority."

ciliatory and yet tenacious way in which they pursued their object.

It is of the essence of *Sunnî* mentality—and implied in the very term—that what has been established by sound tradition as good and true must not be departed from. But this conservative (or, as some would put it, reactionary) element in the intellectual outlook of the *'Ulemâ* was, and has continued to be, counterbalanced amongst at least a proportion of them by a certain openness of mind as to what might be regarded as consistent with this postulate. This flexibility enabled the orthodox church to take in successive centuries a series of steps by which it incorporated one by one all but its irreducible opponents, even if at a price. It is outside the scope of this work to enter into this process in detail, but a glance at the manner in which it was accomplished is not without importance. . . .

The first task of the early *Sunnî* *'Ulemâ* was to close the breach in their own ranks caused by the intrusion of Greek philosophy and dialectic. The conservative majority, in reaction against the "advanced" and non-traditional theses of its admirers, refused at first to have anything to do with scholasticism. But when it was proved, after a century and more of controversy, that scholasticism might be used as a weapon in defence of tradition, the battle was virtually won, though its echoes were to rumble on for a long time to come.

The problem of Ṣî'ism was more complex. But the *Sunnîs, 'Ulemâ* and laymen alike, had from very early days shared the sympathy of the Ṣî'a for the house of 'Alî, though not their political or dogmatic tenets. This sympathy offered a bridge by which, in the fifth and sixth centuries of the Hegira era, when revolutionary Ṣî'ism had spent itself, the orthodox church (by means of the alliance with Ṣûfism which will be referred to immediately) was able to win over a large proportion of those who had been attracted to Ṣî'ism for social or political reasons. Henceforth Ṣî'ism seemed to be the creed of a dying sect, until Ṣâh Ismâ'îl the Safavid in the sixteenth century A.D. fanned the embers into a blaze and made it the national or "established" church in Persia. But within the Ottoman Empire, Ṣî'ism survived only as the religion of small and isolated groups of mountain-dwellers in parts of Anatolia, Syria, and Yemen, except for the strong Ṣî'î bloc in lower 'Irâk.

In both these advances the orthodox establishment had yielded little in comparison with what it had gained; it had not compromised its rigid adherence to the Tradition of the Community, though it had admitted, on the one hand, a vein of arid scholasticism and, on the other, a vein of sentimental attachment to the House of the Prophet. In the third, and most difficult, task which lay before it, the incorporation of the mystical doctrine of the *ṣufî* adepts, it was led into a path of compromise which in the long run threatened to submerge the orthodox teachings entirely. This danger, though implicit from the beginning, was not immediately obvious. Ṣûfism, in its theological aspect a compound of asceticism and gnosticism, represented in its social aspect a movement for social justice and equality by appealing to the conscience of individuals. Like Ṣî'ism, it spread mainly amongst the lower middle classes (and in these circles it retained down to the nineteenth century several traces of this early association); unlike Ṣî'ism, it relied on pacific methods and was relatively disorganized. But since they relied on religious conversion for the attainment of their ends, the *ṣûfî* leaders were strongly opposed to the worldliness of the orthodox *'Ulemâ*, and it was this opposition that formed the chief obstacle to more harmonious relations. On the other hand, there were many features in the life of orthodox circles in the fourth and fifth centuries that drove earnest religious teachers to seek in Ṣûfism a means of deepening religious conviction, and through their efforts a bridge was built. The orthodox, though with some hesitation, agreed to countenance the *ṣûfî* methods, on the understanding that the *Ṣûfîs* would observe the rites and subscribe to the official teaching of the established church.

It must not, of course, be imagined that any agreement was drawn up, or that an arrangement of this kind was ever formally sanctioned. The Islamic religious structure, true to its egalitarian principles and conscience, had never countenanced any form of external organization or any kind of hierarchy. Although it recognized *icmâʿ*, the "Consensus" of the doctors, as a valid source of doctrine, there was neither Council nor Curia to promulgate its decisions. The volitional element that runs through all the pre-Ottoman Islamic institutions, and that made their efficacy dependent on their appeal to the will rather than on careful regulation of duties and powers, was naturally at its strongest in this sphere. To "broaden down from precedent to precedent" was characteristic of Islamic usage long before the birth of the British Constitution. Each forward step was secured by tacit assent on the part of those who were most qualified to express an opinion, and from whom the rank and file took their cue. No one was prevented from opposing and from trying to gain support for his opposition, but within a generation or two controversy on the point at issue would die out. So it was in this

instance also, although the magnitude of the issues involved and the events which followed raised up a current of opposition, more especially on the part of the *Hanbalîs* (the most hostile to "innovations" of the orthodox "schools"), which lasted for some centuries. But in the long run the *Manbalîs* were routed, and their school sank to the position of a tiny remnant until the events of the nineteenth century brought fresh life to it.

At first, however, the compromise with *taṣawwuf* offered little ground for serious apprehension and much for congratulation. It seemed that the *'Ulemâ* would henceforth be in a position to exercise some control over the movement and restrain it from dangerous excesses, and they had gained in return valuable allies in their task of creating a united community. It was a moment of opportunity, and there were many indications that it was being put to good use. The first results, indeed, were all that could be hoped for. Within the ancient boundaries of Islâm the *ṣûfî* teachers took the lead in a new campaign, which captured a large share of the former *ṣîʿî* organizations, and for the first time brought the great mass of the population within the fold of the orthodox Community. Simultaneously, in the vast territories which were in process of annexation to the Domain of Islâm, notably in Anatolia, Central Asia, India, and Indonesia, they were the real missionaries of the conquering faith.

Yet for all this success, there were several elements in the movement that disturbed the confidence of the *'Ulemâ*. The leaders in this campaign were often men who, though of undoubted piety and purity of character, were rude and unlettered, and sometimes set little store by the rituals and dogmas of the orthodox. In many instances they were men who themselves sprang from the people amongst whom they laboured, and who shared in consequence their deep-seated religious traits and traditions; and these traits showed themselves in a tendency to relax the strict principles of orthodox Islâm, and to compromise with ideas and practices incompatible with them, although they had the merit of easing the path of conversion. All over the Islamic world there were to be found larger or smaller groups which acknowledged their adherence to the Community, but whose conceptions of orthodoxy were derived from the teachings of such preachers and their followers, who revered them as saints and ranked them above the official *'Ulemâ*. The legacies of animism, of paganism, of Christianity, of Hinduism, often remained almost intact under a thin veneer of Islâm.

Simultaneously, in the old-established lands of Islâm, the *ṣûfî* movement began to create an organization for itself, as noted teachers formed groups of disciples in convents and these in turn founded daughter-convents in other lands and cities. Thus, by an unpremeditated process, in both town and country, great "brotherhoods" or *tarîkas* were established with loose hierarchies of teachers and their own independent schools, rituals, and meeting-houses, each with a vast body of adherents who looked mainly or entirely to them for spiritual guidance. Sûfism became a profession, with a body of teachers rivalling the *'Ulemâ* and often enjoying a wide influence, especially amongst the artisans and lower classes. But the penalty had to be paid in a gradual hardening of the entire structure, as each order relapsed into a rigid traditionalism; and it was not long before the seeds of decay began to appear.

A third factor which contributed to give Sûfism the character of an organization rivalling the orthodox church was the elaboration of its theology along independent lines. This was the work of Ibnu 'l-'Arabî (d. 1240), a Spanish Moslem whose spiritual affiliation goes back to the pious but unlettered Berber revivalists of the preceding century, and whose tomb is still one of the principal sanctuaries of Damascus. His monist doctrines intensified the natural pantheistic bent of *ṣûfî* thought and supplied the philosophic basis for a vast literature in the next centuries.

The *'Ulemâ*, having opened the gates to "orthodox" Sûfism, were but little prepared for the flood which poured through them. Nevertheless, they could not (and there is no evidence that they desired to) repudiate the alliance, and their only means of counteraction—since all hopes of controlling the *tarîkas* were illusory—was to utilize the influence of the moderate *tarîkas*, such as the *Kâdirî* brotherhood, and to strengthen their own instrument of education and propaganda, the *madrasas* or religious seminaries. The enormous numbers of *madrasas* founded during the thirteenth, fourteenth, and fifteenth centuries in almost all the Islamic lands give evidence of the vigour with which this policy was carried out.

It was during this period that the Ottoman Empire came into existence. ...It bestowed its patronage on both [rival religious organizations] alike, while the policy to which we shall refer in a moment led the *'Ulemâ* to place a greater value upon their association with the brotherhoods. The outcome was a kind of symbiosis of the two institutions, each contributing to the support of the other, though not without occasional friction. The outward sign of their closer co-operation was not so much the spread of the more "orthodox" *tarîkas*...over the whole central area of the Empire, as the gradual inclusion of the whole body of the '*Ulemâ* in one or other (and sometimes more than one) of these brotherhoods, a process which reached its culmination during the eighteenth century. By this time, membership of the religious orders was practically synonymous with the profession of Islâm; there were so few who stood outside them that when it occurs the fact excites remark. The more considerable *şeyh*ly families had their private *tarîkas,* affiliated to one or other order, and even the *Hanbalîs* no longer remained unaffected.[3] In return, the orders taught their members the ritual and ethics of Sunnism, and to pay due respect to the '*Ulemâ*; and at the principal religious festivals and ceremonies '*Ulemâ* and *dervîşes* with their brotherhoods participated on an equal footing.

It was thus only within the Ottoman period that the ideal of unity was at length achieved within the *sunnî* Islamic fold, even if at a price and in a way which the fathers of the church could not have foreseen. With the effects of this compromise in dogmatics and religious ethics we are not at present concerned, except to note that in all circles the primitive teachings were to a greater or less extent overlaid by a superstructure of Sûfism, and that, as in all other religious systems, a wide gulf existed between the conceptions and principles of the doctors and the ideas and practices of the proletariat. But the social effects were correspondingly great, since, almost for the first time, the religious institution embraced the whole fabric of Moslem society.

It has already been pointed out that that society was composed of a vast number of small social groups, almost self-governing, with a wide gap interposed between the governing class of soldiers and officials and the governed class of merchants, artisans, and cultivators. The religious institution was thus charged with a double task: on the one hand, to fill the major gap, and, on the other, to knit the separate small groups together by supplying a common ideal and a common organization superimposed upon the group loyalties and if need be overriding them in a wider common loyalty. One other institution also embraced them all, that of administration, but its function, as we have seen, was negative and oppressive. The necessities of economic life linked individual groups together, more closely perhaps than religion did, but their range was narrowly limited. Even language was a dividing rather than uniting factor, since Turk and Arab were mutually unintelligible, and the dialects of each region stamped their speakers as foreigners to the men of the others. Religion alone offered that positive link which enabled the Turk, the 'Irâkî, and the Egyptian to feel the warmth of a common possession, and brought the peasant into organic relation with the Sultan.

But it is not enough to regard the relationship as one solely of a common religious allegiance, important as that aspect may have been in creating a common ground and softening the asperities of official intercourse. Nor must the binding element of common obligation to the *Şerî'a* be over-emphasized; for, as we shall see, there were limits to the community of law, and the *Kâdî*'s functions went beyond the simple administration of

---

[3] Note also the large proportion of Sûfistic works in the lists of books written by '*Ulemâ* as given by Cabartî and Murâdî. The term *şeyh*ly here and below is applied to families which were hereditarily associated with the religious institution.

justice. The teachings of orthodox Islâm, by their pursuit of the egalitalian ideal and consequent emphasis on the dignity of the individual believer, might even be said to have had a dissociative effect so far as the ordinary urban and agricultural populations were concerned. When all were equal and co-ordinate the purely pan-Islamic appeal could produce only accumulation without cohesion. It could focus opinion, but it lacked the means of action. The great benefit which the alliance of orthodoxy with Sûfism had brought to the religious institution was that it supplied a concrete organization which spread over all ranks of society and found a place in it for every member. Each village, each craft, each group had its own *ṣûfî* "lodge," affiliated to one of the great *tarîkas*, and enrolled in its brotherhood. It was behind the banner of its *tarîka* that each took part in the religious festival, and the ceremony both symbolized their conviction that all were indeed parts of a single continent, and expressed the means whereby that association was nourished and sustained. The connexion which existed between the craft-guilds and the orders has already been described, and it was the existence of similar connexions throughout the social range which in reality constituted the cement of the whole system.

It must be admitted, however, that even with this support, the religious institution fell short of creating a complete unity. For the orders themselves, though well organized internally, lacked an organization to knit them to one another, other than their common membership of the Community. Each was an autonomous unit, and, more serious still, there were marked lines of cleavage between them. . . . The moderate or orthodox orders were sharply opposed to the antinomian orders, with the grave consequence that the Janissaries, who belonged to the antinomian *Bektâşî* order, were dissociated from the main body of the religious institution to a considerable extent. Another significant line of cleavage was between the principal Turkish orders, the *Mevlevîs* and *Bektâşîs*, and those which had the widest following in the Arab provinces, the *Kâdirîs*, *Rifâ'îs*, *Şâdilîs*, and various local orders. During the seventeenth and eighteenth centuries, it is true, an attempt was made to remedy this division by the *Halwetî* and *Nakşbendî* orders, but though they met with some success, especially amongst the *'Ulemâ*, they did not materially affect the situation. Moreover, full co-operation between *'Ulemâ* and *Sûfîs* was hindered by the contempt with which the former regarded the popular orders and their practices.

Yet when all due allowance is made for these elements of weakness, the fact remains that the religious institution was successful to a remarkable degree in creating a sense of corporate unity between the varied racial and social groups, hitherto often antagonistic, which came within the range of its influence. The measure of its success can be most fully gauged from the contrast offered by those who stood outside it. The Ottoman government, by leaving the task of social unification to the religious institution, condemned the non-Moslem and heterodox Moslem groups under its control to exclusion from effective incorporation in the Ottoman structure of society; and it was for this reason, and not from deliberate anti-Christian policy, that the *billet* system proved fatal to it in the end. The same considerations apply to the *Şî'îs* of 'Irâk and Syria, to the *Yezîdîs* of Mesopotamia, and to all other dissident Moslem groups, except that in these cases it was their own hostility to the *ṣûfî* orders rather than any regulation on the part of the government that condemned them to isolation. Since it had come about that only through membership —direct or indirect—of the *sunnî* community could the individual achieve his social orientation in the *Dawla,* the more successful the *sunnî* religious institution was in this office the more it emphasized the relegation of all others to the outer margins.

While it was true, however, that the Empire was officially the patron and protector of Islâm and the *Şerî'a,* the development we have just traced was not due to its initiative or even to its encouragement. For we must be careful to avoid confusing the religious institution in its social aspects with the political state. Church and state in Islâm were one only in the realms of theory. The religious institution, it is true, claimed not merely to control the state but to be itself the state; but long experience had compelled it to recognize the existence of a civil power which it did not in fact control. Hence it was another characteristic feature of the *sunnî* religious institution that from the early days of Islâm it was not only inclined to hold aloof from the state, but had shown more than a tinge of hostility towards it. Fear of anarchy ...had led the *'Ulemâ* to condone the steady encroachment of the military power and the usurpation of authority by military Sultans, but they pursued with all the more determination the task of building up their own institution on independent lines. Moreover, the feeling of hostility to the state was even more marked in *ṣûfî* circles, although they consistently preached a doctrine of quietism; and the alliance of orthodoxy with Sûfism tended in consequence to strengthen the current of opposition to state interference.

The effect of this was to create eventually a sharp line of demarcation between the state and the religious institution. Each had its own functions and rarely overstepped them. The state was concerned with military, administrative, and economic affairs; the religious institution with doctrine, law, education, intellectual life, and social relations. The universalism of the Church, with its converse of exclusivism, was therefore independent of and unaffected by the local political situation. While it taught submission to established authority—especially when, as in the Ottoman Empire, that authority endeavoured to govern in accordance with the *Şerî'a*—it was no part of its duty to organize the life of the community in relation to a particular political structure, least of all amongst those who stood outside its own borders. On the contrary, the fundamental task of the *'Ulemâ* was to ensure that, no matter what political changes might come about, the religious institution, with all that it stood for, should remain unshaken.

Moslem Sultans and governors, too, for their part, had learned to reckon with this situation, and had consequently adopted a peculiar two-sided attitude towards the religious leaders. On the one hand, they were careful to cultivate goodwill by outward deference, by giving their support to religious activities, by creating endowments and building mosques and *madrasas,* and by avoiding as far as possible any violation of religious usages or of the persons of the *'Ulemâ.* On the other hand, they endeavoured to exercise some form of control over them through the officers to whom they "delegated" their own religious functions. Of these officers the two most important were the *Kâdî* and the *Muhtasib*. Both were in principle religious functionaries—the one charged with administering the legal provisions of the *Şerî'a*, the other with maintaining public morality. In reality they had much more extensive duties. The *Kâdî*...took but a small personal share in legal business, but was expected to maintain a close supervision over all administrative acts; and in particular, himself an *'Alim*, he was the intermediary of the government in its dealings with the *'Ulemâ*. The *Muhtasib* was a subordinate judicial officer whose function of preventing and punishing all sorts of fraudulent and dishonest dealings made him a valuable instrument of control over the guilds and lodges of the artisans and other classes of townsmen.

This dual policy was inherited by the Ottoman state amongst its other legacies from earlier Islamic states, and was developed with characteristic thoroughness by the Ottoman Sultans. The genuineness of their religious conviction and of their patronage of the religious life need not be called in question; but with that tendency towards centralized organization which is seen in all their administrative enactments, it is not to be wondered at that they attempted to apply it also to the religious institution.

Government and the Social Structure

HAMILTON GIBB   HAROLD BOWEN

The paradox remains of a government, generally apathetic, unprogressive, and careless of the welfare of its subjects, and often arbitrary and violent in its dealings with them, and a society upon whose institutions and activities such a government had little or no effect. The explanation is to be found in the very lack of a complex, all-embracing political organization. . . . We may visualize Moslem society as composed of two coexisting groups, the relations between which were for the most part formal and superficial. One group formed the governing class of soldiers and officials, the other the governed class of merchants, artisans, and cultivators. Each was organized internally on independent lines, and neither group interfered with the organization of the other in normal circumstances. From time immemorial the governing class had lived on a percentage of the produce of the land, supplemented by various duties on goods, and the social structure of the other class had accommodated itself to this situation. In spite of political and dynastic revolutions, stability was ensured by the fact that under all changes of sovereignty the existing bureaucracy remained in being, and maintained the traditional practices with a minimum of alteration. The new masters stepped into the places vacated by their predecessors; the titles to assignments of land were redistributed,

Reprinted from Gibb and Bowen, *Islamic Society,* Part I, pp. 209–16. [Some footnotes omitted]

but the relations between landlord and peasant, official and artisan, remained on the whole unchanged. The extreme conservatism of the bureaucracy is nowhere more clearly seen than in Egypt, where the respective functions of the Moslem accountants, the Jewish gold-dealers and bookkeepers, and the Coptic tax-assessors and collectors in the eighteenth century were practically what they had been in the tenth. From the outside it looked as though the *Paşa* or Bey could do as he pleased; in practice he was restrained from excessive abuse of his power partly by his own reverence for tradition and acceptance of traditional usage as binding, partly by the steady pressure of the bureaucracy, who had learned by experience that a certain standard of agricultural and industrial productivity was in their own best interests. Changes of dynasty, even, were not without their compensations. During a long period of uninterrupted dynastic rule, abuses naturally crept in and multiplied, sometimes to an extent which threatened social stability. The advent of a new dynasty swept these away and revitalized the old system; usually the energy and foresight of its founder resulted in a number of minor reforms in addition. Such had been the case in the Ottoman conquest, and the real defect of Ottoman rule was that it had lasted too long.

A further consequence of this state of affairs was that the Ottoman conquest did not result in the Ottomanization of the Arabic lands. A Turkish military aristocracy was no new phenomenon in either Egypt or Arab Asia, but even the bureaucracy never became thoroughly Turcicized. On the contrary, we find that the Turkish (or rather Bosniak) garrisons, intermarrying generation after generation with the Arab inhabitants, became absorbed into the local population, apparently even to the extent of forgetting their Turkish tongue. The old administrative cadres retained both their traditional functions and their Arabic idiom. The careful reader of Cabartî's chronicle cannot fail to be struck by the persistence of the technical administrative terms of the medieval Mamlûk Sultanate, and it is very questionable whether a knowledge of Turkish extended far outside the ranks of the senior officials. The increasing predominance of the Mamlûk troops still further, if anything, counteracted any tendency towards Ottomanization, since they deliberately cultivated the tradition of pre-Ottoman times. In Syria, however, Ottoman influence was much stronger, but here too, except in Aleppo and the northern districts, it scarcely penetrated below the ranks of the governing class. Even the aristocratic families among the *'Ulemâ* of Damascus, though in frequent relations with the Turkish *'Ulemâ* and intermarrying with Turkish families, resented the introduction of Turkish usages, and only those who had studied in Constantinople were familiar with the Turkish language.

The interposition of the bureaucracy thus shielded the mass of the population—cultivator, artisans, merchants—from the effective intervention of the military power in their organization and activities. Over a long period of centuries they had created an independent organism, so solidly based and yet so resilient that its stability was never in danger. On this social and economic basis the structure of Islamic society was built up; the foreign slaves, foreign rulers and administators, and foreign merchants formed only the superstructure, which could be supported without risk of collapse, so long as the foundations remained intact.

To describe the structure of this society in any detail would as yet be premature. It is evident upon closer examination that we have to deal, not with a closely knitted organism, even within the restricted limits of a single province, but rather with a vast number of small social groups, which may almost be described as self-governing. A recent investigator has defined such a society as "consisting mainly of territorial and genealogical communities, rooted in thousands of more or less isolated centres, mostly village, which are autonomous units, almost self-sufficient in their religious, social, political, and economic life.". . .

In the first place the groups carried none of the social and religious exclusiveness of the Indian castes, and are not to be regarded as in any way analogous to the latter. There is indeed a tendency towards the marking-off of the military forces as a superior caste, but even this is offset very considerably by their normal social relationships; and amongst the social groups themselves any similar tendencies seem to be foreign to the mentality of Western Asia. This is again reflected in the religious equalitarianism adopted by Islâm, which has in turn strengthened the resistance to caste ideas, if it has not wholly prevented the classification of social grades. The absence of rigid caste barriers gave sufficient flexibility to the system to allow exceptional talent or personality to make its way up; and there are enough examples in our very restricted material of persons who, born into one group, attained to some position in another, to justify us in asserting that there was at all times a certain movement within and between the individual groups.

Nevertheless, for the enormous majority of persons, their station in life, their occupation, and their economic position were regulated by the accident of birth. A son normally followed his father, a daughter was generally married within the village or craft group. Consequently where these groups were of long standing (and there were few which were not), the tie of common occupation was almost always strengthened by that of blood, and the craft or village community—if not too large—was constituted by members of a single family more or less widely branched. Such a constitution enabled the effect of the rigid Islamic law of inheritance, namely to decompose property into minute fractions, to be mitigated by constant recombination, and rendered the community more compact and homogeneous. On the other hand, the already powerful control of tradition over the conduct of the individual member of the group was intensified by the family ties which linked him to the other members, and by the disciplinary sanctions which the family was in a position to exercise. In these circumstances initiative was not so much stifled as non-existent, since every consideration combined to persuade each member that in the maintenance of the established order lay his own best interests, and nothing ever came to his observation or knowledge which might induce a belief that a better order could exist.

The relations in which the separate groups stood to one another were less uniform. Groups with different economic functions—such as cultivator and artisan, artisan and merchant— were obviously linked by the natural or traditional economy of their provinces, which was almost always of a simple and direct kind. The normal interchange of services was conducted in the cities usually on a money basis, in the country districts very often for produce in kind. Except for these, and for the common participation of local groups in local religious ceremonies or the more specialized association of two or three groups in a religious fraternity, there seems to have been extraordinarily little direct contact between the various groups. Each inhabited its own quarter in the city, or its own village or section of a village in the country, and, in certain districts at least, the existence of factional feuds set up a positive barrier to social intercourse.

Administratively, each group had a chief member, an elected or appointed *şeyh* or leader, through whom all its relations with the governing authorities were conducted. The holder of an assignment of land acted through the village *şeyh* or *şeyhs*, who were held responsible for the maintenance of order and the collection of the taxes. Each industrial and merchant corporation had likewise its *şeyh*, with the same administrative and taxing functions, who dealt with the relevant officer of government either directly or through a superior *şeyh* possessing jurisdiction over a number of corporations. In every case, again, these relations were fixed by tradition, and for the most part strictly adhered to. The very looseness of this organization was one of the chief safeguards of the social structure. Any violence on the part of a military officer, a government official, or a band of Arab marauders could normally affect only individual groups; when it expended itself, the groups rapidly recovered. In extreme cases, if the original group were entirely dissolved, a fresh group was formed, and—provided the violence was not renewed—set to work to rebuild the shattered economic tissue. When this happened too frequently (as was the case in the later medieval period) it caused a shrinkage in the numerical strength and economic capacity of the social structure as a whole, but did not destroy it. In general, therefore, the conduct of government touched only the surface of its life; here and there temporary dislocations might be caused, and a grasping and short-sighted policy might and did produce local contractions by allowing land to fall out of cultivation or forcing the stoppage or transfer of a branch of industry. But so long as the groups themselves, with their traditional organs of administration, remained intact, and so long as the intervention and extortions of the military governors were limited to the profits and spared the capital and the means of livelihood themselves, the social organism showed a marvellous power of recuperation.

The predominating role of traditional usage in all these relations, internal and external, has been sufficiently emphasized above. Its precise character necessarily varied from group to group and from place to place, even within the same district. There can be little doubt that in many groups this tradition went back far behind the Islamic era; in Upper Egypt, especially, its roots lay in the ancient Pharaonic civilization. Among the industrial groups, on the other hand, the traditional usages as a whole derived from the Middle Ages, though specific practices might be of earlier origin. But it was not merely the fact of its antiquity that made traditional usage all but absolute; indeed it was generally quite sufficient for a usage to be once established, even at a most recent date, for it to enjoy the same prescriptive character. Its potency lay in its association with the religious ideas of governors and governed alike;

not primarily in the sense that the religious authorities of Islâm gave a religious or quasi-religious sanction to each and every usage,[4] but rather that reverence for tradition was the doctrine most characteristic of and most strongly stressed in Islamic teaching. The close association of the religious and social structures will be examined later, but enough has been said to show that, for all its apparent fragility, even a Turkish or Mamlûk governor might hesitate to lay a sacrilegious hand on tradition.

It is not surprising that so intimate an association, governed by unwritten sanctions, should have escaped the notice of European travellers, whose contacts with Moslem society were of the most superficial. But it is of importance for us to appreciate it thoroughly, as it is typical of the institutions of Islamic society and government generally. "Point de lois fixes. . . ." No written laws, whether with penal or other sanctions; in their place a network of traditional relations, maintained only by the common will, yet which had survived eight centuries of dynastic vicissitudes and conquering armies, and still regulated the conduct of both society and government. Similarly in other fields, where at first sight there appears to be nothing but unregulated confusion, and ever, to the Western eye, a total disregard of law and justice, we shall find custom and tradition setting recognized limits to conflicting jurisdic-

____

4 It might be questioned whether they ever expressly sanctioned a great many of the traditional usages in village and town, but there can be no doubt that the local men of religion, whether of the 'Ulemâ, or of the Ṣûfîs, or of both, did in fact throw their weight upon the side of tradition, and officially condoned the traditional usages even when (like those at the cutting of the Halîc at Cairo) they were pre-Islamic and animistic in origin.

tions and dictating what may not be done and what may be done, even though technically against the written law. In the last resort, it is a difference in the conception of law, and in the function of administrative law in particular, that is at the bottom of the misunderstanding.

Such a system, on the other hand, possessed serious and inescapable drawbacks, quite apart from the personal suffering and economic loss resulting from its repeated violation by members of the governing and military classes. It perpetuated the gulf which separated the people from the government, producing at best an apathetic acquiescence in it on their part, as a necessary evil, but not infrequently offering a foothold to elements of social opposition. Their direct relations with it were limited to the field of taxation, often extorted with violence and supplemented by oppressive *avanias*. On the side of the government we have already seen its results in a similar apathy towards the interests of the subjects and an absence of all incentive to improvement or reform. But since the situation could not long remain stationary, the balance was continually shifting against the people by constant small encroachments. One institution, it is true, remained to form a positive link between them, and in a measure endeavoured to redress the balance— the religious institution. . . .

The second criticism to be brought against the system is its hostility to change and consequent stifling of initiative. If we may judge by the analogous situation in intellectual life, originality was not wholly non-existent but it was suppressed in the supposed interests of the group, or if it could not be suppressed was ignored, and its achievements suffered to disappear. We shall never know,

in any probability, whether some Arab Jacquard devised an improved loom or some Turkish Watt discovered the power of steam, but we can confidently assert that, if any such invention had occurred, it would have been entirely without result. The whole social organism, in fact, was one characteristic of, and only possible in, a stationary or retrograde civilization, and herein lay its essential weakness. It is not an exaggeration to say that after so many centuries of immobility the processes of agriculture, industry, exchange, and learning had become little more than automatic, and had resulted in a species of atrophy that rendered those engaged in them all but incapable of changing their methods or outlook in the slightest degree.

It was this incapacity, rather than unwillingness, to learn that above all characterized Asiatic Moslem society in the seventeenth and eighteenth centuries. Its sterilized brain could not effectually conceive any idea that lay outside the narrow range of its experience and tradition, nor could it meet any situation which deviated from the path traced by routine. So long as the Ottoman provinces lived in a closed intellectual, economic, and social order, the system continued to serve its purpose, though with steadily diminishing returns. But during the course of the eighteenth century various factors combined to disturb the existing equilibrium, more especially in the economic and military spheres, and created new problems which the old organization was totally unable to deal with. The result was to render the social order the helpless victim of violent solutions by which its protective covering of tradition was torn away and its institutions were exposed to destruction.

roman law as the law of the world

nineteen

RUDOLF SOHM

Jus Civile and Jus Gentium

Jus civile is the local law of a city. It was destined to be replaced by the jus gentium, a general law for the civilized world.

The local law of Rome had already adopted a number of juristic acts which were all characterized by formlessness, ease of application, and free adaptability.

The Romans themselves had not failed to observe that their law already contained two distinct ingredients, one of which operated by virtue of its form, and was derived from their old jus civile, while the other was free from formal elements, and owed its adoption and validity as law to the contact between the commerce of Rome and that of the world at large. The former bound none but Roman citizens to whose mutual dealings it alone applied, and the latter was binding on, and applicable to, the peregrini as well. The former kind of law, which was specifically Roman, was now called jus civile in the special and narrower sense of the term, the "jus proprium civium

Romanorum."[1] The jus gentium, on the other hand, came to be regarded as a universal law of all mankind, common to all nations, because resting on the nature of things and the general sense of equity which obtains among all men, the "jus gentium quod apud omnes gentes peraeque custoditur," a sort of natural law, exacting recognition everywhere in virtue of its inherent reasonableness. It would, however, be erroneous to suppose that the Romans attempted to introduce a code of nature such as the philosophers had devised. The jus gentium was, and never had been anything else but a portion of *positive Roman law* which commercial usage and other sources of law, more especially the praetorian edict, had clothed in a concrete form. Nor again must it be imagined that the Romans simply transferred a portion of foreign (Hellenic) law bodily into their own system. In the few quite exceptional cases where they did so (as e.g. in the case of hypotheca), they did not fail to impress their institutions with a national Roman character. The antithesis between jus civile and jus gentium was merely the outward ex-

Reprinted from *Institutes of Roman Law,* 3rd ed. (Oxford: Clarendon Press, 1926), pp. 44–99, by permission. [Some footnotes omitted]

[1] In modern phraseology "civil law" is used for "private law" simply; the Romans meant by civil law the law which obtains among "cives."

pression of the growing consciousness that Roman law, in absorbing the element of greater freedom, was commencing to discard its national peculiarities and transform itself from the special local law of a city into a general law for the civilized world. *The jus gentium was that part of the private law of Rome which was essentially in accordance with the private law of other nations,* more especially with that of the Greeks which would naturally predominate along the sea-board of the Mediterranean. In other words, jus gentium was that portion of the positive law of Rome which appeared to the Romans themselves in the light of a "ratio scripta," of a law which obtains among all nations and is common to all mankind.

The value of the division of Roman law into jus civile and jus gentium was not merely theoretical, but also eminently practical. The law which now governed the intercourse of foreigners—Greeks, Phoenicians, Jews— in Rome was, of course, Roman law, but it was Roman jus gentium, and the Roman jus civile, in the new and narrower sense of the term, was confined on principle to the mutual dealings of Roman citizens. The jus gentium was thus, at the same time, the Roman law for foreigners, i.e. the law which governed the transactions of the peregrini. And it was but natural that such should be the case, since it was the influence of foreign intercourse that had given the jus gentium its shape.

There is a moment in the history of every nation when the claims of a natural sense of justice assert themselves and revolt against the hard and fast austerities of ancient traditional forms. The Romans had now arrived at this stage. The jus gentium was in its nature the equitable law whose growth and expansion, in opposition to the jus strictum of ancient tradition, proceeds henceforward with ever increasing volume. The whole tendency of the history of Roman law pointed to the suppression of the jus strictum by this new equitable law, and to the consequent destruction of the ancient jus civile by the jus gentium. But it must not be imagined that the development was a very sudden one. Such a course would have been entirely alien to the legal instinct of the Romans. The jus gentium did not come down like a hurricane and sweep the jus civile. The slow and gradual elaboration of a system of equity alongside the older and stricter law, was rather the work of a patient and uninterrupted development extending over a period of more than five hundred years. When, in the natural course of things, the vitality that once filled the forms of the jus civile had passed from them, leaving them but hollow relics of a bygone age, then, but not till then, were they finally discarded. Slowly, cautiously, and, as it were, bit by bit, portions of a freer and more equitable law were worked out and tested, first one, then another, and finally incorporated in the organism of Roman law. The reform of Roman law was the result of a vast series of small changes of detail. And it was only by painstaking care of this description, by scorning all appeals to vague general principles of equity, that the Romans, aided by that keen sense of form, moderation, and legality, which with them was hereditary, could succeed in reducing the jus aequum to a body of principles lucidly conceived, minutely elaborated, and carefully weighed in all their details. By such a method alone could Roman law, while its contents were freely developing over so vast a field, preserve intact throughout that artistic power which moulds and subdues its materials, and erects them into a firm harmonious structure. It is this power which has made Roman law, and more especially Roman private law, what it is: a model for all times to come such as has never since been equalled.

In working out the jus gentium, i.e. those rules of natural equity which regulate the dealings between man and man, and in reducing these rules to a system of marvellous transparency and lucidity which carries irresistible conviction by its form as well as its matter to the mind of every observer, in doing this, Roman law has performed its mission in the world's history. And it was this achievement, successfully performed for all times to come, that not only fitted Roman law for becoming the general law of the Roman empire, but also endowed it with the power, when once it had emerged from the oblivion of centuries, to conquer the modern world.

There were three agencies whose influence in working simultaneously and successively at this identical task, viz. the developing and importing of the jus gentium, was decisive of the ultimate result. These were the praetorian edict, Roman scientific jurisprudence, and imperial legislation.

. . .

The Praetorian Edict

In the year 367 B.C. the judicial functions were separated from the consular power, and a special officer, the praetor urbanus, was appointed to administer justice in the city. Subsequently (about 242 B.C.) the increase of commerce necessitated the appointment of a second praetor, the praetor peregrinus, to whom all disputes were assigned where one or both of the parties were peregrini. The jurisdiction of the praetor urbanus was henceforth confined to matters in dispute between Roman citizens themselves.

During his year of office, the praetor, like the consuls before him, was invested with the ancient judicial power of the king.[2] That is to say, in administering justice he was authorized to exercise his sovereign judicial discretion, being, formally, only bound by the letter of the leges or popular enactments, and by such customs as ancient tradition had endowed with the force of laws. It is important to bear this fact in mind in order to appreciate the peculiar importance of the praetorian "edict."

An edict is an order promulgated by a magistratus populi Romani. A praetorian edict, therefore, is an order promulgated by the praetor. It deals with the principles by which the praetor intends to be guided in his administration of justice, in other words, in the exercise of his free judicial discretion. It is not likely that the praetor began to proclaim such edicts from the very outset. He would, of course, in the first instance consider the administration of the existing law his sole task, so that it was naturally a very gradual process by which definite principles peculiar to the praetorian jurisdiction were developed—principles which, when developed, tended more and more to constitute the praetorian power the organ of

---

2 The word "praetor" means literally a general, and is a title of honour accorded to the consuls in the first centuries of the Republic. . . . The praetor was really a third consul who was specially entrusted, not with the military command, but with the administration of justice. This is the reason why, in point of rank (and in the number of his lictors), he was inferior to the consul, though, on principle, his power was consular. . . .

reaction against the principles of civil law. It was thus but gradually that an occasion arose for the praetor to promulgate any orders in regard to the granting of legal assistance. It would seem, however, that, even at an early period, it was usual to post up in the praetor's court a list of legal formulae for the better information of the parties to an action, e.g. of formulae for the interdicts for which application had to be made to the praetor—interdicts being commands by means of which the praetor, in the exercise of his executive powers, granted an extraordinary remedy—and, again, of formulae for the processual sponsiones (processual agreements) which the praetor, under certain circumstances, compelled the parties to enter on. In addition to this tablet of formulae other tablets gradually came into use, which contained the orders of the praetor concerning matters of law, i.e. the edicts. After the introduction of the formulary procedure the "actiones" or formulae for commencing an action were also published in tablets. A kind of new Tables of Law thus arose side by side with the twelve bronze tables which were to be seen, not far away, in the forum Romanum, and on which was engraven the old jus civile of Rome. The praetorian tables being only intended to last for a year were simply made of wood painted white, and were for this reason called collectively "album." Nevertheless these wooden tablets were destined to outlast the bronze ones. For they represented those principles of law which metamorphosed and finally swept away the ancient laws of the decemviri. The term "album" or "edict of the praetor," as applied to the whole, is due to its outward form, the formulae prescribed by the praetor (the publication of which was not, in the legal sense, an edict) being thus included with the edicts proper under the collective title of "the Edict."

It is probable that, from an early date, it was the business of every new praetor, on taking office, to revise the tablets of formulae and put up new ones. For it was obvious that these tablets, being made of wood, would serve, at most, for the one year of office. What had been a traditional usage in the case of the formulae became, from the very outset, a matter of necessity in the case of the edicts. For the edict was only valid during the year of office of the praetor who issued it. Thus when the new praetor came in, he had to publish anew "the Edict" as a whole.

The edict which the praetor issues on taking office is called the "edictum perpetuum." It is intended to be valid for the whole term of his year of office. The opposite of the edictum perpetuum is an extraordinary order issued by the praetor during the year of office for such unforeseen occasions as may arise. The edictum perpetuum or, as we shall in future call it, the "edict" simply, is not a statute, nor is it originally even a source of law at all. For the very magistrate who had issued the edict might arbitrarily disregard it, till a lex Cornelia (67 B.C.) made it illegal for a praetor to depart from his edictum perpetuum. But even then the validity of the edict expired with the year of office of the praetor who had issued it. The new praetor was not bound by the edict of his predecessor. He could repeat it or alter it, as he chose. It was, however, but natural that a custom should soon establish itself for each praetor, on taking office, regularly to repeat a large portion of the edict (the "edictum tralaticium"), and confine himself merely to additions (nova edicta, novae clausulae). Thus a regular system of judge-made law grew up in the praetorian court which, in addition to the statutory and customary law already in force, became, in point of fact, one of the most potent factors in the legal system.

The praetor peregrinus had to decide disputes between aliens, and between citizens and aliens, i.e. the law he administered was the jus gentium. In the edict of the praetor peregrinus, therefore, the jus gentium acquired a written, fixed and tangible form, and was thus, at the same time, placed in a position to exert a more powerful influence on the general development of Roman law. On the other hand, the praetor urbanus only had jurisdiction in disputes between Roman citizens. His edict dealt with Roman law in its entirety, i.e. both with the jus gentium (which of course also applied to Roman citizens) and the jus civile, in the narrower sense. The form in which the jus civile really attained to practical vitality in the praetor's court became clearly apparent in the edict of the praetor urbanus.

The praetor had no power to legislate, but he might grant or refuse an action. The old action at law (legis actio) was confined within certain inflexible formulae which had been developed by the practice of the courts in conformity with the words of the statute. All the magistrate could here do was to grant or disallow the action (legis actio). Hence it was a most important event when, by the enactment of the lex Aebutia towards the middle of the second century B.C., the formulary procedure established itself. This procedure derived its name from the fact that, under it, the lodging of the complaint resulted in a written precept (formula) being addressed by the magistrate to the judex, containing an authoritative statement of the issue in dispute, together with the principles on which the judex was to decide it. The judex who heard the case (i.e. the private individual to whom the praetor, in accordance with traditional custom, referred the matter in litigation for trial and decision) was now far more dependent than formerly on the magistrate's instructions. He might be directed, under certain conditions, to disallow an action which, nevertheless, lay as civil law, or, on the other hand, to admit a claim of which the civil law knew nothing whatever. Again, as against the parties themselves, the position of the praetor was now one of much greater freedom than before. He had the power, not merely to refuse the action, but also to allow it, subject, however, to such conditions as to make it in certain cases tantamount to a refusal. The entire procedure was thus brought under the control of the praetor.

We can now understand how it came to pass that the praetorian law soon began to advance with rapid strides. By the time of Cicero the praetorian edict had already become the leading organ for the development of Roman law. But the praetorian reform achieved its most essential result by working out that equitable law (the jus gentium) which was tending more and more to displace the harsh rigours of the old jus civile. The praetorian edict was the engine best fitted for effecting this reform—a task as important as it was difficult. As the edict was never valid for more than one year, it was a convenient instrument for giving new principles a trial. If the innovations did not answer, they could be dropped again at once. The praetors in general showed little taste for the sudden adoption of far-reaching general principles. They confined themselves rather, in the first instance, to laying down rules for a perfectly definite case, the conditions of which were clearly apprehended. The next praetor might then add some further clause to the edict of his predecessor, the third might take yet another step in advance, and so on. It was precisely on account of this objection to far-reaching generalizations that they always hesitated to strike out anything that had once found its way into the edict. They preferred the method of adding a second concrete case to the first, a method which had this further advantage that it secured accuracy of verbal expression,—an important consideration, since the praetorian edict, like the statutes, was interpreted according to its letter. Thus there grew up in the edict a kind of code of private law; on the face of it, a collection of rules on the granting of actions, admission of pleas, and so on, couched, moreover, in a style, which was not exactly Ciceronian, nor even pleasant to read. Nevertheless it was by means of this code, with all its old-fashioned jargon and cumbrous phraseology, that the wisdom, experience, and foresight of bygone ages were handed down from generation to generation. It was a code which combined conservatism with a ready susceptibility of change, thus standing at the same time firmly rooted in the experience of the past and the life and movement of the present.

Praetorian law, in the shape it assumed in the edict, was not, strictly speaking, *law,* but the power involved in the right to allow or disallow actions and other legal remedies virtually raised it to the position of law. Thus we find Cicero declaring that even at his time the edict was felt to be a kind of law. The praetorian law, being a law made by officials ("jus honorarium"), was opposed to the jus civile, i.e. law in the strict and proper sense of the term, the law made by the people, developed by popular enactments and popular customs. Thus both the jus civile and the jus honorarium contained elements of jus gentium, but in the jus honorarium the influence of the jus gentium predominated. The praetorian edict was, in the main, the instrument by means of which the free principles of jus aequum gained their victory over the older jus strictum. Though at first the edict may merely have served the purpose of giving fuller effect to the jus civile (juris civilis adjuvandi gratia), and then of supplementing the jus civile (juris civilis supplendi gratia), nevertheless, in the end, borne along by the current of the times, it boldly assumed the function of *reforming* the civil law (juris civilis corrigendi gratia).

The development of the praetorian edict reached its climax in the last century of the Republic. In the main the problem had now been solved. It was universally felt that the jus honorarium, fully matured as it was (it was already for the most part "tralaticium"), was now entitled to rank as a second great power, equal in importance to the jus civile. But the constitutional changes which were now beginning to take place soon opposed a barrier to the further creation of law by the praetor. For we must bear in mind that the praetor's jus edicendi was the outcome of that autocratic power which was peculiar to the ancient *republican* magistracies. The rising imperial power could not permanently tolerate any rival independent authority. But, as in all other branches of public life, so here the old forms were preserved, though in substance the way was being prepared for the new monarchical ideas. The far-seeing genius of Hadrian, at this point, recognized and, at the same time, gave effect to the necessary results of the altered political circumstances. It was never, from the outset, considered anything very abnormal for the supreme power in the state to instruct the magistrates as to how they should exercise their official power. Thus some leges, and subsequently (more especially in the first centuries of the empire) a series of senatusconsulta, had laid down instructions which were binding on the praetors in the administration of justice and the granting or refusing of rights of action, and in so doing had indirectly contributed to determine the contents of the praetorian edict. It was from this fact that Hadrian took his cue. The time had come to prescribe to the praetor the *entire* contents of his edict. The regular reissue of the edict of the magistrate had already sunk to a mere matter of form. It would have been inconsistent with the actual position of the princeps and praetor respectively, if the latter had ventured to make important alterations in the edict without the assent of the former. And, moreover, if the praetor had attempted to make any change in his edict, which the emperor did not approve, the latter was legally empowered to disallow it by virtue of his jus intercedendi. The result was that the praetorian edict became stereotyped and barren. Its task was done. All that remained was to cast it into a final shape and, at the same time, to define, in a legal form, the relations subsisting between the imperial power and the edict. With a view to this purpose, Hadrian (before the year 129 A.D.) instructed the great jurist Salvius Julianus definitely to revise the edicts of the praetor urbanus and praetor peregrinus, adding, at the same time, the market-regulations (as to the liability of the vendor for faults, etc.) contained in the edict of the curule aediles. By order of the emperor, the whole was then ratified by a senatusconsultum.

This is the so-called Edictum Hadrianum or Julianum. The edict issued by the provincial governors—praesides provinciarum—in the administration of justice (edictum provinciale) was similarly dealt with and finally reduced to a definite form. Thus the imperial power—the effect of which was extended to the senatorial provinces by means of the senatusconsultum—rose supreme above the magistracies, appropriating, as its own, the contents of the edict with its rules on the administration of justice. Formally, however, the change was slight. The magistrate continued to administer justice and the edictal law was still, in theory, derived from his official power as its source. The praetor and, in the provinces, the praeses provinciae continued, on taking office, to issue their edict and the contents of the edict were still jus honorarium, i.e. law which existed only in virtue of the official authority of the magistrate entrusted with the administration of justice. The jus honorarium had not been converted into jus civile, because the contents of the edict had not been declared law for the whole empire. The semblance of the power of the old republican magistrates remained as heretofore. But the emperor and senate, by means of their legislative authority, had compelled the magistrate to issue the edict in the new form as finally established and in no other. In substance, therefore, it was not the will of the magistrate, but the will of the emperor that determined the contents of the magisterial edict. Thus, if it appeared that any provision of the edict was ambiguous, it was the emperor who had to be appealed to, with a view to deciding the matter by means of imperial rescript. In like manner it was reserved for the emperor to have the edict, when necessary, supplemented. The edict of the praetor had become unchangeable

—an edictum perpetuum in a new sense of the term, and the edictal law, in its further stages of development, was to appear in the form, not of praetorian, but of imperial law.

The praetorian law was finished. The time had come for a fresh power to enter on the scene, in order to solve a new problem which had now arisen. This power was Roman Scientific Jurisprudence.

. . .

Roman Jurisprudence

The beginnings of Roman jurisprudence date from the pontifices, who acted as skilled legal advisers in the court, first of the king, then of the consul, lastly of the praetor. Their science of law was closely bound up with their science of religion and astronomy. Theirs was the knowledge of the jus sacrum and the calendar, they alone could tell the dies fasti and nefasti, i.e. the days on which an action at law might or might not be commenced. It was a consequence of their functions as consulting assessors in the law courts that the knowledge, control and development of the formulae relating to actions (legis actiones) and to juristic acts came to rest entirely with them. Their science was the science of the letter of the law and of its technical application, interpretation and utilization (interpretatio). The development of this science was exclusively confined to the college of pontifices, and its knowledge was preserved and handed down, within the same limits, by tradition and by instruction of the new members who joined. Moreover, the precedents, i.e. the early legal opinions (responsa, decreta) of the college, which formed the basis and norm of the existing practice, were preserved in the archives of the pontifices, and to these archives none but members of the college had access. Thus the business of interpretation, which was, of course, in each separate case, decisive of the form of action or juristic act, was confined to a few, and the pontifical jurisprudence came positively to be regarded as a kind of occult science, and as constituting, at the same time, a powerful weapon in the hands of the patricians (to whom the pontifices belonged) in their struggle with the plebeians. No wonder, then, that the publication by Flavius (304 B.C.) and Aelisu (about 204 B.C.) of the legis actiones (i.e. the formulae of actions, in the shape which the pontifices had given them; the so-called "jus Flavianum" and "jus Aelianum") was regarded as a great popular act. Accordingly it marked an important turning-point, when Tiberius Coruncanius (about 254 B.C.), the first plebeian pontifex maximus, proclaimed his readiness to give information to anybody on legal questions. True, the pontifices had, before this time, given information on enquiry, not however to every one, but only to magistrates and to persons who, as parties to an action, were practically concerned in some question of law; in other words, the information vouchsafed only applied to a particular case; it was fragmentary and afforded no insight into the system as a whole. The announcement made of Tiberius Coruncanius meant that he was also prepared to answer questions addressed to him by persons whose interest was purely theoretical, in other words, questions put by those whose object was to know law and study the existing jus civile. The knowledge of law was to be opened up to all. Here, then, we have the first beginnings of a system of public legal instruction and—as its necessary consequence—a juristic literature. The same Aelius whom we just mentioned, surnamed "Catus," "the cunning" (Sextus Aelius Paetus

Catus, Consul 198 B.C.), had already composed a work, called the "commentaria tripertita," in which the author, not confining himself to a mere collection of formulae, offered a commentary on the Twelve Tables and the formulae for actions and juristic acts. It represents the first attempt to set forth the pontifical jus civile in a literary form, in the form, it is true, of mere explanatory or exegetic notes, but nevertheless a book —the first book dealing with law, the "cradle of juristic literature." From this time onward the technical knowledge of law passed more and more out of the hands of the pontifices and became an ingredient in national culture. At the same time the influence of Greek literature, and, more especially, the scientific methods of the Stoic philosophy, operated as a powerful and ennobling stimulant. The idea now suggested itself of casting the hard materials of law into a suitable artistic form. Thus, at an early date, we find M. Porcius Cato, the younger (who died 152 B.C.), making a conscious attempt to work out general principles of law (regulae juris), i.e. to trace in the raw material of legal rules, as presented by history, the underlying legal idea, to shape the statue from the rough block of marble. The most distinguished of all these "veteres" was Qu. Mucius Scaevola, the younger, pontifex maximus. About 100 B.C. he wrote his great treatise on the jus civile, in eighteen books, a work of wide and enduring fame. In this treatise the positive private law was, for the first time, set forth in systematic order, i.e. arranged and classified according to *the nature of the subjects* dealt with. Scaevola's system remained the foundation for the subsequent labours of his successors. He abandoned the traditional legal arrangement, and with it the method of merely interpreting the words of statutes or of formulae relating to procedure or juristic acts. Nor did he confine himself to the discussion of isolated cases or questions of law. He arranged his work according to the subject-matter with which the several rules of law are concerned, and in which they are, so to speak, focussed. He was the first to determine, in clear outline, the nature of the legal institutions (will, legacy, guardianship, partnership, sale, hiring, etc.), and the various kinds (genera) thereof. He made the first attempt to set out general legal conceptions, i.e. those elements which go to make up the checkered and, to all appearances, boundless mass of concrete facts. This is the secret of the great significance and enormous success of his work. His achievements rendered it possible, for first time, to survey private law rising as a whole beyond all the complexities of detail. A mere knowledge of law was beginning to develop into a legal science.

. . .

The chief business of a Roman jurist—apart from the drawing up of formulae for juristic transactions (cavere)—was to give answers to legal questions (respondere). With this he would combine the practice of teaching law and writing on legal subjects.

The authority of the ancient pontifical responsa rested on the position occupied by the college of pontifices, which appointed one of its members every year to give "opinions" on questions of private law. This is the reason why the judges were, as a matter of fact, bound by the pontifical responsa. Since the close of the republic, however, and with the spread of juristic learning, it has become a frequent practice for persons other than members of the college of pontifices freely to give "responsa," though, of course, such responsa were devoid of binding authority. It was clear that such a practice must tend to prejudice the prestige of the responsa and of jurisprudence in general. On the other hand, a return to the old monopoly of all legal learning by the pontifices was out of the question. The Emperor Augustus therefore devised a different remedy. With a view to restoring the authority of professional legal opinions, and at the same time, very probably, to throwing the imperial power into fresh relief, he ordered that in future all responsa should be given ex auctoritate ejus (principis), i.e. with the sanction of the emperor. As Augustus was at the same time pontifex maximus, this ordinance of his might be interpreted as involving both a revival and a reform of the old authoritative responsa, which the rise of the new practice had not, of course, done away with. Through the medium of the emperor, it was now feasible for persons who were not pontifices to deliver *authoritative* responsa. Henceforward the pontifical college ceases to play any part in the development of the civil law, and the princeps together with scientific jurisprudence (which has now definitely passed into the hands of laymen) become the prominent agents in the further development.

From the reign of Tiberius onward the business of giving responsa ex auctoritate principis was invariably carried on in a form which that emperor seems to have been the first to settle definitely. Henceforward it is the usual practice for the emperor to confer the so-called "jus respondendi" (jus publice, populo respondendi) on certain distinguished jurists. The jus respondendi is the privilege of delivering "opinions" *binding on the judge,* both on the magistrate and the appointed judex privatus. The "opinion" of a privileged jurist was required to be delivered in writing and sealed, and if a party submitted such an opinion, in due form, the judge was bound to decide accordingly, unless, indeed, a conflicting opinion of another privileged jurist were also submitted. At first it was only the responsum expressly delivered by the jurist in reference to a particular action that possessed such authoritative force. But it soon became the practice to extend the same authority to previous responsa, i.e. to such as no longer existed in their official form (written and sealed), but were only to be found in the literature of the responsa (the collections of responsa). A rescript of the Emperor Hadrian expressly sanctioned this practice.

The responsa prudentium, i.e. the "opinions" of the privileged jurists, had become a kind of source of law, and their force, as a source of law, was beginning to extend to juristic literature in general.

. . .

Roman jurisprudence was thus placed in a position of commanding influence. It only remained to be seen whether it would be able to utilize the influence it had acquired.

At the outset, a conflict arose between the jurists themselves. Two rival law-schools sprang up, the Sabinians and Proculians, the Sabinians being the followers of C. Atejus Capito, the Proculians the followers of M. Antistius Labeo. Both Capito and Labeo lived under Augustus. The Sabinians derived their name from Masurius Sabinus, an adherent of Capito, who lived in the reign of Tiberius. The Proculians derived their name from Proculus, who lived in the reign of Nero and was acknoledged as the leader of the disciples of Labeo. The successors of Sabinus and Proculus were C. Cassius Longinus and Pegasus respectively, and it is after them that the Sabinians are sometimes called Cassiani, and the Proculians Pegasiani.

It is impossible, at the present day,

to determine, with any certainty, what the essence of this divergence of schools was. But there would seem to be good warrant for one statement, at least, viz. that the influence exercised by Labeo extended in a large measure to the Sabinians. Of the two great jurists of the Augustan age Labeo was beyond doubt the greater. The large number of quotations from his works which the Corpus juris has preserved bear testimony, to this day, to his extraordinary influence on scientific jurisprudence. Capito's name, on the other hand, has practically disappeared from Justinian's collection. Labeo is the author of various new classifications, divisions and definitions—e.g. the definition of "dolus malus," of excusable error, of appurtenances, etc.—which helped to place both the theory and practice of law on a clearer and firmer footing. He is probably the author of the division of all actions into "actiones in rem" and "actiones in personam"—a division which, to this day, affects all juristic thought in matters of private law. As in the domain of scholarship —for he was an accomplished scholar and thoroughly imbued with the Greek and Roman culture of his age —so also in that of jurisprudence, he was an "analogist," i.e. his method was to trace all that was normal, all that was united by a common underlying conception, in order that, by so doing, he might bring positive law under the control of the art of dialectics. He was well qualified, therefore, to perform a useful task in his time. For there were many principles of law floating, as it were, in the air, generally recognized and already universally adopted, but still, maybe, waiting for some one to give them direct utterance. Labeo was the man to grasp them boldly and firmly, to cast them into shape, to give them a terse and vigorous expression which was sometimes, perhaps, too terse, because too sweeping. There was a book of Labeo's in which he had collected what he called the "probabilia," i.e. a number of such "legal principles of universal validity" taken from practical life ("libri pithanon"). This book long continued to exercise a vast practical influence, and it was with a view to softening the exaggerated point of the principles thus formulated that Paulus, as late as two centuries after, wrote a critical commentary on Labeo's work, testing his principles in the light of the actual facts of particular cases, and more especially in the light of the concrete intention of the parties (the "quod actum est"). But it was precisely the vigour and audacity of his definitions and principles that very naturally carried his contemporaries away. The power of definiteness and logical precision were on his side and could not fail to ensure his success. Neither he nor Capito seem to have founded a regular school themselves. They both gave legal instruction, but apparently after the traditional republican fashion of old distinguished Romans, whose practice it was to give public answers to questions in the presence of their pupils, occasionally arguing with them, but very rarely imparting regular private tuition in a series of connected lectures. Sabinus, who (we are told) earned his living by giving legal instruction, seems to have been the first to originate a school of law. It is probable that, at the same time, the method of instruction by means of a corporate organization, such as had been in vogue among the Greek schools of philosophy, found its way into Rome. These schools were societies of which the professor was the president and the pupils the members, each pupil being bound on entering to pay a subscription. The presidency of the school passed by a legal succession from one professor to the other. In opposition to the school of Sabinus, a second school sprang up, organized after the same fashion. This was the school of Proculus. After their respective founders the members of the former called themselves Sabinians, those of the latter Proculians. Tradition subsequently traced back the opposition between the schools to the opposition between the two famous jurists of the age of Augustus, Labeo and Capito. Nevertheless there were many eminent jurists who did not belong to either school and who had learned law in the old fashion, i.e. as "auditores" of some distinguished jurist. But as long as the opposition between them lasted, the organized societies of Sabinus and Proculus were the natural centres of all further development. Sabinus himself was the leading spirit among the chiefs of these schools. He pointed out to his pupils the lines on which Roman law should progress, in the sense of ridding itself of old-fashioned formalism. The Proculians, on the other hand, were inclined to abide by traditional rules, though, in so doing, they often, perhaps, sacrificed the spirit to the letter of Labeo's, their master's, teachings. The following dispute may serve to illustrate the difference between the schools. The Sabinians maintained that the defendant in an action was entitled to an acquittal, even though he only gave satisfaction to the plaintiff *during* the trial. The Proculians, on the other hand, insisted that in the actiones stricti juris, i.e. in those actions where the issue submitted to the judge was simply whether or no the defendant was liable, he (the defendant) ought, in all cases, to be condemned, if he was liable at the time when the issue was formulated (litis contestatio), and that no payment by him, *after* litis contestatio, could affect the result. Sabinus' most important work—the one through

which he exercised the most lasting influence—was his treatise called "libri tres juris civilis." Starting from the law of inheritance and passing on to the several juristic acts, he exhibited the entire body of civil law, classified according to subjects, and succeeded, like Labeo—whose influence he too felt, though in some points he controverted his teachings—in bringing out a number of new points of view, so much so, that his work was adopted henceforward as a fundamental treatise for the study of the jus civile.

The first indications of the so-called "classical jurisprudence" appeared early in the second century. Its task was to reconcile the opposition between the two schools, and its labours resulted in the fusion of the jus civile and jus honorarium (which latter had already become stationary) with the new imperial law into one harmonious whole. The foundations were laid by P. Juventius Celsus in his "Digesta" (in thirty-nine books). He was a follower of Proculus and died probably in the reign of Hadrian. Celsus was succeeded by a more eminent lawyer of the Sabinian school, Salvius Julianus, a native of Hadrumetum in the Roman province of Africa, who flourished under the reigns of Hadrian and Antoninus Pius. The task of his life consisted, in the first place, in the final consolidation of the edical law; and, secondly, in the composition of his great Digest in ninety books. Like Celsus, he adopted the arrangement of the praetorian edict, utilizing it, however, for the purpose of expounding *the whole* of Roman law. His vast acquaintance with practical case-law, the ingenuity of his own countless decisions, his genius for bringing out, in each separate case, the general rule of law which, tersely and pithily put, strikes the mind with all the force of a brilliant aphorism and sheds its light over the whole subject around—these are the features which constitute the power of his work. Roman jurisprudence had completed its dialectic training under Labeo and Sabinus, and the time had now arrived for applying to the vast mass of materials the principles, categories and points of view that had been thus worked out. Julianus' Digest exhibited Roman jurisprudence in all its strength, and its success was proportionately great. Surrounded as he was by numerous friends, all working towards one and the same end, the great jurist's triumph was ensured. Of such fellow-workers we may mention two: one, Sextus Caecilius Africanus, a rugged and weighty writer, the other Sextus Pomponius, a man of extensive reading and learning, who was also interested in historical research. After this, the star of the Proculian school began to set. The jurist Gajus, who died after 180 A.D., and whose institutional treatise was adopted as a model by all subsequent writers of legal text-books, is the last in whom the opposition between the schools is represented. He himself was a Sabinian. He still mentions contemporary teachers "of the other school," i.e. Proculians. But their names have not been handed down to us. The Sabinians gained the day. From the time of Salvius Julianus, and as a consequence of his labours, there was but one jurisprudence, and the lines on which it was progressing were those marked out by him.

The real nature of the task, to fulfil which was the function of Roman jurisprudence, had now become manifest. To unfold the great legal system in all its wealth and multiplicity by means of decisions and opinions, while following up in its details each question that arose, and yet, at the same time, to produce order out of chaos by vindicating the force of firm principles—such was the problem which Roman jurisprudence had to solve. A kind of casuistry of a higher order was required, such as had already been exhibited to the Romans in the great Digest of Celsus, and more especially of Julianus. At this point—it was towards the end of the second century—the Greek-speaking Orient sent its intellectual forces to participate in the creation of a jurisprudence for the whole empire, emphasizing thereby the consciousness of a great internal unity to which the empire had already attained. Under Marcus Aurelius and Commodus, Q. Cervidius Scaevola, a Greek by birth and subsequently a member of Marcus Aurelius' council of state (consilium), wrote his Digest in forty books, in which he set forth Roman law after the casuistic method, in the shape of "responsa," adopting, like others, the arrangement of the edict. His pupils were Septimius Severus, who afterwards became emperor, and, above all, Aemilius Papinianus, the most illustrious and, with Julianus, the greatest of Roman jurists. Papinian, who, like Scaevola, was an Oriental, combined the moral weight attaching to a character of sterling rectitude with the elegance of a Greek and the terseness and precision of a Roman. Like Scaevola he adopted the casuistic method of expounding the law by means of answers to concrete legal cases. He carried this method to its highest perfection. His most important works were eighteen "libri responsorum" and thirty-seven "quaestionum libri," in the latter of which he follows the arrangement of the edict. A mass of detached questions is here treated with the utmost lucidity; the decisions are formulated with great breadth, but, at the same time, with due regard to their proper limitations; the essential facts of each case are thrown into sharp relief and their accordance with the legal principle propounded is so strikingly brought out as to carry conviction, even where no arguments are adduced. Greek and Roman culture, acting and reacting on one another, produced in Papinian the brightest luminary of Roman jurisprudence. What he had taught and demanded throughout his life, viz. that what was immoral should also be thought impossible, he sealed with his death. He was murdered by the servants of Caracalla in 212 A.D. on account of the unswerving resistance which he opposed to the fratricidal designs of that tyrant.

After Papinian the period of decline begins. Roman jurisprudence had accomplished its masterpiece. The era of creative genius is followed by the labours of the compilers. Papinian's pupil, Domitius Ulpianus, a Syrian by descent (he was a native of Tyre), summed up the results achieved by his predecessors in a critical spirit, and embodied them in his voluminous commentary on the praetorian edict in eighty-three books, in his fifty-one "libri ad Sabinum," and in a long series of monographs—most of his works dating from the reign of Caracalla (212–217 A.D.). Next to him, and working in a kindred spirit, we have the jurist Julius Paulus, like Ulpian, an unusually prolific writer and probably a pupil of Scaevola's. His principal works were also a commentary on the edict (in eighty books), and a commentary ad Sabinum (in sixteen books). From this time onward it was in the main through the medium of Ulpian's and Paulus' writings that the labours of the great jurists operated on subsequent ages. The immense intellectual achievements of Roman jurisprudence were there put together in a clear and easily intelligible form. The foundations of Justinian's Digest were thus laid. A touch of the bright Greek spirit illumined the writings of Ulpian and caused them to be preferred to those of Paulus, where the thought is perhaps occasionally more profound, but the struggle with the matter more apparent. Ulpian's writings form the groundwork of Justinian's Digest. They constitute one third, Paulus' writings about one sixth of the Digest (viz. 2462 passages from Ulpian, 2080 from Paulus), so that about one half of that part of our Corpus juris which consists of the Digest owes its origin to the writings of Ulpian and Paulus. After Ulpian only one other jurist, Herennius Modestinus, a pupil of Ulpian's and, like him, a native of the Greek portion of the empire, attained to eminence. Little, however, had been left for him to do. His favourite topics are the law relating to the public officials of the incipient monarchy, and certain subtle questions of theory and practice. It was soon after his time that Roman jurisprudence lost its leading position. The jus respondendi ceased to be conferred after the close of the third century. The emperor alone gave "responsa," in the form of the "rescripta principis," and the last achievement of Roman jurisprudence—for its vitality had not yet passed away—was to infuse its spirit into the numerous rescripts of Diocletian and his successors.

From Labeo and Sabinus down to Celsus and Julianus, i.e. during the first century of the empire, the development of Roman jurisprudence had been steadily progressive. From Celsus and Julianus to Scaevola and Papinian, i.e. during the second century, it stood at the height of its power. From the time of Ulpian and Paulus, i.e. from the third century onwards, a period of uninterrupted decline set in. The treasure of Roman jurisprudence lay henceforth in the wealth which the past had produced. And a wonderful treasure it was which was thus entrusted to the safe-keeping of the jurists, and which they now passed on to the emperors and, through them, to the coming generations.

The task which had devolved upon Roman jurisprudence, and which it had now solved, had been a twofold one, viz. firstly, to consolidate into a uniform system the law which lay stored up in all the manifold sources, from the time of the Twelve Tables downwards; secondly, to develop, in a scientific form, the abundance of matter which these sources of law contained. The time had arrived for a new interpretatio[n]. Just as, at an earlier date, the Twelve Tables had to be "interpreted," so now, it was above all things the praetorian edict that had to be subjected to a similar process. It was only in a rough and ready manner, in a few broad outlines, that the praetorian edict had been able to work out the principles of a free and equitable law for the mutual dealings of man and man. There was a large field for further labour here. Nay, what is more, there were a great many subjects on which no information whatever was to be gained either from the praetorian edict or any other written source of law, for example, on the principles of representation, on the legal effect of conditions, on the contractual liability for negligence and many others. The problem here was to discover the true nature of the dealings themselves, to trace the *unexpressed* and *unconscious intention* underlying all such dealings, and, having done so, to put it into words, to clothe it in a form in which definiteness and lucidity should be coupled with a degree of comprehensiveness sufficient to bring out the broad general principle governing, not merely a large number of cases, but positively *all* cases, including those which were peculiar and exceptional. Such a problem touched rather the creation than the application of law. But it was precisely in performing a task of this kind that the genius of Roman jurisprudence came most strikingly into play. In spite of its innate dialectic strength and discipline, it had but few dogmatic interests in the modern scientific sense of the term. It gave little thought to the abstract conception of law, of ownership, or of liability; and what little it gave, generally yielded but very scanty results. But with regard to the consequences involved in the abstract conception of ownership or liability, its natural instinct was never at fault for a single moment. And nowhere was this unique power more conspicuously displayed than in the way the Roman jurists, so to speak, hit upon the precise requirements of bona fides in human dealings and applied them to individual cases. In such transactions, for instance, as sales, agreements to let and hire, agencies, etc. they seemed to know at once, and instinctively, what it was that the nature of the circumstances themselves required, in all cases and in each separate case, quite apart from any explicit declaration of intention on the part of the persons concerned. It is this wonderful discrimination, this clear-sightedness in the adjustment of conflicting principles, guided by a never-failing power of discerning the common elements; this unique faculty for giving outward expression to the law inherent in the concrete circumstances, which law, when found, supplies the rule—with many practical variations of course—for all other circumstances of the same kind: —these are the features to which the writings of the Roman jurists owe their incomparable charm, and the work they have achieved its indestructible force. It was no mere "arithmetic of abstractions," as it has been called, that made the Roman jurists as great as they were, it was rather that practical tact, which, without always being intellectually conscious of the abstract conception, nevertheless invariably acted in accordance with it, and thus succeeded in bringing out, in the individual case, the general law inherent in all cases of a similar description.

The department of law where the peculiar genius of the Roman jurists found full scope, is the law of obligations, the law of debtor and creditor, the law, in other words, which is most properly concerned with the mutual dealings between man and man; and here again it is more especially the law relating to those contracts, where not merely the expressed, but also the unexpressed intention of the parties has to be taken into account (the so-called negotia bonae fidei). And in regard to this unexpressed intention which is not, for the greater part, present to the mind of the party himself at the moment of concluding the contract, it was the Roman jurists who discovered it, and discovered it for all times to come, and enunciated the laws which result from its existence. This is a task which will never have to be done over again. And, at the same time, they clothed these laws in a form which will remain a model for all future ages. This is the reason why the law of obligations, and it alone,—and more particularly the law of those negotia bonae fidei, and it alone—constitutes what is, in the truest and strictest sense, the imperishable portion of Roman law. . . .

It was just the manner in which the Roman jurists exercised their vocation that enabled them to accomplish these striking results and to secure to Roman law its imperishable and irresistible power. For the centre and pivot of all their learning lay at all times in the art of giving "responsa," i.e. in the treatment of concrete cases. Roman jurisprudence grew up in immediate contact with practical life, immersed, so to speak, in a multitude of concrete cases, but never at a loss to discover the law inherent in each,—a law which, though abstract, met the requirements of details and which, with all its elasticity, was strong and firm enough to govern the vast field of human dealings with triumphant certitude.

The praetorian law was the channel through which the jus gentium had, in the first instance, gained admittance to, and had then rapidly permeated, Roman law. But it was only in the hands of the Roman jurists that the jus gentium, that law of human dealings which, in itself, was so intangible, so shifting and so free, received the tangibleness, the perspicuity and, at the same time, the necessary limitations without which the principles of bona fides, in the form in which the Roman jurists had embodied them, could never have retained their indestructible vitality.

The real task which had devolved on Roman law in its course of development was thus accomplished. The jural reason inherent in the various relations of human intercourse had found an expression of classic beauty in the writings of the Roman jurists. The last touch was all that was wanting. To apply it was reserved for the imperial power.

.   .   .

The Imperial Legislation

The imperial power passed through two stages of development. In its first stage, that of the principatus, the power of the emperor is simply the power of the "first citizen" of the republic; in its second stage, i.e. from the time of Diocletian and Constantine, it is the power of a monarch. This development is reflected in the history of law. The princeps of the first epoch has no legislative powers, but the imperial monarch of the fourth and subsequent centuries has legislative powers. During the period of the principate the emperor's influence on the development of the law is merely incidental and supplementary, whereas during the period of the monarchy he assumes, by means of his legislative authority, the exclusive leadership in all further legal progress.

1. First Stage

During the first stage, which extends down to about 300 A.D., the princeps influences the development of law in four ways: by his decisions of particular cases (decreta, interlocutiones); by his "opinions" on particular cases (rescripta); by his instructions to officials (mandata); by his public ordinances (edicta).

"Decreta" and "Rescripta" must be regarded as means of authentic interpretation. The emperor interprets the law by applying it to a particular case, but the imperial interpretation of law is authoritative, and conclusive for all cases of the same kind. A rescript was granted in reply to an enquiry addressed to the emperor either by a magistrate or—as was far more frequently the case—by a private party. It took the form either of an independent reply (epistola) or of a note appended, by way of answer, to the petition (subscriptio). The quasi-statutory force of decrees and rescripts (legis vicem habent), like that of the responsa prudentium, is not limited to the life of the emperor who issues them. The authentic interpretation shares the legal force of the law it interprets.

The "Mandata" which the emperor addressed to his officials became, as a matter of fact, a source of law in so far as certain portions of them (capita ex mandatis) were regularly repeated in every set of official instructions. The imperial "Edicts" were the outcome of that right to issue public orders which vested in the emperor in his magisterial capacity. By means of his edicts on questions of private law he made known the principles by which he intended, in such cases, to be guided in the exercise of his imperial power. Edicts and mandates were only valid, on principle, during the life of the emperor who issued them; if their validity was to extend any further, the next emperor had to repeat them.

The jurists gave these various manifestations of the imperial power, so far as they bore on the development of law, the collective name of "constitutiones," and assigned to such constitutiones a quasi-statutory force in so far as the conditions of permanent validity had been satisfied, which (as we have seen) was not a matter of course in the case of edicts and mandates. During this epoch, however, a law proper did not ordinarily take the form of an imperial ordinance, nor again of a popular statute—which latter occurred only very exceptionally, and only in the early part of this period—but the form of a senatus-consultum. During the republic, the authority of the senate was still confined to regulating the *execution* of the laws by means of an authoritative interpretation. From the beginning of the empire, however, though at first, in the face of some opposition, the senate exercised an independent legislative power operating, of its own force, as a source of jus civile. The decree of the senate was now regarded as taking the place of the popular statute. The princeps has the right to treat with the senate and to originate a decree of the senate by means of a motion (oratio); since Hadrian, in fact, the power to submit bills to the senate for the purpose of having them enacted as senatusconsulta is exclusively exercised by the emperor. To what extent the right of the senate to agree to a motion of the emperor's had, in the course of this epoch, sunk to a mere matter of form, is apparent from the fact that it could become the practice, at a subsequent date, to quote, not the senatusconsultum, but merely the oratio, i.e. the motion of the emperor.

. . .

2. *Second Stage*

From the close of the third century the power of Roman jurisprudence began to decline. From the same date, i.e. from the reign of Diocletian, the imperial power, which had not definitely become monarchical, commences to exercise an exclusive control over the further development of law. The emperor reserved for himself not merely the right formally to create new law (viz. by legislation), but also the right to interpret the existing law, out of which he was thus able in cases of doubt to develop new principles. The imperial opinions (rescripta) took the place of scientific interpretation and consequently increased enormously in number. (We possess over a thousand rescripts of Diocletian's.) In addition to the rescript, we have, as before, the "decretum" or judicial decision of the emperor, and, above all, the imperial statute, representing the new form in which the development of the law is carried on. The imperial statute originated in the motion which the emperor introduced to the senate (oratio), but the form of communicating it to the senate has now been discarded. Imperial legislation supersedes senatorial legislation. An imperial statute is, so to speak, an "oratio" directly promulgated to the nation at large. Hence it is described as an "edictum" or "lex generalis." When the emperor had acquired the power to legislate, it became necessary to distinguish his merely interpretative or judicial from his legislative functions. Whereas in the earlier epoch every rescript and decree had possessed the force of general law, unless its validity were expressly limited to the particular case ("constitutio personalis"), the position was now reversed, and every rescript and decree, as such, was treated as a "constitutio personalis," i.e. as valid only for the particular case, unless the general validity of the principle applied were expressly ordained. It was only when the emperor chose to act as lawgiver that a law binding on the whole empire ("constitutio generalis") came into existence, and (on principle at least) it was the form which marked and characterized a statute as such. In ordinary cases, then, a law takes the form of an edict, i.e. a law officially promulgated; in extraordinary cases, it takes the form of a rescript or decree (expressly issued with the force of law), i.e. a law not officially promulgated. There are still laws which are not officially promulgated, and which only become known to the people at large through the medium of literature, because the emperor, in legislating, still continues, to some extent, to avail himself of the forms of an earlier period when, formally, he possessed no legislative powers. Nevertheless, the principle of the distinction between a law, as something which requires to be promulgated, and a mere detached decision, as something which needs no promulgating, is already well established; and the decision which is not officially promulgated (the rescript or decree) has only the force of law in exceptional cases. The modern type of monarchical legislation is thus gradually attaining to a consciousness of its own nature and conditions.

. . .

Imperial legislation which henceforth took the lead in all further progress had a twofold task to fulfil: firstly, to complete the development of Roman law; secondly, to gather in the results.

The completion of the development of Roman law involved, on the one hand, a final process of filing down the jus civile by the jus gentium, and, on the other, the removal of the antithesis between jus civile and jus honorarium. Both these tasks were solved, not by the short and sharp method of codification, but by a series of separate statutes. For the same cautious conservative tendency, chary of innovations, which characterizes the history of Roman law in general, is no less characteristic of the methods of imperial legislation. From Diocletian and Constantine to Justinian, i.e. during an interval of over two centuries, the ancient traditional law, the "jus vetus," was subjected to a continuous process of polishing and filing at the hands of successive emperors, till perfect unity and harmony had been established. And the majority of final reforms, which effected alterations of a more far-reaching character in the private law, were only accomplished by Justinian, the last Roman emperor whose own proficiency in the law enabled him, in some measure, to dispense with the aid of his legal advisers, and work independently at the improvement of Roman law. Some of his reforms, e.g. in the law of inheritance, were not even carried out till after the comupletion of the Corpus juris, by means

of his Novels. Down to the Corpus juris the Twelve Tables continued in theory to constitute the basis of the entire body of Roman law. Down to the Corpus juris, again, the antithesis between jus civile and jus honorarium continued in theory to be maintained. Justinian's Corpus juris summed up the results of that continuous development which had commenced centuries ago with the Twelve Tables, and the Twelve Tables themselves, with all that followed them, were now superseded by the great imperial code of Justinian. Theoretically speaking, this code signalized the final victory of the jus civile, for the law begotten by imperial legislation was civil law; in point of fact, however, it was the jus gentium, allied with the jus honorarium, that had triumphed all along the line.

Caracalla had conferred the Roman franchise on all citizens of the empire. There was thus but one nationality in the Roman empire, to wit the Roman—and the Roman nation was coextensive with that portion of mankind upon which the civilization of Western antiquity rested. From the fourth century onwards the tendency to shift the centre of gravity to the Eastern, in other words, to the Greek portion of the empire, became more and more pronounced. Formal expression was thus given to what had already been an accomplished fact: the victory of cosmopolitan Hellenism over the spirit of ancient Rome. It was no longer the traditions of Rome and Italy, but the views and requirements of Greek provincialism that surrounded and influenced the emperor of Constantinople. The provinces had ousted the old premier country, Greece had triumphed over Rome. And so it came to pass that the jus gentium finally displaced the old jus civile. Centuries ago the intercourse with the Greeks had engrafted the jus gentium on the local law of Rome. Now that the native soil of the jus gentium itself had become the scene of legal development, the jus gentium could not fail to put forth all its strength. Thus the jus aequum, having attained to full maturity, received the final form in which it dominated with essential uniformity the whole field of private law. Roman law was finished: the local law of a city had passed into a law available for the world in general.

One thing only remained to be done, and that was to gather in the ripe fruits and store them up for future generations. This task also devolved on the emperors, and was successfully performed by them.

Codification

I. The Stages Preliminary to Codification

In the later empire (which dates from the fourth century) there were two groups of sources of law: firstly, the "jus vetus," or "jus" simply, i.e. the old traditional law, the development of which was completed in the classical period of Roman jurisprudence (in the course of the second and the beginning of the third century); secondly, the "leges" or "jus novum," i.e. the later law which had sprung from imperial legislation. These two classes of law, "jus" and "leges," mutually supplementing each other, constituted the whole body of law as it existed at the time, and, taken together, represented the result of the whole development of Roman law from the earliest times down to the period we have now reached, viz. the epoch of the later empire.

The "jus" was based, indeed, on the Twelve Tables, the plebiscita, the senatusconsulta, the praetorian edict and the ordinances of the earlier emperors. In reality, however, neither the tribunals nor the parties were in the habit of using these sources of law, in their original form, but preferred to resort to the classical juristic literature where they found the results of these sources set forth and worked out. It was not the praetor or the plebiscitum that was now quoted, but Papinian, Ulpian, Paulus, and the other jurists. And, at the same time, no distinction was made as to whether the particular opinion had happened to be conveyed by Paulus or Papinian in the shape of a "responsum" or not. The authority which the responsa, and the literature connected therewith, had acquired since the opening of the second century was now actually transferred to juristic literature in general. To this must be added the fact that the conferring of the jus respondendi on individual jurists was discontinued in the course of the third century; after Diocletian the emperor was the only person entitled to give authoritative responsa, which he did by means of his rescripts. Thus it happened that later ages failed to appreciate the distinction between jurists who had, and jurists who had not, the jus respondendi. The writings of jurists who had not possessed the jus respondendi were cited as entitled to an authority in no way inferior to that of the writings of privileged jurists, provided only they were supported by the same *literary* prestige which distinguished the writings of the illustrious privileged jurists. Thus, for example, in the fourth century, Gajus, who flourished as a professor of law under Antoninus Pius and Marcus Aurelius, and whose writings delighted all subsequent ages by a fluency and lucidity worthy of a Greek, enjoyed, in the courts of law, an authority equal to that, say, of

Paulus or Papinian, in spite of the fact that he had never possessed the jus respondendi. Considering that, in the case of the privileged jurists, their other writings which, of course, had nothing to do with their jus respondendi, were ranked on a par with the writings on the responsa, it was altogether absurd to insist on the jus respondendi as a condition of judicial authority. The practice of not discriminating between the different kinds of writings necessarily led to the practice of not discriminating between the authors themselves—which is only another way of saying that the transfer of the authority of the responsa to juristic literature in general had become an accomplished fact.

A keenly-felt want was satisfied by this development. The old sources of law, and more especially the popular statutes and the praetorian edict, had ceased, by this time, to be generally intelligible, partly on account of their language, partly on account of the bald, sententious, pregnant phraseology in which they were couched. Since people were no longer able to make use of the old sources of law themselves, they were driven, in lieu thereof, to resort, on a more extensive scale, to the juristic literature which had sprung from these sources. In other words, "jus," i.e. the law of the earlier stages of development, ceased to be practically available in any other form but that in which it appeared in the writings of the jurists; the jus (vetus) became identified with jurist-made law.

All the emperors had to do here was, partly to modify, partly to supplement and confirm the law as they found it. This was done by a number of "laws of citations," among which Valentinian the Third's Law of Citations (426 A.D.) is the most important. Valentinian merely sanctioned what had already become an established usage. He enacted that the writings of the jurists, to wit, of Papinian, Paulus, Ulpian, Gajus and Modestinus, as well as of all those who were cited by these writers (the limits of classic literature being thus officially determined) should possess quasi-statutory force so that their opinions should be binding on the judge. If the opinions differed on the same question, that opinion should prevail which was supported by most jurists; if the numbers were equal, Papinian's opinion should prevail, or, if Papinian had expressed no opinion on the question, the judge was to exercise his discretion. Not a word is said about citing the old sources of law themselves; their force as law has passed on to juristic literature. Valentinian the Third's Law of Citations marks the completion, for the time being, of that development which had commenced with the responsa of the old pontifices and the jus respondendi of Augustus. Never did a literary movement achieve a more unqualified success.

.   .   .

The jus (vetus) was traditionally taken to include those collections of early imperial ordinances, more especially of rescripts, among which the Codex Gregorianus—published about 300 A.D.—and the Codex Hermogenianus—a later collection supplementing the former, and published in the course of the fourth century—were preeminent. Both these codices were perhaps due to suggestions from official quarters. Their practical value lay in the fact that they contained such rescripts (including the numerous rescripts of Diocletian) as the classical jurists had not yet been able to take into account.

The real type of the new imperial law (leges) was the "edictum," in the later sense of the term, the "constitutio generalis" promulgated to the public. All that these constitutions of the new kind as well as the rescripts of the post-classical period required was that they should be collected, and this want was supplied by the Codex Theodosianus, published by the Emperor Theodosius II in 438 A.D., and promulgated in the very same year with statutory force for the Western Empire, by Valentinian III. It contained the constitutiones generales issued since Constantine and at the same time abrogated all such constitutions of the same period as had not been adopted.

Between the Codex Theodosianus and Justinian a series of separate imperial laws were issued, which were known as "Novels," and collected under that name (the so-called "Post-Theodosian Novels").

The following sources of law were thus in use at Justinian's time: 1. the writings of the jurists, as determined by Valentinian's Law of Citations; 2. the earlier imperial ordinances (Codex Gregorianus and Hermogenianus); 3. the Codex Theodosianus and its novels.

These are the materials out of which our Corpus juris was constructed.

II. The Corpus Juris of Justinian

The Emperor Justinian, who reigned from 527–565 A.D., conceived the plan of consolidating the entire existing law in one single code. For this purpose he caused two collections to be prepared, one of the "jus," or jurist-made law, the other of the "leges," or emperor-made law. A short text-book (the "institutiones," or "Institutes") was prefixed to the whole by way of introduction to the code and the study of law. Thus the code was divided into three parts: the, Institutes, the Digest (or Pandects), and the Code.

1. The Institutes. The Institutes (in four books) are a short text-book of Justinianian law, its contents being partly of an historical, partly of a theoretical character. It was composed by the imperial minister Tribonian, and, under his supervision, by the two professors Theophilus and Dorotheus. It was founded on earlier institutional treatises, e.g. those of Ulpian and Marcianus, but more especially on the Institutes and Res quotidianae of Gajus. Justinian published the Institutes as part of his code, with the same statutory force as the remaining portions.

. . .

2. The Digest (or Pandects). The Digest (in fifty books) is a collection of excerpts from the writings of the jurists, in other words, a codification of the "jus" or jurist-made law, prepared, by Justinian's orders, by a commission of professors and advocates under the supervision of Tribonian. In their arrangement of the subject-matter the compilers were, generally speaking, guided by the order of the praetorian edict. The commission was divided into three sections, each of which was instructed to extract a particular group of writings. To the first section was assigned the group of works dealing with the jus civile, "the Sabinian group," so called, because the staple of these works consisted of the writings Sabinus and his commentators. To the second section was assigned the group of works dealing with the praetorian edict, the so-called "Edict-group." To the third section was assigned the group of works dealing with separate legal questions and cases, the "Papinianian group," so called, because in this branch the writings of Papinian and his commentators transcended all others in importance. Each section extracted the works alloted to it so far as they bore on each particular subject. Thereupon the whole was consolidated into one work, the extracts of the three groups being pieced together under each rubric, while some extracts from such writings as had, in the first instance, been overlooked or set aside, were subsequently inserted (the so-called "Appendix-group"). Inasmuch as the object of the whole undertaking was not to promote historical research, but to produce a practical code of law, the commission was empowered to make alterations in the excerpts they adopted. This is the explanation of the so-called "interpolations" ("emblemata Triboniani") by means of which the selections from the classical jurists were brought into harmony with the law of Justinian's time. The controversies among the juristic writers were set aside, one view only being accepted—such at least was the intention—in the Digest. All individual features were swept away in favour of a uniform, self-consistent whole. It was but reasonable that Justinian and his advisers should look with pride on their achievement. Their work was, in the main, a success. The results of the development of Roman law extending over more than a thousand years had been summed up. Instead of a wilderness of juristic writings there was a uniform work, easy of survey and methodical in execution. It was forbidden to make any further use of the writings of the jurists in their original form, and the imperial selection—an epitome and, at the same time, a revival of Roman jurisprudence—was published with statutory force. Never had a code been prepared from nobler materials.

. . .

3. The Code. The Code (in twelve books) is a collection of imperial constitutions, including both the separate decisions of the old type since Hadrian, and the general ordinances of the new type; in other words, a codification of imperial law (leges). As early as 528 A.D., Justinian had ordered a new code to be compiled on the basis of the Codex Gregorianus and Hermogenianus (which in this instance, then, were counted among the "leges"), the Codex Theodosianus and the later ordinances. This Code was finished and published in 529 A.D. The subsequent composition of the Digest and Institutes, however, which involved a number of material changes in the law, necessitated a remodelling of the Code. The Code of 529 was repealed and a new Code published in 534. The Code in this its second edition (repetiae praelectionis) is the Code of our Corpus juris. The imperial constitutions which have been admitted are arranged in chronological order under their several titles. Here again, interpolations were, when necessary, resorted to with a view to bringing the contents of the earlier imperial ordinances into accordance with the law prevailing at the time. All earlier constitutions were deprived of validity. Just as the "jus" had no validity except in the form of the Digest, so the "leges" possessed no validity except in the form of the new Code of Justinian.

. . .

The Corpus juris of Justinian was thus finished. The entire positive law had been cast into a final shape. All three parts, Institutes, Digest and Code, though published at different dates, were to have equal validity as parts of one and the same code of law. With a view to preventing new controversies, the writing of commentaries was forbidden. All doubtful points were to be referred to the emperor himself for decision. This explains the necessity for new constitutions (novellae constitutiones) which were already issued, in fairly large numbers, by Justinian himself (536–565). The "novels" were afterwards collected. The collection of novels which was used by the glossators at Bologna (the Authenticum) was "received" in Germany in the sixteenth centry as the *fourth* part of the Corpus juris.

Part 5

the

seedbed

societies

The seedbed type of society stands in somewhat different relation to the general scale of evolutionary advancement than do the other types of society treated in this volume. In terms of the degrees of structural differentiation attained by their systems of social organization, the seedbed societies, namely ancient Israel and classical Greece, might best be classified with the archaic societies. Indeed, they were not especially large, complex, or long enduring as compared to many archaic systems. However, the seedbed societies had a momentous impact upon the long-run course of human evolution that no archaic society could have produced. Whereas the most general complexes of religio-moral culture remained particularistically bound up with or undifferentiated from the constitutive social orders of the archaic systems, the seedbed societies broke through the diffuseness of the "cosmological" beliefs and developed elements of culture of such meaningfulness and sophistication as to provide appealing orientation in quite various social environments. Their cultural traditions generated the especially fruitful philosophic breakthroughs that became the sources of crucial elements in the cultures of later civilizations that attained very high "historic" and then "modern" levels of development. Most importantly, the Christian culture which has constituted the normative foundation of modern Western civilization may be understood to have obtained its characteristic evolutionary dynamism from its synthesis of patterns that originated separately in the two seedbed societies.

We have selected readings on the seedbed societies that explicate major aspects of the processes of philosophic breakthrough in the two cultures, but which also are concerned with cultural components that later proved of special importance to the Christian synthesis. The Hebraic breakthrough and contribution to so-called Judeo-Christian culture focused upon the fundamental conception of transcendental monotheism. We will be concerned with the evolution within Judaism, especially in the religiously dynamic era of the prophets, of the interdependencies and tensions between the belief in a God whose will commands and gives meaning to all events on earth and the ethical understanding of the significance of the human situation and human social action. In the Greek case, the component of the cultural breakthrough that contributed most importantly to the later Christian belief system was the intellectually rationalized secular culture. It emerged only through a very complex concatenation of a number of dynamic elements in Greek culture. In certain respects, the most fundamental element was the grounding of secular concerns and speculation in an essentially religious concept of order, the natural order which classical thought came to see as transcending and imparting significance to the actions of even the gods. However, our attention will focus mainly upon the relationships between the ethical components of the transcendent order of nature, especially the component concerned with social and political justice, and the institutional structuring of the Greek city-states. Given the prominence of political concerns and public discourse in Greek social life, the tensions between the transcendent ideals of justice and the political structure of society were able to generate and sustain a tradition of differentiatedly secular thought. It was the secular grounding of Greek rational speculation that enabled it much later to enter Christian culture both through the capacity of its logic to discipline and systematize theology and through its substantive social ideals concerning the "natural" patterns of human association.

From the Mosaic period on, Hebraic religious thought focused importantly on the concept of convenant or *berith* between God and the Jews, his Chosen People. The enduring core of the covenant conception was that Jahweh, God, promised to bring his people to a special standing among the peoples of the world, but at the same time obligated them to obey his will, commands, and law in special ways. Each of the elements of the covenant—Jahweh's powers, will, and law, the nature of the promised future paradise, the obligations incumbent upon the Jews through their special relation with God, judgments as to whether the holy commands were being fulfilled, the extent to which Jahweh was actually obligated to reward the Jews for their faith—became the subject of much profound theological speculation.

Especially during the more strictly archaic phases of Hebrew thought, Jahweh was, as Weber phrased it, a god of foreign policy (and a Clausewitzian one at that) who was worshipped for his powers in advancing his chosen people over other nations. The belief in his ability to secure collective well-being for his people was served by a gradual magnification and universalization of the conception of his powers. Other peoples and their histories increasingly became significant as vehicles of Jahweh's special plans for the Jews. However, the further the glorification of his powers proceeded, the greater was the theological tension generated by the failure of his people to realize their destiny. Here a voluntaristic element inherent in the conception of covenant came to play a critical role: the disappointments of the people could not be attributed to limitations in the powers of God or to an "immoral" intention on the part of God not to fulfill his promises to Israel, but they could represent his special punishment for a willful and wicked falling away from his commandments. Thus, the covenant conception directed religious speculation to a strong concern with the moral short-comings of the people, generally understood as a voluntary opposition to the will of the Lord, and with calls for them to return to his ways so that their destiny might be realized.

The spiritual tensions structured by the covenant theology generated an intense movement of philosophic breakthrough in the period of political disaster which ancient Israel experienced after the conquest by Babylon. A long series of ethical prophets, some of whose missions are known to us from the Bible, arose from the pastoral sector of Judaic society to inveigh against the estrangement of the sophisticates of the cities and royal courts from the customs of the patriarchs. After the model of Moses, they claimed to act upon personal inspiration from Jahweh in calling the people to return to the commandments of the covenant. The prophets brought new vision to the Hebraic conception of history, formulating it as the record of the meaning of events as revelations about Jahweh's preparations of his people for their salvation. The prophets claimed to enter history as divinely inspired agents who could reveal to the people with certainty the nature of the trials and punishments with which Jahweh tested them, hence as crucial catalysts in the process of preparation for salvation. The prophetic emphasis on moral worthiness for salvation was accompanied by change in the conception of salvation itself. It came to focus less on political preeminence and more on the liberty of the people to live according to the customs and commandments ordained by God, and thus linked up with beliefs about moral-ethical perfection. The later prophets began to project a spiritual conception of salvation that came to be the basis of modern Judeo-Christian beliefs.

Martin Buber discusses the thought of a late prophet who is known as Deutero-Isaiah since he was the author of one of the component documents in the Book of Isaiah. For this prophet, whose theology culminates the evolution of the Old Testament period, the role of prophecy is deeply bound up with the very conception of and belief in God. Buber shows that he is much concerned with validating the universal powers of Jahweh as against the claims made for gods of other peoples. The crux of Deutero-Isaiah's faith is that Jahweh is the God of prophecy. Jahweh has fixed what the future will be and can inspire prophets to foretell it, while other gods cannot affect history and destiny. The ability of the prophets truly to reveal the future is a critical index of the universal powers of their Lord. Although history contains new creations when Jahweh intervenes in the course of events, no other force can determine history. Even wickedness and adversity are entirely the creations and instruments of the Lord. Prophecy is strictly revelatory of what God has set as man's future. For Deutero-Isaiah, it reveals the destiny of men to the exclusion of setting actual moral alternatives before them, for men do not truly create history.

The universalism of Deutero-Isaiah's conception of God leads him to concern with the destinies of peoples other than the Jews. As the redeemer of Israel, Jahweh will liberate his people from the rule of Babylon. However, he will also establish a just order among the nations, thereby becoming the liberator of all enslaved and afflicted peoples. The liberation of all peoples will follow the redemption of Israel, hence, through the covenant, the Jews stand as the instrument for preparing the salvation of all nations.

As Buber strongly emphasizes, the core of Deutero-Isaiah's prophetic thought was the mystery of the "servant of Israel." By the basic terms of the holy covenant, the people of Israel were to be the servant of Jahweh collectively. Since the people had proved disappointing to God and had fallen away from his service, whoever would stand in for them and follow the way of the covenant would become his servant. Deutero-Isaiah's mystery concerned the role of the prophet as the servant who was the stand-in for all of Israel. Ever since Moses, Jahweh had chosen leaders to guide the people back to his true commandments and toward their redemption. Because the prophets had to oppose the false commandments of the kings and courts, their lot necessarily was one of suffering. Hence, the prophetic way to redemption involved the acceptance of a life of suffering out of one's duty to the Lord. Taking up the burden for the sake of becoming God's agent in the redemption of the people came to be itself a redeeming act. The prophet who suffers, as Deutero-Isaiah suffered, can show the people how to fill the role of servant. Despite his worldly lowliness, he alone opens the hard hearts of the people and leads them to the fulfillment of their unique historical role. Only he who is a prophet in his suffering is truly a servant, and he is a forerunner of the Messiah.

Classical Greek civilization emerged out of its Homeric, strictly archaic background through a long process of normative rationalization. Its rationalization was grounded in a system of beliefs, themselves rationalized by early conceptions of logic, concerning a natural order which was the true and right order of all things standing behind the flux of apprehendable reality. The general conception of a natural order provided a core of evaluative principles and standards in terms of which knowledge about diverse aspects of the human condition gained rationalization. The Greeks came to differentiate what they termed *paideia* or philosophically systematized learning from what was merely personal opinion or traditional convention, but lacked rigorous derivation from basic principles. It was believed that man could become truly and fully human, could realize the entire teleological potential of his humanity, only by ordering his life in terms of *paideia*. People other than Greeks were in general considered barbarians precisely because of their ignorance of philosophic learning or knowledge.

While Greek culture thrived on the tensions generated among its many variant forms institutionalized in different city-states, cult centers, alliances, and later "academies," all versions of Greek culture gave primacy to ethical questions concerning the proper nature of institutional arrangements in the *polis* or city-state. The *polis* was for all Greeks the principal framework of social life, aspiration, and activity, and hence the most important complex structure to humanize and rationalize. Moreover, its normative definition as a corporate entity in which men participated—in early times as members of large lineages divided into classes and led by a king, later as heads of households stratified largely on universalistic grounds—on a basis of personal responsibility for the welfare of the commonwealth encouraged public consideration of matters not only of policy but also of institutional arrangement. At issue were the most fundamental questions of how the corporate life should be ordered so as to encourage the maximal development of both individual and collective humanity and virtue. Thus, philosophical speculation about the "natural" organization of the *polis* came to comprise the very core of the more secular aspects of Greek *paideia*. At the same time, it also came to stand at the center of the normative tensions generated by the evolution of Greek society: The development from the Homeric kingdoms to the tyrannies, oligarchies, and democracies of the classical era involved continual controversy which the Greeks attempted to remove from the areas of traditional convention and mere opinion to that of *paideia*.

Werner Jaeger essays the part played by ideals of justice and of legality, as elements of the *paideia*, in the evolution of the city-state to the democratic form exemplified by Athens in the classical era. In the early *poleis*, rights to administer justice were held by heads of the noble families and by kings. However, justice was glorified as an essential basis of the organization of the state and of loyalty to the state. The state that could not provide justice for its citizens attenuated the legitimacy of its claims to their loyalty, obedience, and cooperation. Entitled to assurances that they would receive justice, the common citizens began to demand written laws as a means of delimiting and regulating the elements of arbitrariness which entered into the justice they received from the kings and nobles. Thus, the principle of *themis* or institutional privilege of deciding cases and dispensing justice came to be counterbalanced by a principle of *dike* or justice in the sense of receiving one's due share. As the *paideia* evolved to place stronger emphasis on the humanizing of the individual and of his participation in the *polis, dike* became increasingly important as the principle regulating the articulation of social units into the corporate state.

Appeal to the principle of *dike* constituted perhaps the major normative device by which the common citizenry, through long and often bitter class struggles, asserted its claims to a greater share in the powers of the state. Jaeger shows that the very meaning of the concept contained an important aspect of equality. As *dike* gained the standing of a norm for the measurement of rights recognized by the courts in the determination of cases, it gradually undermined formal discrimination against the common class. As it penetrated the sphere of rights to dispense justice and hold public office, it promoted the access of all citizens to these privileges. It affected educational ideals by undermining the heroic emphasis of the earlier aristocratic morality in favor of a conception of the good citizen who understands, obeys, and is concerned with the law. The virtues of obedience to the promulgated law and of profound involvement in the performance of civic duties emerged as fundamentally democratic ideals which all citizens could hope to emulate in common. The *paideia* as a system of educational learning came to place profound emphasis on the formulation of laws which would promote human self-realization in terms of these civic-democratic virtues. Jaeger underlines the stress of the ethical-educational systems of the classical era upon the philosophical training of the citizen for his civic role in the setting of a right order through the making of laws.

The point of departure for A. H. M. Jones' essay is the striking fact that, against this background, all of the great Athenian philosophers of the classic, democratic period were oligarchic rather than democratic in basic sympathy. In the public controversies over the normative structure of the Athenian *polis,* they tended to argue that democratic rule operated at excessive cost in terms of ideals such as civic discipline, the encouragement and reward of excellence and virtue, the legality of public action, the stability of the law, and fairness (*dike*) to the minority of wealthy citizens. Since we do not have records of the arguments with which the democratic commons countered these charges, Jones argues, our knowledge of the actual workings of the Athenian democracy has become significantly biased. He attempts to redress this bias by reconstructing some of the key arguments to which the commons probably appealed.

Jones cites Pericles' famous funeral oration as evidence that those of democratic sympathy did not agree that excellence and virtue were denied leadership in public affairs. Pericles argued that, although all Athenian citizens held rights to participate in the development of public policy, the emphasis on equality was importantly delimited so that men of proven distinction were given greater honor and influence in civic deliberations. While the offices conducting routine public business were filled by lot, the principal offices concerned with leadership of the state were granted only to prominent citizens of established ability.

Jones shows the charge that democracy undermined the rule of law in favor of the undisciplined rule of the mass to have been based on a conception of an immutable, ideal law which can only be debased when affected by the play of interests. However, this was the conception of law contained in the *paideia,* and seems to have been accepted by all parties. Stability of the basic legal framework was valued by the commons as a crucial bulwark against tyranny and oligarchy. Constitutional provisions assured that the procedures for changing the laws were awkward and complex. Yet, in the area of taxation and economic control of the rich, Jones does find some derogation of legality. If taxes were not steeply "progressive" and if large expenditures on the public were required mainly as liturgies from those who aspired to leadership, the state often acted in questionable ways in times of financial difficulty, e.g., condemning the rich and confiscating their property. Informers and blackmailers were apparently active enough to heighten the sense of the insecurity of property and of democratic manipulation of the laws.

the god of the sufferers

twenty

MARTIN BUBER

Deutero-Isaiah is, in spite of the teaching of Amos, Isaiah and Jeremiah, the originator of a theology of world-history, for he is the first to base his particular message again and again on declarations about the rule of God over the nations and his works among them, the first to found the particular on this universal, and to deduce it, so to speak, from this. His God is not merely One Who reveals Himself according to His nature—as in all Israelite prophecy—but also a God Who declares His nature theologically. There is no sense at all in calling Deutero-Isaiah "the first monotheist of Israel," but certainly he is the first concerned with a monotheistic theology, because he is concerned with a theology of world-history. And he is concerned with it, because here for the first time the prophet's task is to repel as vain the claims of other gods to the leadership of the world and its destiny; and it is his task, especially because this claim influences the problematic character of this hour of history, namely the problematic character of the political program of the man acting in this

hour, Cyrus, lord of the nations. True it was not to him, but about him, the words had to be spoken, proving that the gods, under whose protection Cyrus was inclined to put his program and to let it be sanctioned by them, were powerless in the field of history —this can be proved radically only by showing that they are no gods, but a concoction made by man. Every other kind of criticism would only be liable to produce counter-criticism, every other kind would become entangled in a circle of arguments and answers. No unconditional superiority can appertain to a theology unless it undertakes to demarcate its "all" against a "nothing"; and so that it does not construct this "nothing" dialectically but shows it up perceptibly. In other words, the nonentity of the gods is proved by relegating them into the realm of psychology. The gods, which claim the leadership, have no existence but are "made"; and because of this their so-called claim to leadership and sovereignty over the world is nothing other than the claim of those who "make" them. There are some who ask why Deutero-Isaiah again and again speaks of the gods as images. Did he not know that the religions saw in these images only cases filled with divine life-forces? He needed to speak so, because only so could he express in his concrete language that these gods are not beings but figurations of the human soul;

and only so could he set up over against them a god, who is in no sense at all figuration, but thoroughly Being, that is to say God.

From this we must again understand that, in the words of Deutero-Isaiah, God at every stage stands over against the idols of the nations as He Who knows the coming things and announces them from the beginning whereas they, the idols of the nations, know nothing, and therefore are incapable of announcing anything. YHVH appears here as the God Who inspires prophecy, the prophetic God. And Deutero-Isaiah is the first who can see Him in this capacity; because his conception of prophecy is different from that of all the prophets that preceded him. His prophecy has no longer the character of an alternative; his God no longer sets before men two possibilities, in deciding between which they may have a share; He has decided, and man is only the object of His decision. Although Deutero-Isaiah knows deeply the guilt of Israel, and characterizes it stringently, the question concerning the influence of man's repentance upon the divine activity almost fails to stand; it is the presupposition and the beginning of his message that Israel has already atoned for its iniquity (40:2). His task to prophesy salvation is blended with the fact that his prophecy is in Israel the first prophecy according to the accepted sense, that is to say, he has to foretell things fixed and unchangeable. The sealed announcement of salvation, which his teacher Isaiah had composed against the background of the idea of alternative, Deutero-Isaiah uncovers in a world lacking this background. It is true the prophet knows about the drama between God and man, between YHVH the Holy and His unholy Israel, resisting His hallowing action; but this drama is known to him as a thing of the past only, as a thing overcome by God's forgiveness. And it is clear also that Deutero-Isaiah does not know the mysterious reality of man's resistance that can participate in the determination of his fate. Certainly he knows the mystery of human autonomy in the sight of God, and he knows its importance; but this particular side of the mystery is closed for him: the real opposition of God and man which in its operation touches the utmost depths of history. What man devises against God only occurs, in the eyes of this prophet, upon the surface of world history, whereas the depths are God's alone. The terrible thing, which Isaiah recognizes in his vision, that God inexorably gives to the creature of His hands the power to stand up against Him, is done away for Deutero-Isaiah. The refractoriness against God spreads in history, because God "bears" it (46:4), but its activity is composed of movements, which are mere sham, and in fact YHVH did not raise up an opponent for Himself. God foretells the coming things with mathematical precision, because only He appoints them; He announces history, because He makes it. Yet there is no place in Deutero-Isaiah for apocalyptic subjection before a fate entirely independent of man and powerful over him, and no place for an apocalyptic "removing the veil." He sees, as the prophets that were before him, not a sphere on the yonder side of history only arrayed in its likenesses; he beholds the mighty life of the occurring hour. And with all the vigorous proclamations of the divine master, that He knew from the beginning of the world the becoming and coming of this hour —we see Him setting His omnipotence against the sham force, as if this was a true force, and as if he could not conquer it except in hard battle. In this late prophet's book too, and in his book with a new emphasis, it is shown that YHVH is a God living in history. He does not fix history from the sphere on the yonder side and strange to it, He does not allow history to be unrolled as a scroll, but He Himself enters into it, and conquers it in warfare. The "valiant God" of Isaiah (9:5; 10:21), which Jeremiah (Jer. 32:18) and Deuteronomy (Deut. 10:17) retained only as an attribute among attributes, becomes here a historic reality visible to the eye: as a valiant warrior YHVH goes forth, He stirs up the zealous war (we must recall again the primitive conception of the "zealous" God), raises the battle shout, and prevails over His enemies (Is. 42:13).

We are probably also entitled to find a connection between this undogmatic historical realism of Deutero-Isaiah's faith and the fact that he points with emphasis to the host of heaven; apparently attacking the Babylonian belief in the power of the star-gods' mastery over earthly life, the prophet points to the countless plurality of the powers, which YHVH, Lord of hosts, brings forth with fixed order, calling them all by name, and none of them missing (40: 26). Not as in an apocalyptic poem of uncertain date but to my mind not very far from the time of Deutero-Isaiah (chap. 24), the army of heaven is seen as opposing the absolute sovereignty of God, that only in the hour of His ascent to the royal throne (here as in Deutero-Isaiah, 52:7) He "shall visit" and subdue it, until the moon shall become flushed and the sun pale (24, 21, 23); such an existence of supramundane opposite powers is not to be endured here, even as a passing affair. The gods are creatures of the human mind, but the stars and planets are a living reality: the innumerably vast serving army of the One.

While we are entitled to take the criticism of the astral religion as a warning to Cyrus, that he should guard himself from the spirit of Babylon, in another place Deutero-Isaiah appears to deal boldly and powerfully with the religion of the king of Persia himself. We read in one of the Gathas, in the middle of a series of questions of Zarathustra to the most high God concerning the formation of the world, "Who created with adroit action light and darkness? Who created with adroit action sleeping and working?" The answer "Ahuramazda" is "already given in the manner of the formulation of the questions." In Deutero-Isaiah's book (45: 6f.) YHVH says in the same message directed straight at Cyrus "His anointed" (v. 1), where He promises to him "the treasures of darkness," that is to say the blessings of the time of salvation still hidden in darkness, He says, "I am YHVH, there is none else; former of light and creator of darkness, maker of peace and creator of evil, I YHVH make all these." We do not know when the Gathas were composed, but there is no reason to doubt that the teaching about the most high God, Who created light and darkness, was ancient and widespread in the days of Cyrus. May we therefore suppose that in contrast to the prophet's handling of the Babylonian astral gods (cf. also 46:1f.), he here identifies the one with the other, and proclaims that YHVH is this same creator God? Such an identification would be inconsistent with the severe decisiveness of Deutero-Isaiah's belief in the Unity; it is not possible for him to think of identifying the One with the chief of a world of gods, even if that world be in the eyes of the Achaemenidae still only "a princely household of tribal gods." But the truth of the matter is that the prophet declares of his God something completely different from the Gathas, even though probably the words used refer to their teaching. Mazda did not by himself create good and evil, "he brought forth the creators of these oppositions, but the opposition itself is not his work"; the twin spirits brought forth by him produce the opposition of good and evil by choosing each one of them the world opposite to that of the other. YHVH is absolutely different, as He reveals Himself to Cyrus in the words of the prophet. He creates by Himself not only the cosmic opposition pair light-darkness, but also that which constitutes the human sphere, peace-evil. That *shalom,* "peace," "welfare," and not *tov,* "good," is here contrasted with *ra,* "evil," is obviously in order to keep away the notions of ethical opposition. Evil in the sense of wickedness comes into the world only as a result of resistance to God; but evil in the sense of adversity and affliction —here the prophet gives a theological answer to the question of his generation about the origin of evil—is fashioned by God Himself for purposes of His leadership of the world, without gaining thereby the same standing as peace, since in the last resort this rules alone. It should also be noticed that the verb "to create," reserved for the divine activity, is used by the prophet here only in relation to the negative creations, darkness and evil, and it will be found that the expression is emphasized here still more in its content as a theological declaration.

Certainly it would not be right to say that the sentence is directed against the Persian belief in two powers, as was formerly thought. Certainly "verse 7, closely connected as it is with verse 6, is directed against the nations in general." Certainly the prophet sets out "not against a definite religion, but against the religions of the ancient world in general"; but this, as with everything of his, notwithstanding the universalist pathos of the expression, is determined by historical reality; the motive and the direction of the saying are the reality of the hour.

Deutero-Isaiah certainly knew the first chapter of Genesis. Here he found darkness as primal matter which, according to the text, might be regarded as uncreated. In his zeal for the exclusiveness of his God, the prophet could not content himself with regarding darkness as a negative idea, as the mere absence of light; in argument darkness as evil is a polar fixture, and about darkness with its apparently independent power to consume the light it was necessary to know that it is a created thing. But when YHVH says, by the mouth of the prophet, that He creates darkness as He creates evil, there is in this another meaning than simply that both were created in the beginning. In the eyes of Deutero-Isaiah God's creation is something of all ages and times, something happening again and again, something even historical. God created Israel (43:1,7,15), He creates new things in the historical hour for which the prophet speaks (48:6f.), He creates for the sake of His work of redemption a transformation of nature, which is also symbolic of the spiritual transformation (41:20), He creates salvation and righteousness (45:8). God creates in history. There is no theological boundary in the eyes of this prophet between creation and history.

Just as in the book of Genesis the story of the formation of the world is only the opening of the story of the formation of the people, and obviously the whole connection is aimed at making us follow the meaning of the origin of Israel back to the meaning of the world's origin, so and still more so all that Deutero-Isaiah has to say about the creation points to history; likewise as all that he has to say about history points to the hope of redemption. In some verses the realms even penetrate one another, and this is most clear when the prophet (51:9f.), in a figurative expression taken from what seems to be a common Semitic myth, calls upon YHVH's arm to "awake," for it is that which in days of old pierced the dragon, and that which dried up the "waters of the great deep" and "made the depths of the sea a way for the redeemed to pass over." The creation of the world and the deliverance of Israel at the Red Sea "coincide for the eye of the prophet into one act of God's universal will to save"; and the prophet uses, in order to express as vividly as possible the fusion of both ideas, the same word to describe the depths of the water, *tehom,* as is used both in the beginning of the creation story (Gen. 1:2), and again in the Song of the Sea (Ex. 15:5, 8), and the union of the two realms is decided by a third factor, the act of redemption immediately expected. The same thing is expressed in the composition of the book by the repetition of a definite phrase in another sphere; so for example (I only instance here one of many examples) the acknowledgement of the Creator passes over (Is. 40:12ff.) to an acknowledgement of His absolute superiority over the world of nations, which is as nothing and nought before Him, and afterwards in the promise of redemption (41:12) the words recur to declare that the enemies of Israel shall be then as nothing and nought. The Biblical mode of expression by repetition the prophet uses in a special way, the same words recurring in different realms, and these being connected by peculiar associations of speech and so explaining and completing each other.

So the analogy or even the essential unity of creation, control in history, and redemption imprints itself in the memory of the hearer or reader whose heart is open to receive. Certainly this is no mere artificial means of expression, but the unity of the spheres in the prophet's faith in God transposes itself into a unity of speech and expresses itself in it.

As Deutero-Isaiah links together creation and redemption, so in the matter of redemption he links the redemption of Israel with that of the nations. The prophet's universalism, however, is still more concrete than is generally assumed.

Amos had proclaimed YHVH to be the liberator of the nations, who in contrast to Israel do not know His name or His nature, and who in His stead beheld the wishes of their heart. Deutero-Isaiah proclaims Him as the future liberator of the subject nations, who do not know Him yet as Cyrus, called by Him to begin the work of liberation, does not know Him (45:4f., emphasized by repetition): decisive for the things to come is that the nations should know Him as Cyrus should know Him. The call, "Turn ye unto Me and be saved, all the ends of the earth" (v. 22), is by no means only of religious significance—everything announced and everything demanded is here to be understood both as national-historical, and also as religio-suprahistorical—but it is for the same nations, subjugated by Babylon and other ruthless powers, to turn to YHVH, Who wills to bring them into liberty in the great future historical hour. For He is the only Liberator, and there is none else (v. 21). He is "the just God," and justice in the formation of the order of nations (the word *tsedaqah* has assumed this meaning here) proceeds from Him. The close succession of sayings referring to different circles, and the use of similar ideas in different circles, resulted in important verses being improperly understood. If the prophet announces (49:12) that multitudes should come from far, from the north and from the west, there is no need to see these multitudes as Israel, in spite of a nearby verse where the language does refer to Israel (43:6): he means all those nations, imprisoned in "darkness" (42:7; 49:9), whom God will bring into liberty. They must be made to inherit the desolate heritages upon the restored earth (49:8), that God's "deliverance" shall be "unto the end of the earth" (v. 6). Israel's comfort, with which the book began, here rises to be the comfort of humanity. As in the aforementioned apocalyptic song (25:7f.) "all peoples" are called YHVH's "people," His people whose reproach shall be removed "from off the whole earth," and as in the psalm (Ps. 47), which is apparently from the same age, the psalm that glorifies the moment in which YHVH shall sit upon the throne to reign over the nations of the whole earth, the princes of the assembled peoples are called by the name of "the people of the God of Abraham," the father of many nations, so here all the afflicted of YHVH are raised up (Is. 49:13) to the status of "His people," for He has mercy on them. Only from here can we grasp the function of the "servant of YHVH," who is called to be a "light of nations," and a "covenant of the people," that is a covenant of the people made up out of the peoples (vv. 6 and 8; 42:6; for the word "people" cf. v. 5). He is to establish *mishpat* upon the earth (42:4), that is to say the new world order, in which that same *tsedaqah* of God materializes. Therefore "the shores await His instruction."

Isaiah prophesied (2:1ff.) the days to come, when all nations will flow to YHVH's mountain, and there receive His "instruction," that will make up matters between them and order the new life of the peoples; he saw in his imagination representatives of the Ethiopians coming up then to Mount Zion, and bringing presents to its God (18:7). Deutero-Isaiah prophesies that representatives of nations in subjection, whom Egypt made to toil, and whom Ethiopia did sell (so, I think, the difficult verse 45:14, must be understood), will come when they are freed, albeit of their own will in chains of iron, to show that they are passing over to YHVH's service, and pray in the direction of Mount Zion, (v. 15 also belongs to the prayer, and perhaps even vv. 16 and 17): "Truly Thou art a God that hides Himself, God of Israel, Savior." YHVH, according to their opinion, had hidden Himself on the other side of history, so to speak, but now He has shone forth as the liberator of Israel and all of them. So, too, Israel had thought their way to be hid from YHVH (40:27). Over against this stands YHVH's word (45:19), that not in secret did He declare to the heathen world His message which He handed down to Israel (cf. 48:16)— and now (45:20): "Gather yourselves together and come, draw near together, ye escaped of the nations."

What in Isaiah was only alluded to, is here fully expressed; Israel's redemption and the redemption of the nations are merely different stages in the one great act of redemption which God performs in the world of men. What will happen now to Israel presupposes what will happen to the nations. Israel will prepare for God the proper instrument for His work among mankind. From this may be understood what is meant by the "servant of YHVH."

The many attempts to explain the figure of the servant of YHVH are essentially of three classes.

Supporters of the first class regard the "servant" corporately: as the actual Israel, or as the "ideal Israel," or as the nucleus or remnant of the people faithful to YHVH; but this interpretation among other things does not agree with the ponderous passage, where at the beginning (49:5) the original function of the servant is depicted as being to "bring back" Israel to YHVH, and afterwards in a certainly important expansion of this function the restoration of the tribes of Israel is portrayed as a matter "too light" for him. It is certainly right that in the Bible we may see "the corporate personality as a pattern and as an educator," but this does not prove "that this ideal entity can exercise a function upon the real one." The Israel conception living in the people can act educationally, but a real function such as this "to assign desolate heritages" (v. 8) cannot be entrusted to it by God, just as it cannot take upon itself the real suffering of the people. What the prophet says (53:8–12) about the servant's death and future cannot be connected with a corporate part of the community.

Supporters of the second class see in the servant of YHVH a historic figure. This is either the figure of a well-known person: here a whole line of historical personages has been mentioned, beginning with Moses and proceeding to Deutero-Isaiah himself, and even after his time to one of the martyrs in the Maccabean age (presuming a date of the songs as late as this); or it is a contemporary of the prophet, otherwise unknown to us. This view again is upset principally by the fact that not only is the death of this person related (53:9), but also a future promised to him after his death (v. 10ff.). The language, just here most precise and sober, precludes any thought of a resurrection of the dead.

The third, the Messianic, is also an individualistic interpretation. We find it, as well as the second interpretation, already in the Acts of the Apostles (Acts 8:30ff.). Although in the essential point this interpretation approximates closely in my view to the prophet's true intention, it is opposed by an unsurmountable difficulty, namely that the servant's testimony about himself, his toil, and his struggles hitherto (Is. 49:1ff.) cannot well be understood as of the future, that is to say as an anticipation of a future utterance of a man not yet existing, or at any rate not yet visible. And so they attempt to attribute the last song to another and later author, and to interpret this song only as Messianic, and to explain the remaining three songs as relating to a historical personage, for example the prophet himself. But this view, that the man of whom it is said (53:7) that he was led as a sheep to the slaughter and opened not his mouth, is different from the man who says of himself (50:6), "My back have I given to the smiters," is contrary to a straightforward and plain understanding of the text.

Generally speaking the interpretations are forced either into making omissions or alterations, for which there is no reason as far as the songs themselves are concerned, or into assigning them to different authors. But no statistical analysis of words has been able to uproot the impression of a stylistic unity prevailing in the songs themselves and linking them with the rest of the book. The one thing to which the investigation points again and again, is that the songs may be from another period in the life of the prophet than the rest of the book, and apparently from a later period.

For a more exact understanding of the personality of the servant of YHVH the following things should be taken into consideration:

1. In the book of Deutero-Isaiah the changing proclamations come to three recipients, Israel, Cyrus, and the servant. Between these recipients different orders of relationship prevail; expressions recur here and there in due proportion, and their recurrence cannot be regarded as accidental. This connection in the choice of words is greatest between Israel and the servant: both are "chosen" by God (cf. on the one hand 41:8f.; 44:1f.; 48:10; and on the other hand 42:1; 49:7), both are fashioned by Him "from the womb" (44:2; 49:5), both are "preserved" (49:6; 42:6; 49:8), both are "upheld" (41:10; 42:1), both are "honored" (43:4; 49:5) and in both YHVH "glorifies Himself" (44:23; 49:3), both are to act according to the divine "instruction" (42:21; 42:4), on both God's Spirit is bestowed or poured (44:3; 42:1). But we also find linguistic connections between Israel and Cyrus: both "are called by name" by YHVH (43:1; 45:1, 4), and both are ignorant of what God is preparing for them, or who it is that is preparing (48:8; 45:4f.). Furthermore there are some expressions that connect the three of them; the most characteristic of them is this, that it is YHVH's "desire," His purpose, which it is Israel's task to execute (42:21), which Cyrus is considered to accomplish (44:28; 46:10; cf. also 48:14), and finally which will prosper in the hand of "the servant" (53:10). Over against this there is no special connection between Cyrus and the servant, apart from the fact (if we take together here the fragment, 61:1, which has become fused with later parts) that both are "anointed," as Elijah was bidden (1 Kings 19:15) to anoint an alien king and also his own successor; only the king of Israel is missing, characteristically, among those anointed in Deutero-Isaiah's words. This fact, that there is no connection between Cyrus and the servant, apart from the personal divine charge symbolized in the act of anointing, is significant; these two, acting to a certain extent in the same age, have nothing common to both of them alone; apart from the general concept of divine charge (this is common to both of them, as also to Israel and others) they differ quite essentially in their character, their destiny, and their acts. To Israel and Cyrus there is nothing common, except that both of them are called by God, though neither of them know it. It is different with Israel and the servant; here the servant succeeds and replaces Israel, so that being and activity belonging to Israel pass over onto him. To Cyrus the servant is related as the charge of the one is related to the charge of the other; to Israel he is related as the charge conceived in accomplishment is related to the unaccomplished one.

2. Many times in the book of Deutero-Isaiah the "coming" things or the "new" things are set over against the "former" things. These latter are prophecies of former times, prophecies which now have been, or are being, fulfilled, whereas the former are prophecies now uttered, or hinted at, which will be fulfilled with the same certitude as are now the others. Often the nations or their idols, the products of the nations' desires, are asked whether they have made known or have known aforetime anything of the things now being fulfilled, whereas Israel is witness of the prophecy spoken aforetime; or the nations and their idols are asked whether they understand the course of things, and whether they can interpret the announcement now proceeding forth into the world. In connection with the confrontation of the two (that sometimes is only hinted at) always one of them, the former or the new things, or both of them, are elucidated by means of present or future events. So the call of Cyrus, recorded in 41:25, which has already taken place, belongs to the confrontation in vv. 22f., 26; 42:9, in connection with the "new things" looks back to the proclamation of the servant's mission, vv. 1–8; the "former things" of 43:9, are elucidated by the once announced and now approaching return of the exiles, vv. 5f., whereas the "new things" of 43:19, are only revealed in the prophecy of the outpouring of the Spirit, 44:3, which is again summarized in v. 7 as the "coming things"; the "former things" of 46:9 refer again to the "hawk" from the east, v. 11; and finally the contrast of the "new things" and the "former things" of 48:3–6, is expanded in the following: the former things are God's imminent work in Babylon by Cyrus (v. 14f.), whereas the new things express themselves in a saying that clearly interrupts the sense (v. 16), but that at all events cannot be said to be a later interpolation, but only an addition of the author himself, and obviously is to be understood as a saying of the servant of YHVH: "And now my Lord YHVH has sent me and His Spirit."

If we now examine all the "former things" together, we see that they are definitely related to the verses in Isaiah's song of the child (9:3f.) about the redemption from the oppressor's rod, that is to say, to the prophecy of the people's liberation, which the *limmud* Deutero-Isaiah understands as the liberation from the Babylonian exile. Over against this Isaiah's prophecy concerning the future ruler is interpreted of Cyrus, the "anointed one" (the "man of my counsel," 46:11, compare the "counsellor of the valiant God" of 9:5, EV 6). David's throne (9:6, EV 7) man shall no more sit upon; the "faithful graces (promised) to David" (53:3) pass over to Israel ("to you"); the king of Israel, in accordance with the primal convenant, is now none other than YHVH Himself (52:7; cf. 41:21; 43:15; 44:6). The "shoot" that comes out of "Jesse's stump" (11:1) is no offspring of David; this is no natural seed, but a "holy seed" (6:13). This is the man, on whom YHVH's Spirit rests (11:2), as it is "put upon him" (42:1; cf. 61:1) and sent together with him (48:16), the man who "vindicates with equity the weak of the earth" (11:4), just as he is sent "to bring good tidings to the weak" (61:1), the man who "judges" (11:3f.), and "sets justice in the earth" (42:3f.), the man who does not smite except with the rod of his mouth, and does not slay the wicked except with the breath of his lips (11:4), who does not cry, nor make his voice to be heard in the street, who does not break the crushed reed, nor quench the smoking flax (42:2f.), that is to say the servant.

3. It has been, I think, rightly observed, that in the second half of the book of Deutero-Isaiah the person of Cyrus withdraws, as the prophet becomes disappointed with the lord of the nations. Perhaps Deutero-Isaiah, who apparently handed on his message to Cyrus either from his proximity to the court or by another way, had received "a clear and definite rejection of his suggestions," even before the overthrow of Babylon. But the text itself leads us farther than this explanation. Not only did Cyrus not call upon YHVH's name at all (41:25), but after the conquest he venerated the former gods of Babylon. By this act he explicitly stated that he, Cyrus, "did not know" YHVH, nor wished to know Him, at all events as the One. In the first servant song, which apparently was the first composed as well as the first in order, the prophet supplies the answer to this. Here his God says (42:8): "I am YHVH, that is my name (this means, my name testifies to me as the One Who, in contrast to all the idols, is really there), and my glory (*kabhod*) I will not give to another, nor my praise to graven images" (cf. 48:11). Bel and Nebo, idols of Babylon (46:1), that are carried on the shoulder (v. 7), must not boast themselves, as Cyrus glorifies them, that they are those who called and empowered him to go forth in punitive battle against Babylon. The whole of this world historical spectacle, which YHVH devised for the hour of turning, and which Cyrus imperfectly executed, was only a prelude. "Behold the former things are come to pass, and new things do I declare, before they spring forth I tell you" (42:9). The hour of the king of Persia, who has liberated Israel from the yoke of Babylon, passes away and the hour of the "servant" begins, he who attends to YHVH's "desire" to redeem the world of the nations from the yoke of its guilt.

4. From this point it becomes clear not only that in the second half of the book the figure of the servant ousts that of Cyrus, but also that the first song is placed so much earlier than the rest; the song (42:1ff.) follows immediately the first declaration of the deeds of Cyrus (41:25). In the days when the book was being composed out of the speeches and pamphlets, there must certainly have been everywhere a feeling of disappointment, and therefore it was necessary to connect with the recognition of the unsatisfactory character of the work of Cyrus the announcement of the future satisfactory work of the servant. This, and one further point. In 41:8ff., God addresses Israel as His servant, whom He has chosen and held. Here in the first part of the book Israel receives only comfort and encouragement, but soon, perhaps on account of certain negative experiences of the people, the dispute with Israel begins (42:18ff.). In order to guard the hearer and reader against errors liable to arise from restricted horizon, and to enlarge his vision in the revealed ways of God, it was necessary to set up over against the inadequate servant, Israel, the anonymous servant, who has been "chosen" and "held" as Israel but unlike Israel was one in whom YHVH also delighted, and upon whom He put His Spirit (42:1). This contrast recurs again and again during the course of the book. The stubborn is contrasted with the submissive, the timid with the bold, the blind with the enlightening, and for all this God calls both of them without distinction "my servant" (for Cyrus the prophet avoids this epithet, although Nebuchadrezzar is so called by Jeremiah, 25:9), and promises to both of them His protection, His assistance, and the future gift of His bliss. This contrast is a strong paradox of the book, and again it is not surprising that often the attempt has been made to identify them. There are also those who try to overcome the difficulty by means of positing a later fusion of different elements, and further that the verses among them which speak of the personality of the servant have been adapted to refer to Israel. Especially have they stressed the verse (49:3) in which the servant tells that YHVH said to him: "My servant art thou, Israel in whom I glorify myself." These words are not to be regarded as proof of the truth of the corporate interpretation, nor is the word "Israel"

to be omitted as a later insertion. If the saying really was directed to Israel, there was no need to say: "Thou art Israel." If, however, what is meant by the servant is a person, but a person standing in a quite peculiarly close relationship to Israel, it is fairly evident that God speaks to him: "*Thou* art the Israel in whom I glorify myself." The paradox of the two "servants" cannot be solved or dispelled. It is intended to be a paradox. In it we recognize the supposition necessary in order that Isaiah's Messianic prophecy should be transformed into the Messianic mystery of Deutero-Isaiah.

. . .

After the speech of the rulers, the prophet announces at first in his own name, and afterwards in YHVH's name, about the servant's future, about the future that fits God's "desire," His plan (v. 10), which will prosper in the servant's hand. This closing saying links on to the opening one: the servant must now accomplish his active work after the passive, he must exalt himself highly, enjoy the new blessings among the "many" (v. 12), whose iniquities he bare, and see a succession ("seed") which shall prolong his work (so we are certainly entitled to complete what is said). But how can all this come to pass, since we have been told of his death and burial (v. 9)? One is inclined to think that here a resurrection of the dead is spoken of; but in such a case a direct exposition would necessarily have been given of this supernatural conception, for individual resurrection was utterly unfamiliar to the thought of the Israelite hearer or reader of the prophet. We can only understand the real meaning, if we conjure up in our minds what we have already discovered in the second song and which we can here recognize even more clearly—that is, that the substance of the servant is more than a single human person without, however, having a corporate character. Here we infer that this person takes shape in many likenesses and life-ways, the bearers of which are identical in their innermost essence, but no supernatural event, no resurrection of the dead leads from one of these figures to the next. It seems to me that we are permitted to take the remarkable phrase "in his deaths" (v. 9) quite literally: it is not a single death that comes upon the servant on his way, he goes from death to death, and to new life again.

There are three stages on this way. The first is the prophetic stage. In the futile labor of the Israelite prophet in Israel, he sees himself as an arrow which, it is decreed, is to remain in its quiver; but he is promised that a great work will be preserved for him in the future, reaching far beyond the confines of Israel, and compared with which all that he now does and endures is mere preparation. The prophet does not know when and how this will take place; but because God offers him to bear an immense affliction, he who is accustomed and willing to suffer, loads it upon himself not asking how and why, for he knows that he has to bear it for God's sake. The second stage is the *acting* of the affliction. Since the servant not only endures the affliction loaded upon him without kicking against it but also, as it were, accomplishes it, it becomes as though changed into an *act*. Job recognized that affliction is a mystery of God, and the Psalmist recognized that God loves those who suffer willingly; YHVH's servant recognizes the mystery of affliction in this that it is affliction for God's sake and for the sake of His "desire." And the third stage is the "success" of the desire: the work born out of affliction, the liberation of the subject peoples, laid upon the servant, the divine order of the expiated world of the nations, which the purified servant as its "light" has to bring in, the covenant of the people of the human beings with God, the human center of which is the servant. Only now the sharp arrow is expelled from the darkness of the quiver and hurled forth. The Spirit of his Lord is on the "anointed" servant and reveals him. It is still laid upon him, who was a prophet from the foundation on, to proclaim a message (61:1); but this message ends in the inauguration of God's new order of justice for the world (42:3).

These three stages are not to be comprehended in the life span of a single man. They are the way of the one servant, passing through all the different likenesses and life cycles. We do not know how many of them the prophet himself saw in his vision; it is to be supposed that it was not given him to know very much about what he saw. Neither can we presume what historical figures he included in the servant's way; it was laid upon the anonymous prophet to announce a mystery, not to interpret it. But one thing is clear to us, that he saw himself at one point on the way. It can never be proved that these two, the servant and his announcer, are one; but many sayings in the two songs written in the first person tell us that "Deutero-Isaiah" felt himself as one of the figurations of the servant, and that he felt himself as the one among them before whom was uncovered the mystery of the servant's being concealed and of his future being revealed. We may assume that, after he had despaired of Cyrus, he recognized his own being as one of the temporal elements in the way of the person for whom the very work of the redemption of world history was reserved. He was able to recognize it because he was in truth a prophet, a *nabi,* and in so far as he was such.

The Israelite *nabi* was in former days a leader, a prophetic leader; it was as a *nabi* that the first liberator lived in the memory of the people. According to the book of Deuteronomy (Deut. 18:15, 18), Moses received God's word and transmitted it to the people, that in time of necessity there would be raised up for them again and again a *nabi* "like him," that is, there would again and again appear a prophetic leader. Certainly in the time of Judges we do not generally find the *nabi* as leader, but in order to lead it was necessary to receive the divine Spirit, and therefore it was laid upon the "judge" to pass through the *nabi* stage. After the kingdom had been firmly established, the *nabi* was pushed from his place if he was not willing to be paid court minister of spiritual affairs, and instead he became a powerless opposition to the powerful; instead of leading, he had to expound what true leadership is and what it is not. And from the nature of things this meant for the *nabi* an increasingly dangerous venture. God's truth, which he had to prophesy, is opposed to all that the court and princes wish to hear, and in the sphere of foreign affairs also opposed to what the people wish to hear. The *nabi* has more and more to be prepared not only for scornful rejection of his message, but also for ill treatment, imprisonment, and even death. The Messianic promise of a king, who will fulfill his task, hints at things beyond this state. Nothing is said about prophets in the Messianic days, possibly because it seemed that in future there would be no need of them. But at the time of the catastrophe, the disappointment with kings grew into disappointment with the kingdom in Israel. In Ezekiel's plan for a temple theocracy, God's vice-gerent, the prince, becomes a figure without other meaning than external representation. But the *nabi* begins anew to acquire in prophetic thought the vocation to lead, the same vocation of which tradition told in former days. Certainly the *nebiim* now too frequently fail to find an attentive ear, now too they are reviled and tormented, but now they see the state of martyrdom as a transition to a new leadership; not the king but the *nabi* is appointed to be deputy of God's kingdom, and this kingdom now signifies in reality all the human world. Now there is no more need, as there was in his former prophetic career, to make his voice heard in his cry over the transgressors. Neither is there any need to break the bruised reeds from among the nations nor to quench the smoking flax, as the men of Cyrus' sort were used to do; the order which he "brings forth" sets up everything in its true place. He himself, un-quenched and unbruised, establishes the order in the earth, and the most distant shores wait for his instruction. But the realization of this new vocation is laid upon the prophet himself to achieve—by making an act of the enduring of his sufferings. The suffering *nabi* is the antecedent type of the acting Messiah.

Perhaps we may see here the explanation of the enigmatical epithet of the servant, *meshullam* (Is. 42: 19). *Meshullam,* that is to say "the perfected one," he is called after the maturity of his vocation, inasmuch as he is sent by God as His "messenger" to the world of nations. The fact that he is called in this place "blind" and "deaf" is apparently to be explained by the fact that at the moment God speaks he, the *nabi,* has not yet proved able to grasp fully his own destiny and the way to its accomplishment in spite of his many experiences and of the fact that his ears are open to receive God's word. His readiness to serve in his appointment is in advance of his "knowledge" (53:11; a colon must be put after this word: the servant recognizes and knows the intention of God concerning him that is expressed in the following verses). Deutero-Isaiah sees himself as the figure the servant assumes in the hour of knowledge, the hour when the great connection of things is made known.

Admittedly the aforementioned verse about *meshullam* belongs to the verses which speak of the servant of Israel and of the personal servant in the same expressions, and the dividing line between them appears somewhat blurred. So there are passages before this (42:16, 18) speaking of the people as blind and deaf, as this passage speaks of the blind and deaf servant. But just as we must nevertheless distinguish between them, so on the other hand we cannot overcome the difficulty by the supposition of later additions or alterations. The prophet wishes us never to forget the special tie between the personal servant and the servant Israel. They are closely fastened one to the other. The personal servant is that Israel in whom YHVH glorifies Himself as in His faithful one (49:3), but just because he is that, YHVH can glorify Himself in Israel generally as in that which is redeemed by Him (44:23). YHVH's love for faithless Israel, a hurt and suffering love, renews itself from the prophet's love of God, a love hurt and suffering for God's sake. There is a nucleus of Israel, preserved through the generations, that does not betray the election, that belongs to God and remains His. Through this nucleus the living connection between God and the people is upheld, in spite of the very great guilt: not alone by interposing on behalf of Israel, but far more by being the true Israel. God's purpose for Israel has put on skin and flesh in these powerless combatants. They are the small beginning of the kingdom of God before Israel becomes a beginning of it; they are the beginning before the beginning. The anointing of the kings was unfulfilled, and Deutero-Isaiah no longer awaits a king in whom this anointing should be fulfilled; the anointing of the *nebiim* has been fulfilled, and therefore it is from their midst that the figure of the perfected one will arise. All arise. All that the *nabi* in this his ultimate form shall establish in the world of the nations, Israel shall establish by him. For through him, through his word and life, Israel turns to God, and becomes God's people. No more will these two, Israel and the prophet, be opposed one to the other, and there will not even be any more distinction between them. Now not only, as up to this time, the truth of Israel, but the reality of Israel in its purity, will be embodied in the *nabi,* the reality of *Jeshurun* (44:2), the upright people, in the reality of *Meshullam,* the perfected one. At the same hour when this man is allowed to go up, after persevering again and again in the hiddenness and migrating through afflictions and deaths unto true life; when he is allowed to go up and be a light for the nations, at that hour the servant Israel and the personal servant will have become one.

Time and again, when God addresses Israel as his servant, He speaks to one chosen by Him. The servant here denotes a person—individual or corporate—whom God chose to fulfil a special function, as anointing denotes the empowering to fulfil permanently a special function. We do not find in any other prophet in the same way as in Deutero-Isaiah the belief in the election as the basis of all his declarations. Israel was chosen from of old, and it is as a "chosen one" that the personal servant too appears in the first saying addressed to him (42:1). The two elections mean designation to service and action. But the work to which Israel had been elected aforetime was a work complete in itself: the establishment of Israel as God's people, that is to say as a people building its whole common life under God's order and rule; it was laid upon Israel to work not on others but on itself, this work, however, was to shine in the midst of the world of nations, to win souls for God and thus to become the beginning of His kingdom, "the first of His harvest" (this conception of Jeremiah's is taken for granted by Deutero-Isaiah). This work, which Israel was called upon to do for itself and thereby for mankind, it did not do. For this reason the *nabi* was now called, who in former generations had worked continually not for himself but for Israel, to fulfil a work that had to be done directly for the world of nations, first the "bearing" of affliction, afterwards the setting up of the order of the kingdom. But the people of Israel, redeemed from the sovereignty of strangers, and cleansed from iniquity, this people has now been set up by YHVH as His kingdom (52: 7); it will establish God's sovereignty upon itself and serve as the beginning of His kingdom in the world. The suffering and acting servant acts now no more, as in his earlier form as *nabi,* from opposition to Israel, and he suffers no more because of this opposition: he suffers and acts in the name of Israel initiating the kingdom, yes, he suffers and acts as Israel. And rightly the kings speak of him and of Israel in one breath, in one utterance.

He is Israel as servant. When the nations look at him, they look at the truth of Israel, the truth chosen from the very beginning.

The *nabi* as an early form of the Messiah we find as late as a Christian apocryphal fragment, in which the Spirit says to the Christ that It has been waiting for Him "in all the prophets" (*in omnibus prophetis*) that He should come and It should rest in Him (*requiescerem in te;* cf. Is. 11:2; and 42:1). But the figure of the suffering Messiah that appears from generation to generation, and goes from martyrdom and death to martyrdom and death, has recognizable traces up to the latest popular tradition of Judaism: still in Hasidism the tale is told of this or that *tsaddiq,* dying a violent death, that he was Messiah, son of Joseph.

But the unity between the personal servant and the servant Israel passes over to their unity in suffering. As far as the great suffering of Israel's dispersion was not compulsory suffering only, but suffering in truth willingly borne, not passive but active, it is interpreted in the image of the servant. Whosoever accomplishes in Israel the active suffering of Israel, he is the servant, and he is Israel, in whom YHVH "glorifies Himself." The mystery of history is the mystery of a representation which at bottom is identity. The arrow, which is still concealed in the quiver, is people and man as one.

The anonymous prophet's hope that his Messianic message might be realized in his age, was not fulfilled. In the building of the Jewish state in the days of the Second Temple, in the life of the community that returned from Babylon, there was little evidence of it, in spite of all the honest attempts made by Israel to take upon itself YHVH's commandments. But the great scattering, which followed the splitting up of the state and became the essential form of the people, is endowed with the mystery of suffering as with the promise of the God of sufferers.

The God, Who in the days of old caused the first father to "stray" from his father's house and went before him in his wanderings of set purpose as a faithful shepherd, is acknowledged by suffering generations in their way, the way of exile, to be their Shepherd (40:11). They do this in the strength of the prophetic faith: "YHVH goes before them" (52:12). He Whom the *nabi* Abraham had recognized in days of old as the God of the way, remained the leader in the way in the anonymous prophet's message (48:17), which the suffering generations have carried with them on their wanderings.

the greek city-state
and its ideal of justice

twenty-one

WERNER JAEGER

Athens was the last of the great Greek cities to appear in history, and her constitutional ideals presuppose a long anterior development. Throughout Solon's life and work [which expressed the new spirit in Athens at the beginning of the sixth century] it is clear that he was deeply influenced by Ionian civilization. Accordingly, we cannot doubt that these new political ideals also originated in Ionia, the intellectual and critical centre of Greece. Unfortunately, the information which we possess about the political history of the Ionian colonies is very poor: so that we must fall back on inferences *a posteriori,* based on the facts which we know to have existed at a later period, and on parallel situations in other countries.

With the exception of Callinus, . . . it would seem that Ionia produced no truly political poetry comparable to that of Tyrtaeus and Solon. We cannot put this fact down to pure chance: it was clearly deep-rooted in

Reprinted from *Paideia: The Ideals of Greek Culture,* vol. I (Oxford: Blackwell, 1947), pp. 99–114. Copyright © 1939 by the Oxford University Press; second edition by Blackwell, 1947. Reprinted by permission of Basil Blackwell and Mott, Ltd.

the Ionian character. Like all the Greeks of Asia Minor, the Ionians lacked constructive political energy, and never succeeded in forming a permanent and historically active state. They did, indeed, pass through a heroic age at the period of their immigration into the country—the period which is reflected in the Homeric poems: and it would be wrong to believe that they were always the weak sensual people which we know in the time just before the Persian wars. They fought many fierce wars with one another and with foreign foes. Their poets, Callinus, Archilochus, Alcaeus, and Mimnermus, were true warrior-bards. But they never held the polis to be the supreme absolute, as Spartans and Athenians did. Their work in the development of the Greek spirit was to set the individual free—and it was so even in political life. In general, then, the Ionian colonies were incapable of co-ordinating the energies of their free individual citizens, and of using them to strengthen their own power; but it was Ionia which first released the political forces which, in the firmer framework of the mainland Greek cities, helped to create a vitally new ideal of the state.

The life of the Ionian polis is first known to us from the Homeric epics. The Trojan war itself did not allow

Homer to depict a Greek state, for he considered the Trojans to be barbarians. But he involuntarily gave Troy, in its struggle to defend itself, some of the traits of an Ionian city-state; and Hector, the guardian of his country, was the pattern of heroism for Callinus and Tyrtaeus. In this stage of Ionian culture, especially as reflected in Callinus, we can trace many resemblances to the Spartan ideal. But at an early period the Ionian city-state began to develop in another direction, and that movement is also shown in the epic. In the only passage where the *Iliad* depicts a city at peace—the late description of the shield of Achilles—we find that, in the marketplace at the centre of the city, a lawsuit is in process: "the elders" sit on polished stones in a holy circle and give judgment. That means that the heads of noble families now held an important part in the administration of justice, which had originally been the province of the king. The famous condemnation of divided government argues that kings still existed, but their position was clearly precarious. The shield of Achilles also pictured a royal demesne, with a king admiring his harvest; but he was probably only a landowning nobleman, for the epic often gives the title *basileus*, "king" or "prince," to members of the nobility. As in Greece proper, agrarian civilization (which is the basis of a landed aristocracy) at first obtained throughout Ionia. Another example of limited monarchy is Alcinous, king of the Phaeacians. Among the elders of his council, he is only the chairman, although he is the legitimate and hereditary king. Therefore, the transition from monarchy to aristocracy is not far off: the king is soon to become only a high-priest or an eponymous official, with no peculiar privileges attaching to his rank. This transition is mentioned in several cities, but we can see it most clearly in Athens. There the royal family of the Codridae is gradually pushed into the background by the advancing power of the aristocracy, which is still dominant in the age of Solon. But our knowledge is insufficient to determine how long after the migrations this characteristic development took place in Ionia.

The Ionian coastal strip, on which the constant streams of immigrants landed, was not wide; and the hinterland, occupied by disorganized but warlike native peoples (like the Lydians, Phrygians, and Carians), was impossible to penetrate. Hence, the coastal cities were more and more driven to engage in seafaring, especially as the art of navigation was developed. To this new enterprise many rich nobles turned their energy, and they became its leaders. The Greek colonists had always been much less attached to the soil, after they had torn themselves loose from their motherland. The *Odyssey* shows the vast increase in geographical knowledge and the new type of personality created by the sailors of Ionia. Odysseus himself is not so much a knightly warrior as the embodiment of the adventurous spirit, the explorer's energy, and the clever practical wisdom of the Ionian: he has seen men and cities, and he is never at a loss in any difficulty or danger. The *Odyssey* looks eastward as far as Phoenicia and Colchis, southward to Egypt, westward to Sicily and the westerly Ethiopians, and northward over the Black Sea to the land of the Cimmerians. There is nothing strange or unusual in the tale of the sailor hero's meeting with crowds of Phoenician seafarers and merchants: the Phoenicians traded all over the Mediterranean, and were the most dangerous competitors of the Greeks. Another sailor epic was the tale of the voyage of the Argonauts, with its wonderful stories of the distant countries and nations whom they visited. Ionian trade grew with the growing industrialization of the cities of Asia Minor, a process which took them still further away from their early agricultural civilization. And it made a great and decisive advance when gold coinage was introduced from neighbouring Lydia, and when monetary exchange replaced barter. By our standards, the coastal towns of Ionia were small; and the surest sign that they were over-populated is the fact that, like the cities of Greece proper, they sent out numerous colonies in the eighth, the seventh and the sixth centuries to the coasts of the Mediterranean, the Sea of Marmora, and the Black Sea. Although other historical evidence is lacking, the astounding number of colonies planted by one city like Miletus bears witness to the enterprise, the expansive energy, and the pulsating life which filled the Greek cities of Asia Minor during those centuries.

Versatility, individual initiative, and wide vision are the chief characteristics of the new men created by these new conditions. As the physical horizon expanded, their spiritual horizon had grown too, and their sense of their own powers made them capable of wider and higher thoughts and ideals. The spirit of independent criticism which we see in Ionia both in the personal poetry of Archilochus and in the theories of the Milesian philosophers must have affected public life also. We have no records of the civil conflicts which must have taken place in Ionia as they did elsewhere in the Greek world. But the long succession of Ionian epigrams and poems which extol Justice as the basis of human society runs from the later portions of the Homeric epics through Archilochus and Anaximan-

der down to Heraclitus. As we might imagine, such praise of justice by poets and philosophers did not precede the struggle to realize the ideal, but was plainly a natural repercussion of the political struggles which lasted from the eighth century to the beginning of the fifth. The poets of Greece proper, from Hesiod downwards, spoke of Justice in the same tone, and none more clearly than Solon of Athens.

Until these struggles began, the right of the nobles to administer justice—in accordance with traditional usage, not by any written code of laws—had been unchallenged. But as the economic position of the common people improved, the conflict between the freeman of low birth and the nobleman was naturally intensified. Judicial power could easily be misused for political ends. The people demanded written laws. Hesiod's complaints against the corrupt princes who turn justice askew were the necessary preliminary to this general demand. They made the word Justice, *diké,* the war-cry of the class-conflict. The process of the codification of law in the various Greek cities went on for centuries, and we know little of its history. But here we are concerned chiefly with the principle which inspired it. Laws which are written down mean the same law for all, high and low alike. After the laws are written, the judges may still be noblemen and not commoners; but they are now bound to administer justice in accordance with the established standards of diké.

Homer shows us the earlier situation. He usually describes justice by another word—*themis*. Zeus gave to the Homeric kings "the sceptre and themis." Themis is the epitome of the judicial supremacy of the early kings and nobles. Etymologically, the word means "institution." The feudal judge gives his decisions in accordance with the institutions set up by Zeus, and derives their rules from his knowledge of customary law and from his own intuition. The etymology of diké is not clear. The word belongs to Greek legal terminology, and is no less old than themis. The parties to a dispute were said to "give and take diké," so that the word contained the ideas of determining and of paying the penalty. The guilty man "gives diké," which originally meant "makes compensation" for his act; the injured party, whose rights are re-established by the judgment, "takes diké," and the judge "allots diké." Hence, the fundamental meaning of diké is much the same as "due share." Besides that, it also signifies the lawsuit, the judgment, and the penalty; but these meanings are derivative, not primary. The higher significance which the word acquires in the post-Homeric city-state is developed not from these more or less technical meanings, but from the normative element which must be assumed to be behind the ancient and familiar formulæ. Diké means the due share which each man can rightly claim; and then, the principle which guarantees that claim, the principle on which one can rely when one is injured by *hybris*—which originally signifies illegal action. The meaning of themis is confined rather to the *authority* of justice, to its established position and validity, while diké means the legal enforceability of justice. It is obvious how, during the struggles of a class which had always been compelled to receive justice as themis—that is, as an inevitable authority imposed on it from above— the word diké became the battle-cry. Throughout these centuries we hear the call for diké, growing constantly more widespread, more passionate, and more imperative.

The word diké contained another meaning, which was to make it still more useful in these struggles—the meaning of equality. This sense must have been innate in the word: we can best understand it by thinking of the old popular ideal of justice—compensation with an eye for an eye, and a tooth for a tooth. Obviously, that sense of equality must have been derived from the use of diké in legal proceedings; the derivation is confirmed by the history of law in other nations. Throughout all Greek thought, the word retained this original significance. Even the political philosophers of later centuries depend on it, and seek only to redefine the concept of equality, which had been so mechanized by the rise of democracy as to become repugnant to Plato and Aristotle, with their aristocratic belief in the natural inequality of mankind.

Early Greece strove, above everything else, for equal justice. Every trifling dispute above *meum* and *tuum* called for a standard by which the claims of the parties could be measured. This is the same problem in the sphere of law as that which had, in the same age, been solved in the economic sphere by the introduction of fixed standards of weight and measure for the exchange of goods. What was needed was a correct norm to measure legal rights, and that norm was found in the concept of equality which was implicit in the idea of diké.

Of course, that norm could be applied in far more ways than the Greeks thought; but perhaps that made it even more suitable for use as a political platform. It could, for instance, be taken to mean that an unprivileged class (that is, the commons) should be equal to the privileged class in the eyes of the judge, or before the law where law existed. Again, it could mean that each citizen ought to have an active part in the administration of justice; or that the votes of all citizens in affairs of state should be constitutionally equal; or, finally, that an ordinary citizen should have equal right to hold the principal public offices which were actually occupied by the aristocrats. This is, in fact, the beginning of a long process during which the concept of equality grew wider and more mechanical until it came to signify extreme democracy. Yet democracy is not a necessary consequence of the demand for equal justice or for a written law. Both equal justice and codified law have existed in monarchic and oligarchic states; while it is characteristic of extreme democracy that the state is ruled not by the law but by the mob. But hundreds of years were to pass until the democratic type of constitution developed and grew common in the Greek world.

Before that could happen, a long historical process was to be completed. Its first stage is still a kind of aristocracy—but a changed aristocracy. For now the ideal of diké is used as a standard in public life by which both high-born and low-born men are measured as "equals." The nobles were compelled to admit the new civic ideal created by the demand for justice, and based on diké as a norm. In the struggles of the approaching social conflict, and in the violence of revolution, they themselves were often compelled to appeal to diké for help. Even the Greek language bears traces of the formation of the new ideal. For centuries it had contained words to signify concrete offences—murder, theft, adultery; but it had had no general word for the quality through which one might avoid committing these offences and escape transgression. For that quality the new age coined the word "righteousness" or "justice," *dikaiosyné*— just as in its enthusiasm for the athletic virtues it had coined abstract

words (which have no parallel in English) to correspond to the concretes "wrestling," "boxing," and so forth. This new word was created as the sense of justice was more and more sharply intensified, and as the ideal of justice was embodied in a special type of human character and a peculiar areté. Originally, an areté was any kind of excellence. When the areté of a man was considered equivalent to courage, areté came to mean an ethical quality to which all other human excellences were subordinate and subservient. The new dikaiosyné was a more objective quality; but it became areté *par excellence* as soon as the Greeks believed that they had found, in written law, a reliable criterion for right and wrong. After *nomos*—that is, current legal usage— was codified, the general idea of righteousness acquired a palpable content. It consisted in obedience to the laws of the state, just as Christian "virtue" consisted in obedience to the commands of God.

So then the will to justice, which grew up in the communal life of the city-state, was a new educational force comparable to the ideal of warlike courage in the old aristocratic culture. In the elegies of Tyrtaeus, that old ideal had been taken over by the Spartan state and raised to an all-embracing ideal of citizenship. In the new state, based on law and justice, which was struggling through hard conflicts into life, the warrior-ideal of Sparta could not be accepted as the sole and universal embodiment of citizenship. Yet, as is shown by the summons of the Ephesian poet Callinus to his unwarlike fellow-citizens to resist the invading barbarians, even in the Ionian cities warlike courage was still needed at moments of crisis. Courage had in fact only changed its place within the general scheme of areté. From now on the law commands the citizen to show courage in face of the enemy, to the point of dying in defence of his country; and the law punishes failure to obey that command by heavy penalties: but it is only one of many commands. In order to be *just,* in the concrete sense which justice now has in Greek political thought (that is, in order to obey the law and to mould one's conduct by its pattern), the citizen must do his duty in war as he must do his duty in other matters. The old free ideal of the heroic areté of the Homeric champion now becomes a duty to the state, a duty to which all citizens alike are bound, as they are bound to observe the limits of *meum* and *tuum* in matters of property. One of the most famous poetic utterances of the sixth century is the line, often quoted by later philosophers, which says that all virtues are summed up in righteousness. The line is a close and exhaustive definition of the essence of the new constitutional city-state.

The new conception that righteousness is the areté of the perfect citizen, embracing and transcending all others, naturally supplanted previous ideals. But the earlier aretai were not superseded by it: they were raised to a new power. That is what Plato means in the *Laws,* when he says that in the ideal state Tyrtaeus' poem praising courage as the highest virtue must be rewritten so as to put righteousness in the place of courage. He does not exclude the Spartan warrior's virtue: he relegates it to its proper place, as subordinate to righteousness. Courage in a civil war, he says, must be estimated differently from courage exerted against a foreign enemy. To show that all areté is embraced by the ideal of the righteous man, Plato gives a very enlightening example. Usually he speaks of four cardinal virtues: courage, godliness, righteousness, and prudence. (It is here irrelevant that in the *Republic* and often elsewhere he mentions philosophical wisdom instead of godliness.) As early as Aeschylus, we find this canon of the four so-called Platonic virtues mentioned as the sum of a citizen's virtue. Plato took it over *en bloc* from the ethical system of the early Greek city-state. But he recognized that, although the canon mentioned four virtues, righteousness really embraced all areté. The same thing happened in the case of Aristotle. He defines many more species of aretai than Plato; but when he comes to righteousness, he says that the name signifies two conceptions: there is righteousness in the narrow sense, the juristic sense, and general righteousness which includes all political and moral virtue. It is easy to see that this is the idea which was born in the early city-state. Aristotle then quotes, with considerable emphasis, the verse mentioned above, to the effect that righteousness embraces all virtue. The precepts of law regulate the relations of every citizen to the gods of the polis, to its enemies, and to his fellow-citizens.

. . .

The process of assimilation which we have—in anticipation—described, the process by which the morality of the early polis and its ideal of character is taken over by fourth-century philosophy, has an exact analogy in the rise of the city-state itself. For the city-state culture also assimilated the morality of an earlier age. It took over not only Homer's heroic areté but the athletic virtues too—the whole ideal of aristocracy; the same assimilation took place in Sparta too at the age when she first appeared in history. The city-state encouraged its citizens to compete in the Olympic games and other such contests. It crowned with its highest honours the citizens who returned victorious. Victory in such a contest had once glorified only the family of the winner; but now, the whole citizen-community felt itself to be one family, victory served *ad maiorem patriae gloriam*. And the city encouraged its sons to share not only in athletic contests but in the musical and artistic heritage of the past. It created *isonomia* not only in legal matters but in the higher things of life, which had been created by aristocratic civilization and now became the common property of the citizen-family.

The enormous influence of the polis upon individual life was based on the fact that it was an ideal. The state was a spiritual entity, which assimilated all the loftiest aspects of human life and gave them out as its own gifts. Nowadays, we naturally think first of the state's claim to educate all its citizens during their youth. But public education was not advocated in Greece until it became a thesis of fourth century philosophy: Sparta alone, at this early period, paid direct attention to the education of the young. Nevertheless, even outside Sparta, the early city-state educated the members of its community, by utilizing the athletic and musical competitions which were held during the festivals of the gods. These competitions were the noblest reflection of the physical and spiritual culture of the age. Plato rightly calls gymnastics and music "the old-established culture." That culture, which had originally been aristocratic, was fostered by the state through great and costly competitions; and these competitions did more than encourage musical taste and gymnastic skill. They really created the sense of community in the city. Once that sense has been established, it is easy to understand the Greek citizen's pride in membership of his state. To describe a Greek fully, not only his own name and his father's are needed, but also the name of his city. Membership in a city-state had for the Greeks the same ideal value that nationality has for men of to-day.

The polis is the sum of all its citizens and of all the aspects of their lives. It gives each citizen much, but it can demand all in return. Relentless and powerful, it imposes its way of life on each individual, and marks him for its own. From it are derived all the norms which govern the life of its citizens. Conduct that injures it is bad, conduct that helps it is good. This is the paradoxical result of the passionate effort to obtain the rights and equal status of each individual. All these efforts have forged the new chains of Law, to hold together the centrifugal energies of mankind, and to co-ordinate them far more successfully than in the old social order. Law is the objective expression of the state, and now Law has become king, as the Greeks later said—an invisible ruler who does not only prevent the strong from transgressing and bring the wrongdoer to justice, but issues positive commands in all the spheres of life which had once been governed by individual will and preference. Even the most intimate acts of the private life and the moral conduct of its citizens are by law prescribed and limited and defined. Thus, through the struggle to obtain law, the development of the state brings into being new and more sharply differentiated principles of public and private life.

And that is the significance of the new city-state in the shaping of Greek character. Plato says, and rightly, that every type of constitution produces its own type of man; both he and Aristotle claim that all education should, in the perfect state, bear the imprint of the spirit of the state. Again and again the great Athenian political philosophers of the fourth century formulate this ideal in the words "education in the spirit of the laws." The words show that to establish a legal standard by written law was for the Greeks an *educational* act. Law is the most important stage in the development of Greek culture from the social ideal of aristocracy to the fundamental conception of man as an individual, as expressed by the philosophers. And the ethical and educational systems constructed by philosophers constantly recall, in both form and content, the legislation of earlier periods. Such systems do not come into being in the empty air of pure thought: they are rooted in the historical life of the nation—as the ancient philosophers themselves said— and do but translate it into the region of abstract and general ideas. Law was the most universal and permanent form of Greek moral and legal experience. The culmination of Plato's work as a philosophical educator comes in his last and greatest book, when he himself turns lawgiver; and Aristotle closes the *Ethics* by calling for a legislator to realize the ideal he has formulated. Law is the mother of philosophy, for another reason—because in Greece lawmaking was always the work of great individuals. They were rightly considered to be the educators of their people; it is typical of Greek ideas that the lawgiver is often named beside the poet, and the formulas which define the law are often mentioned beside the wise utterances of the poet: the two activities were essentially akin to each other.

The rule of law was later criticized, in the epoch of degenerate democracy, when many rash and despotic laws were hurried into existence; but such criticism is meanwhile irrelevant. All the thinkers of this early period unite in praising law. It is the soul of the city. Heraclitus says "the people must fight for their law as for their walls": evoking, behind the visible city defended by its walls, the invisible polis with its sure rampart of law. But there is an even earlier reflection of the ideal of law, in the work of the natural philosopher Anaximander of Miletus, about the middle of the sixth century. Transferring the concept of diké from the social life of the city-state to the realm of nature, he explains the causal connexion between coming-to-be and passing-away as equivalent to a lawsuit, in which things are compelled by the decision of Time to compensate each other for their unrighteousness. This is the origin of the philosophical idea of the *cosmos:* for the word originally signifies the *right order* in a state or other community. The philosopher, by projecting the idea of a political cosmos upon the whole of nature, claims that isonomia and not pleonexia must be the leading principle not only of human life but of the nature of things; and his claim is a striking witness to the fact that in his age the new political ideal of justice and law had become the centre of all thought, the basis of existence, the real source of men's faith in the purpose and meaning of the world. Anaximander's projection of law upon nature is an important philosophical conception of the world, and will be studied in detail elsewhere. Here we can only show in general how clearly it illuminates the function of the state and the new ideal of man as a citizen. At the same time we can see the close connexion between the origins of Ionian philosophy and the birth of the constitutional city-state. Both are rooted in the universal idea which, starting from this point, inspires

Greek civilization more and more deeply—the idea that the world and life in all their appearances can be interpreted by one fundamental standard.

In conclusion, we must trace the process by which the Ionian city-states came into being, with special reference to the development of the old aristocratic civilization into the idea of universal culture. It should be specially noted that these general remarks are not fully applicable to the early city-state: they are a preliminary diagnosis of the process whose bases we have analysed above. But it will be valuable to define the range and tendency of the process, and to keep it as a whole before our minds.

The polis gives each individual his due place in its political cosmos, and thereby gives him, besides his private life, a sort of second life, his $\beta\iota\sigma\varsigma$ $\pi o\lambda\iota\tau\iota\kappa\acute{o}\varsigma$ Now, every citizen belongs to two orders of existence; and there is a sharp distinction in his life between what is *his own* and what is *communal.* Man is not only "idiotic," he is also "politic." As well as his ability in his own profession or trade, he has his share of the universal ability of the citizen, by which he is fitted to co-operate and sympathize with the rest of the citizens in the life of the polis. It is obvious why the new ideal of the individual as citizen cannot be based (like Hesiod's ideal of popular education) on the conception of man's daily work. Hesiod's idea of areté was inspired by the facts of real life and by the vocational morality of the working-class, his audience. From the standpoint of the present time, we should be inclined to say that the new movement ought to have taken over the Hesiodic ideal *en bloc:* by doing so, we might think, it would have substituted a new concept of the people's education for the aristocratic ideal of the education of the entire personality; the new concept would have valued each individual by the work he did in the world, and would have taught that the good of the community was achieved when each individual did his work as well as possible. That was the system proposed by the aristocrat Plato when he described, in the *Republic,* a state based on legal order, governed by a few intellectually superior men. It would have been in harmony with the life and work of the people. It would have emphasized the fact that hard work is no shame, but is the sole basis of each man's citizenship. That fact was indeed recognized; but the actual development of the citizen ideal followed quite different lines.

The new factor in the development of the city-state, which at last made every man a political being, was the compulsion laid on each male citizen to take an active part in the public life of his community, and to recognize and accept his civic duties— which were quite different from his duties as a private person and a working man. Previously, it was only the nobleman who had possessed this "universal" political ability. For centuries power had been in the hands of the aristocrats, and they had a vastly superior system of political education and experience, which was still indispensable. The new city-state could not, without injuring itself, ignore the areté of the aristocracy; but it was bound to repress its selfish and unjust misuse. That was at least the ideal of the polis, as expressed by Pericles in Thucydides. Thus, in free Ionia as in authoritarian Sparta, the culture of the city-state was based on the old aristocratic culture—on the ideal of areté which embraced the whole personality and all its powers. The working-class morality of Hesiod was not abandoned; but the citizen of the polis aimed above all at the ideal which Phoenix had taught Achilles: to be a speaker of words and a doer of deeds. Certainly the leading men in each state were bound to move towards that ideal, and the ordinary citizens too came to sympathize with it.

This fact had great results. Socrates, as we know, introduced his criticism of democracy by discussing the relationship of technical or professional knowledge to political ability. For Socrates, the mason's son, the simple working man, thought it was a startling paradox that the cobbler, the tailor, and the carpenter should need special knowledge to practise their own honest trades, while the politician needed only a general and rather indefinite education to engage in politics, although his "craft" dealt with much more important things. Obviously the problem could not have been posed in these terms, except in an age which held that political areté was naturally a branch of *knowledge*. From that point of view, the essence of democracy was the lack of any special knowledge. But as a matter of fact the early city-states had never considered the question of political ability to be a predominantly *intellectual problem*. We have seen what they considered civic virtue to mean. When the constitutional city-state came into being, the virtue of its citizens really consisted in their voluntary submission to the new authority of the law, without distinction of rank or birth. In that conception of political virtue, ethos was still far more important than logos. Obedience to the laws and discipline were far more important qualifications for an ordinary citizen than knowledge of the

administration and aims of the state. To co-operate was, for him, to join others in submission to the law, and not to govern.

The early city-state was, in the eyes of its citizens, the guarantee of all the ideals which made life worth living. πολιτεύεσθαι means "to take part in communal life"; but besides that it simply means "to live"—for the two meanings were one and the same. At no time was the state more closely identified with all human values. Aristotle calls man "a political being," so as to differentiate him from animals by his power of living in a state: he is in fact identifying *humanitas,* "being human," with the life in a state. His definition can be understood only by studying the structure of the early polis: for its citizens held their communal existence to be the sum of all the higher things of life—in fact to be something divine. In the *Laws* Plato constructs just such an old Hellenic cosmos based on law, a city in which the polis *is* the spirit, and in which all spiritual activity is referred to the polis as its final end. There he defines the essence of all true culture, or paideia (in contrast to the specialized knowledge of tradesmen such as the shopkeeper and the travelling merchant), as "the education in areté from youth onwards, which makes men passionately desire to become perfect citizens, knowing both how to rule and how to be ruled on a basis of justice."

Plato's words are a true description of the original meaning of "universal" culture as conceived in the early city-state. In his conception of culture he does include the Socratic ideal of a craft of politics; but he does not think of it as a special branch of knowledge comparable to the craftsman's professional cunning. He believes that true culture is "universal" culture, because political understanding is the understanding of universal questions. As we have shown, the contrast between the factual knowledge of the craftsman and the ideal culture of the citizen, with its reference to his entire personality and life, goes back to the aristocratic ideal of early Greece. But its deeper meaning first appears in the city-state, because there that ideal was imposed upon the whole community, and aristocratic culture became the force which formed every man as a citizen. Aristocracy is the first, and the early city-state is the second, of the vital stages in the development of the "humanistic" ideal of a universal ethico-political culture: in fact, the historical mission of the city-state was to lead Greece towards that ideal. And although the early city-state developed into mass-rule, an extreme democracy guided by quite different forces, that development does not alter the true nature of city-state culture; for throughout its political evolution that culture kept its original aristocratic character. Its value should be estimated neither by contrast with the genius of individual political leaders—who are always produced by exceptional conditions—nor by its value for the mass of mankind to whom it cannot be communicated without becoming less rich and less potent. With characteristic good sense the Greeks always shunned such comparisons. The ideal of universal political areté is indispensable because it implies the constant creation and regeneration of a governing class; and without such a governing class no nation and no state, whatever be its constitution, can long survive.

the athenian democracy
and its critics

twenty-two

A. H. M. JONES

It is curious that in the abundant literature produced in the greatest democracy of Greece there survives no statement of democratic political theory. All the Athenian political philosophers and publicists whose works we possess were in various degrees oligarchic in sympathy. The author of the pamphlet on the "Constitution of the Athenians" preserved among Xenophon's works is bitterly hostile to democracy. Socrates, so far as we can trace his views from the works of Xenophon and Plato, was at least highly critical of democracy. Plato's views on the subject are too well known to need stating. Isocrates in his earlier years wrote panegyrics of Athens, but in his old age, when he wrote his more philosophical works, became increasingly embittered against the political régime of his native city. Aristotle is the most judicial in his attitude, and states the pros and cons, but his ideal was a widely based oligarchy. With the historians of Athens, the same bias is evident. Only Herodotus is a democrat, but his views have not carried

Reprinted from *Athenian Democracy* (Oxford: Basil Blackwell and Mott, Ltd., 1957), pp. 41–61, by permission. [Footnotes omitted]

much weight, partly because of his reputation for naïveté, and partly because his explicit evidence refers to a period before the full democracy had evolved. Thucydides is hostile: in one of the very few passages in which he reveals his personal views he expresses approval of a régime which disfranchised about two-thirds of the citizens, those who manned the fleet on which the survival of Athens depended. Xenophon was an ardent admirer of the Spartan régime. Aristotle, in the historical part of his monograph on the Constitution of Athens, followed—rather uncritically —a source with a marked oligarchic bias. Only the fourth-century orators were democrats; and their speeches, being concerned with practical political issues—mostly of foreign policy— or with private litigation, have little to say on the basic principles of democracy, which they take for granted.

This surviving literature is certainly not representative of Athenian public opinion. The majority of Athenians were proud of their constitution and deeply attached to it. The few counter-revolutions—in 411, 404, 322 and 317—were carried out by small extremist cliques, in 411 after a carefully planned campaign of deception and terror, in the other three cases with the aid of a foreign conqueror, and all were short-lived, being rapidly overwhelmed by the mass of the citizens. Nor was it only the poor majority, who most obviously benefited from the system, that were its supporters. Most of the great statesmen and generals of Athens came from wealthy families, and a substantial number from the nobility of birth; the leaders of the popular risings which unseated the oligarchic governments of 411 and 403 were men of substance.

Since, however, the majority were mute—in the literature which has survived—it is not an easy task to discern what they considered the merits of democracy to be, or, indeed, on what principles they thought that a good constitution should be based. Democratic political theory can only be tentatively reconstructed from scattered allusions. For the basic ideals of democracy the best source is the series of panegyrics on Athens. The most famous of these, Pericles' Funeral Speech, as recorded by Thucydides, is also the most instructive; its peculiarities of diction and its general tone, which is in conflict with Thucydides' own outlook, suggest that it is a fairly faithful reproduction of what Pericles really said. There is an early fourth-century Funeral Speech attributed to Lysias, which contains some useful material. Little for our purposes can be drawn from Isocrates' *Panegyricus* and *Panathenaicus*. A curious document of this class is the skit on a Funeral Speech contained in Plato's *Menexenus,* which seems close enough to type to be used—with reservations —as a statement of democratic principles. To these documents, which too often only repeat banal generalities, may be added *obiter dicta* in the political and forensic speeches of the orators, when they appeal to some general principle. Among these may be included some political speeches in Thucydides, which, though placed in a Sicilian setting, doubtless are modelled on Athenian prototypes. Another important source is the actual constitution of Athens, from whose rules general principles can sometimes be deduced. But our most valuable evidence comes from the criticisms of adversaries, which are so much more fully reported than anything from the democratic side. This evidence, though copious, is tricky to evaluate and must be used with caution. We must distinguish criticism on points of principle, where a democrat would have accepted his opponent's statement of the democratic point of view as correct, and would have argued that the principle or institution criticised was in fact a good one; and criticism on points of practice, which a democrat would have endeavoured to rebut, arguing that the accusations were untrue, or alternatively that the abuses alleged were regrettable but accidental and remediable defects of democracy.

It is the object of this paper to reconstruct from these sources democratic political theory and then to determine how far in practice the Athenian people lived up to its principles. The procedure will be to take up the various lines of criticism advanced by oligarchic critics, and to work out on what lines democrats would have answered them, using for this purpose the scattered evidence outlined above. . . .

The first and most basic charge brought by the philosophers against democracy is best expressed by Aristotle in his characteristic terse direct style: "in such democracies each person lives as he likes; or in the words of Euripides 'according to his fancy.' This is a bad thing." This is no isolated text. Aristotle returns to the point elsewhere. Isocrates in the *Areopagiticus* declares that in the good old days it was not the case that the citizens "had many supervisors in their education but as soon as they reached man's estate were allowed to do what they liked," and urges that the Areopagus should recover its alleged pristine power of controlling the private lives of all the citizens. Plato in the *Republic* complains that under a democracy "the city is full of liberty and free speech and everyone in it is allowed to do what he likes... each man in it could plan his own life as he pleases." He then enlarges on the deplorable results of this, that the citizens are various, instead of conforming to one type, and that foreigners and even women and slaves are as free as the citizens.

An Athenian democrat would no doubt have demurred at the last charge, though admitting with some pride that foreigners and slaves were exceptionally well treated at Athens, but he certainly gloried in the accusation of liberty. Freedom of action and of speech were the proudest slogans of Athens, and not only political but personal freedom; as Pericles says in the Funeral Speech, "we live as free citizens both in our public life and in our attitude to one another in the affairs of daily life; we are not angry with our neighbour if he behaves as he pleases, we do not cast sour looks at him, which, if they can do no harm, cause pain." Freedom of speech was particularly prized. As Demosthenes says, "in Sparta you are not allowed to praise the laws of Athens or of this state or that, far from it, you have to praise what agrees with their constitution," whereas in Athens criticism of the democracy was freely permitted. One only has to read the works of Isocrates, Plato and Aristotle to see that this is true. The condemnation of Socrates is an apparent exception to the rule, but as Xenophon's account of the matter shows, the real gravamen of the charge against Socrates was that, of his pupils, Alcibiades had done more than any other one man to ruin Athens in the recent war, and Critias had been the ruthless ringleader of the Thirty, who had massacred thousands of Athenians a few years before.

The second main charge against democracy is most neatly stated by Plato: that "it distributes a kind of equality to the equal and the unequal alike." The same point is made by Isocrates, who distinguishes "two equalities; one allots the same to every one and the other what is appropriate to each," and alleges that in the good old days the Athenians "rejected as unjust the equality which considers the good and the bad worthy of the same rights, and chose that which honours each according to his worth." Aristotle argues similarly, though he is justifiably sceptical about the criterion according to which rights are to be scaled; in democracy freedom is the criterion, that is, all free men are equal, and this is in Aristotle's view unjust, but so in his opinion are the only practical alternative criteria, wealth or birth.

Democrats in general approved of the egalitarian principle. Demosthenes in one passage argues that what makes all citizens public spirited and generous is "that in a democracy each man considers that he himself has a share in equality and justice," and in another praises a law forbidding legislation directed against individuals as being good democratic doctrine, "for as everyone has an equal share in the rest of the constitution, so everyone is entitled to an equal share in the laws." The Athenians were not, however, either in theory or in practice, absolute egalitarians, but drew a distinction between different political functions. On one point they admitted no compromise—equality before the law; as Pericles says, "in their private disputes all share equality according to the laws." This to us elementary principle needed emphasis, for Plato's friends in the Thirty, when they drew up a new constitution, ordained that only the 3,000 full citizens were entitled to a legal trial and that all others might be summarily executed by order of the government. It was secured in the Athenian constitution not only by the right of every citizen to seek redress in the courts, but by the character of the courts, which consisted of large juries drawn by lot from the whole body of the citizens.

The Athenians also attached great importance to the equality of all citizens in formulating and deciding public policy. This was secured by the right of every citizen to speak and vote in the assembly, and by the composition of the council of Five Hundred, which prepared the agenda of the assembly; this body was annually chosen by lot from all the demes of Attica. Here democratic principle came into conflict with the oligarchic view, developed at length by Plato, that government was an art, demanding the highest skill, and should therefore be entrusted to a select few. On this question Aristotle, whose ideal was a broadly based oligarchy, whose members would not all be experts, took issue with Plato, and the arguments which he uses are applicable to a fully democratic régime, and probably drawn from democratic theory. In the first place he argues that, though each individual in a large assembly may be of poor quality, the sum of their virtue and wisdom taken together may exceed the virtue and wisdom of a select few, just as dinners provided by joint contributions may be better than those provided by one rich host. His second argument is rather more cogent. Politics, he suggests, is one of those arts in which the best judge is not the artist himself but the user of the product. The householder is a better judge of a house than the architect, the steersman of a rudder rather than the carpenter, the eater of a meal rather than the cook. A third justification for democratic practice is put into the mouth of Protagoras by Plato in a passage which so well illustrates the tone of the Athenian assembly that it is worth quoting in full. Socrates is expressing his doubts as to whether political wisdom is teachable.

I, like the other Greeks (he says), think that the Athenians are wise. Well, I see that when we gather for the assembly, when the city has to do something about buildings, they call for the builders as advisers and when it is about ship construction, the shipwrights, and so on with everything else that can be taught and learned. And if anyone else tries to advise them, whom they do not think an expert, even if he be quite a gentleman, rich and aristocratic, they none the less refuse to listen, but jeer and boo, until either the speaker himself is shouted down and gives up, or the sergeants at arms, on the order of the presidents, drag him off or remove him. That is how they behave on technical questions. But when the debate is on the general government of the city, anyone gets up and advises them, whether he be a carpenter or a smith or a leather worker, a merchant or a sea-captain, rich or poor, noble or humble, and no one blames them like the others for trying to give advice, when they have not learned from any source and have had no teacher.

Protagoras' reply is in mythological form. Zeus when he created men gave various talents to each, but to all he gave a sense of decency and fair play, since without them any society would be impossible.

So, Socrates, (he concludes) that is why the Athenians and the others, when the debate is about architecture or any other technical question, think that few should take part in the discussion, and if anyone outside the few joins in, do not tolerate it, as you say—rightly in my opinion. But when they come to discuss political questions, which must be determined by justice and moderation, they properly listen to everyone, thinking that everyone shares in these qualities—or cities wouldn't exist.

The Athenians went yet further in their egalitarian principles in that they entrusted the routine administration of the city to boards of magistrates chosen by lot. This aroused the irony of Socrates, who declared that "it was silly that the rulers of the city should be appointed by lot, when no one would be willing to employ a pilot or a carpenter or a flautist chosen by lot." It is a proof of the poverty of our information on democratic theory that no reasoned defence of this cardinal institution, the lot, has survived. The nearest thing to it is a comic passage in a private speech of Demosthenes where Mantitheus, pleading against the assumption of his name by his half-brother, raises the hypothetical case that both might put in their names for the ballot for an office or the council, and that the name Mantitheus might be drawn. There would have to be a lawsuit "and we shall be deprived of our common equality, that the man who wins the ballot holds office: we shall abuse one another and the cleverer speaker will hold the office." It is implied that the lot was employed to give every citizen an equal chance, without regard to wealth, birth or even popularity or eloquence. This may seem to be carrying principle to extremes, but Socrates' comment is not altogether fair. It was not "the rulers of the city" who were chosen by lot, but officials charged with limited routine duties, for which little more than "a sense of decency and fair play" was required. Furthermore, it must be remembered that a magistrate had to pass a preliminary examination, which was, it is true, usually formal, but gave his enemies an opportunity for raking up his past; was liable to be deposed by a vote of the assembly taken ten times a year; and after his year was subject to a scrutiny in which his accounts were audited and any citizen could charge him with inefficiency or abuse of authority. It is unlikely that many rogues or nincompoops would expose themselves to these risks.

Athenian democrats did not believe that all should share alike in the important offices, whose holders to some extent controlled policy. Pericles, after affirming the equality before the law of all citizens, goes on: "but in public esteem, when a man is distinguished in any way, he is more highly honoured in public life, not as a matter of privilege but in recognition of merit; on the other hand any one who can benefit the city is not debarred by poverty or by the obscurity of his position." This point is even more strongly put in the mock panegyric in the *Menexenus*:

For in the main the same constitution existed then as now, an aristocracy, under which we now live and have always lived since then. A man may call it democracy, and another what he will. But in truth it is an aristocracy with the approval of the majority. We have always had kings: sometimes they were hereditary, sometimes elective. In most things the majority is in control of the city, and bestows office and power on those whom it thinks to be the best. No one is rejected for weakness or poverty or humble birth, nor honoured for their opposites, as in other cities. There is one criterion: the man who is thought to be wise and good holds power and rule.

These principles were embodied in the Athenian constitution, whereby all the important magistrates—the ten generals, who not only commanded the army and the fleet but exercised a general control over defence and foreign policy, the other military commanders, and in the fourth century the principal financial magistrates—were elected by the people; a procedure which could be regarded as aristocratic. In fact, the Athenian people were rather snobbish in their choice of leaders. The "Old Oligarch" sneeringly remarks, "they do not think that they ought to share by lot in the offices of general or commander of the horse, for the people knows that it gains more by not holding these offices itself but allowing the leading citizens to hold them." Xenophon records the complaints of Nicomachides, an experienced soldier, that he has been beaten in the elections for the generalship by a rich man who knows nothing about military affairs. Demosthenes, a strong democrat, rakes up Aeschines' humble origins in a fashion which we should hardly consider in good taste, but apparently did not offend an Athenian jury. "We have judged you, a painter of alabaster boxes and drums, and these junior clerks and nobodies (and there is no harm in such occupations, but on the other hand they are not deserving of a generalship) worthy of ambassadorships, generalships and the highest honours."

Besides the lot the other instrument whereby the Athenians secured the effective political equality of the citizens was pay. The 6,000 jurors, the council of 500 and the 350 odd magistrates were all paid for their services at various rates; it may be noted that elective magistrates—the military commanders and ambassadors—were paid, and at higher rates than the ordinary magistrates chosen by lot, so that the claim that poverty was no barrier to political power was justified. During the fourth century citizens who attended the assembly—or at least a quorum who arrived first—were also paid. The philosophers objected to this practice. Aristotle criticises it precisely because it fulfilled its purpose of enabling the poor to exercise their political rights. It may, however, be doubted if by his day it was fully effective. The assembly and the juries seem, from the tone in which the orators address them, to have consisted predominantly of middle-class citizens rather than of the poor, and there is evidence that the council also was mainly filled by the well-to-do. The real value of the State pay had, owing to the progressive rise of prices, sunk considerably by the latter part of the fourth century, and the poor probably preferred more profitable employment. Plato also objects to State pay: "I am told," he says, "that Pericles made the Athenians idle and lazy and garrulous and avaricious by first putting them on State pay." This is an oft-repeated accusation but has very little substance. In a population which never sank below 20,000 adult males and probably reached twice that figure at its peak, the council and the magistracies did not provide employment except on rare occasions; a man might not hold any magistracy more than once, or sit on the council more than twice in his life. Assemblies were held only on forty days in the year. It was only as a juror that a citizen could obtain more or less continuous employment, and here the rate of remuneration was so low—half a labourer's wage in the fifth century and a third in the late fourth, in fact little more than bare subsistence—that in the fifth century, if the picture drawn in Aristophanes' *Wasps* is true, it attracted only the elderly, past hard work, and in the early fourth century, when economic conditions were worse, according to Isocrates, the unemployed.

The third main criticism of democracy comes from Aristotle, that in its extreme (that is, Athenian) form "the mass of the people (or the "majority") is sovereign instead of the law; this happens when decrees are valid instead of the law." It is not entirely clear what Aristotle means by this. He appears here and elsewhere to conceive of the law as an immutable code, laid down by an impartial legislator, against which the will of the citizens, assumed always to be self-interested, should not in an ideal State be allowed to prevail. He may therefore be objecting to any legislation by decision of the majority—or, for that matter, by any constitutional procedure. But this meaning seems to slide into another, that in an extreme democracy the majority in the assembly habitually overrides the existing laws, however established, by arbitrary executive action in particular cases, acting, as he puts it, like the traditional Greek tyrant.

The doctrine of the immobility of law was naturally favoured by oligarchs, who were generally conservative, or, when they wanted to alter the law, professed to be restoring an "ancestral constitution." Democrats, who more often wished to change things, might have been expected to work out a more progressive theory. Some thinkers in the fifth century did indeed propound the doctrine that the law was the will of the sovereign. Socrates, according to Xenophon, defined law as "what the citizens have by agreement enacted on what must be done and what avoided," and was quite prepared to admit that what the citizens enacted they could revoke, just as having declared war they could make peace. Xenophon also reports a no doubt imaginary conversation between Pericles and Alcibiades, in which the former defined law as "what the mass of the people (or "the majority"), having come to-gether and approved it, decrees, declaring what must and what must not be done." Led on by Alcibiades he extends this definition to oligarchies and tyrannies, declaring that what the sovereign body or person decrees is law. Asked by Alcibiades what then is violence and lawlessness, Pericles replies "when the stronger does not persuade the weaker but compels him by force to do what he wants." This enables Alcibiades after suitable leading questions about tyrants and oligarchies, to ask: "Would what the whole mass of the people, overpowering the holders of property, enacts without persuading them, be violence rather than law?" Pericles at this point tells Alcibiades to go away and play, leaving the ambiguity in his theory of law unresolved. In the fourth century Demosthenes enunciates a similar view in one passage, asserting that "the laws lay down about the future (he is denouncing retrospective legislation as undemocratic) what must be done, being enacted by persuasion as they will benefit their users." Some democrats then conceived of law as the considered will of the majority, adding the rider that the majority should persuade the minority and consider the interests of all.

In general, however, democrats tended like Aristotle to regard the laws as a code laid down once for all by a wise legislator, in their case Solon, which, immutable in principle, might occasionally require to be clarified or supplemented. These were the terms of reference given to the legislative commission set up after the restoration of the democracy in 403, and the standing rules governing legislation show the same spirit. At no time was it legal to alter the law by a simple decree of the assembly. The mover of such a decree was liable to the famous "indictment for illegal proceedings," which, if upheld by the courts, quashed the decree, and also, if brought within a year, exposed the mover to heavy penalties. In the fifth century additions to the law were prepared by special legislative commissions, and then submitted to the council and assembly, but there seems to have been no constitutional means of altering the existing law. After 403 an elaborate procedure was introduced for revising the law, which took the matter out of the hands of the assembly. Every year the assembly passed the laws under review, and voted on them, section by section, whether they should stand or be revised. If a revision of any section was voted, any citizen was entitled to propound alternative laws, which were given due publicity, and a court of 501 or 1,001 legislators was empanelled. The issue between the old and the proposed laws was then argued judicially (counsel for the old laws being appointed by the assembly), and the legislators, acting as a jury under oath, gave their verdict.

Such was the Athenian theory on legislation. How far it was observed in practice is disputable. Both Demosthenes and Aeschines, when bringing indictments for illegal proceedings, inveigh against the unscrupulous politicians (their opponents) who flout the law, and Demosthenes alleges that as a result "there are so many contradictory laws that you have for a long while past been electing commissions to resolve the conflict, and none the less the problem can have no end. Laws are no different from decrees, and the laws, according to which decrees ought to be indicted, are more recent than the decrees themselves." These strictures may be taken with a grain of salt. Politicians no doubt often tried to bypass the rather cumbrous procedure for legislation—Demosthenes did so himself through Apollodorus over the allocation of the theoric fund. But the indictment for illegal proceedings was a favourite political weapon, often invoked, as by Aeschines against Demosthenes on the famous issue of the Crown, on very technical grounds. And Aristophon's boast that he had been indicted (unsuccessfully) seventy-five times, if it proves that some politicians often sailed near the wind, also proves that there were many jealous watchdogs of the constitution; Demosthenes' attempt to evade the law was, incidentally, foiled and Apollodorus suffered.

On the other aspect of the rule of law Athenian democrats held exactly the opposite view to Aristotle's. "Tyrannies and oligarchies," according to Aeschines, "are governed by the ways of their governments, democratic cities by the established laws." "No one, I think, would assert," says Demosthenes, "that there is any more important cause for the blessings which the city enjoys and for its being democratic and free, than the laws." In another passage Demosthenes contrasts law and oligarchy, declaring that in the latter any member of the government can revoke existing rules and make arbitrary enactments about the future, whereas the laws lay down what must be done for the future and are passed by persuasion in the interests of all. To Lycurgus of "the three most important factors which maintain and preserve democracy," the first is the law. Hypereides declares it all-important "that in a democracy the laws shall be sovereign."

Both sides were naturally thinking of the worst specimens of the opposite party. Athenian democrats inevitably called to mind the arbitrary excesses of their own Four Hundred and

Thirty when they spoke of oligarchies, and oligarchs could no doubt cite democracies whose acts were as brutal and illegal. On the whole the Athenian democracy seems to have lived up to its principles. Xenophon has given us a vivid picture of one occasion when the assembly in a hysterical mood rode roughshod over its own rules of procedure and condemned the generals in command at Arginusae to death by one summary vote. But the emphasis given to this incident suggests that it was very exceptional. And Xenophon, no favourable witness to the democracy, also testifies that after the restoration of the democracy in 403 the people religiously observed the amnesty agreed with the supporters of the Thirty. When one reads Xenophon's and Aristotle's record of the doings of the Thirty, one cannot but be amazed at the steadfast forbearance of the Athenian people.

The final and principal charge brought by the philosophers against democracy was that it meant the rule of the poor majority over the rich minority in their own interest. This is the main thesis of the "Old Oligarch," whose treatise on the Athenian constitution takes the form of an ironical appreciation of its efficiency in promoting the interests of "the bad" (the poor) at the expense of "the good" (the rich); he is equally cynical in assuming that "the good," if they got the chance, would govern in their own interest to the detriment of "the bad." Plato in the *Republic* declares that "democracy results when the poor defeat the others and kill or expel them and share the constitution and the offices equally with the rest." Aristotle is very insistent that democracy is directed to the advantage of the indigent, going so far as to say that if, *per impossibile,* there

should be more rich than poor in a city, the rule of the poor minority should be called democracy, and that of the rich majority oligarchy.

This view was naturally not accepted by democrats. Their views are doubtless reflected in the speech put into the mouth of the Syracusan democrat Athenagoras by Thucydides:

It will be said that democracy is neither wise nor fair, and that the possessors of property are best qualified to rule well. My opinion is first that the people is the name of the whole, and oligarchy of a part, and secondly that the rich are the best guardians of property, the wise the best councillors, and the masses can best hear and judge, and that all these elements alike, jointly and severally, have an equal share in democracy.

It is more difficult to answer the question whether the Athenian democracy did or did not in fact exploit the rich for the benefit of the poor. In the distribution of political power and influence the rich seem to have fared well. In the minor offices and on the council and in the juries the poor no doubt predominated, though even here it would seem that by the fourth century the well-to-do were by no means crowded out. To the important military, diplomatic and financial offices men of birth and wealth were generally elected. The orators, who, normally holding no office, guided policy by their speeches in the assembly were also mostly well-to-do, and many of them of good family. It was comparatively rarely that a self-made man like Phrynichus or Aeschines achieved political influence. A rich man or an aristocrat certainly did not find that his political career was prejudiced by his wealth or birth, while poor and humbly born politicians had to face a good deal of abuse from comedians and orators.

Isocrates complains bitterly of the fiscal exploitation of the rich. In the *de Pace* he rolls out a list of taxes and charges "which cause so much vexation that property owners lead a harder life than utter paupers," and in the *Antidosis* he declares: "when I was a boy it was thought to be such a secure and grand thing to be rich that practically everyone pretended to possess a larger property than he actually did, in his desire to acquire this reputation. But now one has to prepare a defence to prove that one is not rich, as if it were a great crime." From the meagre figures which we possess it is difficult to check these allegations. Normal peace-time expenditure (including the pay of citizens for political services) was defrayed from a variety of indirect taxes, a tax on resident aliens, royalties from the silver mines, rents of public and sacred land, court fees and fines and confiscations imposed by the courts. Certain religious festivals were financed by the system of liturgies, whereby rich men were nominated to produce plays, train teams of athletes and the like. In time of war it was often necessary to raise a property tax, which fell, it would seem, on about 6,000 persons, or a third to a quarter of the citizen body. In war time also the richest of the citizens were nominated as trierarchs, in which capacity they had to maintain a trireme in seaworthy condition for a year.

The war tax, of which great complaints were made, averaged over twenty years in the fourth century at a rate equivalent to a 5d. or 6d. in the pound income tax. We need not therefore take the laments of Isocrates and his like very seriously. The tax seems in fact to have been too widely spread, and did cause hardship to the poorest of those liable. It was, as appears from Demosthenes' speeches, very difficult to get the assembly, a substantial proportion of whom were taxpayers, to vote a levy, and hence wars were always inadequately financed. Liturgies are much more difficult to calculate, as it depended greatly on the individual concerned how often he undertook them and how much he spent on each. It was useful political advertisement, almost a form of canvassing, to put up good shows, and rich men were often very willing to acquire popularity by serving frequently and spending lavishly on gorgeous costumes and high salaries to stars. An evidently very rich man for whom Lysias wrote a speech boasts that he undertook eleven liturgies in six years, spending in all nearly $3\frac{1}{2}$ talents—a middle-class fortune. But, as he remarks, he need not have spent on them a quarter of this sum if he had confined himself to the strict requirements of the law; nor need he have performed more than a maximum of four liturgies. At the other extreme another very rich man, Meidias, had, according to Demosthenes, performed only one liturgy at the age of nearly fifty, and Dicaeogenes, another wealthy man, only undertook two minor ones in ten years. The trierarchy was a heavier burden than the ordinary liturgies, costing from 40 to 60 minae ($\frac{2}{3}$ to 1 talent) a year, and as it might fall on fortunes of 5 talents, the temporary strain on a poor trierarch's resources would be severe. For this reason the burden was usually from the end of the fifth century shared between two holders, and from 357 the 1,200 persons liable to trierarchic service were divided into twenty groups, whose members shared the expense: thus, if a fleet of 100 ships were commissioned, twelve men would share the charge for each trierarchy. Here again the incidence of the burden varied greatly. The same man who performed eleven liturgies served seven years as trierarch during the Ionian war, spending 6 talents, and a certain Aristophanes (with his father) served three trierarchies in four or five years in the Corinthian War, spending 80 minae in all. Isocrates, on the other hand, who complains so bitterly of the oppression of the rich, and had made a large fortune by his rhetorical teaching, could at the age of 80 boast of only three trierarchies (including those performed by his son). But it would be unfair to the Athenian upper classes to take the parsimonious orator as typical. As a public-spirited citizen we may instance the father of one of Lysias' clients, who in a career of fifty years (which included the Peloponnesian and Corinthian wars) was trierarch seven times. His son proudly displayed to the jury his father's accounts, which showed that he had altogether disbursed on trierarchies, liturgies and war tax 9 talents 20 minae, an average of over 11 minae per annum. His fortune is not stated, but he certainly was a very rich man, since he entered chariots for the Isthmia and Nemea, and is likely to have possessed substantially more than 15 talents, which Demosthenes implies would qualify a man to be called really rich. If so, his contribution to the state would not have exceeded one-eighth of his income.

The taxation of the rich was very erratic, falling heavily in war years, and was badly distributed; before 357 all persons on the trierarchic register took their turn, though some were much richer than others, and after 357 all members of a group contributed equally. This lack of system enabled some rich men to escape very lightly, and was on occasions oppressive to those with moderate fortunes. On the other hand, many rich men liked to make a splash, undertaking more trierarchies and liturgies than their legal quota, and thereby easing the burden of the others. In general, it would seem that the average burden borne by the well-to-do in Athens was well within their means, though its erratic incidence might cause them temporary embarrassment.

The critics, however, allege that a more sinister method of soaking the rich than taxation was in vogue at Athens—that of condemning them on trumped-up charges and confiscating their property. There is reason to believe that this abuse of the law courts did sometimes occur, but it is very difficult to say whether it was common.

Some general considerations need to be clarified. Athens, like all ancient States, relied for the enforcement of the law on the services of informers, and was obliged to reward them for convictions. Professional informers seem to have been a pest at Athens; but so they were everywhere—one has only to think of the reputation of *delatores* in imperial Rome. The State did not encourage frivolous accusations, subjecting to severe penalties an informer who failed to win a fifth of the jury's votes, or who abandoned a prosecution which he had instituted. Nor does it appear that informers were popular with juries. Defendants try to insinuate that their prosecutors are informers, and prosecutors, in their anxiety to prove they are not informers, sometimes go so far as to claim to be personal enemies, or even hereditary enemies, of the accused. Nevertheless, informers seem to have plied a busy trade, principally in blackmailing rich men who had guilty consciences or disliked facing the ordeal of public trial. This state of affairs naturally caused the propertied classes much anxiety, and perhaps caused them to exaggerate the real scope of the evil.

Secondly, Athens, like all ancient States, lived from hand to mouth, and reckoned on the penalties inflicted by the courts as a regular source of income. It was therefore a temptation to jurors to vote in the interests of the treasury when money was short, and an informer dangled before their eyes a fat estate whose owner, he alleged, had been guilty of some serious offence. In this respect also Athens was not unique; Roman emperors short of money are alleged to have encouraged *delatores* and made good the finances by confiscation. Nor need one go so far afield as the Roman empire for a parallel. The Athenian oligarchs in the Thirty filled their treasury by condemning a number of innocuous but wealthy citizens and metics to death and seizing their property. This situation also made the propertied classes nervous, and probably made them exaggerate the evil. There is no reason to believe that all large estates confiscated were confiscated because they were large. Rich Athenians were quite capable of cheating the treasury or betraying the interests of the State; and it is, for instance, very unlikely that a statesman of such severe probity as Lycurgus would have secured the confiscation of the huge estate—160 talents—of Diphilus, unless he had been guilty of a serious breach of the mining laws.

There are three passages in Lysias which allude to the abuse. In a speech written in 399 a litigant states that "the council for the time being, when it has enough money for the administration, behaves correctly, but when it gets into difficulties it is obliged to receive impeachments and confiscate the property of the citizens and listen to the worst of the politicians." In another speech, written about ten years later, another litigant says to the jury: "You must remember that you have often heard them (his opponents) saying, when they wanted to ruin someone unjustly, that, if you would not condemn the people they tell you to condemn, your pay will fail." And in a third speech, delivered in 387, a man accused of detaining the confiscated estate of a relative complains: "My defence is difficult in view of the opinion some hold about Nicophemus' estate, and the present shortage of money in the city, my case being against the treasury." These are serious allegations, and indicate an unhealthy state of affairs. But it is to be noted that they all occur in the period following the fall of Athens, when the State was almost bankrupt, and when, despite the amnesty, feeling against the rich, many of whom had backed the Thirty, was very bitter among the mass of the citizens. I have not detected any other similar suggestion in all the later speeches, forensic or political, of the orators, except one sentence in the Fourth Philippic of Demosthenes, when, after appealing to the rich not to grudge to the poor their theoric payments, he turns to the poor, and says: "But where does the difficulty arise? What is the trouble? It is when they see some people transferring to private fortunes the practice established for public moneys, and a speaker is great in your eyes at the moment, and immortal as far as security goes—but the secret vote is different from the open applause. This breeds distrust and anger." This very guarded passage seems to mean that the rich suspected that the poor wished to increase their payments from public funds by confiscating private property, and that rich men who were applauded in the assembly were condemned by the secret ballot of the juries. Hypereides, a few years later, takes pride in the disinterested justice of Athenian juries:

There is no people or king or nation in the world more magnanimous than the people of Athens. It does not abandon to their fate those of the citizens, whether individuals or classes, who are falsely accused, but goes to their rescue. In the first place when Teisis denounced the estate of Euthycrates, which was worth more than sixty talents, as being public property, and after that again promised to denounce the estate of Philip and Nausicles, alleging that they acquired their wealth from unregistered mines, the jury, so far from welcoming such a speech or coveting other men's goods, promptly disfranchised the false accuser, not giving him a fifth of the votes. And again does not the recent action of the jurors last month deserve great praise? When Lysander denounced the mine of Epicrates as having been sunk within the boundaries—the mine he had been working for three years and pretty well all the richest men in the city were his partners—and Lysander promised to bring in 300 talents for the city—that is what he said they had got out of the mine—nevertheless the jury paid no attention to the accuser's promise but looked only to justice and declared the mine private.

Hypereides perhaps protests too much, but he does at least provide concrete instances when Athenian juries resisted very tempting baits.

If one may attempt to draw a general conclusion it would be that informers were a nuisance to the rich at Athens, and that the Athenian courts were sometimes tempted, especially in financial crises, to increase the revenue by condemning rich defendants on insufficient evidence. Neither of these abuses was, however, peculiar to a democratic régime.